The History of Spanish
A Student's Introduction

This concise textbook provides students with an engaging and thorough overview of the history of Spanish and its development from Latin. Presupposing no prior knowledge of Latin or linguistics, students are provided with the background necessary to understand the history of Spanish. Short, easy-to-digest chapters feature numerous practice exercises and activities. Chapter "lead-in" questions draw comparisons between English and Spanish, enabling students to use their intuition about their native language to gain a deeper understanding of Spanish. Each chapter features further reading suggestions, an outline, and a summary. Highlighted key terms are collated in a glossary. Boxes on linguistic debates teach students to evaluate arguments and think critically about linguistics. Supporting online resources include Word files of all the practices and activities in the book and an instructor's manual featuring a sample syllabus, answer key to the practices and activities, sample exams and teaching suggestions. This book is ideal for a range of courses on the history of Spanish and Spanish linguistics.

Diana L. Ranson is Professor of French and Spanish at the University of Georgia. Her publications include *Change and Compensation: Parallel Weakening of /s/ in Italian, French and Spanish* (1989) and articles on Spanish historical linguistics, syntactic variation in Modern Spanish, and phonological variation in Modern French. She has taught the history of Spanish, the history of French, comparative Romance linguistics, and Old Spanish for over thirty years.

Margaret Lubbers Quesada is Professor of Spanish at the University of Georgia. Her recent publications include *The L2 Acquisition of Spanish Subjects Multiple Perspectives* (2015), and articles in journals, such as the *International Review of Applied Linguistics, Journal of Pragmatics and Language Learning, The Handbook of Spanish Second Language Acquisition*, and *Estudios de Lingüística Aplicada*. She teaches courses in theoretical, applied, and historical linguistics.

The History of Spanish

A Student's Introduction

DIANA L. RANSON
MARGARET LUBBERS QUESADA

CAMBRIDGE
UNIVERSITY PRESS

University Printing House, Cambridge CB2 8BS, United Kingdom

One Liberty Plaza, 20th Floor, New York, NY 10006, USA

477 Williamstown Road, Port Melbourne, VIC 3207, Australia

314-321, 3rd Floor, Plot 3, Splendor Forum, Jasola District Centre, New Delhi – 110025, India

79 Anson Road, #06–04/06, Singapore 079906

Cambridge University Press is part of the University of Cambridge.

It furthers the University's mission by disseminating knowledge in the pursuit of
education, learning, and research at the highest international levels of excellence.

www.cambridge.org
Information on this title: www.cambridge.org/9781107144729
DOI: 10.1017/9781316534793

First published 2018

Printed in the United Kingdom by TJ International Ltd. Padstow Cornwall

A catalogue record for this publication is available from the British Library.

Library of Congress Cataloging-in-Publication Data
Names: Ranson, Diana L. author. | Lubbers Quesada, Margaret author.
Title: The history of Spanish : a student's introduction / Diana L. Ranson,
University of Georgia ; Margaret Lubbers Quesada, University of Georgia.
Description: Cambridge; New York, NY : Cambridge University Press, 2018.
Identifiers: LCCN 2017058252 | ISBN 9781107144729
Subjects: LCSH: Spanish language – Textbooks for foreign speakers – English. |
Spanish language – History.
Classification: LCC PC4129.E5 .R37 2018 | DDC 460.9–dc23
LC record available at https://lccn.loc.gov/2017058252

ISBN 978-1-107-14472-9 Hardback
ISBN 978-1-316-50794-0 Paperback

Additional resources for this publication at www.cambridge.org/RansonQuesada.

Cambridge University Press has no responsibility for the persistence or accuracy of
URLs for external or third-party internet websites referred to in this publication
and does not guarantee that any content on such websites is, or will remain,
accurate or appropriate.

This book is dedicated to the memory of my father,
Guy H. Ranson (1916–2000),
and my academic fathers,
Clifford S. Leonard, Jr. (1928–1999) and
Ernst Pulgram (1915–2005)

DLR

And also to the memory of my mother,
Marion Jean Snow (1927–2016),
and to the beginning of great memories with
Elsi Margaret Williams Quesada (2014–)

MLQ

Contents

Figures

Maps

Tables

Preface for Students

This book is a user-friendly introduction to the history of the Spanish language. It is written for "students," whether enrolled in a course or not, who are curious about the Spanish language. We hope that understanding the evolution of Spanish will help satisfy your curiosity and that it will at the same time inspire you to continue asking questions while observing and analyzing the use of language all around you. If you teach the Spanish language, we hope this book will make it possible for you to answer many of your students' questions about Spanish so that you can satisfy and foster their curiosity as well.

The most user-friendly feature of the book is its style. We have written it as if we were sitting down with you chatting about these topics. Other features include the lead-in questions at the beginning of each chapter to help you reflect on your own use of language and relate it to the chapter's topics. The text of each chapter is organized so that you can learn concepts step by step. We present all the background information you need to understand these concepts, so that you do not need any prior knowledge of Latin or linguistics or even a high degree of proficiency in Spanish. Within the chapters you will find textboxes that offer deeper explanations, additional information, or controversies on certain points. Each chapter ends with a summary to help you review its main points. Following the text of the chapter you will find a variety of activities to help you engage further with the concepts. Some of these help you review and reinforce what you have learned, whereas others provide new material to expand your understanding. We are delighted that you have decided to take this first step toward learning how Spanish has evolved. We would love to hear from you about your journey. Please feel free to email us if you have questions, suggestions, or fan mail.

Preface for Instructors

By writing a "student's introduction" to the history of the Spanish language, we have sought to present in an accessible and engaging way material that has gained a reputation for being dry and difficult. We have learned from experience that students are genuinely interested in learning why *duermo* has one stem and *dormimos* has another and why *mano* is feminine and *día* is masculine. We hope with this book to foster their curiosity by providing them with the tools they need to find answers to their questions and relate them to their daily lives. We also hope that the accessibility of this book will make it easier for instructors, even those who are not experts in this field, to offer a course in the history of the Spanish language.

So as to make the material accessible we have written in a conversational style as if we were sitting down in our offices explaining these concepts to our readers. In fact, we have often found ourselves providing our students with exactly this kind of explication of the other textbooks we have used. The text of each of the seventeen chapters is a step-by-step presentation, supplemented by tables and figures for visual learners, and by textboxes with extra details, additional material, or the sides of a debate. The pedagogical features include lead-in questions at the beginning of each chapter, practice exercises at certain points in the chapter, end-of-chapter summaries, follow-up activities, and suggestions for further reading.

We have designed the book to be adaptable to the preferences of individual instructors. We assume that each of the seventeen chapters provides material for one week of course work, except Chapters 1 and 2, which can be completed together in the first week. Therefore, you may decide to omit two or three chapters, according to your interests and those of your students, and the amount of class time you devote to testing, oral presentations, and other activities. You will almost certainly want to cover Chapters 1–3, which provide an essential foundation, Chapters 6–7, which cover all the regular sound changes, and Chapters 10, 11, and 13, which cover the essentials of noun and verb morphology. You can then choose whether to include external history (Chapters 4 and 5), special sound changes (Chapters 8 and 9), other nominal elements (Chapter 12), regular and irregular verb forms (Chapter 14), syntactic changes (Chapter 15), semantic changes (Chapter 16), and lexical changes (Chapter 17).

You can assign the lead-in questions for each chapter as homework, or begin the lesson on that chapter by discussing them in class, or – and this may be the best approach – discuss them in class the day before you assign a particular chapter. The follow-up activities help to verify and consolidate students' learning, so these work well as homework assignments. In our own practice, though, we have adopted a flipped classroom model where we ask students to read the chapter and complete certain activities as homework before they come to class. Then in class we verify students' understanding by having them present and discuss the assigned activities. Sometimes when an activity has many items – more than we would expect a single student to complete – we assign different items to different students either as homework or for presentation after they come to class. In order to accommodate different preferences, we have provided more activities than students could reasonably complete for one class meeting. Therefore, you can select the ones best suited to your classroom.

One follow-up activity in most chapters is a corpus search. If you decide to include these, we recommend spending class time showing students the websites for the corpora, their organization, and then walking them through a sample search to illustrate search terms and the types of results they return. Some of the corpus searches are more time-intensive than a regular homework assignment and could instead serve as the basis for a research paper. We also enjoy in our own classes having students give oral presentations that take a deeper look at one of the topics covered. The suggestions for further reading at the end of each chapter provide articles and web resources that could serve as a basis for these presentations or for research papers and self-guided learning.

We hope that these materials will allow you to make the history of the Spanish language an accessible and enjoyable course for your students. Please feel free to contact us if we can support your use of these materials and if we can make changes in future editions to tailor these materials to your needs.

Diana L. Ranson: dranson@uga.edu
Margaret Lubbers Quesada: quesadam@uga.edu

Acknowledgments

From both authors:

It is a pleasure to recognize and thank the many people who have supported us during the writing of this book

We would like first to thank the people who contributed directly to this book. Dallin Larsen, a doctoral student at the University of Georgia, contributed to its content by writing textboxes and research summaries, by reading and providing feedback on all the chapters, and generally by serving as an insightful consultant. Dallin also shared with us the handouts from his course on the history of the Spanish language with Jeffrey S. Turley of Brigham Young University, whom we would like to thank as well. Joy Peltier, a recent BA/MA graduate, provided valuable feedback regarding content and style on several chapters. Marissa Baer, a recent BA graduate, provided suggestions for further reading for five of the chapters. She and the ten other students in the undergraduate history of the Spanish language course and the twelve students in the equivalent graduate course in spring 2017 all made valuable contributions to this book through their reactions to and comments on the materials we piloted with them, and their suggestions for improvement. Furthermore, all of our former students at the University of Georgia on courses in the history of Spanish, the history of French, and comparative Romance linguistics and in *gramática histórica del español* at the Universidad Autónoma de Querétaro have helped shape the final form of this book and we are deeply grateful to them. We would like to mention in particular our former student Charo Pozo-Hurtado (1969–2016). We hope that this book will honor her memory.

We are also indebted to all the members of the Department of Romance Languages and the Department of Linguistics at the University of Georgia for their many tangible and intangible contributions. We would like to thank in particular, Stacey Casado, our department head, our colleagues in Romance linguistics, Gary Baker, Sarah Blackwell, Pilar Chamorro, Kelly Farmer Ford, Leslie Gordon, Tim Gupton, Chad Howe, Hilda Mata, Teresa Pérez-Gamboa, Peggy Renwick, and other colleagues with whom we have engaged in enlightening discussions on the topics in this book, including Amélia Hutchinson, Catherine Jones, Keith Langston, Jared Klein, William Kretzschmar, and Jan Pendergrass.

It has been a pleasure to work with the staff at Cambridge University Press, in particular, Helen Barton, Commissioning Editor for Language and Linguistics, and Rosemary Crawley, Development Editor, Higher Education Division. We thank them for their professionalism, insight, and enthusiasm for the project. We also thank Hetty Marx for the extremely useful development assessment and Dominic Stock, senior content manager, Kay McKechnie, copy editor, and Revathi Thirunavukkarasu, typesetter, for their care in seeing the manuscript through to its final form. Finally, we thank the eight anonymous reviewers of our book proposal and the anonymous clearance reader for their suggestions and encouragement.

From Diana Ranson:

The material in this book has also been shaped by many hours of discussion on these topics with colleagues whose work I admire tremendously. First among them, of course, is my co-author and friend, Margaret Quesada, who graciously accepted to accompany me on this journey. Her substantial contributions have been decisive in seeing the book to completion. Special thanks go also to Joel Rini who helped launch this book when I was a visiting professor at the University of Virginia in 2013. I also thank Omar Velázquez Mendoza for his gracious hospitality on that occasion and Mark Elson and Gladys Saunders. Roger Wright has also been a special source of inspiration to me along with my other colleagues across the Atlantic, Dana Allen, Ralph Penny, Chris Pountain, and Miranda Stewart. I have also been fortunate to enjoy many hours of conviviality and conversation on topics related to this book with Janice Aski, Robert Blake, José del Valle, Toni Espòsito, Matt Juge, Enrique Pato Maldonado, David Pharies, Birte Stengaard, Natalya Stolova, Fernando Tejedo-Herrero, Don Tuten, Dieter Wanner, and Kenneth Wireback, and more recently with Marisa Carpenter, Jason Doroga, Sonia Kania, and Cynthia Kauffeld. I also cherish the memory of Ray Harris-Northall and Paul Lloyd, first-rate human beings whose scholarship stands as a memorial to them, and of Tom Lathrop, a good friend whose textbook I used for many years. I also want to extend heartfelt thanks to Steven Dworkin, my first professor of the history of Spanish at the University of Michigan, to whom I dedicate Chapter 17 of this book.

Tremendous thanks go of course to my family for their love, encouragement, numerous sacrifices, and patience in happily enduring far too many conversations on the topics in this book: my mother, Rose Ranson, who also helped with proof-reading, my brothers, Ken and Kelly Ranson, my daughter, Catherine, her husband, Bill, and their three children, Daniel (10), Susanna (8), and Calvin (1), my other three grandchildren, Thomas (12), Aniah and Olivia (both 10), and my husband, Ron Miller, the renowned R. Baxter Miller, for his support and deep understanding of the rigors of scholarship, the craft of writing, and the art of teaching.

From Margaret Quesada:

My deep gratitude goes to my co-author, colleague and friend, Diana Ranson, for inviting me to collaborate with her on this project. As a specialist in second language acquisition studies, I have always considered the history of Spanish to be another of my scholarly interests and working with Diana has deepened my understanding of the historical and linguistic processes that impact language change and has given me new insights into the emergence of linguistic form in language acquisition. It has been a delight and an inspiration to work with her. I am indebted to my professors and mentors from Michigan State University who set me on the path to a rewarding life of scholarship and teaching: Grover Hudson, Ruth M. Brend (1926–2002), Julia S. Falk, Barbara Abbott, Carol Myers-Scotton, Patricia Lunn, Bill VanPatten, George Mansour, and Paul Munsell. I am grateful to my colleagues and students in Mexico for playing an integral role in my professional development during the twenty-plus years I spent there. I would like to mention specifically José Alfredo Zepeda, Silvia Yreri Mendoza, and Alma Rosa Sánchez of the Universidad Autónoma de Querétaro, and Chantal Melis and Beatriz Arias Álvarez of the Universidad Nacional Autónoma de México, whose scholarship on the history of Spanish has served as a special inspiration for material in this book.

To my family goes my deepest appreciation and gratitude for their encouragement, patience, and unconditional support, especially to Sergio Quesada, anthropologist, field-researcher, scholar, teacher, life-long partner in adventures, both academic and non-academic, from Michigan to Mexico, from California and finally to Georgia; to my children, who all have their own lives now but are still a part of me every day: Sarah Quesada Williams, Sergio J. Quesada, Amanda Quesada, and son-in-law Kyle Williams; and finally (but not least of all) to granddaughter and emerging linguist, Elsi Margaret, who will now at last get to spend more time with *abuelita*.

Athens, Georgia, September 2017

1 | Why Do Spanish Speakers Say *el arte* but *las artes*?

The Value of Studying the History of Spanish

Lead-in Question

1-1 Certain questions about the Spanish language have probably come to mind since you began speaking it, like the question in this chapter's title. As an example, here are two questions you might have about English: Why is *mice* the plural of *mouse*, but *houses* is the plural of *house*? Why do similar words in English and Spanish have different meanings, like *embarrassed* and *embarazada*? Please write down two questions – or as many as you can think of – about the Spanish language. Be sure they are questions that really interest you.

In order to start you on the path to learning about the history of Spanish, this chapter presents some interesting questions about the Spanish language that you will be able to answer after learning about its history. One such question, explored in this chapter, is why the noun arte *can be either masculine or feminine in Spanish, as in* el arte abstracto, *where it is masculine, and* las bellas artes, *where it is feminine. The answer to this question illustrates how understanding its history can increase your understanding of Spanish today.*

1.1 Why Study the History of Spanish?

If you are interested in learning about the history of the Spanish language, then it is likely that you have developed some proficiency in Spanish. You may have studied it in a classroom or on your own, or you may have grown up speaking Spanish with your family or in your community. Your ability to communicate in Spanish means that you have an understanding of how Spanish is spoken today by a particular group of people in a particular place. You know, for example, that the letters *ue* are pronounced [we] and that this diphthong occurs in *duermo* but not *dormimos*. You also know that the letters *ch* are pronounced [tʃ] and that this sound occurs in the noun *noche* but not in the adjective *nocturno*. You know the different forms for nouns, like the plural *tamales* and the singular *tamal*; pronoun forms, like *sin mí* and *conmigo*; and irregular verb forms like *soy, quepo, pongo*, and *tuve*. You also know that the words *fábrica* and *carpeta* have different meanings from English *fabric* and *carpet*. Your knowledge of Spanish as it is spoken now allows you to use the language and to describe how you use it. You are able to provide what linguists call a **synchronic description** (*una descripción sincrónica*) of Spanish, a description of the language at one point in time. But you have probably asked yourself questions about Spanish that a synchronic description could not answer. And, if you teach Spanish, then your students have no doubt generated further questions that you might not have been able to answer. You may have asked or heard questions such as:

- Why do some speakers pronounce *caza* like *catha* [ˈka-θa], whereas others pronounce it like *casa* [ˈka-sa]?
- Why are all nouns in Spanish either masculine or feminine?
- Why are there so many irregular verbs in Spanish?
- Why does Spanish have two ways of expressing the future: *iré* and *voy a ir*?
- Why do a lot of words that look the same in Spanish and English not mean the same thing, like *exit* and *éxito*?
- Is the English word *cotton* related to the Spanish word *algodón*?

The goal of this book is to answer these questions about the Spanish language and many more by offering a **diachronic description** (*una descripción* *diacrónica*), or even a diachronic analysis, that compares Spanish at two or more points in time. By comparing the features of Spanish over time, a diachronic analysis can explain the changes that have resulted in the many varieties of Spanish spoken in the world today.

1.2 Why Do Spanish Speakers Say *el arte* but *las artes?*

The title question for this chapter can illustrate how understanding the history of the language can provide a deeper understanding of contemporary Spanish. One possible answer is that the noun *arte* is masculine in the singular and feminine in the plural. Another possibility is that *arte* is always feminine, both in the singular and the plural, like *el agua/las aguas*, but one says *el arte* because the noun begins with a stressed /a/. In order to determine which description is more accurate, we can look at examples where *arte* is modified by an adjective. If a feminine adjective is used with *arte*, as in *el arte poética*, then we can conclude that *arte* is feminine in these cases, but if a masculine adjective is used, as in *el arte poético*, then we can conclude that *arte* is masculine in these examples. The results of a search on www.google.es of *arte* accompanied by the adjectives *abstracto, poético, plástico,* and *mecánico* are shown in Table 1.1.

Let us look more closely at the information in Table 1.1. The number in parentheses in each cell of the table shows the number of **tokens** (*las occurrencias*) found in the search on www.google.es of *arte* with a particular adjective form.

TABLE 1.1 Masculine and feminine adjectives with *arte*

Adjective form:	m. sg. in -*o*	f. sg. in -*a*	m. pl. in -*os*	f. pl. in -*as*
Adjective				
abstracto	71% (321,000)	29% (129,000)	49% (3510)	51% (3700)
poético	66% (25,000)	34% (13,000)	0% (10)	100% (5650)
plástico	41% (2620)	59% (3820)	13% (26,700)	87% (186,000)
mecánico	6% (3290)	94% (48,400)	1% (221)	99% (43500)

m. = masculine, f. = feminine, sg. = singular, pl. = plural

Since we want to know whether *arte* is being used as a masculine or feminine noun, we want to compare the number of tokens of *arte* with masculine and feminine adjectives. We look at both singular and plural adjectives to see whether the differences in gender are the same in the singular or plural. Therefore, each column across the top shows whether the adjective modifying *arte* is masculine singular, feminine singular, masculine plural, or feminine plural. If we look at the first row of the table, we see the number of tokens of *arte* with the adjective *abstracto*. The numbers in the cell to the left show that we found 321,000 tokens of *arte* with *abstracto*, as in *el arte abstracto*, and in the next cell to the right we see that we found only 129,000 tokens of *arte* with *abstracta*, as in *el arte abstracta*. Then we calculate the percentage of masculine and feminine tokens in the singular by adding together the total number of tokens (321,000 + 129,000 = 450,000) and then dividing the number of tokens for *abstracto* by the total number (321,000/ 450,000 = 71%) and the number of tokens for the feminine *abstracta* by the total number (129,000/450,000 = 29%). We see then that in the singular, the masculine *el arte abstracto* is far more frequent than *el arte abstracta*. But we also observe that we find large numbers of tokens for both genders. If you continue looking at the numbers of tokens and percentages for the other adjectives in Table 1.1, you will detect other patterns regarding the use of *arte* as a masculine or feminine noun.

One conclusion we can draw from these results is that *arte* is an exceptional word that can be either gender. It can be either masculine or feminine in the singular and is usually feminine in the plural, as confirmed by the results of our internet search and also by its entry in the *Diccionario Panhispánico de Dudas*. This dictionary states that *arte* can be used in both genders, but that it is most often masculine in the singular. However, it is feminine when it refers to "el conjunto de normas y principios para hacer bien algo" 'the set of norms and principles for doing something well,' so that one speaks of *arte amatoria* 'the art of love' and *arte poética* 'poetic art.' Our internet search does not bear this out, though. The noun *arte* occurs more often with *poético* than with *poética*, even though this refers to a set of principles. On the other hand, *arte* occurs more often with the feminine adjectives *plástica* and *mecánica*, which do not refer to a set of norms. In the plural, *arte* is most often feminine, especially with the adjectives *poéticas*, *mecánicas*, and *plásticas*, but less often with *abstractas*.

1.3 How Does the History of Spanish Explain the Two Genders of *arte*?

We can begin by observing that the Latin noun ARS 'art,' whose accusative form ARTEM changed into Spanish *arte*, was feminine. If *arte* was originally a feminine noun, how then might it have become masculine in some of its uses? The most likely reason is its use in the singular with the definite article *el*. You are no doubt aware that *el* is used before feminine nouns in Modern Spanish that begin with a stressed /a/, like *el agua* 'the water,' *el águila* 'the eagle,' and *el hacha* 'the ax.' But you probably were not aware that *el* is historically a feminine definite article, as well as a masculine definite article. The feminine definite article *el* came from the first syllable of the Latin feminine singular demonstrative adjective ILLAM, meaning 'that' or 'yon.' Latin ILLAM first changed to *ela* through regular sound changes. Before feminine nouns beginning with a consonant, the form *ela* lost its initial vowel to become *la* so that *ela mesa* became *la mesa*. However, before feminine nouns beginning with a vowel, the final vowel of *ela* could merge with the initial vowel of the following noun, so that the first syllable of *ela* was kept. Thus, the feminine definite article *el* came about through the following process:

ILLAM ARTEM [il-lam-ˈar-tem] > [e-la-ˈar-te] > [e-ˈlar-te] > *el arte*

Historically then, *el* is a feminine form of the definite article as well as a masculine form.

The feminine definite article *el* was limited in its use, though, compared to the more widespread *la*, which came from the second syllable of ILLAM. At first, feminine *el* was used with feminine nouns beginning with any vowel, as in *el entrada* 'the entrance,' *el obra* 'the work,' and *el imagen* 'the image,' first attested in 1196, 1256, and 1444, respectively, according to the *Corpus diacrónico del español* (CORDE) 'Diachronic corpus of Spanish' of the Real Academia Española (RAE) 'Royal Spanish Academy.' You can also see an example in the Appendix of Old Spanish texts: *sobre'll oreia* 'sobre la oreja' 'over the ear' (Appendix C, line 59, henceforth Appendix C59). Later, feminine *el* was further limited to nouns beginning only with a stressed /a/, as is true today. Since the masculine definite article *el* was used with all masculine nouns, masculine *el* was far more widespread in its use than feminine *el*. Therefore, speakers came to consider *el* and any noun used with it to be masculine, and so in this way *arte* came to be considered masculine by some speakers and writers. This association may have been further encouraged by the fact that the noun *arte* does not have a distinctive feminine ending in /a/, like *agua* and *águila*, for example.

The same association of *el* with masculine gender still occurs today. Many native speakers of Spanish will readily say, when asked, that *el agua* is masculine, but they are then at a loss to explain the plural form *las aguas* and their use of a feminine adjective in *el agua está fría*. The explanation, of course, is that *agua* is a feminine noun, but the feminine definite article *el* is used before feminine nouns beginning with a stressed /a/.

1.4 Chapter Summary

- By studying the history of the Spanish language, you will be able to find answers to many of your questions about Spanish which will lead you to a deeper understanding of this language.
- You are probably able to describe many aspects of Spanish as it is spoken now, such as the alternation between the stems of *duermo* and *dormimos*. Thus, you can provide a synchronic description of Spanish, one which describes Spanish at one point in time.
- A diachronic description, one which compares the language in at least two different points in time, can increase your understanding of Spanish.
- The changing gender of the noun *arte* provided an example of the value of adding historical information to your understanding of Spanish.
- A Google search of the noun *arte* followed by the adjectives *abstracto*, *poético*, *plástico*, and *mecánico* provided the synchronic description that *arte* can be either masculine or feminine in Modern Spanish. One finds people writing, for example, *el arte abstracto* or *el arte abstracta* in the singular and *los artes abstractos* or *las artes abstractas* in the plural. If we consider only Modern Spanish, we are unable to explain why *arte* is sometimes masculine and sometimes feminine.

- A study of the history of Spanish offers an answer. The noun *arte* was originally feminine in Latin. However, the definite article *el* was used with *arte*, since the Latin feminine definite article ILLAM became *el* before any noun beginning with a vowel in Old Spanish. In Modern Spanish the feminine article *el* was kept only before nouns beginning with a stressed /a/, like *arte*. Some speakers then interpreted the article *el*, which was originally feminine, to be a masculine article and so they assumed that *arte* was masculine. Thus, one finds *arte* used as either masculine or feminine because some speakers assume that *arte* is masculine because it takes the article *el*, while others continue to consider it to be a feminine noun.

Complete Activities 1-1 to 1-5 below.

Activities

Activity 1-1

After reading this chapter, write down any additional questions that have come to mind about the Spanish language. For at least one of the questions you wrote here or in answer to the Lead-in question, check the index to this book to see whether it will provide an answer to your question. If so, make a note of the chapter or page number. If not, ask your professor to answer this question or send your questions to the authors at the email addresses listed in the preface.

Activity 1-2

What are your first impressions of the importance of written records, such as the documents containing examples like *el entrada* and *el arte poético*, to the study of the history of the Spanish language?

Activity 1-3

If a friend asks you why Spanish speakers say *el arte* but *las artes*, what do you say? Give as simple and concise an answer as you can.

Activity 1-4

Corpus Search

We mentioned that Spanish speakers gradually came to consider the definite article, *el*, to be masculine and so certain feminine nouns used with *el* came to be perceived as masculine. This was especially true of feminine nouns that did not end in /a/, like *arte*. But do speakers also consider some feminine words ending in /a/ to be masculine? Do your own search on google.es with the following combinations of words in italics. How do the results for *agua* compare to those for *arte* in Table 1.1?

el agua fría   *el agua frío*
las aguas frías   *los aguas fríos*

Activity 1-5

Question for Thought

Many people think that language change is bad. For example, you may have heard someone say "young people don't know how to speak properly anymore." What are your thoughts on this? What are some of the ways that the English language has changed for the better or for the worse, in your opinion? This question and others will be discussed in Chapter 2.

Further Reading

blog.oxforddictionaries.com: a great site for answers to your linguistic questions about English

udep.edu.pe/castellanoactual/seccion/dudas/: a site in Spanish in Piura, Peru, where you can send questions and find answers about questions of use in Spanish

Rini, Joel 1990. "The application of historical linguistic information to the foreign language classroom," *Hispania* 73: 842–44

2 Is It Wrong to Say *cantastes* instead of *cantaste?*

A Linguist's Attitude and Approach to Language

Lead-in Questions

2-1 Give an example of a time when someone corrected your use of your native language. He or she might have said, for example, "don't say *me and him went to the store*, say *he and I*." What was his or her reason for correcting you?

2-2 Now recall a time when you corrected someone else's use of his or her native language. What did you say? Why?

2-3 If you are not a native speaker of Spanish, recount an incident where someone corrected your use of Spanish or, if you are a native speaker of Spanish, when someone corrected your use of a language that is not your native language. What did he or she say? Why?

Chapter 1 *provided a diachronic explanation for the modern forms* el arte *and* las artes *while at the same time illustrating how linguists approach the task of arriving at this type of explanation. In this chapter, we will take a closer look at a linguist's approach to the study of language. The most fundamental principle of linguists is that all linguistic varieties of a language are equally valid. Following this principle will enable you to learn to think linguistically so that you can analyze what you read and hear in Spanish, or any language, and ultimately find answers to the questions you may have about the languages you encounter in your daily life.*

2.1 Does a Linguist Tell a Cat How to Meow?

A fundamental principle of any linguistic analysis is that linguists do not make **value judgments** (*juicios de valor*) about language. This means that linguists do not consider what native speakers say to be good or bad or correct or incorrect. In fact, linguists do not even use these words. A linguist listens to everything a native speaker says without judging. Let's take the example of *ain't* in English. You have no doubt heard that it is wrong or incorrect to say *ain't*. But this idea does not come from a linguist. It comes instead from a grammarian whose goal is to develop a **prescriptive grammar** (*una gramática prescriptiva*) of the language that tells native speakers how they should speak. A linguist's job, on the other hand, is to **describe** what native speakers say, and eventually to analyze and explain it in a **descriptive grammar** (*una gramática descriptiva*). So, rather than advising you not to say *ain't* like a grammarian would, a linguist accepts that many native speakers of English do say *ain't* and describes which speakers use this form and in which contexts.

Unless you have studied linguistics before, the only times you thought about language use may have been when your parents or grandparents or teachers corrected you or when you corrected someone else. During your school years, for example, your English teachers may have told you to say *drive slowly* and not *drive slow* or to say *they don't have any* instead of *they don't got none*. Because these are the only times that many of us have focused our attention on our use of language, we tend to recall these grammatical rules when we begin to study linguistics. It is for this reason that it is important to begin our journey toward understanding Spanish by discussing how a grammarian's goal of prescribing language use is very different from a linguist's goal of describing, analyzing, and explaining native speakers' use of their own language.

The following story of Big Boy can serve to illustrate the difference between the grammarian's prescriptive approach and the linguist's descriptive approach.

The Story of Big Boy the Cat

When the first author, Diana, was a little girl growing up in San Antonio, Texas, her neighbor, Mary, had a fat Siamese cat named Big Boy. One day, Diana was at Mary's house when she heard a strange rumbling sound: "Raouw-Raouw! Raouw-Raouw!" It sounded more like a person imitating a cat than a real cat, so she said: "Mary, that's the worst imitation of a cat I've ever heard!" But when she looked down, to her great surprise, there was Big Boy himself looking up at her saying: "Raouw-Raouw! Raouw-Raouw!" Her first reaction was to respond like a grammarian would: "Listen, Big Boy, that's not how you meow. You're supposed to make a nice kitty-cat sound like 'meow, meow'." Then the absurdity of the situation hit her. How was she – a human – going to tell a cat how to meow? Certainly a cat would know how to meow better than she would. This realization led her to think like a linguist: "Well, that's the strangest meow I've ever heard, but since a cat is making it, it must be a meow. I'll just have to expand my idea of what a meow sounds like."

To linguists, native speakers are like the cat in this story. From a linguist's point of view language is made up of everything native speakers say. So, if a native speaker says something that the linguist has never heard, then the linguist has to expand the definition of what is possible in that language. Let's say that the second author, Margaret, thinks that *azúcar* is masculine for all native speakers of Spanish. Then one day she hears a Puerto Rican say: *¿Tú quieres azúcar morena?* Rather than telling this native speaker that he is wrong and that he should say *azúcar moreno*, Margaret concludes that *azúcar* can be feminine in this variety of Spanish. She may even set out to determine for which speakers and in which situations this is true. A linguist doesn't tell a native speaker how to speak any more than a person tells a cat how to meow. Whatever a native speaker says is part of his or her language in the same way that certain sounds a cat makes are meows.

Complete Activities 2-1 and 2-2 on pages 16–17.

2.2 What Does a Linguist's Attitude Mean in Real Life?

Some of you may delight in correcting your friends' use of English or Spanish. You may enjoy telling people to say, for example, *where is it?* rather than *where's it at?* If you become a linguist, does that mean that you can no longer correct your friends? A simple answer is that you can still correct your friends, if you really want to, but you will no longer consider their way of speaking to be bad or incorrect. And so when you correct them, you are really only pointing out to them that there is another way of saying the same thing. This will allow you to observe and appreciate these differences. Maybe speakers like to say *where's it at?* because placing the preposition at the end allows them to emphasize the fact that they are asking for a location.

If you have ever suffered from people's corrections of your speech or ever been made to feel inferior for the variety of English or Spanish that you speak, you will find the linguist's attitude to be liberating. You now know that anything you say as a native speaker is part of your language and that your way of speaking is neither worse nor better than the speech of the person correcting you. You may have been subjected to social judgments from other people about your speech, but these have nothing to do with its value from a linguistic point of view. We have heard many heartwarming stories from our own students over the years who were relieved to discover in our classes that there was nothing linguistically inferior about their variety of Spanish or English.

Even though linguists do not make value judgments about language, is it possible for a native speaker to make a mistake? We might say that a native speaker has made a mistake when he suffers from a slip of the tongue. If a native speaker of English were to say *I have tooken my time*, he would no doubt quickly correct this to *I have taken*, realizing that this is not a form he normally uses. A native speaker can also say something inappropriate, for example, by using informal speech in a formal situation. This is why even a linguist would tell a student who is a native Spanish speaker to say *no sé la respuesta* 'I don't know the answer' in response to a question asked in class rather than *no me importa un bledo* 'I couldn't care less.' The latter response is not a grammatical mistake, since it exists in the speech of native speakers, but it is inappropriate because it is too informal and disrespectful for the classroom setting.

There is another case where we might say that a native speaker has made a mistake, because what she said did not achieve her goals for saying it. This happens when a native speaker produces a **hypercorrection** (*una hipercorrección*), a form that results from an erroneous attempt to correct a perceived error or less desirable form. Suppose that an Andalusian speaker, who normally deletes [s] at the ends of syllables and words, pronounces *este* as ['es-te] instead of ['e-te] when she thinks that pronouncing the [s] is more appropriate. But this same speaker may produce a hypercorrection when she adds an [s] to words where it does not occur in the speech of native speakers who usually maintain it. She might say *quiero hablar más fisno* 'I want to speak in a more refined way.' However, by saying *fisno* rather than *fino*, she has produced a hypercorrection that ironically does not achieve her goal of speaking in a more refined way.

An example from English would be a speaker, who often says *takin'* ['tekɪn] instead of *taking* ['tekɪŋ], producing the hypercorrect form *chicking* for *chicken*. She might do this under the erroneous belief that her pronunciation of *chicken* can be improved by replacing the final consonant [n] with [ŋ] (Nordquist 2017). Speakers are most likely to produce hypercorrect forms when a feeling of linguistic insecurity leads them to try to follow prescriptions that they have not fully understood. Even though hypercorrection is a normal process, we can consider it to be a mistake, since it does not achieve the speaker's goal in producing it.

Another application of the linguist's attitude occurs in the classroom. You may be wondering whether having a linguist for a Spanish teacher would mean she has an "anything goes" attitude. Some students assume this would be good since they would not lose points for their grammatical errors. Others assume that this would be bad because they want to learn to speak Spanish "correctly." But both of these ideas are based on a misunderstanding. Recall that linguists believe that native speakers determine what is possible in their language. If Spanish is not your native language, then you are capable of making errors in Spanish. A linguist who is helping you improve your Spanish will correct these errors (and take points off, if need be) so that your Spanish will become more like that of a native speaker. She can also teach you to speak "correctly," but without using this judgmental term. She will instead teach you to speak like a native speaker. A linguist will not judge your Spanish to be bad, but rather non-native, when you make mistakes. Mistakes are after all a normal part of the language learning process. So, a linguist can do everything that a grammarian can do in the classroom except place value judgments on language. Furthermore, a linguist can do more than a grammarian because a linguist observes, describes, and analyzes all varieties of language, not just the variety that the grammarian judges to be "correct."

Complete Activities 2-3 and 2-4 on pages 17-19.

2.3 Why Are There Grammarians?

Now that you have learned that linguists can do everything grammarians can do except make value judgments, you may be wondering why anyone is a grammarian. In Chapter 5 you will learn that grammarians play an important role in society of helping to create what we can call **a standard language** (*una lengua estándar*). A standard language, though, to a linguist is just one of many varieties of Spanish or English. Some speakers, especially if their profession requires it, pay careful attention to the prescriptions of grammarians, and so a language changes less quickly than it might otherwise. However, most speakers pay very little attention to grammarians' prescriptions, which explains why languages keep changing in spite of these prescriptions.

One of the most famous linguistic documents in the history of the Romance languages can serve to illustrate the fact that grammarians usually do not succeed in preventing changes. This document, known as the *Appendix Probi* ('Probus's Appendix'), is one of five appendices added to a first-century Latin grammar by Marcus Valerius Probus. In it an anonymous author in the third or fourth century attempts to correct what he considers to be common errors in the Latin language of his time. The document consists of 227 pairs of words in the form "A *non* B" 'A not B' where A is the Classical Latin form, the one preferred by the author, and B is a form the author judged to be incorrect. This document is especially valuable because it provides some insight into popular speech at that time by setting down in writing the forms that earned the author's disapproval.

Two examples from this document are cases where the author is disapproving of hypercorrection: FORMOSUS NON FORMUNSUS and OCCASIO NON OCCANSIO. In the Latin spoken in his time, speakers often deleted an /n/ in the middle of words, so that a word like MĒNSAM 'table' would be pronounced *mesa*, just like the word for 'table' in Spanish. This prompted some speakers to pronounce an /n/ in words that did not have one in Classical Latin, represented by the *n* added by the author in the words above. These words evolved to *hermoso* and *ocasión* in Spanish, so we can see that the original form survived, not the hypercorrect one with the added /n/.

There are other examples, though, where the censured form survived. The Latin word for 'mother-in-law' was SOCRUS, whose ending made it look like a masculine noun. The same was true of NURUS 'daughter-in-law.' Despite the grammarian's admonishments of SOCRUS NON SOCRA and NURUS NON NURA, it is the censured member of each pair, created by adding the feminine ending -A, that survived in Spanish as *suegra* and *nuera*.

2.4 Chapter Summary

- Linguists have a descriptive rather than a prescriptive approach to language. This means that they describe what a language is like rather than prescribing what it should be like.
- Linguists' descriptive approach also means that they do not make value judgments about language. Rather they consider everything a native speaker says to be part of his or her language without judging any variety to be superior or inferior to another. In fact, linguists do not even use evaluative terms like *correct* and *incorrect* or *better* and *worse*.

- In practical terms this means that linguists do not correct native speakers. If you adopt the attitude of a linguist, you will learn not to correct your friends either, but rather to appreciate and analyze the differences between their speech and yours.
- Linguists can, however, correct non-native speakers. If you have a Spanish teacher who is a linguist, he or she will be able to correct your speech where it differs from that of a native speaker. As a teacher, a linguist can do everything a grammarian can do, except make value judgments.
- A linguist can even do more than a grammarian because a linguist observes, describes, and analyzes all varieties of language, not just the variety that the grammarian judges to be "correct."
- Grammarians have the important function in society of formulating rules for the standard variety of a language, but speakers continue to change their speech in spite of grammarians' admonitions.
- Some examples from the third- or fourth-century *Appendix Probi* show that the grammarian's preferred forms were not necessarily the ones that survived in Spanish.

Complete Activities 2-5 and 2-6 on pages 20-22.

Activities

Activity 2-1

Who is the grammarian in the comic strip in Figure 2.1? What is the perceived error he is trying to correct? Does the author of the comic strip think his behavior is appropriate in this situation?

Figure 2.1 *Candorville* comic strip
(*Candorville* used with the permission of Darrin Bell, the Washington Post Writers Group and the Cartoonist Group. All rights reserved.)

Activity 2-2

A. In your own words, explain the difference between a linguist and a grammarian.

B. Ask three people you know "what is a linguist?" Write below who you asked in the underlined space and then what he or she said. If the person you asked did not give a satisfactory answer, write what you said to educate him or her.

1. Person 1: _____

2. Person 2: _____

3. Person 3: _____

C. Do you prefer for your Spanish professors to be linguists or grammarians? Explain why.

Activity 2-3

The examples below present two ways of saying more or less the same thing, in pairs such as A1 and A2.

1. Place a check mark next to all the options you say yourself. If you say more than one option, try to determine when you say one and when you say the other.

2. Place an asterisk next to the ones a grammarian would think are "correct."

3. For at least two groups of examples, practice thinking like a linguist and describe the difference between the two options and try to explain why speakers might say each one.

For example, here are some possible responses for Group 1 in English:

1. I say all of these. I tend to say A1, B1, and C1 in informal comfortable situations, like when I'm at home with my family. I tend to say A2, B2, and C2 in more formal situations where I tend to monitor my speech, like in a classroom or at a religious service.
2. A grammarian would think that only A2, B2, and C2 are correct, especially in writing.
3. A1 *They're gonna do it* and A2 *They are going to do it.* The difference is that speakers pronounce fewer sounds in A1. Not only does the contraction *they're* delete the vowel /a/ in *they are*, but saying *gonna* deletes the /i/, /ŋ/, and /t/ in *going to.* One explanation is that speakers produce A1 so as to have fewer sounds to pronounce. It's striking to see how many fewer sounds are pronounced in B1 and C1 than in B2 and C2.

Examples in English	Examples in Spanish
Group 1:	Group 1:
A1. They're gonna do it.	A1. Yo no ahpiro la ese. Soy purihta.
A2. They are going to do it.	A2. Yo no aspiro la ese. Soy purista.
B1. I dunno.	B1. No he encontrao ná.
B2. I don't know.	B2. No he encontrado nada.
C1. Jeet jet?	C1. Uno dice « los sapatos ».
C2. Did you eat yet?	C2. Otro dithe « los thapatos ».
Group 2:	Group 2:
A1. It's more simple and more fair.	A1. Este ladrillo es más más malo.
A2. It's simpler and fairer.	A2. Este ladrillo es peor.
B1. It's funner.	B1. Es más bueno que el pan.
B2. It's more fun.	B2. Es mejor que el pan.
C1. It's more good.	C1. La gente de aquí habla peor.
C2. It's better.	C2. La gente de aquí habla mucho peor.
C3. It's more better.	
Group 3:	Group 3:
A1. Honey, I shrunk the kids.	A1. Cantastes bien ayer
A2. Honey, I shrank the kids.	A2. Cantaste bien ayer.

Examples in English	Examples in Spanish
B1. I swang at the ball.	B1. Hubieron dificultades.
B2. I swung at the ball.	B2. Hubo dificultades.
C1. I have swam 5 laps already.	C1. ... y Lázaro andó.
C2. I have swum 5 laps already.	C2. ... y Lázaro anduvo.
Group 4: A1. Where are you going? A2. Where is it you're going? A3. Where you('re) going? A4. You're going where?	Group 4: A1. ¿Adónde vas tú? A2. ¿Adónde tú vas? B1. Lo voy a hacer. B2. Voy a hacerlo.
Group 5: A1. Adios, amigos. See you later. A2. Bye, guys. See you later. B1. Look at Chad's sombrero. B2. Look at the hat Chad is wearing.	Group 5: A1. Traje mi lonche hoy. A2. Traje mi almuerzo hoy. B1. ¿Vas a ir al pari en el bar esta noche? B2. ¿Vas a ir a la fiesta en casa de Omar esta noche?
Group 6: A1. This cake is sweet. A2. What a sweet shot! B1. I'm mad about what you did. B2. That goalkeeper has mad skills.	Group 6: A1. Mi padre ya tiene sesenta años. A2. ¡Qué padre tu nuevo auto! B1. ¿Quieres una mordida de mi pastel? B2. El policía aceptó mi mordida y no me dio una multa.
An extra group in English just for fun: A1. Athen's Coffee Shop A2. Athens' Coffee Shop B1. Employee's Only B2. Employees Only	An extra group in Spanish just for fun: A1. Enrique no a escuchado la noticia. A2. Enrique no ha escuchado la noticia. B1. Se bende esta casa. B2. Se vende esta casa.

Activity 2-4

Explain why a linguist would reject the following myths and why it is important to debunk them, even if you were (or still are!) in agreement with these ideas.

1. Grammarians and language academicians, like the members of the Real Academia Española (RAE), are the highest authorities on language. They decide what you should and shouldn't say.
2. Spanish dialects like Andalusian, Argentinean, and Puerto Rican are corruptions of real Spanish, the Castilian dialect.
3. With the loss of word-final /s/ and intervocalic /d/, as in *estao* (instead of *estado*), the Spanish language is going downhill.
4. Spanish is just bad Latin.
5. Written Spanish is more correct than spoken Spanish.
6. People who are illiterate don't learn their own language well and so they make a lot of mistakes when they speak it.
7. You shouldn't use foreign words, like words from English, when you speak Spanish. It sounds silly to say things like, "Voy a ir de *shopping* el sábado."
8. Spanish is the most logical language in the world, French the most romantic, Italian the most beautiful, and German the most difficult.

Activity 2-5

Here are some more examples from the *Appendix Probi.* For each one:

1. a. Write the resulting form in Spanish. (If you need help, choose from among these words listed in alphabetical order: *ajo, ánfora, autor, cámara, columna, espejo, flagelo, hormiga, hostia, mesa, ojo, plebe, río, senado, verde, viejo, viña.*)
   b. Write A or B next to the Spanish word to indicate whether it comes from the form A or B of the *Appendix Probi.* Explain how you decided.
2. The examples are arranged according to the type of change they represent. Study the changes and add a heading to each group in the space provided choosing from among the following options:
   a. Loss of a vowel, like the u in TABULA NON TABLA. The loss of an unstressed sound in the middle of the word is called **syncope** (*la síncopa*).

b. Loss of a consonant, like the M in NUNQUAM NON NUNQUA

c. Change of a vowel, like I to E in SIRENA NON SERENA

d. Change of a consonant, like V to B in VAPULO NON BAPLO (in this case a vowel is lost as well) (like Modern Spanish *vápulo* 'beating, scolding')

Selected examples from the *Appendix Probi*	
Change: _____	Change: _____
VIRIDIS NON VIRDIS	MENSA NON MESA
SPECULUM NON SPECLUM	AUCTOR NON AUTOR
OCULUS NON OCLUS	RIVUS NON RIUS
VETULUS NON VECLUS	HOSTIAE NON OSTIAE
Change: _____	Change: _____
VINEA NON VINIA	PLEBES NON PLEVIS
ALIUM NON ALEUM	AMFORA NON AMPORA
COLUMNA NON COLOMNA	FLAGELLUM NON FRAGELLUM
FORMICA NON FURMICA	
SENATUS NON SINATUS	
CAMERA NON CAMMARA	

3. If you were to write a modern version of the *Appendix Probi,* which items would you include? Give at least two items in Spanish and two items in English.

If the item you propose is like an item in the *Appendix Probi,* state how the two items are alike.

Item 1 in English:
Item 2 in English:
Item 1 in Spanish:
Item 2 in Spanish:

Here are two examples in English and two in Spanish to get you started:

English: *family not famly*
            between you and me not between you and I

Like *tabula non tabla, family not famly* is a case of syncope. *Between you and me not between you and I,* the subject of the comic strip in Activity

2-1, is a case of hypercorrection like *occasio non occansio*, but one involving forms and not just sounds. When some speakers of English say "you and me are friends," someone corrects this to "you and I are friends" because in this sentence *you and I* is the subject of the verb *are*. These speakers then conclude that it is always right to say *you and I* and so they end up saying *between you and I*. This is a case of hypercorrection because the speaker has made an erroneous attempt to correct a perceived error. The correct form according to prescriptive grammar is *between you and me*, since *you* and *me* are the objects of the preposition *between*.

Spanish: *bacalao no bacalado*

             cantaste no cantastes

Bacalao no bacalado is a case of hypercorrection like *occasio non occansio*. Many speakers of Modern Spanish delete the sound /d/ between vowels, so that *hablado* becomes *hablao*. Thinking erroneously that the vowel sequence [ao] represents [aðo] with a deleted [ð], some speakers change *bacalao* to *bacalado* by hypercorrection, in the same way that an English speaker might change *chicken* to *chicking*.

Cantaste no cantastes illustrates a change in Modern Spanish by **analogy** (*la analogía*), that is, the change of the form of one word following the model of another word. Since all second person singular or *tú* verb forms end in /s/ except the preterit *cantaste* and the imperative *canta*, some speakers add an /s/ to *cantaste* to form *cantastes*, so that it will end in an /s/ like all other second person singular verb forms.

Activity 2-6

Write a brief answer to the title question for this chapter: Is it wrong to say *cantastes*?

Further Reading

"What is correct language?" www.linguisticsociety.org/resource/what-correct-language www.sil.org: This is an excellent site for exploring general information on languages and linguistics. The section on attitudes is particularly relevant to this chapter: www.sil.org/language-assessment/language-attitudes

"Good grammar, bad grammar – prescriptivism vs. descriptivism – Linguistics 101." YouTube video

Powell, J. G. F. 2007. "A new text of the 'Appendix Probi,'" *The Classical Quarterly* 57(2): 687–700

3 How and Why Do Languages Change and How Do Linguists Know?

Lead-in Questions

3-1 Can you think of a change you have made in the way you speak English or Spanish? Have you started using a new word or pronouncing a word differently? What might explain this change? Maybe you started using the word *beanie* in English along with *ski cap* or you started saying *zumo* in Spanish along with *jugo* because you have a friend who uses this word. Write down at least two such changes and what you think motivated you to make them.

3-2 Now think of cases where you vary the way you say something in English or Spanish. For example, you may pronounce the word *route* two different ways, so that sometimes it rhymes with *boot* and sometimes with *bout*. Or you may sometimes refer to your footwear as *shoes* and sometimes as *kicks*. Write down at least two such examples and try to determine when you use one variant and when you use another.

Now that you have learned to think like a linguist in Chapter 2, *you are ready in this chapter to delve into the core concern of a book on the history of Spanish: how and why languages change. We will start with the premise that languages do not change on their own, but rather speakers change their language in line with their goals. We will also see that changes take place in different aspects of a language – in spelling, sounds, forms, the order of forms and words, the words themselves, and the meanings of these words – and that the speakers have different reasons for changing each of these aspects of their language. Finally, you will learn that historical linguists study language change by formulating hypotheses about changes and then testing them by collecting data from written texts.*

3.1 What Is Language Change?

Language change (*el cambio lingüístico*) is of course a change in a language, like the creation of a new word such as *selfie* in English or *autofoto* in Spanish. But when we talk about any change in a language, like the creation of a new word, we must keep in mind two important points. The first is that languages do not change by themselves; rather, people change them. A new word doesn't just appear on its own; instead, someone says it to a friend or records it in a song or sends it in a tweet. People are of paramount importance in language change for the simple reason that languages exist only when speakers open their mouths to speak or when writers put pen to paper or fingers to keyboard. In short, languages exist only when speakers or writers produce them, and whenever people use their language they make decisions – conscious or unconscious – about which sounds or letters to produce, which forms to use, which words to choose, and which order to put them in. We can say then that languages change when people change them by creating new features and choosing them over old ones.

The second point is that a change in language use by one or even several individuals does not constitute a change in the language. The first documented use of *selfie*, for example, was in 2002 in the post of a 21-year-old man in a science forum on the website of the Australian Broadcasting Corporation (Zimmer 2013). However, if he had been the only person who ever used the term, then this would not have constituted a change in the English language. We consider that a change has occurred only after a significant number of speakers begin using a particular feature in a regular fashion. As we all know, the word *selfie* has enjoyed great success, so much so that in 2013 it was named the word of the year by the *Oxford Dictionaries*. As a result, we can say by now that this new word or **neologism** (*un neologismo*) for the product of the technology that makes it possible for people to take, send, or upload photos of themselves constitutes a change in the English language. There is no precise formula for the number of speakers or frequency of use of a particular linguistic feature that allows linguists to say that a change has occurred, but as individuals we no doubt think this has happened when we become aware of a new term or start using it ourselves.

Practice 3-1

Conduct an internet search on the word *selfie*, or any other word you use and are curious about, to discover an interesting piece of information about it, like when it was first used, how to say it in Spanish or other languages, or the proposed terms for different types of selfies, like *wesies* or *groupies*. What does your discovery say about language change?

The word *selfie* is a lexical change since it involves a change in the vocabulary or **lexicon** (*el léxico*) of the English language, but changes can occur in other aspects of a language as well. In order to appreciate some changes that have occurred in the history of the Spanish language, let us take a look at a fourteenth-century Spanish text, *El Conde Lucanor*, and compare it to a Modern Spanish translation in order to identify some changes that have taken place.

El Conde Lucanor

Original text	Modern Spanish translation
1. Exemplo Quinto: De lo que contesçió	Cuento Cinco: De lo que sucedió
2. a un raposo con un cuervo que teníe	a un zorro con un cuervo que tenía
3. un pedaço de queso en el pico.	un pedazo de queso en el pico.
4. Otra vez fablava el conde Lucanor con	Otra vez hablaba el conde Lucanor con
5. Patronio, su conseiero, et díxol así...	Patronio, su consejero, y le dijo así...

Original text	Modern Spanish translation
6. –Señor conde Lucanor –dixo Patronio–	–Señor conde Lucanor –dijo Patronio–
7. el cuervo falló una vegada un grant pedaço	el cuervo halló una vez un gran pedazo
8. de queso et subió en un árbol porque	de queso y subió en un árbol para que
9. pudiese comer el queso más a su guisa	pudiera comer el queso más a su manera
10. et sin reçelo et sin enbargo de ninguno.	y sin miedo y sin molestia de nadie.
11. Et en quanto el cuervo assí estava,	Y en cuanto (mientras) el cuervo así estaba,
12. passó el raposo por el pie del árbol,	pasó el zorro por el pie del árbol,
13. et desque vio el queso que el cuervo tenía,	y desde que vio el queso que el cuervo tenía,
14. començó a cuydar en quál manera	comenzó a pensar en de cuál manera
15. lo podría levar dél.	podría quitárselo (llevarlo de él).

We can identify the following types of changes by comparing the original text with the Modern Spanish translation.

A. A purely **orthographic change** (*un cambio ortográfico*) is a change only in **orthography** (*la ortografía*) or spelling but not in pronunciation. A purely orthographic change occurs when writers of a language use new or different letters or delete letters in the representation of certain sounds without changing the sounds themselves.

In order to identify a purely orthographic change you need to know that the following different sets of letters represented the same sounds in Old Spanish and in Modern Spanish:

Sound	Old Spanish spelling	Modern Spanish spelling
[s]	*ss*	*s*
[β] between vowels	*b* or *v*	*b* or *v*
[kwa]	*qua*	*cua*

Example: Old Spanish *assí*, Modern Spanish *así* (line 11). Whereas writers generally used a double *s* in Old Spanish to represent the sound [s] between vowels, in Modern Spanish they use *s*.

B. A **phonological change** (*un cambio fonológico*) or sound change is a change in **phonology** (*la fonología*) or pronunciation. A phonological change occurs when speakers use new or different sounds in the pronunciation of a word or when they delete certain sounds.

In order to identify a sound change on the basis of a written text, you need to know the sounds represented by the letters. Here are some letters that represent different sounds in Old Spanish than in Modern Spanish, if indeed these letters are still used in Modern Spanish.

Spelling	Old Spanish sound	Modern Spanish sound
ç, z	[ts] (as in English *pizza*)	[s] or [θ]
s between vowels	[z]	[s]
x	[ʃ] (as in English *shell*)	[x]
f	[h]	[f] or Ø
ll	[ʎ] (as in Italian *figlio*)	[j] in most dialects

Example: Old Spanish *dixo* [ˈdi-ʃo] > Modern Spanish *dijo* [ˈdi-xo] (lines 5 and 6). The sound that used to be pronounced /ʃ/ in Old Spanish is now pronounced farther back in the throat as the jota [x] in Modern Spanish.

C. A **morphological change** (*un cambio morfológico*) is a change in **morphology** (*la morfología*) or the form of a word. A morphological change occurs when speakers use new or different forms or lose forms that they used to use. The forms that speakers may change are made up of **morphemes** (*los morfemas*), the smallest meaningful units in a language. A simple example from English is the past morpheme -*d* at the end of words like *wined* and *dined*. One type of morphological change occurs when speakers change one form following the model of another form through the process of analogy. For example, when the past tense of English *shine* changes from *shone* to *shined*, this form follows the model of regular verbs like *wined* and *dined*.

Example: Old Spanish *levar* → Modern Spanish *llevar* (line 15). The Old Spanish infinitive *levar* changed its form to *llevar* in Modern Spanish following the model of other verb forms in the paradigm of this same verb, like *llevo, llevas, lleva,* and *llevan*.

Further explanation: Through regular sound changes, Old Spanish *levar* would have remained *levar* in Modern Spanish. The Modern Spanish form *llevar* is the result of analogy of the infinitive to certain forms of the verb in the present indicative, namely 1sg. *llevo*, 2sg. *llevas*, 3sg. *lleva*, and 3pl. *llevan*. These forms, which serve as the model for the morphological change from *levar* to *llevar*, get the initial *ll* through regular sound change. For example, in the 1sg. form *llevo* from Latin LĔVŌ, the vowel ĕ, in tonic position, the position that bears the stress, is articulated as the diphthong /je/ (and the Latin /w/ written as *v* becomes [β] between vowels), so that LĔVŌ becomes ['lje-βo]. Then [lj] changes to the palatal consonant [ʎ] resulting in the form *llevo*. The infinitive, Latin LĔVĀRE, which would have become *levar* [le-'βar] through regular sound change, becomes instead *llevar* [ʎe-'βar] through analogy, so that it begins with the same consonant as *llevo*, *llevas*, *lleva*, and *llevan*.

D. A **syntactic change** (*un cambio sintáctico*) is a change in **syntax** (*la sintaxis*), the order of morphemes or their grammatical function. A syntactic change occurs when speakers change the order of elements, like the change in English from *What time is it?* to *What time it is?*, or when speakers change the function of a grammatical form, like the change of function of *fuera* from pluperfect in Old Spanish, meaning 'had been,' to imperfect subjunctive in Modern Spanish.

Example: Old Spanish *et díxol así*, Modern Spanish *y le dijo así* (line 5). The pronoun *le* followed the verb in Old Spanish, but it precedes the verb in Modern Spanish.

Further explanation: In Old Spanish a **clitic pronoun** (*un pronombre clítico*), a pronoun that cannot stand alone but is always accompanied by a verb, like the indirect object pronoun *le*, could not appear in clause-initial position or after *et* 'and.' So, when a clause began with a verb or *et*, any accompanying clitic pronoun was placed after the verb (*díxo-l(e)*). A syntactic change occurred so that clitic pronouns, like *le*, are now placed before the verb in Modern Spanish even in clause-initial position (*le dijo*).

E. A **lexical change** (*un cambio léxico*), which affects the lexicon or vocabulary of a language, is the change of a **lexical item** (*una unidad léxica*) or word used to express a certain idea. A lexical change occurs when speakers create new words or lose existing words.

Example: Old Spanish *guisa* (< Germanic *wisa*, related to English *wise*, as in *lengthwise*) is lost and replaced by *manera* (line 9).

F. A **semantic change** (*un cambio semántico*) is a change in **semantics** (*la semántica*) or meaning. One type of semantic change occurs when a word takes on a new meaning or loses a previous meaning.
Example: *cuydar,* now spelled *cuidar,* changed its meaning from 'to think' to its current meaning of 'to care for' (line 14).

Through these examples, we have seen that language change occurs when a certain number of speakers discard existing structures for new ones or create new spellings, sounds, forms, words, word orders, or meanings for existing words.

Complete Activities 3-1 and 3-2 on pages 42-43.

3.2 Why Do Languages Change?

Having considered examples of language change in the previous section and the change of *arte* from feminine to masculine in Chapter 1, we can now ask "Why did these changes occur?" For example, why did the Latin feminine noun ARTEM not simply continue unchanged? If we accept that all language change depends ultimately on speakers, then our next step is to determine why a speaker might alter his or her language. Perhaps the most basic reason is that people like variety. This idea goes back at least as far as Dante, who wrote in Latin at the beginning of the fourteenth century that a human being is a very unstable and variable animal and so all human institutions, like customs and clothing, must change over place and time. In the same way that we humans enjoy trying out different fashions in clothing, food, or technology, we also enjoy trying out new words, forms, and sounds. We are conscious of some of these changes, like when we use a new word, such as *bromance* in English, which combines *brother* and *romance*, or *burrocracia* in Spanish, which combines *burro* and *burocracia*. Yet, we are unaware of other changes, like the change in the pronunciation of *where* from [hw̥ɛɹ] to [wɛɹ], so that *where* now sounds like *wear* and *ware*. In Spanish, for example, many speakers who aspirate the /s/ saying *ehte* [ˈeh-te] instead of *este* are unaware of this change. A graduate school classmate of the first author once said in class: "Yo no ahpiro. Soy purihta." His very denial of his aspiration confirmed that he did indeed aspirate, but that he was not aware of it. If we want to dig deeper for a reason for people's fondness for variety and change, we could cite the reason given by the Greek philosopher Heraclitus of Ephesus (c. 535–475 BC) that "everything changes and nothing stands still." Similarly, we could quote the first author's former professor, Ernst Pulgram (1983: 111), who echoed Heraclitus by writing: "[for] the cause of linguistic change in the abstract … as good an explanation as any is the fact that in this universe everything changes … "

Of course, even once we accept that people change language because they enjoy variety or because change is inevitable, we still have to explain why certain speakers make certain changes to their language at a certain time. This challenge for historical linguistics, referred to as the **actuation problem** (*el problema de actuación*), has been particularly difficult, if not impossible, to solve. This problem was stated in Weinreich, Labov, and Herzog's (1968: 102) groundbreaking article as follows: "Why do changes in a structural feature take place in a particular language at a given time, but not in other languages with the same feature, or in the same language at other times?" Despite this difficulty, we agree with Tuten and Tejedo-Herrero (2011: 287) that the best path forward in finding an answer to this question is to identify the first users or innovators of a particular change along with the later adopters, so that we can identify their motivations for implementing this change.

Perhaps the best place to begin looking for motivations is in the speech situation itself. Since speakers and writers use language in a particular situation, the language they use will logically depend on their goals for this situation and their perception of the linguistic output that will achieve these goals. The first author referred to the idea that speakers adapt their language use to their goals as the Principle of Efficiency (Seklaoui 1989: 4). This revises the Principle of Least Effort (Zipf 1949) to clarify that speakers do not reduce their effort indiscriminately; they do so only when this reduction is in line with their goals. In order to determine the most effective means of communication in a given situation, a speaker considers the entire situation, which, according to one model (Jakobson 1960: 353), includes at least six elements:

CONTEXT

MESSAGE

ADDRESSER _____ADDRESSEE

CONTACT

CODE

Each of these elements can of course affect the speaker's, or addresser's, choices.

Taking as an example a Puerto Rican Spanish speaker's decision to pronounce *este* either as [ˈes-te] or with aspiration as [ˈeh-te], or another weakened variant, such as gemination [ˈet-te] or deletion [ˈe-te], we can see how this choice might depend on the various elements in the speech situation. We can first consider the speaker herself. Poplack (1979: 69) found, for example, that among Puerto Rican speakers living in Philadelphia, the weakened variant in a word like *este* was favored by younger speakers, by those from the western part of Puerto Rico, and those who knew only Spanish and had no proficiency in English. We can also assume that a speaker who uses both variants might adapt her speech to that of her addressee, so that she might aspirate the /s/ in a conversation with a fellow Puerto Rican but not with a speaker from Mexico City who never aspirates the /s/. The means of contact could also play a role, so that this same Puerto Rican speaker might spell the word as *este* in an email or letter, even though she would pronounce the word as [ˈeh-te] in a conversation.

The **code** (*el código*) or language spoken might also have an effect. A speaker who may aspirate the /s/ in Spanish might not do so in an English word like *esteem*. Depending on her message, she might pronounce an /s/ when giving a friend an urgent warning about *este perro* 'this dog,' yet aspirate the /s/ when referring to the same dog in a less urgent message. Finally, the **context** (*el contexto*) can also enter into the speaker's decision. This includes the physical setting where the conversation takes place, the **cotext** (*el cotexto*) which is all the "text" or speech before and after the exchange in question, and shared knowledge, the information shared among the conversational participants that has not been expressed in the conversation. For example, the speaker might pronounce the /s/ when speaking to a friend in a formal meeting, even though she would aspirate it if she and her friend were at her home. In fact, Poplack (1979: 69) found that vernacular speech greatly favored a weakened variant of /s/ whereas formal speech greatly disfavored this variant. Poplack found that the sounds following the /s/ in question, known as the **phonological context** (*el contexto fonológico*), also had an effect. Weakening was favored by a following voiced consonant, like the /g/ in *rasgo* 'trait,' and disfavored by a voiceless consonant, like the /k/ in *rasco* 'I scratch.'

The discussion of the different pronunciations of *este* has shown how a speaker might choose a certain pronunciation in line with her conversational goals. If she wants to show solidarity, for example, she can choose the pronunciation her addressee would use. Or if she wants to mark the formality of a meeting, or present herself as more intelligent, she can choose the pronunciation that she perceives as being more formal or more educated. A speaker might also choose a variant because she thinks it will show that she is up-to-date, like using the word *cardi* instead of *cardigan* or *publi* instead of *publicidad* in Spanish. Of course, as we mentioned earlier, one use of a new pronunciation or word by one speaker does not constitute a change in the language, so at some point a variant must increase in popularity in order to constitute a linguistic change. Therefore, in order for a variant to become established in the language, it will spread from speaker to speaker throughout a community as people hear or read these innovations and then adopt them, no doubt because they perceive them consciously or subconsciously as compatible with their linguistic goals. Thus, language change takes place when people innovate by using a new pronunciation, form, or word or by making novel use of an existing feature, and this innovation then spreads through a community of speakers as more members adopt it.

Complete Activity 3-3 on page 43.

3.3 How Do Languages Change?

Having considered what constitutes a linguistic change and some reasons why a speaker might adopt a change, let us now consider how speakers may create a new variant and eventually lose an old one. Here the reasons are somewhat different depending on the type of variant, so we will consider in turn changes in phonology, morphology, syntax, the lexicon, and semantics.

3.3.1 How Do Sounds Change?

When speakers introduce a new pronunciation by modifying existing sounds they create a phonological change. The majority of these new pronunciations, but not all, result in a reduction of **articulatory movement** (*el movimiento articulatorio*), that is the movement of the tongue, lips, jaws, and vocal cords in ways that produce certain sounds. If we consider once again the change from *este* to *ehte* in Spanish, we observe that the more recent variant, *ehte*, requires less movement. The tongue has to rise toward the alveolar ridge behind the teeth to produce the [s] in ['es-te], but in ['eh-te] it can remain at the bottom of the mouth in the same position as for the vowel [e]. You can observe this yourself by repeating *este* and *ehte* several times and comparing the movement of your tongue during the two words. The reduction of movement is perhaps even more obvious in words like *chispa* or *rasco* where the following consonant [p] or [k] is not pronounced in the same place in the mouth as the [s]. Whenever a sound is deleted completely, this of course reduces the movement even more, as when *este* is pronounced as ['e-te] or the word-final [s] is deleted in *casas* so that it becomes ['ka-sa].

3.3.2 How Do Forms Change?

When speakers create a new form, they produce a morphological change. Often speakers create this new form based on the model of another form through analogy, as noted in Section 3.1 in the change of Old Spanish *levar* to Modern Spanish *llevar* following the model of *llevo, llevas, lleva,* and *llevan*. Children, for example, are experts at analogy, since they tend to regularize irregular verbs. An English-speaking child might produce regular forms like *teached* and *catched* instead of the irregular forms *taught* and *caught*, while a Spanish-speaking child might say *sabo* and *cabo* instead of *sé* and *quepo*. In fact the second author's daughter, when she was three, at first said *no sé* in response to her mother's question about who had made a mess in the house. When her mother responded with disbelief with *¿no sabes?*, the daughter then replied *no,* *no sabo.* This happens because children master the rules of regular conjugation before they learn all the irregular verb forms. Adult speakers create new analogical forms, too, especially for verbs they use infrequently. Thus, an adult speaker of English might say *I treaded* rather than *I trod* for the past tense of *to tread,* just like an adult Spanish speaker might say *andé* instead of *anduve* for the preterit of *andar.* Of course, analogy does not always result in regular forms. An English speaker might say *dreamt* instead of *dreamed* on the model of *slept* or *dove* instead of *dived* on the model of *drove.* It is interesting to note that when speakers create new forms through analogy, whether these new forms are regular or not, they reduce the number of forms that must be stored in memory.

A speaker can also create a new expression out of existing forms. For example, in English, speakers created the new expression *I'm going to read a book* to express the future alongside *I will read a book.* Similarly, Spanish speakers say *voy a leer un libro* alongside *leeré un libro.* In both English and Spanish, speakers use an existing word, namely the verb *to go* or *ir* in what was at the beginning a novel use, so that movement toward a concrete spatial location is used to express movement toward a more abstract temporal "location" or futurity. This new expression has the advantage over the old expression of a more transparent meaning, making the desire for a more meaningful form a possible motivation for its creation. Any native speaker can analyze the elements of *I'm going to read* or *voy a leer* as a form of the verb *to go* or *ir* plus the infinitive for 'to read.' However, this is not true for the form *leeré,* which a Spanish speaker is likely to analyze as the stem *leer-,* which he may rightly identify as the infinitive, plus the ending *-é* whose origin he will probably not be able to identify. An English speaker might or might not recognize *I will read* as the verb *to will* as in *to will something to happen* plus the infinitive *read.*

Once the new expression is created, the distinct words that form it may become grammatical elements through the process of **grammaticalization** (*la gramaticalización*). During this process, these elements lose their individual identity as their sounds are reduced and their original meaning changes. Note, for example, that *I'm going to read a book* can be reduced to *I'm gonna read a book* or even *Ima read a book* so that the verb *to go* in this expression is no longer interchangeable with the full form. If someone says *I'm gonna Mexico* instead of *I'm going to Mexico,* the hearer will have to assume that Mexico is some kind of action rather than a place. So, new grammatical forms are usually created either through analogy to existing forms or through new expressions that then undergo grammaticalization.

It is also possible for a grammatical form to be lost when its functions are taken over by another form. For example, in English a change is in progress that may lead to the eventual loss of *fewer* in favor of *less*. It used to be the norm to use the comparative *less* with non-count nouns, such as *less coffee*, and to use *fewer* with count nouns, as in *fewer cups of coffee*. Now many speakers say *less students* rather than *fewer students* for the opposite of *more students*. One sees signs in supermarkets that read "Ten items or less" (not "Ten items or fewer"). Thus, English speakers are eliminating the distinction between count and non-count nouns by using *less* with both. As it happens, this change makes English more like Spanish, which has only one comparative, *menos*, for both count and non-count nouns, as in *menos café* and *menos tazas de café*.

3.3.3 How Does Word Order Change?

When speakers change the order of words and morphemes or when they assign a new function to a form, a syntactic change occurs. One possible explanation for changes in word order in Spanish, for example, may be found in current linguistic theory, known as the *Interface Hypothesis* (*la hipótesis de la interfaz*) within minimalist theory. Spanish is generally considered to have the basic word order subject-verb-object (SVO), as does English. But Spanish is also flexible in its word order, depending partially on certain verbal features. When Spanish speakers construct sentences, they take into account the type of verb (whether transitive or intransitive) and whether or not the subject of the sentence is known information or old information. Thus, a speaker's syntactic knowledge of word order, lexico-semantic knowledge of type of verb, and pragmatic knowledge of information structure all interact in what are called *interfaces* to produce variable word orders in Spanish (Lozano 2006). Basic declarative sentences with transitive verbs and unknown subjects follow the SVO word order as in *María llamó al policía*, and sentences with certain kinds of intransitive verbs, those that do not take a direct object, such as *Llegó María a las tres*, are more common with a VS order. The word order of transitive sentences (usually SVO), however, can be altered when the subject (*María*) is the unknown information. In answer to a question such as *¿Quién llamó al policía?*, the tendency among native speakers is to respond *Llamó al policía María*, with the new information at the end of the sentence, which results in a VOS order

(Zubizarreta 1998). Syntactic changes such as these can begin in a small number of contexts and with a certain type of verb and then gradually spread throughout the language. Speakers' preferences for different word orders depends then on their interpretation of certain features at the syntactic, lexico-semantic, and pragmatic interfaces. A change in these preferences can lead to a change in word order (Sorace 2004).

3.3.4 How Do Meanings Change?

In **semantic change** (*el cambio semántico*) new meanings become associated with existing words. This happens, for example, through **metaphor** (*la metáfora*), which occurs when speakers perceive a similarity between two objects and extend one meaning to another. For example, they call the handheld device that controls the cursor on a computer screen a *mouse* or *ratón* because it's about the same size as this small rodent with a long, narrow "tail." Similarly, Spanish speakers call a mountain range a *sierra* because the peaks of the mountains resemble the teeth on a saw, and English speakers *comb* through evidence in the same way one would run a comb through sand looking for a physical object. Speakers can also associate the meanings of objects that are in physical contact through the process known as **metonymy** (*la metonimia*). Thus, one can refer to the part of one's pants that comes in contact with a physical seat as the *seat* of the pants in the same way that Latin CATHEDRAM, a word meaning 'chair,' changed meaning to become Spanish *cadera* 'thigh,' a part of the body in contact with a chair. Another interesting case of semantic change in English is the word *literally* which has ironically acquired a non-literal meaning. Speakers use *literally* in its original literal meaning to assure the hearer that something has actually happened as stated, as unbelievable as it might seem, so that *I laughed so hard, I literally fell out of my chair* means that the speaker physically fell out of her chair. *Literally* in its new meaning continues to assure the hearer that something seemingly unbelievable has happened, but now it no longer means that this actually happened, as when a speaker says *I literally died laughing*. Thus, speakers can attribute new meanings to existing words through their associations with other words or their use in certain expressions.

3.3.5 How Do Words Change?

In the same way that phonological change occurs when speakers introduce new sounds and morphological change occurs when speakers create new forms, lexical change occurs when speakers adopt or create new words. These new words are often borrowed from other languages or they are created from existing words through the addition of prefixes or suffixes or the fusion of two words to create **blends** (*los acrónimos*). Speakers often adopt new words to go along with new concepts, as when Spaniards arrived in the New World and adopted words such as *patata, tomate, coyote*, and *puma* for the previously unknown flora and fauna of the Americas (Dworkin 2012: 203) or when Spanish speakers adopted words such as *internet, web, software*, and *hardware* from English (Asención 2000: 14) to refer to new technological inventions. Speakers can also create new words by combining prefixes with existing words, as in *teletrabajo* 'telecommuting' (prefix *tele-* 'distance' + *trabajo*) and *agroturismo* 'agrotourism' (prefix *agro-* 'agricultural' + *turismo*), or by adding suffixes, as in *basurita* 'speck of dirt' (*basura* + diminutive suffix *-ita*) or *pantallazo* 'screen shot' (*pantalla* + suffix *-azo*). Blends can be formed by combining two existing words, as in *amigovio/amigovia*, which combines *amigo/amiga* and *novio/novia*, or the word *burrocracia*, mentioned above, which combines *burro* and *burrocracia* to refer to a bureaucracy that one considers to be as dumb as a donkey. Thus, we will see throughout our study of the history of Spanish that speakers adopt new words from other languages, create new words from words already in their language, or even adopt new words and then create new words from the borrowed words, such as *tuitear* and *tuitero* from *tuit* borrowed from English *tweet*.

3.3.6 What Is a Change in Progress?

Having looked at the various ways that speakers create new sounds, forms, orders of linguistic elements, words, and meanings, it is important to realize that the creation of the new element can be said to constitute a change in the language if adopted by a large enough number of speakers, but that this is not the end of the process of change. Rather, the introduction of the new element usually signals the beginning of a period of variation during which the newer variant and the older variant coexist. As we saw above in Poplack's (1979) study, the variant pronunciations ['es-te] and ['eh-te] coexist within a community of speakers and most likely also within the speech of a single speaker for a certain period of time. This is also true of the variants *leeré* and *voy a leer* and the two meanings of *ratón* 'mouse.' Over time, one of the variants may be lost completely at which point the loss of this form constitutes another change in the language as it completes the change in progress. While the two variants coexist, if linguists think that one of them will be lost eventually, for example, the variant *este* or *leeré*, then they speak of a **change in progress** (*un cambio en progreso* or *un cambio en curso*). So, whenever two variants coexist, one can wonder whether this variation represents a change in progress whereby one variant will eventually be lost or whether it represents stable variation that will continue indefinitely. For the changes you will encounter in this book, it is important to keep in mind that they usually proceed through the following steps: introduction of a new variant, a period of variation when the new variant coexists with the older variant, and finally the loss of the older variant. For every example of a completed change or a change in progress in Spanish, we can consider how new variants are created, how various factors affect the choice of one variant over another during the period of variation, and finally why one variant is eventually lost, if indeed the information is available to answer these questions.

3.4 How Do Linguists Study Language Change?

The goal of research, whether in the academic realm or in everyday life, is to learn something that you did not know already. Anyone can create knowledge by conducting research. The process begins by asking a question you want to find an answer to. Then you collect, analyze, and interpret the information you need to answer your research question. In order to study linguistic changes that took place before the end of the nineteenth century, when audio recordings became possible, the information you collect to answer your research question must come from written sources. This reliance on written records creates certain challenges. First of all, the number of written records is finite, so we cannot produce new data to study earlier periods of Spanish in the way that researchers studying Modern Spanish can record conversations with additional speakers to add to their set of data. Secondly, we do not know the age, sex, and social class or, in many cases, even the identity of the writers who produced many of the documents we rely on, making it impossible to correlate these writers' social characteristics with the variants they choose. Because of the limited number of historical documents and the incomplete information that often accompanies them, Labov (1972: 98) once said that "the great art of the historical linguist is to make the best of this [sic] bad data."

In order to do our best with these written data, as Labov advised, the researcher first identifies appropriate corpora and texts from which to extract data for a particular research question and then takes care in interpreting the data in these sources. Such care is required because the written text is never an exact representation of the spoken language of the time. To illustrate, we can consider a modern example from English. On a pole sign outside Checker's fast food restaurant in Athens, Georgia, there was once this announcement: "Cole slaw 15¢ on any sandwhich." One observes immediately the spelling *sandwhich* instead of *sandwich*. But what does this tell us about the way the author of this sign pronounced this word? Do we take the letters to be an accurate representation of speech and conclude that this author pronounced *sandwich* as [ˈsænd-hwɪtʃ]? Since we have first-hand knowledge of current pronunciation, we know that this is unlikely. Given that the majority of speakers no longer make a distinction between words like *whales* and *Wales*, it is more likely that the speaker pronounced *which* and the second syllable of *sandwich*, *-wich,* in the same way. Therefore, this spelling indicates that the first *h* in *sandwhich* was a silent letter added by the author. The astute linguist of the future would conclude from this spelling that the distinction between [hw] and [w] had already been lost for some speakers.

Two useful corpora for studies on diachronic changes in Spanish are the *Corpus del español* (Davies 2002) and the *Corpus diacrónico del español* (CORDE; Real Academia Española). Each corpus allows the researcher to look for certain strings of letters in the written documents by date. For example, for our corpus study of *arte* with masculine and feminine adjectives in Chapter 1, we could search combinations of *arte* plus an adjective like *abstracto* or *mecánico* in the *Corpus del español* and the CORDE to see how the gender of *arte* has changed over time.

3.5 Chapter Summary

- Languages do not change on their own; rather, people change languages when they change the way they speak and write.
- A change in a language has occurred when the majority of people in a community adopt a change.
- We can identify the following types of changes:
  - A purely orthographic change is a change in spelling, but not pronunciation, as from Old Spanish *assí* to Modern Spanish *así*.
  - A phonological change is a change in sounds, as from Old Spanish *dixo* [ˈdiʃo] to Modern Spanish *dijo* [ˈdi-xo].
  - A morphological change is a change in form, as from Old Spanish *levar* to Modern Spanish *llevar*.
  - A syntactic change is a change in word order or grammatical function, as from Old Spanish *et díxol(e)* to Modern Spanish *y le dijo*.
  - A lexical change is a change in vocabulary, as from Old Spansh *guisa* to Modern Spanish *manera*.
  - A semantic change is a change in meaning, as from Old Spanish *cuydar* 'to think' to Modern Spanish *cuidar* 'to care for.'
- People change languages because people like variety and change.
- Even when we accept change as inevitable, there remains the actuation problem, namely why certain changes occur in a certain place at a certain time.
- Since people change language we need to look to the speech situation itself in determining motivations for change. The speech situation includes at least these six elements: speaker or addresser, addressee, context, message, contact, and code. Each of these elements determines how the speaker or addresser will use language.
- Phonological changes often result from a reduction of articulatory movement.

- Morphological changes often result from analogy, the process by which speakers change the form of one word so that it resembles the form of another word. They may also result from innovation, whereby speakers create a new expression from existing forms.
- Syntactic changes may result from the desire to structure the information words convey in a certain way.
- Semantic change occurs when words change meaning by being applied to something similar, through metaphor, or by being applied to something they are in contact with, through metonymy.
- Lexical change is motivated by the desire to create names for new objects and concepts or to name existing objects or concepts in new ways.
- A change in progress means that one of two variants, alternative ways of saying the same thing, is being lost, which will eventually result in a change in the language.
- Historical linguists rely on written records to study language change. Two important collections of texts across different time periods are the *Corpus del español* and the CORDE.

Complete Activity 3-4 on page 43.

Activities

Activity 3-1

Looking back at the text of *El Conde Lucanor* in the original and in the Modern Spanish translation, identify at least one other example of each type of linguistic change. Write your example below along with the line number where this example occurs in the text. If you are unable to find another example in this text, think of an example in Spanish or English from your own experience or an online search.

A. purely orthographic change
B. phonological change

C. morphological change
D. syntactic change
E. lexical change
F. semantic change

Activity 3-2
Classify the following according to the type of linguistic change they represent:

Your questions about the Spanish language from Lead-in question 1-1 on
   page 1 and Activity 1-1 on page 7.
The examples in Activity 2-3 on page 17.

Activity 3-3
Recount a conversation you have had recently. For this conversation, identify
the six elements of this speech act, namely the speaker or addresser, the
addressee, the message, the context, the contact, and the code, as outlined
above by Jakobson. Now give an example of how your language use might be
different if you changed each one of these elements.

Activity 3-4

Corpus Search
Think of something you would like to know about the history of Spanish that
would benefit from a corpus search in the *Corpus del español* or the CORDE.
For example, in order to gather further information for the title question in
Chapter 1 on whether *arte* was masculine or feminine, we could conduct
a search in the *Corpus del español* of *arte* with different following adjectives.
Keep in mind that if you have trouble finding results in one corpus, you can try
the other corpus. If you have trouble coming up with ideas, here are some
searches to try:

a. Search a word which used to be written with initial *f-* which is now written
   with *h-*, like *fremosa/fermosa* ~ *hermosa, fablar* ~ *hablar*, or *fallar* ~
   hallar. What is the date of the text with the first appearance of the word
   with *h-*? What is the date of the last text with the word with *f-*? How long
   then was the period when both coexisted in written texts?

b. Search the word *aqueste* (or *aquesta, aquestos, aquestas,* or even better *aquest** which allows for any of the endings). In older texts one finds the demonstrative adjective *aqueste* alongside *este.* Write down the date and text where it first appears and/or see which century it appears in the most often. (Further information on this topic can be found in Ranson 2005.)

c. Search *la origen* to determine when this word was feminine rather than masculine as in Modern Spanish *el origen.*

d. Search *más bueno,* instead of *mejor,* to determine when it first appears and whether it is becoming more frequent in use.

e. Search *dixole* to determine the last date of this form and therefore the last date when the pronoun *le* could follow the verb *dijo* rather than preceding it as in Modern Spanish *le dijo.*

Reflect on this exercise. What did you learn about how to conduct a search in these corpora?

Further Reading

Crawford, Jackson. "How does language change?" YouTube video

Crystal, David. "How is the internet changing language today?" YouTube video

Lightfoot, David 2006. "Internal languages and the outside world," *How new languages emerge.* Cambridge University Press

Wright, Roger 2011. "Divergence, fragmentation, and the 'locus' of change," *Anuario del Seminario de Filología Vasca "Julio de Urquijo"* 40(1–2): 993–1004

4 | Did /f/ Change to /h/ in Spanish because of Basque?

Four Moments of Language Contact in the History of Spanish

Lead-in Question

4-1 Do any of your non-Spanish-speaking friends ever use Spanish words when speaking English? They might say *Adios, amigos* or use food terms like *salsa* and *burrito*. Make a list of at least three Spanish words that English speakers use. Think of different aspects of culture like food, music, dance, art, literature, clothing, and housing that these words could come from. Why would someone prefer a Spanish word when speaking English? Now switch the languages around and give three examples of English words used by Spanish speakers. Why do you think Spanish speakers borrowed these words from English?

In this chapter, you will learn about four major moments of language contact in the history of Spanish. The first moment is the arrival of Romans in the Iberian Peninsula, which puts speakers of Latin in contact with speakers of Basque, Iberian, Celtic, and other languages. A second moment of contact is the arrival of Germanic tribes in the Iberian Peninsula, who encounter the speakers of Latin who had settled there. A third moment of contact is the arrival of Arabic speakers in the Iberian Peninsula. The fourth and final moment of contact is the arrival of Spanish speakers in the Americas, who encounter speakers of indigenous Amerindian languages. For each moment of contact, we will consider its effects on the sounds and words of Spanish. We will see that we can identify borrowed words and place names with a higher degree of certainty than borrowed sounds.

4.1 What Is Language Contact?

Language contact can be defined quite simply as "the use of more than one language in the same place at the same time ... [where] at least some people use more than one language" (Thomason 2001: 1). Thus, language contact occurs when speakers of different languages occupy the same territory, as was the case for example when the Romans arrived in the Iberian Peninsula in 218 BC. In these situations, speakers need to communicate with speakers of another language and so they accommodate their speech by learning the other language to a greater or lesser degree. The speakers who learn both languages fluently are the most likely to adopt features from the other language, in the same way that you might use Spanish words when you are speaking English. In this way, certain features become part of the other language and may eventually be used even by monolingual speakers.

4.2 Where Did Spanish Come from?

It is important to take a closer look at the origins of Spanish before we address the four moments of contact. Spanish evolved from the varieties of Latin spoken by the Romans when they arrived in the Iberian Peninsula more than two thousand years ago. Spanish is a modern form of Latin, in the same way that the English you speak is a modern form of Old English. It does not make sense to say that Spanish is influenced by Latin, because Spanish is Latin. As a modern form of Latin, Spanish belongs to the family of Romance languages, which also includes French, Italian,

Portuguese, Romanian, Catalan, Occitan, Rhaeto-Romance, Sard, and the now extinct Dalmatian, spoken until the late nineteenth century in what is now Croatia. If we go back farther in time, we will see that Spanish is also related to such diverse languages as English, Danish, Greek, Russian, and even Hindi and Farsi. All of these languages have a common ancestor known as Indo-European, the language spoken by nomadic tribes that inhabited parts of Eastern Europe in the region near the Black Sea approximately 5,000 years ago (Penny 2002: 2, Martinet 1986: 18–19). When these peoples spread over vast territories of Europe and Asia, the varieties of Indo-European diversified as speakers of each variety made changes not shared by the others.

According to Ethnologue, there are 439 living Indo-European languages spoken by approximately 47 percent of the world's population. These languages are divided into several language families, among them the Italic family from which Spoken Latin, the language of the Roman Empire, and ultimately Spanish have derived. Figure 4.1 shows a summary of the Indo-European languages.

To our knowledge, there is no physical evidence of Indo-European; no inscriptions on cave walls, gravesites, or buildings (Alatorre 1989: 12). How do we know then that Indo-European existed and that the descendants of this language are related? We determine this from the remarkable resemblance in basic vocabulary and grammatical structure of the surviving languages. Linguists have been able to propose a reconstruction of the original language, known as Proto-Indo-European (PIE), by comparing lexical, grammatical, and phonological similarities among Indo-European languages in their modern forms and in older texts.

Complete Activity 4-1 on page 69.

4.3 What Are the Four Moments of Language Contact in the History of Spanish?

The first three moments of contact between speakers of the language that would become Modern Spanish and speakers of other languages took place in the

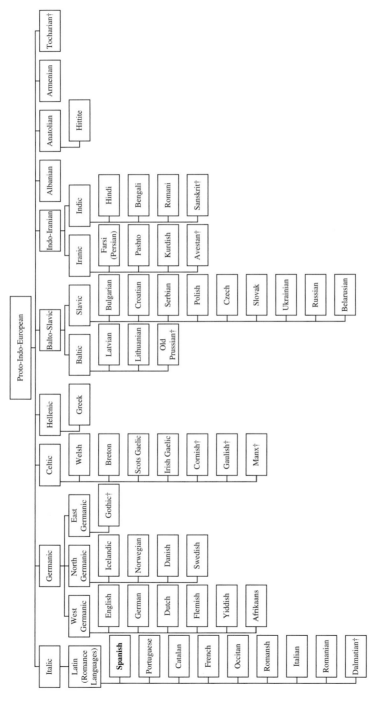

Figure 4.1 Indo-European language families with representative languages (adapted from Algeo 2010 and Jasanoff and Cowgill 2017)

† indicates an extinct language whose last native speaker has died.

Iberian Peninsula. The first is the arrival of the Romans in the Iberian Peninsula in 218 BC, which brought Romans in contact with the indigenous peoples of Iberia. The next two important migrations are the subsequent arrivals into this same territory of Germanic tribes in the fifth century AD and of Muslims in 711. The last migration is the arrival of Spaniards in the Americas beginning in 1492. We will label these four moments of contact according to the languages whose speakers came in contact with speakers of Latin or Spanish, as the indigenous Iberian period, the Germanic period, the Muslim period, and the American period.

Practice 4-1

Look at a map of the modern-day Mediterranean region and make a list of the possible places from closest to farthest from which different peoples could have arrived in the Iberian Peninsula by land and by sea.

For each of these moments of contact we will seek to answer the following questions:

- What were the historical events that led to contact between speakers of different languages?
- Who did speakers of Latin and Spanish encounter and what were the characteristics of their languages?
- What has been the lasting impact of the languages of these different groups on Spanish today?

4.3.1 The First Moment of Contact: The Indigenous Iberian Period

In 218 BC the Romans disembarked on the northeastern coast of the peninsula to stop the northward advancement of an army from Carthage (Lapesa 1980: 53), now modern-day Tunis in North Africa. The Roman invasion of the Iberian Peninsula was thus the result of the Punic Wars, the struggle for trade routes and colonies in the Mediterranean between the Romans and Carthaginians from 264 to 146 BC. You are no doubt familiar with another event from these wars in 218

BC, namely Hannibal's famous crossing of the Alps with horses and elephants in order to invade Rome from the north. After the capture in 206 BC of Cádiz (then Gades), the last Carthaginian stronghold in Hispania, the Romans began their gradual takeover of the peninsula. The conquest and pacification of Hispania was not complete, however, until 19 BC when Augustus conquered the northern coastal areas of Cantabria and Asturias. By this time, the Roman Empire extended from Western Europe across the north of Africa to the Greek archipelago.

The Romans' arrival led of course to the coexistence of speakers of Latin with speakers of other languages. Even though many scholars, such as Lapesa (1980), refer to the peoples the Romans encountered in Iberia as pre-Roman peoples, we will refer to them as indigenous Iberian peoples. This does not mean that these peoples originated in Iberia, but rather that they were already established there before the arrival of the Romans, in the same way that the indigenous peoples of the Americas were already established there before the arrival of the Europeans. Lapesa (1980: 56) points out that the indigenous inhabitants of the peninsula learned Latin voluntarily because it served as a common language for the different groups and because its knowledge led to social advancement. The adoption of Latin and the eventual disappearance of the indigenous languages were not abrupt of course; instead there was a more or less extended period of bilingualism according to the region and social status of speakers (Lapesa 1980: 56). The Romanization of the peninsula was earlier and more intense in the southern and eastern areas and then spread more slowly to central, western, and northern regions where the Romans met with greater resistance (Lapesa 1980: 55–56). Speakers of indigenous languages probably used Latin at first only in interactions with the Romans, while speaking their original language on other occasions. Over time they began to use Latin on more and more occasions until finally children no longer learned the indigenous language of their parents.

Complete Activity 4-2 on page 69.

When the Romans arrived in the Iberian Peninsula in 218 BC, "the peninsula was a linguistic mosaic," according to Alatorre (1989: 28), as shown in Map 4.1,

Map 4.1 The Iberian Peninsula around 300 BC (adapted from Domínguez Monedero 1984)

but little is actually known about the peoples who inhabited the region at the time and their languages. Lapesa (1980: 13) laments that the prehistory of the peninsula has to be pieced together from ambiguous miscellaneous data from myths; imprecise writings of Greek and Roman authors; human remains and archeological fragments of coins, instruments, and artistic objects; inscriptions in undecipherable languages; and the names of peoples, tribes, and geographical designations of remote and diverse origins. The three most important groups we can identify are the Basques, the Iberians, and the Celts. Some scholars also speak of Celtiberians, a people resulting from intermarriage between the latter two groups.

The Iberians, who spoke a non-Indo-European language, arrived in the Iberian Peninsula from Africa (Lapesa 1980: 26), but the date of their arrival is uncertain. Their territory extended from the south of the peninsula to at least the *río Iber,* the modern Ebro River, from which they derive their name. Another indigenous Iberian language, the only one still spoken in the Iberian Peninsula, is Basque. Recent evidence that modern-day Basques are partially genetically related to the Paleolithic/Mesolithic inhabitants of Iberia suggests that they arrived in the Iberian Peninsula in about 6000 BC. This would mean that they arrived at least one millennium or more before Indo-European groups spread across Europe and the Iberian Peninsula (Behar et al. 2012: 1). We are less sure, however, where the Basques originated. Some believe that they were related to the Iberians (Lapesa 1980: 28, Alatorre 1989: 25). Others believe that they came from the area of the Caucasus Mountains in southern Russia between the Black and Caspian seas (Penny 2002: 2).

As early as the eighth century BC, the third important indigenous group, the Celts, migrated in waves from the territory that is now France and occupied the peninsula (Alatorre 1989: 22). They were part of the Indo-European migration that began in Eastern Europe and spread throughout Western Europe and Great Britain. After their arrival, the Celts lived among the Iberians, which has led some scholars, such as Núñez Méndez (2012: 9), to speak of Celtiberian peoples and their language. The Celtiberians remained a dominant force in the central plateau area of the peninsula until the invasion of the Carthaginians in 237 BC.

4.3.2 The Second Moment of Contact: The Germanic Period

Even though the Roman conquest of the Iberian Peninsula established what is now Spanish as the language of the majority of speakers in Spain, there were two subsequent groups who arrived in Iberia in large numbers. The first of these was a band of Germanic tribes consisting of Vandals, Suevians (or Swabians), Alemanni, and Visigoths who crossed into Spain from their kingdom in southern France (then Gaul) in 409. The following year, on the other side of the empire, Germanic tribes sacked the city of Rome. Upon the collapse of the Roman Empire in the west in 476, the Visigoths declared an independent kingdom in Gaul and Iberia. In the early sixth century, they were expelled from most of Gaul, and in the seventh century were driven out of eastern and southern Spain. Nonetheless, they maintained control of a major part of Iberia until the

Map 4.2 The Visigothic kingdom in Spain c. 560

beginning of the eighth century. Map 4.2 shows the greatest extent of the Visigothic kingdom in Spain.

From the first to the fourth century there had been a sustained interaction between Romans and Visigoths, who were technically subjects of the Roman state, so it is likely that they were bilingual in Latin and their Germanic vernacular at the time of the invasion in 409. Theirs was a spoken language that never had a written form in the Iberian Peninsula. Throughout the Visigothic era, Latin was the language used for official and cultural interactions and so their linguistic influence on the Latin of Spain was not extensive.

The Visigothic invasions are important, though, for two non-linguistic reasons. According to Lapesa (1980: 123), following the establishment of the independent Visigothic kingdom, communication with the Peninsula was cut off from the rest of the Roman world. Without the unifying force of the Romans, the differences among the varieties of spoken Latin in different parts of Iberia increased. In addition, the inhabitants of Cantabria became isolated and their speech diverged from the Hispano-Romance spoken elsewhere. This is important because, as we will see in Chapter 5, standard Spanish is based on the dialect of this region. Also significant was the establishment of Toledo as the center of government under the Visigoths (Penny 2002: 16). This made its capture from the Muslims by the Christian kings a notable event, as we will also see in the next chapter.

4.3.3 The Third Moment of Contact: The Muslim Period

The Muslims defeated Roderic, the last of the Visigothic kings, in the battle of Guadalete in 711 just a few short weeks after their armies crossed into the Iberian Peninsula from the north of Africa. By 718, most of the peninsula was under Islamic rule. This conquest was not a difficult task, as the invaders quickly made alliances among the Christian population. For example, since Roderic had usurped the throne from the rightful heir of his predecessor, King Witiza, one of Witiza's brothers joined the Muslims to defeat Roderic in the battle of Guadalete (Alatorre 1989: 72).

The Muslims brought with them an advanced knowledge of science, music, art, architecture, literature, and philosophy. For this reason, many people already living in the Iberian Peninsula admired their conquerors and adopted their ways of life. The Muslim period also ushered in an era of tolerance toward religious beliefs so that Christians, Jews, and Muslims lived side by side in relative harmony for more than seven hundred years. Those who embraced the Islamic faith did so of their own free will without coercion. The tolerance shown to religion also applied to language use, so that the inhabitants of the peninsula were not forced to abandon their language (Alatorre 1989: 77).

4.3.4 The Fourth Moment of Contact: The American Period

Although Spanish became an official language of Spain's conquered territories in the Americas after Christopher Columbus's arrival in 1492, many indigenous languages have survived to the present day. Maps 4.3 and 4.4 show the names and locations of Amerindian languages in Mexico, Central,

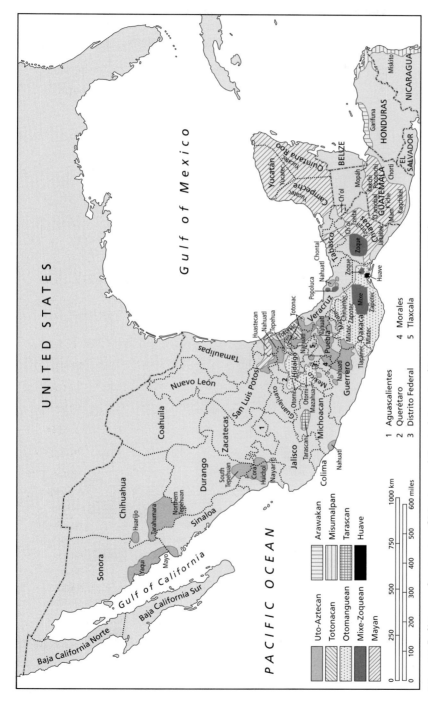

Map 4.3 Indigenous languages of Mexico and Central America (Gutman and Avanzati 2013a)

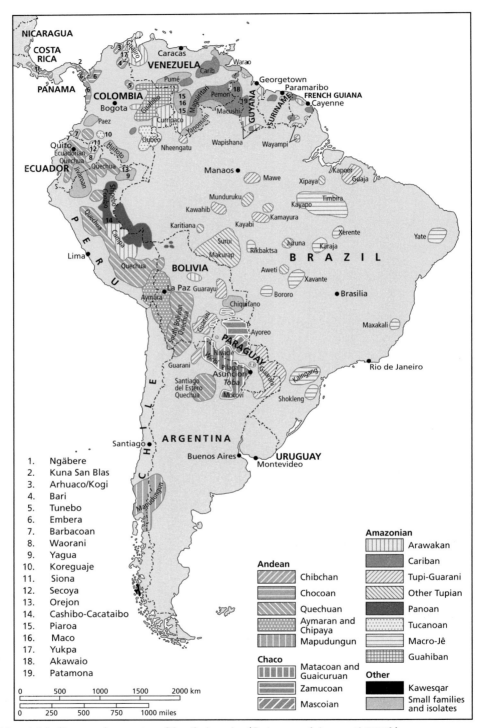

Map 4.4 Indigenous languages of South America (Gutman and Avanzati 2013b)

and South America. Most speakers of indigenous communities are bilingual and use their native language for familiar situations and Spanish for official interactions. We can assume that this situation was similar to that of the speakers of indigenous languages of the Iberian Peninsula after the arrival of the Romans. While many indigenous languages, such as Quechua and Guaraní, have robust numbers of speakers, others are declining, as younger people use Spanish for more and more situations. Of the 1,062 living languages of the Americas, 645 are in danger of extinction (Simons and Fenning 2017).

Practice 4-2

When the Spanish came into contact with many different indigenous cultures in the Americas, they encountered a diverse range of previously unknown flora, fauna, foods, and customs for which they had no names. To what situation is this similar? Will the end result be the same or different? In what ways?

Complete Activities 4-3 and 4-4 on pages 70-72.

4.4 What Were the Effects of Language Contact on Spanish?

When people from different cultures come in contact, they naturally share and borrow objects, customs, foods, manners of dress, and especially their languages. English speakers in the United States adopt Mexican foods along with the terms for them, such as *salsa, enchilada*, and *chalupa*. Spanish speakers also borrow words from English, especially in the area of technology, such as *tuit* 'tweet,' *bloguero* 'blogger,' and *hipervínculo* 'hyperlink.' In the examples just mentioned, we can be certain that a word like *salsa* was borrowed from Spanish because we know that this word existed in Spanish and we know that English and Spanish speakers were living in the same place at the same time. Thus, the following three criteria for interlanguage influence proposed by Lloyd (1987: 45–48) have been met in this case:

1. The feature in question must have existed in the influencing or **donor language** (*la lengua donante*).
2. There must be geographical correspondence between the donor language and the borrowing or **recipient language** (*la lengua recipiente*).
3. There must be chronological correspondence between the two languages so that the change occurred during a period of active bilingualism when a large number of speakers spoke both languages.

These criteria ensure that the key requirement for language contact is met, namely that more than one language is spoken in the same place at the same time. They also ensure logically that the donor language has the feature attributed to it.

Language contact may also have an effect on the sounds of a language, but this type of contact is more difficult to establish with certainty. Most often speakers of the recipient language adapt the borrowed words to the sounds already existing in their language. For example, English speakers adapt the Spanish word *amigo* to the sounds of English by pronouncing the initial vowel as a schwa [ə], as in *uh*, the middle stressed vowel as a diphthong [ij], as in *sea*, and the final vowel as the diphthong in *row* [ow]. This happens because English speakers tend to reduce vowels in unstressed syllables and produce diphthongs in stressed and final syllables. English speakers also pronounce the *g* as [g], rather than [ɣ], the voiced velar fricative or approximant, which does not exist in English. However, as far as we know, such changes in pronunciation by English speakers have not yet caused changes in the pronunciation of these words in Spanish. However, if one day Spanish speakers began to pronounce the initial [a] of *amigo* and other unstressed vowels as schwa, then we would be able to attribute this change to their contact with English speakers.

Before we consider specific changes based on language contact, it is important to keep in mind that such changes are more the exception than the rule. We will see beginning in Chapter 6 that internal changes, those that occur naturally in a language without any influence from other languages, are much more frequent than the changes that can be attributed to contact with speakers of other languages.

Language contact can lead to changes in a language at any level (Thomason 2001: 11), but three types of changes most often occurred in the history of Spanish. One is the adoption of place names, or **toponyms** (*topónimos*), such as the names of cities, states, and rivers. Many toponyms in the Iberian Peninsula come from indigenous words just as many toponyms in the Americas come from Native American words, such as the cities of Chicago and Milwaukee, the states of Mississippi and Michigan, and the Atchafalaya and Potomac Rivers in the United States. Place names allow us to identify the places where speakers of other languages once lived. The second and most prevalent result of language contact is lexical borrowing, the adoption of words or parts of words from other languages. These borrowings often refer to cultural products and customs of the peoples speaking the donor languages, such as the adoption of *salsa* and *siesta* by English speakers. A third possible effect of contact among speakers is the adoption of new sounds or a change in pronunciation of existing sounds. We will see that such phonological effects are the most difficult to establish with any certainty.

4.4.1 Toponyms

Throughout the Iberian Peninsula and throughout the Americas one finds toponyms that attest to the presence of speakers of languages other than Spanish or Latin. We can begin with the name *Iberia* itself, which comes from the Latin word ɪBĒRɪA, derived from the Greek word for a Celtic tribe of people living there, the *Iberes*. The Greeks also named the cities of *Rhodes*, now *Rosas*, and *Emporion*, now *Ampurias*, since these were once Greek colonies. The name for Spain, originally *Hispania*, is believed to be a Latinization of the Carthaginian name for 'place of rabbits.' *Cartagena* 'New Carthage' and *Ibiza* 'island of pine trees' also come from the

Carthaginians. The Phoenicians, the ancestors of the Carthaginians, contributed *Gades*, now *Cádiz*, and *Malaka*, now *Málaga*, founded as far back as the eighth century BC. The Celts provided many toponyms ending in -*briga*, meaning 'city,' such as *Segobriga*, now *Segovia*, and *Conimbriga*, now *Coimbra*, in Portugal.

The Germanic tribes left the name of the city *Burgos*, from the Germanic word *burg* 'castle,' found in many German place names as well, such as *Hamburg* and *Salzburg*. There are place names throughout Spain from Arabic. Some of the most notable ones are the names of rivers that begin with *Guad-*, from Arabic *wad* 'river,' like the *Guadalquivir* 'great river' and the *Guadalmedina* 'river of the city.'

In Latin America, one finds numerous place names from indigenous languages, such as *Tlaxcala* from Nahuatl *Tlaxcallan* 'the place of corn tortillas,' *Arequipa* from Quechua *Ari qhipay* 'Yes, please stay,' and *Campeche* from Mayan *Ah-Kin-Pech* 'place of snakes and ticks.'

4.4.2 Lexical Borrowings

Throughout history speakers have borrowed words from indigenous groups for previously unknown plants and animals, objects, technologies, and customs. Table 4.1 presents some of the more common words Spanish has borrowed from other languages. For example, when the Romans arrived in the Iberian Peninsula they borrowed words to refer to "physical features of the terrain, meteorological phenomena, plants, tree names, domesticated and wild animals, foodstuffs, clothing, [and] social practices" (Dworkin 2012: 30–31). In similar fashion, Spaniards arriving in the Americas borrowed words from the indigenous American peoples for the new flora and fauna and cultural practices they encountered there, such as *patata* and *alpaca* from Quechua and *chile* and *coyote* from Nahuatl (Dworkin 2012: 203, 205). In these two situations, the Latin or Spanish speakers were the invading group who eventually had their language adopted by a majority of the speakers in those areas.

TABLE 4.1 Selected lexical borrowings in Spanish

- From the indigenous Iberian period beginning in 218 BC (Dworkin 2012: 30–31):

  ardilla 'squirrel,' *barro* 'mud,' *berro* 'watercress,' *cama* 'bed,' *cigarra* 'cicada,' *cueto* 'craggy hill,' *charco* 'puddle,' *galápago* 'giant tortoise,' *gorra* 'cap,' *manteca* 'lard,' *pizarra* 'slate,' *sapo* 'toad,' *zarza* 'brambles,' *zorro* 'fox'

- From the Germanic period. Even though Germanic tribes did not enter Spain until the fifth century, borrowings that were transmitted first to Latin go back as early as the first century (Dworkin 2012: 67–73):

  albergar 'to lodge,' *blanco* 'white,' *eslabón* 'link,' *espuela* 'spur,' *esquina* 'corner,' *estribo* 'stirrup,' *fresco* 'fresh, cool,' *gana* 'desire,' *ganso* 'goose,' *guardar* 'to keep, preserve,' *guerra* 'war,' *rico* 'rich,' *robar* 'to rob,' *tregua* 'truce'

- From the Arabic period beginning in AD 711 (Dworkin 2012: 82, 84–85, 90, 102):

  aceite 'oil,' *ajedrez* 'chess,' *albaricoque* 'apricot,' *alcázar* 'castle, fortress,' *alcohol* 'alcohol,' *algodón* 'cotton,' *almacén* 'warehouse, store,' *almohada* 'pillow,' *alquimia* 'alchemy,' *arroz* 'rice,' *atún* 'tuna,' *azul* 'blue,' *azúcar* 'sugar,' *barrio* 'neighborhood,' *berenjena* 'eggplant,' *espinaca* 'spinach,' *hasta* 'until,' *limón* 'lemon,' *naranja* 'orange,' *sandía* 'watermelon,' *tarea* 'task,' *taza* 'cup,' *zanahoria* 'carrot'

- From the American period beginning in 1492 (Dworkin 2012: 201–07):
  - From Taíno: *canoa* 'canoe,' *hamaca* 'hammock,' *tiburón* 'shark' (from Columbus's *Diario a bordo*)
  - From Taíno or Arawak: *batata* 'sweet potato,' *huracán* 'hurricane,' *maíz* 'maize, corn,' *tuna* 'prickly pear,' *yuca* 'yucca'
  - From Nahuatl: *aguacate* 'avocado,' *cacahuete* 'peanut,' *chocolate* 'chocolate,' *coyote* 'coyote,' *guajolote* 'turkey,' *tomate* 'tomato'
  - From Quechua: *alpaca* 'alpaca,' *cancha* 'open unencumbered space,' *chinchilla* 'chinchilla,' *coca* 'coca leaf or plant,' *cóndor* 'condor,' *patata* 'potato,' *puma* 'puma'

- From Gallo-Romance from circa AD 1000 (Dworkin 2012: 120–23):
  - Medieval loanwords: *flecha* 'arrow,' *batalla* 'battle,' *libre* 'free,' *ligero* 'easy, light,' *perejil* 'parsley'

TABLE 4.1 (cont.)

- ○ Seventeenth-century loanwords: *asamblea* 'legislative assembly,' *bagaje* 'baggage,' *banquete* 'banquet,' *bayoneta* 'bayonet,' *billete* 'ticket,' *bloquear* 'to blockade,' *burgués* 'inhabitant of a city,' *café* 'coffee,' *crema* 'cream,' *equipaje* 'baggage,' *fila* 'line, queue,' *fumar* 'to smoke,' *jefe* 'leader,' *lotería* 'lottery,' *paquete* 'packet,' *placa* 'plate, plaque'

  - ○ Eighteenth-century and on loanwords: *apartamento* 'apartment,' *avión* 'airplane,' *bebé* 'baby,' *botella* 'bottle,' *camión* 'truck,' *carnet* 'identity card,' *chalé* 'chalet,' *champaña* 'champagne,' *champiñón* 'mushroom,' *chófer* 'chauffeur,' *cognac* 'cognac,' *complot* 'plot,' *croissant* 'croissant,' *detalle* 'detail,' *élite* 'elite,' *interesante* 'interesting,' *menú* 'menu,' *pantalón* 'pants,' *peluca* 'wig,' *ruta* 'route,' *sofá* 'sofa'

  - ○ Eighteenth-century and on loan translations: *alta costura* 'high fashion,' *falso amigo* 'false friend,' *palabra clave* 'key word,' *golpe de estado* 'coup d'état,' *último grito* 'latest novelty (in fashion)'

- • From Italian, especially from 1500 to 1700 (Dworkin 2012: 151–53): *actitud* 'position, posture,' *acuarela* 'watercolor,' *banco* 'bank,' *bancarrota* 'bankrupt,' *crédito* 'credit,' *diseñar* 'to design,' *modelo* 'model,' *balcón* 'balcony,' *fachada* 'facade,' *mosaico* 'mosaic,' *compositor* 'composer,' *ópera* 'opera,' *soprano* 'soprano,' *tenor* 'tenor,' *alerta* 'alert, warning,' *batallón* 'batallion,' *bombardear* 'to bombard,' *emboscada* 'ambush,' *pistola* 'pistol,' *mercante* 'merchant,' *millón* 'million'

- • From English, since the 1950s (Dworkin 2012: 220, 224, 226, 227): *fútbol* 'football, soccer,' *béisbol* 'baseball,' *básquetbol* 'basketball,' *tenis* 'tennis,' *bádminton* 'badminton,' *boxear* 'to box,' *bate* '(baseball or cricket) bat,' *gol* 'goal,' *córner* 'corner kick,' *gangster* 'gangster,' *esnifar* 'to sniff,' *flipar* 'to flip out,' *ponerse alto* 'to get high,' *hamburguesa* 'hamburger,' *esnob* 'snob,' *póster* 'poster,' *puzzle* 'puzzle,' *líder* 'leader,' *suéter* 'sweater'

This list was compiled from the words listed in Dworkin (2012). Other such lists of words are found in Spaulding (1943), Resnick (1981: 133–46), Lapesa (1980), Penny (2002: 255–84), and Resnick and Hammond (2011: 292–323). Words with a controversial origin are excluded from this list and appear instead in Box 17.1.

Box 4.1 What is meant by the terms substratum, superstratum, and adstratum languages? And why is it better not to use them?

Some scholars of the history of the Spanish language use the term **substratum** (*el sustrato*) to refer to the indigenous languages spoken before the arrival of the Romans in the Iberian Peninsula, like Iberian, Basque, Phoenician, Celtic, and Greek, and before the arrival of Spaniards in the Americas, like Tupi, Arawak, Caribe, and Chibcha (Lapesa 1980: 4ff., 537ff.). They also use the term **superstratum** (*el superestrato*) to refer to languages, such as Visigothic and Arabic, that were placed over the existing Spanish layer of sediment, but that did not succeed in replacing Spanish. The term **adstratum** (*el adstrato*) refers to languages that coexist in the same area, such as Spanish and Basque. Oddly no one ever speaks of a stratum language, even though within this geographical metaphor Spanish would be the stratum, the language that displaces the substratum languages and resists the attempts of superstratum languages to displace it. Keep in mind that in historical linguistics these terms are meant to indicate chronology rather than prestige or superiority, so that a substratum refers to a language spoken in an area before the arrival of speakers of another language without implying that the first language was somehow inferior.

Despite their widespread use, the terms substratum and superstratum, and even adstratum, are insufficient to capture the complex situations of contact among speakers of different languages. For example, is Basque a substratum language or an adstratum language with respect to Spanish? One could ask the same question regarding Quechua and Spanish in South America. For this reason, we agree with Lloyd (1987: 41) that it is preferable to refer to situations of language contact and their effects as interlanguage influence and to specify the nature and duration of the contact rather than to refer to substratum and superstratum languages.

The concept of substratum and superstratum languages probably originated in the late eighteenth century in the work of Lorenzo Hervás y Panduro (1784, 1800–04) (cited by Craddock 1969: 21). Of particular interest are the critical evaluations by Craddock (1969: 18–47), Izzo (1972), and Cassano (1977), summarized by Lloyd (1987: 42–48).

Spanish has also borrowed words from speakers of Germanic languages and Arabic who entered their territory in the Iberian Peninsula. Words from Germanic may have entered the Spanish lexicon not only during the Germanic presence in Iberia from the fifth to the eighth century, but also during contact between Germanic and Latin speakers in Rome in the first century AD and during a later wave of Germanic borrowings from Gallo-Romance, what is now French (Dworkin 2012: 67–69). It is often difficult to determine with certainty the exact path of transmission of a particular word and so we will not assign Germanic borrowings into Spanish to one of these three contact situations. Given the long contact between speakers of Arabic and Hispano-Romance in the Iberian Peninsula, it is not surprising that Arabic is the largest source of borrowings in the Spanish lexicon (Dworkin 2012: 83).

Spanish speakers have also borrowed words from languages such as French, Italian and English. These were not mentioned above as moments of contact since no territorial conquest was involved in these cases; instead contact occurred through cultural exchange. French speakers began to enter the Iberian Peninsula in about 1000 either as clergy reorganizing the Spanish church or as pilgrims to Santiago de Compostela (Dworkin 2012: 119). This led to the adoption of a relatively small number of "Medieval Gallicisms," such as *flecha* 'arrow' (Fr. *flèche*) and *jardín* 'garden' (Fr. *jardin*) (Dworkin 2012: 120–23). The largest number of Gallicisms entered Spanish beginning in the seventeenth century because of France's growing prestige in the world, especially after the French Bourbon royal house ascended to the throne in Spain (Dworkin 2012: 128–29). In fact, "Gallicisms constitute the largest single group of borrowings into the postmedieval language until the mid-twentieth century, when Anglicisms became the most frequent borrowings" (Dworkin 2012: 128). Borrowings from Italian into Spanish were also motivated by the prestige that Italians enjoyed in certain fields, such as art, music, and banking, beginning in the sixteenth century.

Borrowings from English have become especially prevalent in Spanish and in other languages in the past sixty years or so as the United States has risen on the world stage and English-language exports, such as popular music, television, films, print and broadcast media, drugs, fashion, and technology, have increased. Many of these language exports do not require face-to-face contact between Spanish and English speakers so that "[t]he sociocultural background for the introduction of Anglicisms in Spanish is very different from that of the earlier lexical strata of the Spanish lexicon" (Dworkin 2012: 218). Spanish speakers can therefore borrow words from English without actually coming into contact with English speakers. Many of these borrowings are loan translations, such as *año luz* 'light year,' *ciudad dormitorio* 'bedroom city,' *fecha límite* 'expiration or expiry date,' *hora punta* or *hora pico* 'peak or rush hour' (Dworkin 2012: 222).

Complete Activity 4-5 on page 73.

4.4.3 Phonological Influence

As mentioned above, it is more difficult to prove that one language has had a phonological influence on another language than it is to prove lexical borrowing. Even when Lloyd's criteria for interlanguage influence are met, it is difficult to prove that the sound change in question resulted from language contact rather than from sound changes that could occur naturally in the language.

A case in point is the aspiration and loss of initial /f/, the change from /f/ > /h/ > Ø, which is often attributed to Basque influence. It is certain that a word like Latin FĪLUM became ['hi-lo] and then *hilo* ['i-lo] in Spanish, but whether Basque speakers had a decisive role in this change is the subject of much debate. The argument in favor of Basque influence is based on the lack of a word-initial /f/ in Basque. The assumption is that since Basque speakers did not have a word-initial /f/, they would be likely to change Latin /f/ to a different sound. Further support comes from the fact that aspiration of /f/ is also found on the other side of the Pyrenees in southern France where the result of Latin FĪLUM in Gascon, a variety of Occitan with a great deal of influence from Basque, is *hil* [hil]. However, the change of /f/ to /h/ has also been documented in areas far from the Basque country, which suggests that the change from a labio-dental fricative /f/ to a glottal fricative /h/ is a natural change that occurs without interlanguage influence. Activity 4-6 asks you to indicate whether certain pieces of information regarding the change of /f/ to /h/ argue in favor of or against Basque influence so that you can draw your own conclusions about the role of Basque in this change.

Complete Activity 4-6 on page 73.

Another change attributed to Basque is the addition of a vowel before the trilled /r/ at the beginning of a word. Since Basque does not allow /r/ in this position, Basque speakers add an /e/ to Latin words beginning with /r/. Therefore, RĒGEM 'king,' which became Spanish *rey*, was borrowed into Basque as *errege*; and ROTAM 'wheel,' Spanish *rueda*, was borrowed into Basque as *errota*. This Basque pronunciation pattern may also have led to the addition of an initial /a/ in other Spanish words of Latin origin, such as *arrugar* 'to wrinkle,' *arrancar* 'to uproot, start up, tear off,' and *arrepentir* 'to regret' (Alatorre 1989: 24).

Another proposed interlanguage influence, one attributed to Celtic, is the vocalization of /k/ > [j] before a consonant (Alatorre 1989: 23): The argument in favor of Celtic influence is that /k/ palatalizes to [j] in Romance languages whose speakers were in contact with speakers of Celtic, so that Latin NOCTEM became Spanish *noche*, Portuguese *noite*, Provençal *noite*, French *nuit*, and Catalan *nit*. In Romance languages spoken in areas with few Celtic speakers, /k/ remained as a stop as in Italian *notte* and Romanian *noapte*.

Another change attributed to Celtic is the voicing of intervocalic voiceless stops, since this change also appears to coincide with populations where there was a strong Celtic presence, evidenced by the alternating spelling in such names as *Doitena/ Doidena, Ambatus/Ambadus* and the ending *-brica/-briga* (Lapesa 1980: 42).

A possible example of Arabic influence is the change of the initial consonant in certain words, such as *jabón* and *jugo* from /s/ to /ʃ/, which later becomes /x/ (Posner 1966: 84). The fact that we know that the sound /ʃ/ existed in Arabic and the rather infrequent natural change of /s/ to /ʃ/ lends support to the assumption of Arabic influence.

An example from an indigenous language of Mexico is the borrowing of the Nahuatl consonant /tɬ/ as [tl] into Mexican Spanish. This is a clear case of borrowing, since the sound is used only in Nahuatl names, such as *Tlaxcala, Quetzalcoatl,* and *Cuautla*. Note that in Nahuatl *xocolatl* [ʃo-ˈko-laːtɬ], borrowed into Spanish as *chocolate* [tʃo-ko-ˈla-te], the final /tɬ/ was changed to /t/ and a final /e/ was added.

In these possible cases of interlanguage phonological influence, we can trace the ones of more limited scope to a particular language, such as Arabic for *jabón* and Nahuatl for *Tlaxcala*. When the sound change occurs throughout the language and is one that could occur naturally in any case, such as initial /f/ to /h/, then it is impossible to state conclusively that these changes occurred because of the pronunciation habits of bilingual speakers. At the same time, it is impossible to prove that interlanguage influence had no effect.

Box 4.2 Languages in contact: Spanish–Otomí

In this chapter, we discussed how the Romans borrowed words from indigenous Iberian groups to expand the lexicon of Latin and how Spaniards borrowed words from indigenous Amerindian languages. Borrowing can also move in the opposite direction. Recall that Basque adopted Latin words such as RĒGEM 'king' and ROTAM 'wheel' which, after undergoing phonological changes, became *errege* and *errota*. This same process has occurred in the indigenous Amerindian languages in their over 500 years of contact with Spanish. In fact, there are far more borrowings from Spanish into the indigenous languages than there are from these languages into Spanish. Just as the history of the Basque language is a mystery because there are no written records of the language before the Roman conquest, so it is with the origins and development of many of the Amerindian languages. However, by examining linguists' transcriptions of these languages today, we can clearly identify the impact that Spanish has had on them.

Below are fragments from oral stories of speakers of Otomí, an indigenous language of Querétaro, Mexico, written in the orthographic convention approved by the Commission of Indigenous Communities of Querétaro and based on the International Phonetic Alphabet. Some Spanish words have been borrowed into the language with apparently no changes, while others have undergone phonological changes. Look for the words: *gustaban, ajo, sopa, todavía,* and *maestro*. Which words have undergone some phonological change?

(1) ko xa gustabi no hme'na
porque dice que le gustaba la tortilla 'because she says she liked tortillas'

(2) mí 'ra^{h}je ñ'i, axo, ju, so^{h}pa
nos daba chile, ajo, frijol, sopa 'she would give us chile, garlic, bean, soup'

(3) to'be ja ga tsoni
todavía llego allí 'I still go there'

(4) dá xi^{h}pa nor maestro
le dije al maestro 'I told the teacher'

(All examples taken from Palancar 2009: 83–84 and 94; our English translations)

4.5 Chapter Summary

- This chapter has explored the major moments of language contact in the history of Spanish and their impact on the evolution of Spanish.
- The major moments of language contact include:
  - The indigenous Iberian period: 218 BC–AD 409
  - The Germanic period: 409–711
  - The Muslim period: 711–1492
  - The American period: 1492 to the present
- During each period speakers of different languages came together so that features of one language were borrowed by speakers of the other.
- In order to establish interlanguage influence, a borrowing must meet three criteria:
  - The feature must have existed in the donor language.
  - The donor and the recipient languages must have been spoken at the same time.
  - The donor and recipient languages must have been spoken in the same place.

In other words, there must have been chronological and geographical coexistence for interlanguage influence to take place.

- Three types of change most often resulted from interlanguage influence in the history of Spanish: the adoption of toponyms, lexical items, and, more rarely, new sounds.
- We can establish borrowing more conclusively for toponyms and words than for sounds. This is because many sound changes attributed to borrowing may occur naturally in a language, whereas a particular word, similar to a word in another language, will not be created naturally by speakers.
- Keep in mind that, even though this chapter has presented examples of external changes through interlanguage influence, the vast majority of changes in a language occur naturally and are therefore internal changes.

Complete Activity 4-7 on page 74.

Activities

Activity 4-1
Identify the branch of Indo-European for each of the languages in Table 4.2 by consulting Figure 4.1. For example, Latin belongs to the Italic branch. For each of the common words in these languages write at the bottom of the table two sounds they have in common that indicate common ancestry.

Activity 4-2
1. Can you think of some modern examples of bilingualism where one language is used more for official business and another is used for more intimate or familiar interactions similar to the way Latin was used for official business and the indigenous languages were used in family life in Iberia after the arrival of the Romans? Explain this situation. How do you think these uses will impact these languages in 100 years?

TABLE 4.2 Common words in Indo-European languages (adapted from Wheelock 1963: xx)

	Branch	'I'	'me'	'is'	'mother'	'brother'	'ten'
Sanskrit		aham	ma	asti	matar	bhratar	daca
Iranian		azem	ma	asti	matar	bratar	dasa
Greek		ego	me	esti	meter	phrater	deka
Anglo-Saxon		ic	me	is	moder	brothor	tien
Old Irish			me	is	mathir	brathir	deich
Lithuanian		asz	mi	esti	mote	broterelis	deszimtis
Russian		ia	menya	jest'	mat'	brat'	desiat'
Latin	Italic	ego	me	est	mater	frater	decem
Spanish		yo	me	es	madre	fraile	diez
sound 1:		initial vowel [a], [i], [e]					
sound 2:		medial consonant [h], [z], [g]					

2. Think about your own language use. Do you ever use a more formal register or style of your language with people you might want to impress, such as professors or employers? How does your language change? Why? Why do you think the inhabitants of the Iberian Peninsula might have wanted to use Latin during the first centuries of the Romanization of the peninsula, even when speaking with other bilingual speakers?

Activity 4-3

1. Below is a vertical timeline of important dates for interlanguage contact in the history of Spanish. Next to each date write the letter of the corresponding event choosing from among the options after the timeline. In the column titled "Key words" write a few words to describe this event. Finally, write the numbers for the beginning of each of the four moments of contact described in this chapter in the column "Moment of contact": 1 for the Roman period, 2 for the Germanic period, 3 for the

Muslim period, and 4 for the American period. There will only be these four numbers in this column.

Date	Event	Key words	Moment of contact
around 6000 BC			
around 3000 BC			
eighth century BC			
264–146 BC			
237 BC			
218 BC			
206 BC			
19 BC			
409			
476			
711			
718			
1492			

A. The Arabs arrived in the Iberian Peninsula across the strait of Gibraltar and defeated the Visigoths and their leader Roderic at the battle of Guadalete.

B. The Carthaginians arrived in the Iberian Peninsula. They were able to conquer large territories until their expansion was stopped by the Romans.

C. Nomadic tribes, known as Indo-Europeans, inhabited parts of Eastern Europe in the region near the Black Sea.

D. The Romans had conquered the northern coastal areas of Cantabria and Asturias thereby completing their conquest of the Iberian Peninsula.

E. Spaniards led by Christopher Columbus arrived in the Americas.

F. The Basques arrived in the Iberian Peninsula.

G. The Romans arrived in the northeastern coast of the Iberian Peninsula to stop the Carthaginians' advancement.

H. Germanic tribes, especially the Visigoths, arrived in the Iberian Peninsula from what is now France and occupied most of the peninsula.

I. The Celts arrived in the Iberian Peninsula.

J. Fall of the Roman Empire in the west.

K. By this time, almost the entire peninsula is under Arab rule except for certain remote Christian enclaves in the north and northwest.

L. The Romans conquered Cádiz (Gades), the last Carthaginian stronghold in the Iberian Peninsula.

M. Three Punic Wars were waged between the Romans and the Carthaginians for control of the trade routes and colonies established on the coasts of the Mediterranean.

Activity 4-4

Complete the following table with the dates of each contact language, the geographical area of contact, and some of your favorite examples of borrowing from that language into Spanish.

Contact language	Period of contact	Geographical area of contact	Borrowings
Iberian period Iberian Celtic Basque			
Germanic period			
Muslim period			
American period Taino Nahuatl Quechua			
Gallo-Romance			
Italian			
English			

Activity 4-5

Martin Haspelmath (2008: 6–11), coeditor, along with Uri Tadmor, of the *World Loanword Database* (wold.clld.org), proposes linguistic and extralinguistic factors that favor borrowings among languages. Based on the discussion of borrowings in Section 4.4.2 and the list in Table 4.1, state whether these factors favor borrowings into Spanish. Be prepared to cite examples to support your claim.

A. Linguistic factors that favor borrowing:
   1. the borrowing is a noun rather than another part of speech, like a verb or adjective
   2. the borrowing refers to a cultural product or practice rather than core vocabulary
   3. "victorious invaders will typically borrow place-names, names for local plant and animal species, [whereas] the language of people ruled by foreign invaders will typically adopt military terms … " (Haspelmath 2008: 9).
B. Extralinguistic factors that favor borrowing:
   1. intensity of contact
   2. the prestige of the donor language
   3. a less purist attitude on the part of speakers of the recipient language

Activity 4-6

In order to evaluate further the possible Basque influence on the change of /f/ > /h/ in Spanish, as in FORMOSUS > *hermoso*, indicate whether each of the following statements is evidence in favor of Basque influence in this change by writing P for *pro* or whether it is evidence against this change by writing C for *contra*. (These ideas come from Lloyd 1987: 212–23. See also further discussion in Tuten 2003: 133–36.)

_____ 1. The consonant /f/ does not exist in Basque.

_____ 2. The first written documentation of *h* for *f* occurs in the northern part of Castile and La Rioja in northern Spain.

_____ 3. We do not know whether the sound /h/ existed in Basque. Lapesa (1980: 38) writes, "Basque had an aspirated /h/ that could also be used in place of /f/, and which alternates with it at times," but he does not give examples.

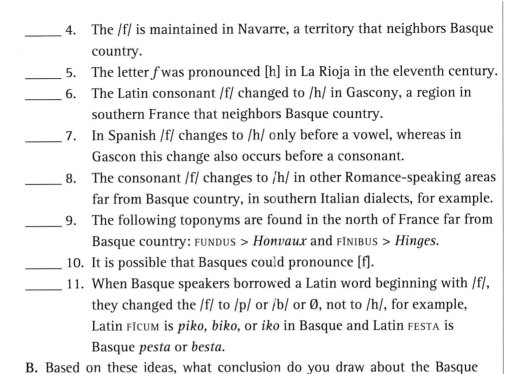

_____ 4. The /f/ is maintained in Navarre, a territory that neighbors Basque country.

_____ 5. The letter *f* was pronounced [h] in La Rioja in the eleventh century.

_____ 6. The Latin consonant /f/ changed to /h/ in Gascony, a region in southern France that neighbors Basque country.

_____ 7. In Spanish /f/ changes to /h/ only before a vowel, whereas in Gascon this change also occurs before a consonant.

_____ 8. The consonant /f/ changes to /h/ in other Romance-speaking areas far from Basque country, in southern Italian dialects, for example.

_____ 9. The following toponyms are found in the north of France far from Basque country: FUNDUS > *Honvaux* and FĪNIBUS > *Hinges*.

_____ 10. It is possible that Basques could pronounce [f].

_____ 11. When Basque speakers borrowed a Latin word beginning with /f/, they changed the /f/ to /p/ or /b/ or Ø, not to /h/, for example, Latin FĪCUM is *piko, biko,* or *iko* in Basque and Latin FESTA is Basque *pesta* or *besta*.

B. Based on these ideas, what conclusion do you draw about the Basque influence on the change from /f/ to /h/ in the history of Spanish?

Activity 4–7

Write down three topics in this chapter about which you would like to have more information. It could be a people, like the Iberians, or a language, like Gothic, or a type of interlanguage influence, like toponyms from indigenous languages of the Americas. Then conduct an internet search on one of these topics and write a short paragraph about what you learned. Why did you choose this topic?

Further Reading

The YouTube video "The history of the Romans: Every year" shows the year-by-year expansion of the Roman Empire. By minute 2:45 the conquest of the Iberian Peninsula is complete.

Gendler, Alex. "How do languages change and evolve?" TedEd. Online at ed.ted.com/lessons/how-languages-evolve-alex-gendler

Haspelmath, Martin, and Uri Tadmor, *World Loanword Database*, wold.clld.org

Le Roux, Patrick 2004. "Questioning Romanization," *Annales. Histoire, Sciences Sociales* 59(2): 287–311 Available online at www.cairn-int.info

Poplack, Shana 1980. "Sometimes I'll start a sentence in Spanish Y TERMINO EN ESPAÑOL: Toward a typology of code-switching," *Linguistics* 18(7–8): 581–618

Webster, Jane 2001. "Creolizing the Roman provinces," *American Journal of Archaeology* 105(2): 209–25

5 Why Is Spanish Also Called Castilian?

The Standardization Process and Its Effects

Lead-in Questions

5-1 What name would you give to the variety of English that you speak most often? What are its distinctive features? Which other varieties of English are you familiar with?

5-2 Which variety of English is considered to be the most prestigious by members of your community? Keep in mind that we are talking about how members of society, not linguists, view language. How do you think this variety came to be prestigious? For example, is this the variety spoken by people in positions of power, such as political, business, and religious leaders? Is it used by language professionals, such as journalists and authors? Is it taught in schools and used in grammar books?

5-3 Now ask yourself these same questions about Spanish. Which dialect of Spanish do you speak? What are its distinctive features? Which variety of Spanish do you consider to be the most prestigious? Make a list of reasons for its prestige then make a list of other varieties of Spanish you know and think about why you consider them to be more or less prestigious.

Chapter 4 focused on the contact between speakers of what is now Spanish and speakers of other languages from the third century BC to the present. Here we will focus more closely on events from the tenth to the fifteenth century AD in order to understand the historical events that led to the selection and establishment of Castilian as the standard variety of Spanish. At the beginning of this time, Castilian was just one of many different speech varieties spoken in the Iberian Peninsula along with other Romance varieties, such as Galician, Leonese, Asturian, Navarrese, Aragonese, Catalan, and Mozarabic, and other non-Romance varieties, such as Basque and Arabic. It is important to realize that Castilian became the basis for the standard dialect for historical reasons and not for linguistic reasons. As you learned in Chapter 2, one variety of Spanish is not linguistically superior to any other. Instead it is societal events, external to the linguistic features of a particular variety, that led to its selection as the basis for the standard dialect.

5.1 What Are Languages and Dialects?

In Chapter 4 we considered the contact between Spanish speakers and speakers of other languages. In situations of contact, speakers develop a certain degree of bilingualism, so that they can use the features of either their native language or their second language. Once they become fluent in both languages, they even have a choice of which language to use. The story of the external history of Spanish, then, is a story of competition among different languages and their features in the minds and mouths of speakers.

In this chapter, we will also focus on competition, but now we are concerned with competition among different Hispanic dialects and the various sounds, forms, words, and even spellings available to their speakers. But since we were concerned with languages in Chapter 4 and we are concerned primarily with dialects in this chapter, we must first ask: What is the difference between a language and a dialect?

Max Weinrich, a sociolinguist and Yiddish scholar, popularized the following quotation that he heard at one of his talks from an audience member, who may have been Joshua Fishman: "A language is a dialect with an army and navy" (Bright 1997: 469). This statement makes the point that there is no linguistic difference between a language and a dialect; the difference is instead social and political. We tend to use the term **language** (*una lengua* or *un idioma*) to refer to the linguistic variety used by a political entity, especially one that has military power or social prestige. We tend to use **dialect** (*un dialecto*) to refer to linguistic varieties with less prestige or more limited use. In linguistic terms, though, we could call every linguistic variety a dialect and not use the term *language* at all. But if we don't use the word *language*, then how would we refer to "the Spanish language"? If by "Spanish language" we mean the collection of linguistic varieties that we wish to classify as Spanish, then we could call this "the Spanish diasystem," where **diasystem** (*un diasistema*) refers to a collection of dialects. If by "Spanish language" we mean the standard language, the one approved by grammarians, then we could call this "the standard Spanish dialect." Therefore, the terms *diasystem, dialect,* and *standard dialect* can be used instead of the term *language*, which we can reserve for the human capacity for language (*el lenguaje*).

Students often propose that we can decide which dialects belong to the same diasystem using the criterion of **mutual intelligibility** (*la comprensión mutua*). However, this criterion is likely to fail on linguistic grounds. In one experiment, speakers of Spanish and Portuguese were able to understand 50–60 percent of what was said by a speaker of the other language (Jensen 1989: 850). This rate is likely to be even higher for speakers of Norwegian and Swedish, yet we consider these to be different languages because they are the official linguistic varieties of separate nations. In contrast, there are many Italian dialects that have much lower rates of mutual intelligibility than Spanish or Portuguese. We consider them to be dialects of Italian, though, because they are all spoken in Italy and therefore not associated with separate political units.

It is important to recognize that the classification of dialects into diasystems does not exist in nature, but is created by people. Speakers all around the world continue speaking in the ways that suit their purposes regardless of the classifications linguists or other people make of their speech. Classifications do not change linguistic reality; they are rather a reflection of how we interpret this reality in order to group linguistic varieties together. Like the story of the three umpires, language families or diasystems are what we agree that they are, whether this follows linguistic reality or not.

The Story of the Three Umpires: A Lesson in Classification

A reporter decided to ask three baseball umpires how they knew whether a pitch was a strike or a ball. The first umpire said: "I call them the way they are." The second fellow, a little more enlightened, said: "I call them the way I see them." The third umpire, who fully understood the role of human beings in classification, said: "They ain't nothin' till I call 'em." Even though the trajectory of the pitch is an observable fact, in the rules of baseball a pitch is a ball or a strike according to the umpire's call.

(Recounted by the late Ernst Pulgram to his students at the University of Michigan)

Complete Activity 5-1 on page 99.

Having recognized that classifications are a human creation, we can now discuss how the variety of Hispano-Romance classified as Castilian came to serve as the basis for the standard dialect of Spanish. We will see how Castilian went through the four stages necessary for standardization, according to Haugen (1972): **selection** (*la selección*), **elaboration** (*la elaboración*), **codification** (*la codificación*), and **acceptance** (*la aceptación*). Selection refers to the reasons why a particular variety is chosen as the basis for the standard. Elaboration is the process by which speakers and writers expand the functions of this variety so that it is used in all spheres of life. Codification is the process of establishing the norms for the standard dialect by selecting certain variants over others. Finally, acceptance occurs when speakers of other varieties adopt a certain dialect as the standard either voluntarily or by force. In the rest of this chapter we will consider each of these steps in the standardization of Castilian. (The information on the history of Spain in this chapter has been verified in O'Callaghan (1975) and Barton (2004).)

5.2 Why Was Castilian Selected as the Basis for the Standard Dialect?

By the early Middle Ages, the Latin that had been brought to the Iberian Peninsula by the Romans beginning in 218 BC had changed in different ways in different regions of the peninsula. Around the year 1000, the dialects spoken in the Iberian Peninsula included Galician, Leonese, Castilian, Navarrese, Aragonese, and Catalan in the north and Mozarabic in the south in al-Andalus, the part of the peninsula under Muslim control. These Hispano-Romance dialects were spoken along with Basque in the north and Arabic in the south. Given the linguistic variety in the peninsula, how then did Castilian come to be the dialect that would serve as the basis for Standard Spanish?

The territorial expansion of Castile is no doubt the single most important reason for its selection as the basis for the standard dialect. Whether this expansion can appropriately be called the **Reconquest** (*la Reconquista*) is a source of debate, as discussed in Box 5.1. What is not debatable, however, is that this southward movement of Castilians through the center of the peninsula increased the economic and political power of Castile while at the same time increasing the number of speakers and the prestige of this variety. It also brought speakers of the Castilian dialect into contact with speakers of other Hispano-Romance varieties.

Box 5.1 Was the *Reconquista* really a Re-conquest?

You may not have realized that the term *Reconquista* is controversial. The first author, for example, had never questioned this term until an elderly Andalusian man told her in 1987 that the *Reconquista* was a northern invasion that destroyed the thriving culture of al-Andalus. It is always important to remember that people hold different views of historical events depending on their own circumstances.

As summarized in García Fitz (2009), the pro-*Reconquista* view is based on the idea that the northern Christian kingdoms, including Castile, were reclaiming the Iberian Peninsula from the Muslims who had displaced the Christian Visigoths. If one views this as a transfer of power according to religion from Christian to Muslim then to Christian again, then the notion of reconquest is justified (Lomax 1984). An underlying assumption here, though, is that the Iberian Peninsula needed to be returned to its rightful owners, the Christians.

However, if one takes a more literal view of reconquest, then the Castilians were not conquering lands they had once held, since scholars agree that these lands were held instead by the Visigoths. The anti-*Reconquista* scholars argue that the Castilians certainly did not identify with the Visigoths, since they had a long history of resisting them (Barbero and Vigil 1988), while the pro-*Reconquista* scholars argue that the culture and politics of these regions, especially Asturias, were more Visigothic than previously thought (Ruiz de la Peña 1995, González Jiménez 2002).

What is the ideology behind the pro-*Reconquista* view? And the anti-*Reconquista* view? Which side do you take?

5.2.1 Where Did Castilian Come from?

After the Muslim conquest of the Iberian Peninsula from the Visigoths from 711 to 718, only a small stretch of land in the northernmost part of the peninsula remained under Christian control. Recall that we mentioned in Chapter 4 that the importance of the Visigothic rule was more political in nature than linguistic. Their success in having established and maintained independent kingdoms in the north of the peninsula was to have an enormous impact on the success of the southward expansion of Castilian. Legend has it that a Visigothic nobleman, Pelagius (*Pelayo*) (born 690, died 737), was responsible for keeping the northern lands in Christian hands, in part by defeating the Muslims in the battle of Covadonga in 722. As founder of the Kingdom of Asturias, Pelagius ruled over it until his death. During the ninth century, in order to defend the middle part of this area from attacks by the Basques to the east and the Muslims to the south, fortifications were built. This is how this area came to be known as *Castella* 'Castile' (later *Castiella* and then *Castilla*), the 'land of forts.' In 884 Alfonso III of

Asturias (848–910) ordered the founding of Burgos, which would later serve as the capital of Castile. By 912 the Castilians had extended their territory to the Duero River, some 50 miles south of Burgos, and settlers had come to Castile from surrounding areas (Tuten 2003: 99). This first southward expansion was relatively easy, since these border lands between Christian and Muslim territory were mostly uninhabited.

In the early days of the historical record, the rulers of the counties that comprised Castile were selected by the kings of Asturias and then by the kings of León, after the region changed its name in 910 when the capital moved from Oviedo to León. Castile as an autonomous entity dates from 931 when Fernán González (*c.* 910–70) became Count of Castile having acquired enough power to act independently from the Leonese king. When he died, the rule of Castile passed to his son, García Fernández (*c.* 938–95), rather than an appointee of the Leonese king. However, in 1028 Castile fell under the rule of Sancho Garces III of Navarre (*c.* 992–1035). In a surprising turn of events, this led to the establishment of Castile as a kingdom. When Sancho died, he divided his kingdom among his three sons. His second son, García, became king of Navarre, his eighth and youngest son, Ramiro, king of Aragon, and his sixth son, Ferdinand I (*Fernando I*) (*c.* 1015–65), king of Castile where he ruled until his death in 1065.

5.2.2 How Did Castile Expand Its Territory?

The first major victory of the Christians against the Muslims was the capture of the city of Toledo in 1085 by Alfonso VI (1040–1109), who had become king of León in 1065 upon the death of the Ferdinand I and then king of Castile-León when the two kingdoms united. The capture of Toledo was a symbolic victory for the Christians, as well as a real one, since Toledo had been the Christian capital of the Visigoths. In 1031 the powerful caliphate of Córdoba, established in 756 under the Umayyad dynasty, had broken up into smaller states, known as *taifas*, making the Muslim-held land more vulnerable to Christian attacks. In order to strengthen their position, the *taifa* leaders invited another Muslim group, the Almoravids, whose capital was in Marrakesh in North Africa, to enter Spain. In 1086, the year following the Christians' capture of Toledo, the Almoravids defeated Alfonso VI at Sagrajas, some 225 miles southwest of Toledo outside Badajoz.

The struggles between Christians and Muslims continued during the eleventh and twelfth centuries with neither side having the upper hand. When Almoravid rule in al-Andalus ended in 1143, the Iberian Muslims turned again to North Africa for help, this time calling on the Almohads, who arrived in Iberia in 1145. In 1195 they defeated Alfonso VIII of Castile (1155–1214) at Alarcos, about 150 miles southeast of Toledo. Since Alfonso VIII knew that the Castilians were not strong enough to defeat the Almohads by themselves, he turned to the Pope for help. In 1197 Pope Celestine issued a call for a crusade against the Muslims in Spain, which was reiterated by Pope Innocent II in 1206. This persuaded soldiers from Aragon and Navarre to join forces with the Castilians, even though they were otherwise rivals. Soldiers from France and Italy also joined the cause. The combined Christian forces scored a decisive victory over the Muslims on July 16, 1212 in the battle of Las Navas de Tolosa, only 100 miles northeast of Córdoba. This battle tipped the tide in favor of the Christians. Soon thereafter in 1230 Castile-León became reunited under Ferdinand III of Castile (*Fernando III*) (c. 1201–52), who moved quickly to capture important cities in the southern part of the peninsula that had been under Muslim control. These included Córdoba in 1236, the kingdom of Murcia in 1243, Seville in 1248, and Cádiz in 1250. Around the same time the Aragonese extended their territories southward at the expense of the Muslims, capturing Valencia in 1238, and the Portuguese captured the Algarve in the 1240s.

After the major southward expansion of the Christians in the mid-thirteenth century, more than two hundred years would go by until their final victory against the Muslims. On January 2, 1492, Muhammad XII (c. 1460–1533), also known as King Boabdil, surrendered the emirate of Granada to Isabella I of Castile (*Isabel I de Castilla*) (1451–1504) and Ferdinand II of Aragon (*Fernando II de Aragón*) (1452–1516). You are certainly acquainted with the Christian monarchs (*los Reyes Católicos*) for their role in financing Christopher Columbus's first voyage to the Americas later that same year. At a time when Castilian was beginning its overseas expansion, it was also the most widely spoken language in the Iberian Peninsula. The Catholic monarchs also took steps to ensure the dominance of Catholicism by issuing the Edict of Expulsion on March 31, 1492, giving the Jews under their rule four months to convert to Christianity or leave. The same decree was later issued against the Muslims, but not until 1609. See Maps 5.1a–d for a visual representation of the expansion of Castile from 1030 until around 1516.

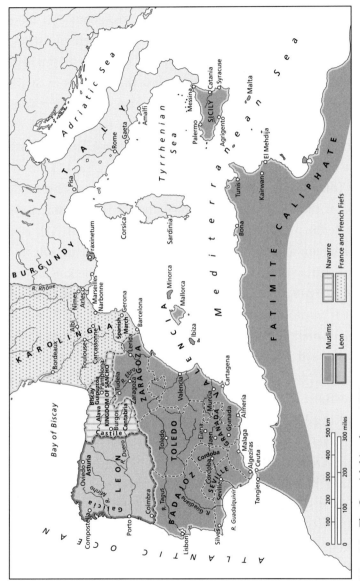

Map 5.1a The Spanish kingdoms 1030

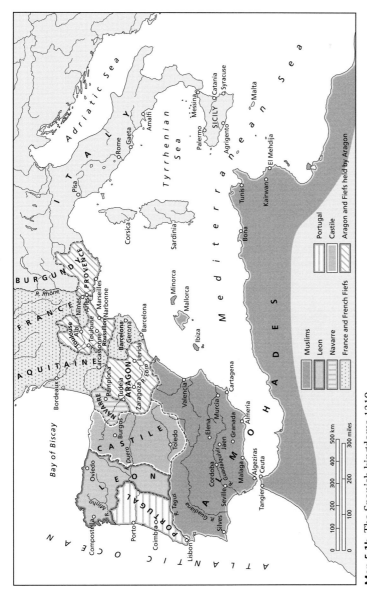

Map 5.1b The Spanish kingdoms 1210

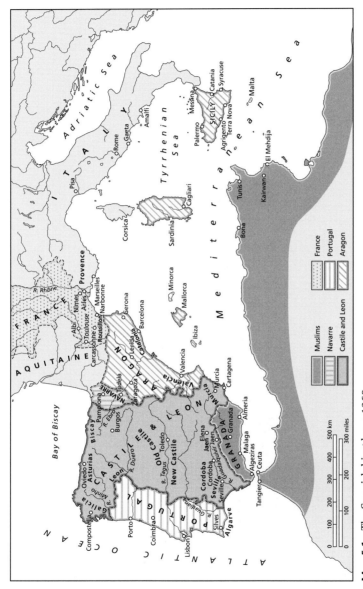

Map 5.1c The Spanish kingdoms 1360

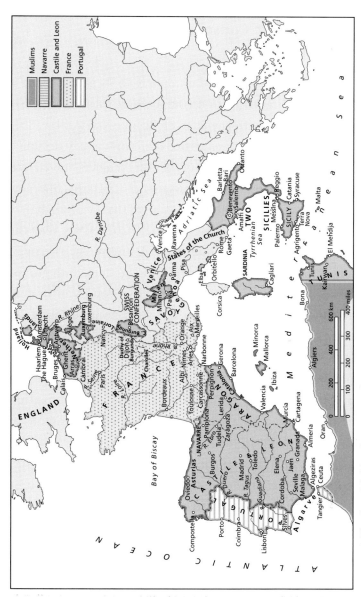

Map 5.1d The Spanish kingdoms around 1516

Complete Activity 5-2 on page 99.

5.2.3 What Were the Linguistic Consequences of the Expansion of Castile?

Not only did Castile's territorial expansion lead ultimately to its prestige, but it also meant that speakers of Castilian came into contact with speakers of other Hispano-Romance dialects and also with speakers of Basque and Arabic. This contact came about, of course, when Castilians settled lands previously occupied by speakers of other dialects and also when speakers of other dialects moved into lands occupied by Castilians. Even though the movement of Castilians into new territories has sometimes been portrayed as the extension of the Castilian dialect into these areas and its imposition there, Tuten (2003) cautions us that the linguistic realities of this situation were no doubt more complex. As we saw in Chapter 4, when speakers of different languages come into contact, both groups accommodate their speech to that of the other group. This results in mutual influences between the two languages, as many speakers become bilingual. We should expect that the same types of mutual influences would result when related dialects come into contact as well, as was the case during movements of peoples in medieval Spain.

The type of dialect mixing that Tuten (2003) proposes is called **koineization** (*la koineización*). The term koine of Greek origin means a common or supraregional dialect, a lingua franca that is spoken across a wider territory than a regional language variety. When speakers of different dialects accommodate their speech to each other, features that seem exceptional may be abandoned and those that seem less stigmatized may be adopted by increasing numbers of speakers. This is a situation where competing linguistic forms are plentiful and enforcement of norms by society is scarce. The process of koineization in the history of Spanish means that some features of the Castilian dialect may have been abandoned by speakers, whereas some features of non-Castilian dialects may have been adopted. Thus, even though Castilian serves as the basis for standard Spanish, we should not assume that all the features of Standard Spanish are in every case the original features of

Castilian. Of course, the reverse may also have happened. Koineization may also explain why certain features of Castilian not shared by other Hispano-Romance dialects may have survived.

Let us consider two cases. The first comes from the repopulation of Burgos from the ninth to the eleventh century. In this situation, speakers would have heard different variants for combinations of the preposition plus an article. For example, the preposition *en* plus the definite article *el*, could have a non-contracted form, *en el*, as was the case in Castilian, or it could have a contracted form, such as *no* in Galician and Portuguese, *enno*, *eno*, or *enne* in Leonese, *enno* or *no* in Aragonese, and *eno* in La Rioja. Other prepositions also had contracted forms. In Leonese, for example, one finds *pollo* for *por lo*, *del* for *de lo*, *al* for *a lo*, and *conno* for *con lo* (Tuten 2003: 115). One can imagine that non-native speakers might have had greater difficulty understanding and learning the contracted forms of another dialect than the non-contracted forms. This could explain why the non-contracted forms, which also happen to be the Castilian forms, would eventually come to be used by the entire community.

In another case of koineization proposed by Tuten (2003: 238–42), it is the non-Castilian form that ends up being adopted. One finds in Old Spanish texts the form *mio*, also written *mjo*, for the possessive adjective 'my' before a noun, as in the title of the famous epic poem, *Cantar de mio Cid*. The shortened variant *mi*, more prevalent in documents from Toledo and Seville, is the variant that ends up being adopted, rather than the form *mio* which was more prevalent in Burgos. We see then that the expansion of Castilian territory did not result simply in the imposition of the Castilian dialect on the people living in those territories. Rather the speakers of the various linguistic varieties spoken there selected certain features over others to create a mixed variety.

5.3 How Was the Castilian Dialect Elaborated?

A necessary step in the process of standardization is the elaboration of a written language able to fulfill all the functions of a society. As part of the elaboration of

Castilian, scholars wrote or translated documents on a wide variety of topics in order to extend its previous domains. The person most responsible for the elaboration of the Castilian dialect was Alfonso X the Wise (*Alfonso X el Sabio*) (1221–84), king of Castile and León from 1252 until his death at age 62 in 1284.

Before this time all official and scientific documents in the Romance-speaking parts of the Iberian Peninsula were written in Latin, or at least a spelling system that looked like Latin (see Box 5.2). As the language of the Roman Empire, Latin had already been elaborated so that it could be used for any function from administrative documents to academic treatises to literary works. The earliest writings in the Iberian Peninsula that clearly represent the spoken Hispano-Romance dialects are the *Glosas Emilianenses* and the *Glosas Silenses* from the late tenth century. These are not complete texts, but rather translations into Hispano-Romance of isolated Latin words or expressions between the lines and in the margins of Latin manuscripts found in monasteries in La Rioja in northeastern Spain. Figure 5.1 shows the longest gloss from the *Glosas Emilianenses*. The text of the last line of the gloss and its translation are found in Activity 5-3.

Box 5.2 Late Latin or Early Romance?

The great writers of the Roman Empire, such as Cicero, Virgil, and Ovid, wrote in what is called Classical Latin. As you know, the spoken Latin of the Roman Empire changed over time into the different Romance languages. Up until the ninth century, however, the documents written in Romance-speaking areas were written in what appeared to be Latin, but this Latin did not always follow the norms of Classical Latin. There are at least two different explanations for this difference.

The traditional view has been that a writer's failure to follow the norms of Classical Latin was based on his or her imperfect learning. Intensive study was required to learn Classical Latin and so it was understandable that many writers would fall short of these norms.

A different view, advanced by Wright (1982), is that in Spain there was no distinction between Latin and Romance until 1080, the year that the Council of Burgos changed from the Hispanic to the Roman rite for the liturgy. This means that texts before that time written in what traditional scholars would call imperfect Latin were not intended to be written in Classical Latin. Instead speakers of Hispano-Romance were writing their language with the only writing system they knew. We could compare this to the way that speakers of English write the word *knight* with silent letters. It is not because we pronounce these letters or because we are trying to write Old English. It is simply because we learned to spell the word that way.

Wright (1982) believes that the reforms instituted by Charlemagne (c. 747–814), Holy Roman Emperor from 800 to 814, created the distinction between written Latin and written Romance. Because Charlemagne spoke Frankish, a Germanic language, he learned Latin as a foreign language. Therefore, he pronounced Latin phonetically giving a sound to each letter. A speaker of Romance, though, would have pronounced what appeared to be Latin in his or her own variety of Romance, so that many letters would be silent. Charlemagne's insistence on pronouncing each letter in these documents made speakers of Romance realize that they needed a new phonetic way to write their own languages. And so, it is not a coincidence that the first written texts in the Romance languages appeared shortly after the time of Charlemagne.

Complete Activity 5-3 on page 100.

These glosses are followed by literary works, such as the play *Auto de los Reyes Magos* (twelfth century), the epic poem *Cantar de mio Cid* (twelfth century), the courtly love poem *Razon feita d'amor con los denuestos del agua y el vino* (early thirteenth century), and the short religious poems that make up the *Milagros de Nuestra Señora* by Gonzalo de Berceo (thirteenth century). Excerpts of these texts are found in the Appendix. One assumes that literary works were written in Hispano-Romance so that they could be read aloud in order to educate

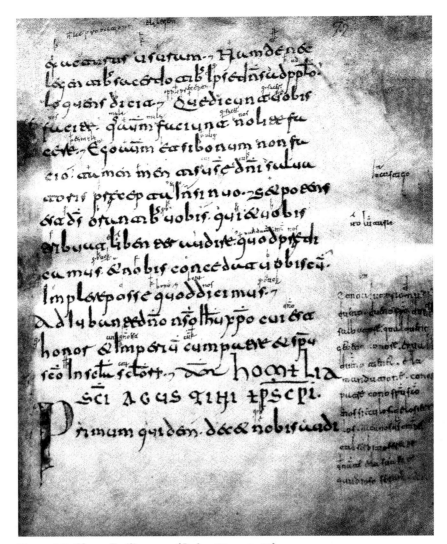

Figure 5.1 *Glosas Emilianenses* (Codex 60, page 72)

and entertain the vast majority of people who could neither read nor understand Latin. Serious prose works, however, such as legal texts and scientific treatises, continued to be written in Latin since these would be read only by scholars who would of course be trained in Latin.

This situation can be compared to the current use of non-standard varieties of modern English. For example, what can be called urban slang is currently used only in informal conversations with friends or in comic strips and certain types of writing that represent the spoken language, in the same way that writing in Castilian was once limited to texts with a close relationship to the spoken word. One teacher in New York City has expanded the function of urban slang by writing an urban slang version of Shakespeare's *Romeo and Juliet*. Her purpose in doing this was to make the work more accessible to her students (Lee 2006), much in the same way that Alfonso X had certain texts translated into Castilian in order to make them accessible to his subjects (Menéndez Pidal, cited by O'Callaghan 1975: 509). Of course, the use of urban slang in writing is still very limited. If we wanted to elevate it to the status of a standard language, we would have to expand its uses by writing urban slang versions of not just plays, but also serious scholarly works and official documents.

Alfonso X oversaw a vast output of writings in Castilian thereby expanding on a practice begun by his father, Ferdinand III of Castile (reigned 1217–52), the first ruler in the Iberian Peninsula to use Castilian rather than Latin in all public documents. Among the works in Castilian was the *Siete Partidas* 'Seven-Part Code,' a legal code completed in 1265 that would not take effect until 1348 under Alfonso XI (1311–50). Alfonso X also supervised the writing of two treatises on history, the *Estoria de España* and the *General estoria*. Many of the scientific works produced under his sponsorship were Castilian translations from Arabic works. These included the *Tablas Alfonsíes*, which provided astronomical data, the *Libros del saber de astronomía*, the *Libro de los juicios de las estrellas*, and the *Lapidario*, a book on rocks and gems. He also oversaw translations of the holy book of Islam, the Koran, and of Judaism, the Talmud, as well as translations of literature. These included *Calila e Dimna*, a collection of popular stories, an excerpt of which can be found in the Appendix, and the *Libro de ajedrez, dados, y tablas,* 'Book of chess, dice, and tables.'

Adapting the language for widespread use during this time required expanding the lexicon and so speakers and writers turned to Classical Latin and Arabic as a source of new words. This practice was no doubt encouraged by the fact that many of the early texts in Castilian were translations from one of these classical languages. Whenever a translation was needed for a Latin word with no equivalent in Castilian, the translator could create a new Castilian word based on the Latin word. These new creations, known as **learnèd words** (*cultismos*), would not have undergone regular sound changes and so they more closely resemble Latin words than the **derived words** (*palabras derivadas*) that have changed over time. In most cases, the new learnèd words did not replace the older derived forms but rather survived along with them. Thus, we have pairs of learnèd and derived words such as *ópera/obra* (< OPĔRA) and *fábula/habla* (< FABŬLAM). Pairs of words that derive from the same Latin word are called **doublets** (*dobletes*). Doublets are not always a learnèd word/derived word pair, though, since many scholars consider both members of pairs like *pensar/pesar, flama/llama*, and *clave/llave* to be derived words. You will also see in Chapter 13 that certain grammatical forms have the same origin, like *ella* and *la* and *mi* and *mío*, and so they are doublets made up of two derived words.

Complete Activity 5-4 on page 101.

5.4 How Was the Castilian Dialect Codified?

Whereas Alfonso X and the scholars under his patronage inevitably contributed to the codification of Castilian by selecting certain forms over others, Antonio de Nebrija (1441–1522) made an even more deliberate act of codification by writing the first grammar of any Romance language, the *Gramática de la lengua española*, based on his native Castilian dialect. He dedicated this work to Isabella I of Castile and presented it to her personally in August 1492. On this occasion the queen asked him why she needed such a book since she already spoke Castilian. Nebrija, more visionary in this regard, pointed out famously that "siempre la lengua fue compañera del imperio" 'language has always been the companion of the empire.' He knew that it would be necessary for others to learn Castilian in order for the Castilian empire to grow and that this grammar would serve as a guide for learners of Spanish as a second language. He also expressed two other equally important ideas in his prologue. He believed that Castilian could be a unifying force for the Spanish nation. In fact, the only time he used the adjective *español* 'Spanish' rather than *castellano* 'Castilian' was in the title of his grammar and when he referred to the Spanish nation. He also believed that a grammar would help to stabilize Castilian, so that it would not undergo what he considered to be the deterioration that Latin had suffered. At the same time, Nebrija also had a more practical concern in mind. This work would help his Castilian-speaking students in Salamanca understand the grammar of Latin better by gaining a clearer understanding of the grammar of their own language (Pountain 2001: 122–23, Gonzalez Nieto 2007: 233–34). Nebrija made further contributions to the codification of Castilian by producing a Latin–Spanish dictionary in 1492, a Spanish–Latin dictionary in 1495, and a guide to spelling in 1517, entitled *Reglas de orthographia de la lengua castellana.*

The organization most responsible for the codification of Castilian, and one which continues to this day, is the Real Academia Española (RAE). Founded in 1713, more than two centuries after Nebrija's grammar, the RAE was modeled after the Académie Française, established in Paris in 1635. In order to carry out its motto, "Limpia, fija, da esplendor" '(it) cleanses, establishes, and gives splendor' to the Spanish language, the RAE produced a dictionary, called the *Diccionario de Autoridades* in 1713, an orthography indicating proper spelling in 1741, and a grammar in 1771. Since its founding, the forty-six members of the RAE have been considered to be the prescriptive authorities on Standard Castilian Spanish. In recognition of the fact that the Spanish spoken outside Spain follows different norms from those of Castilian, in the same way that Romance languages differentiated themselves from Latin, language academies have been created in the other Spanish-speaking countries. These twenty-two academies are listed under the umbrella of the Asociación de Academias de la Lengua Española (ASALE) 'Association of Academies of the Spanish Language.'

5.5 What Led to Acceptance of the Castilian Dialect?

Acceptance of a standard dialect can come about voluntarily or through force. Both of these means of acceptance have occurred in the history of

Spanish. As Castilian extended its territory, speakers of other dialects who lived in these areas would interact with speakers of Castilian in their daily lives. As discussed above, they may also have adopted some of its features in their own speech. In this way Castilian came to be accepted more or less naturally as the predominant language of the areas under the control of Castile by 1492.

The acceptance of a standard dialect is forced rather than voluntary when the government of a nation proclaims a certain dialect to be the standard. There is no clear answer, though, to the question of when Spain became a nation. One answer often given is that Spain became a nation when Isabella and Ferdinand took control of Granada in 1492. It is true that all of the peninsula, except the small region of Navarre and of course Portugal, was united under the Catholic monarchs, but Aragon and Castile were not united in their administrative structure nor were they united in their language. Aragon continued to function independently of Castile with its own government and courts and its people continued to speak Catalan. When Isabella died in 1504 she was succeeded by her daughter, Juana (1479–1555), not by Ferdinand of Aragon, her husband, and the union between Castile and Aragon was dissolved. However, when Juana went mad, her son, who would later become Charles V (*Carlos V*) (1500–58), was only 6, and so Ferdinand served as regent of Castile for ten years until his death in 1516. After Ferdinand's death, Charles V became king over a vast empire that included all of what is modern-day Spain and many other parts of Europe.

Another possibility is that Spain became united politically and linguistically under Philip V (*Felipe V*) (1683–1746), the first Bourbon king of Spain, who came to power as a result of the War of Spanish Succession. From 1707 to 1716 he issued edicts, known as the *Nueva Planta* 'New Plan,' designed to exert control over the inhabitants of Catalonia, Aragon, and Valencia. He abolished their regional councils, replaced local officials with Castilian *corregidores* 'magistrates,' established new laws and courts, shut down Catalan universities, and established Castilian as the language of local administration and courts. A recent history of Spain declares this to be the moment that Spain became a modern state:

At the stroke of a pen, the autonomy of the eastern kingdoms had been erased and in their place was a Spanish monarchy that was stronger, more centralized and, in theory at least, more united than ever before; in this respect the *Nueva Planta* may be said to have marked the birth of Spain as a modern state. (Barton 2004: 138–39)

Other candidates for the unification of Spain include the founding of the First Republic in 1873, but it lasted only until the following year when the Bourbon monarchy was restored, and the Second Republic in 1931, which was also short-lived because Francisco Franco (1892–1975) rose to power in 1939. During his dictatorship, Franco outlawed the use of Basque, Catalan, and Galician, which meant that non-Castilian speakers were forced to accept Castilian, at least in the public sphere. The constitution of the current Spanish democracy, created in 1978, requires in Article 3 the acceptance of Castilian as the official language, while at the same time recognizing other official "lenguas españolas" 'languages of Spain' in their respective autonomous communities and declaring special respect and protection for the "distintas modalidades lingüísticas de España" 'distinct language varieties of Spain.' It is clear then that the official standard language of Spain is based on the Castilian dialect, but that many speakers within the Spanish nation, especially native speakers of Galician, Catalan, and Basque, prefer to express themselves in their native languages.

Complete Activities 5-5, 5-6, and 5-7 on pages 101–03.

5.6 Chapter Summary

- Linguists do not need to distinguish between a language and a dialect.
- To linguists any variety of speech can be called a dialect. Therefore, what non-linguists call a language can be either a diasystem, a collection of dialects, or a standard dialect.

- The classification of dialects into diasystems is a human creation. The features of a dialect do not change if it is classified as a "dialect of Spanish" or a "dialect of Portuguese."
- The process of standardization of a language consists of four steps: selection, elaboration, codification, and acceptance.
- Selection refers to the process by which a certain dialect is selected as the basis for the standard dialect. It is based on political and social reasons, not linguistic ones. The territorial expansion of Castile is a primary reason for its selection as the standard dialect.
- Territorial expansion brought speakers of Castilian into contact with speakers of different Hispano-Romance dialects, such as Galician, Leonese, Asturian, Navarrese, Aragonese, and Catalan, and also with speakers of non-Romance dialects like Basque and Arabic.
- The contact between speakers of Hispano-Romance dialects led to dialect mixing or koineization whereby certain features were adopted by the group and other features were rejected. Therefore, Standard Spanish, which is based primarily on the Castilian dialect, does not have only or all Castilian features.
- Elaboration is the process whereby the functions of a dialect are expanded so that it can serve all the functions of a society. The person most responsible for the elaboration of Castilian was Alfonso X the Wise. During his reign from 1252 to 1284, he oversaw the translation and writing of legal treatises, and historical, scientific, and literary works.
- Codification is the process of formulating rules and norms for the standard dialect. For Castilian, this was done first by Antonio Nebrija who published a grammar of Castilian in 1492 and later Latin–Spanish and Spanish–Latin dictionaries and an orthography or spelling guide.
- From its founding in 1713, the Royal Spanish Academy has overseen the codification of Castilian. In each Spanish-speaking country there is a language academy that oversees the prescriptive norms for the variety of Spanish spoken in that country.
- The acceptance of a standard dialect occurs when speakers of other dialects agree to use it. Acceptance can come about voluntarily, as was the case when speakers of other dialects came into contact with speakers of Castilian during Castile's territorial expansion.

- Acceptance can be forced when a political unit adopts and enforces a language policy that requires the use of a standard dialect. This has happened several times in Spain's history: from 1707 to 1716 through the decrees of the New Plan under Philip V, during Franco's dictatorship from 1939 to 1975, and in the democratic constitution of 1978.

Activities

Activity 5-1

1. Which of the following do you consider to be dialects and which do you consider to be languages? Feel free to look up information on any of these that you are not familiar with. Place a D after the dialects and an L after the languages. Explain your reasoning.

   Basque
   Galician
   Castilian
   Catalan
   Leonese
   Portuguese
   Spanish
   Valencian

2. Now reconsider your classification based on a linguist's view of a dialect and a language. Which ones are dialects? Which ones would you place in the same diasystem? Why?

Activity 5-2

In the timeline below, fill in the events associated with each date in the middle column and then write the name of the ruler during those events in the right column.

Date	Event	Ruler
722		
884		
931		
1035		
1085		
1197		
1212		
1236–50		
1492		

Activity 5-3

In the following pairs of doublets,

• Circle the learnèd word, the one that has changed the least from Latin.

• Try to identify one sound that has changed in the derived word that has not changed in the learnèd word.

• Indicate a difference in meaning for one pair of doublets.

Latin	Spanish word 1	Spanish word 2
1. CATHĔDRAM	cadera	cátedra
2. DĒLICĀTUM	delicado	delgado
3. ARTICŬLUM	artejo	artículo
4. MATERIA	materia	madera
5. COLLOCĀRE	colgar	colocar
6. SPATHŬLAM	espalda	espátula
7. FRĪGĬDUM	frígido	frío
8. MŪSCŬLUM	músculo	muslo
9. SŌLITĀRIUM	soltero	solitario

Latin	Spanish word 1	Spanish word 2
10. RECUPERĀRE	recuperar	recobrar
11. RATIŌNEM	razón	ración
12. RECITĀRE	recitar	rezar
13. HOSPITĀLEM	hostal	hospital
14. VIGILĀRE	velar	vigilar

Activity 5-4

The following is one of the lines from page 72 of Codex 60 of the *Glosas Emilianenses* (see Figure 5.1). Look for and write down 5–10 changes that you can observe between this early version of Hispano-Romance and Modern Spanish:

Hispano-Romance gloss:

> *Facanos Deus Omnipotes tal serbitio fere ke denante ela sua face gaudioso segamus. Amen*

Modern Spanish:

> *Háganos Dios omnipotente hacer tal servicio que delante de su faz gozosos seamos. Amén.*

English:

> God Omnipotent, make us do such service that before His face joyful we are. Amen.

> (*Glosas Emilianenses* 2017)

Activity 5-5

Pick a topic from this chapter that you would like to know more about. This can be a person, like Alfonso X, or an organization, like the RAE, or an event, like the battle of Las Navas de Tolosa. Write down three pieces of information that you found interesting about this topic and explain their importance to the history of Spanish. You could even try to stump your professor or your classmates by finding information that you think even they do not know.

Be sure to write down the source of this information. Say also why you decided to research this topic.

Example: In my research on Isabella and Ferdinand. I discovered these three things:

Isabella and Ferdinand got married in 1469. Isabella was only 18 at the time and Ferdinand was 17.

They were first cousins and so they had to get married in secret.

Neither one of them was a monarch at the time they got married. Isabella became queen in 1474 and Ferdinand became king in 1479.

Source: *Spain then and now*, www.spainthenandnow.com

I decided to research this topic because Isabella and Ferdinand are famous historical figures that I wanted to learn more about.

Activity 5-6

Think of a lingering question that you have after reading this chapter, something that you really want to know. For example, you might want to know why Isabella and Ferdinand decided to sponsor Columbus's voyages to the Americas even though other European leaders had turned him down. Or you might want to know why Aragon turned its attention to Italy after the 1250s rather than strengthening its position in the Iberian Peninsula.

Write down your question and then provide two pieces of information that start you on the path toward finding an answer. Write down also the source where you found this information.

Example: One question I had was why more than 200 years passed between the capture of Cádiz in 1250 and the surrender of Granada in 1492. I found out that the intervening years were troubled times which prevented the Castilians from mounting an attack on Granada. The bubonic plague or Black Death that reached Spain in 1348 may have killed over half the population. There were also famines to contend with and at least five civil wars during this time for the rule of Castile. One of these civil wars was between Isabella 1 of Castile and Juana la Beltraneja, her niece. Source: Barton (2004: 83–88)

Activity 5-7

Questions for thought:

1. What is the role of a standard dialect in a society? What would happen if a country had no standard dialect?

2. The Catholic monarchs called 1492 the ANNUS MĪRĀBILIS 'miracle year.' Which four events took place in 1492? Which of these do you think they considered to be the most important at that time? Which one do you consider to be the most important? How important is each of these events to the consolidation of the Castilian dialect as a national (and now worldwide) language?

3. Thinking back on what you have learned in Chapters 4 and 5, what are the most important historical events in the history of the Spanish language? Make a list of three events and put them in order of importance. Explain your ranking and your criteria for this ranking.

Further Reading

For interactive maps of the expansion of Castile, go to: http://explorethemed.com/reconquista.asp

For a dramatic version of the lives of Isabella I of Castile and Ferdinand II of Aragón (*los Reyes Católicos*), watch the Spanish television series, *Isabel*: www.rtve.es/television/isabel-la-catolica/capitulos-completos/

At www.spainthenandnow.com under the "history" tab, you will find short but detailed articles about Spain's history.

La Rosa, Zhenja 1995. "Language and empire: The vision of Nebrija," *The Student Historical Journal* 27

Tejedo-Herrero, Fernando 2008. "Prácticas estandarizadores en el léxico de las Siete Partidas (1491)," *Romance Philology* 62(1): 29–58

Tuten, Donald N. 2005. "Reflections on dialect mixing and variation in Alfonsine texts," in Roger Wright and Peter Ricketts (eds.), *Studies in Ibero-Romance linguistics dedicated to Ralph Penny*, 85–102. Newark, DE: Juan de la Cuesta

Tuten, Donald N., and Fernando Tejedo-Herrero 2011. "The relationship between historical linguistics and sociolinguistics," in Manuel Díaz-Campos (ed.), *The Handbook of Hispanic Sociolinguistics*, 283–302. Oxford: Wiley-Blackwell

Velázquez-Mendoza, Omar. 2013. "La España altomedieval y su continuo sociolingüístico: ¿Sociedad diglósica o monolingüe?" *Bulletin of Hispanic Studies* 90(6): 627–48

Wright, Roger 1991. "The conceptual difference between Latin and Romance: Invention or evolution?" in Roger Wright (ed.), *Latin and the Romance languages in the Early Middle Ages*, 103–13. New York: Routledge

6 How Did FESTA Become *fiesta* but FESTĪVUM Became *festivo*?

Regular Vowel Changes

Lead-in Question

6-1 Why does the word *fiesta* have a different first vowel from *festivo* 'festive'?
Why don't they both have the same vowel, as in *fiesta/*fiestivo* or **festa/*
festivo? (The asterisk before **fiestivo* and **festa* indicates that these forms
are unattested.) Can you think of a linguistic reason for the difference in
vowels in these pairs of words? In order to answer this question, find at least
three other pairs of Spanish words related in meaning where one has
a **diphthong** (*un diptongo*), a vowel plus a semi-vowel in the same syllable
like /je/ or /we/, and the other has a single vowel or **monophthong** (*un
monoptongo*) like /e/ or /o/. A good way to find these words is to think of
Spanish words with a diphthong and then to look for related words without
a diphthong. What do the words with a diphthong have in common?

*In this chapter, you will learn how Spanish vowels evolved from Latin. Latin had the
same five vowels as Spanish, /i/, /e/, /a/, /o/, and /u/, but there was a long and short
version of each of these vowels. Vowel length in Latin determined whether a vowel was*

stressed or unstressed and this in turn determined its result in Spanish. Knowing the vowel changes in the history of Spanish will allow you to determine the Spanish result or **reflex** *(reflejo) for a Latin word, since these changes are for the most part regular, by which we mean that the same vowels change in the same ways. For example, both of the Latin short mid open vowels, Ĕ and Ŏ, diphthongize to [je] and [we] in Spanish when they are stressed. This regularity is especially remarkable since speakers make no conscious effort to change sounds in a particular way.*

6.1 Where Do the Sounds in Spanish Come from?

The modern varieties of Spanish come from the continuous development of speech varieties going back to Latin and then to the Italic branch of the Indo-European family of languages and ultimately to Proto-Indo-European, as mentioned in Chapter 4. Thus, the sounds that make up Spanish today have a long backstory, but it is typical to begin our discussion of their history with Latin, the oldest language variety in this line of continuous development for which we have ample documentation.

We must remember, as we mentioned in Chapter 3, to use care in interpreting written records, since they are not a faithful representation of the spoken language. We can assume that one variety of Spoken Latin was similar to Classical Latin, but we also know with certainty that many spoken forms of Latin diverged from Classical Latin, as seen in the admonitions of the anonymous author of the *Appendix Probi* in Chapter 2. Our solution then will be to use Classical Latin as evidence of a stage of Latin, since it is well documented, and to refer specifically to Spoken Latin when we know that it diverges from written Classical Latin. Most of the time, however, we will refer simply to Latin, when we assume that Classical and Spoken Latin coincided. In spite of the numerous spoken varieties of Spanish that exist today, we will trace the historical developments to what might be called Castilian or Northern Peninsular Spanish and also to General Latin American Spanish, from which it should be possible to deduce the additional or parallel changes that occurred in other varieties.

This chapter is the first of four chapters devoted to the evolution of the sounds of Spanish, often considered to be the cornerstone of a course in the history of the Spanish language. It is indeed fascinating to think that the members of a speech community, without planning, discussion, or even conscious thought, can end up adopting the same changes in their pronunciation. Over time these changes affect most words in the language and form regular patterns that we can then discern and study using the methods of historical linguistics. We notice, for example, that the vowel written as long ī in Latin is almost always retained as /i/ in Spanish, as in AMĪCUM > *amigo* and CĪVITĀTEM > *ciudad*. As we saw in Chapter 5, there is a distinction between derived words that have undergone natural sound changes over time, like FRĪGĬDUM > *frío*, and learnèd words that were consciously created based on Latin words, like FRĪGĬDUM > *frígido*. In learning about the sound changes in Spanish, it is important to keep in mind that we will be interested in tracing the changes in derived words and not in learnèd ones. Therefore, if you are asked to find the Spanish reflex of RECUPERĀRE, you will want to follow the natural sound changes to *recobrar* rather than falling into the **cultismo** trap (*la trampa del cultismo*) of identifying the learnèd word *recuperar* as the result of these natural sound changes.

6.2 What Are the Vowels in Spanish and How Are They Organized?

It is important to understand the Modern Spanish vowel system before we look at the changes that resulted in this system. We can begin by defining a vowel in articulatory terms. When you pronounce a **vowel** (*una vocal*), the flow of air from the diaphragm through the oral cavity is unobstructed. You can determine that the sound /i/, as in *sí*, is a vowel because you can maintain it without producing any friction until you need to take a breath. If you pronounce the /s/ that begins the word *sí*, you can maintain the sound, but now you hear the hissing sound of friction, caused by obstructing the flow of air in some way. This is what determines the classification of /s/ as a consonant, specifically as a **fricative** (*una fricativa*). If you pronounce the /p/ in *pero*, you don't hear friction like you did for /s/. In fact, you just keep your mouth closed and do not hear any sound at all. This is because /p/ is a **stop** (*una oclusiva*), which like /s/ is a type of consonant. Notice that we represent a sound between slashes, like /a/, when it is a **phoneme** (*un fonema*) or a distinctive sound. We can also write sounds between brackets, like [a], when we wish to represent them as phones or sounds, rather than distinctive sounds. It is important to distinguish between sounds and letters, which we write in italics, because a single letter, like *c*, can represent more than one sound. It can be /k/ in the word *cama*, but /s/ or /θ/ in the word *cero*.

Linguists classify vowels according to the position of the tongue in the mouth, whether it is high or low or in the front or back of the mouth. For example, to pronounce the vowel /i/, you raise your tongue as high in the mouth and as far forward as possible. This position of the tongue gives rise to the classification of /i/ as a high front vowel. To articulate the /u/, you again raise your tongue, but now it is in the back of the mouth, so that /u/ is a high back vowel. Another difference between /i/ and /u/ is that /i/ is articulated with the lips spread out or unrounded, whereas /u/ is pronounced with the lips rounded. In Spanish lip rounding is never distinctive since the front vowels, /i/ and /e/, are unrounded and the back vowels, /u/ and /o/, are rounded.

Practice 6-1

a. We have described the articulation of the high vowels /i/ and /u/. Based on Table 6.1, describe how /e/, /a/, and /o/ are pronounced. What is the difference between /i/ and /e/ and between /u/ and /o/? What is the difference between /e/ and /o/?

b. Pronounce the following pairs of syllables while focusing on the difference in the position of your tongue for each vowel: *qui ~ que, cu ~ co, qui ~ cu, que ~ co, que ~ ca, co ~ ca*. What is the difference between the vowels in each pair?

TABLE 6.1 The Spanish vowel phonemes

	Front (*anterior*)	Central (*central*)	Back (*posterior*)
High (*cerrada*)	/i/		/u/
Mid (*media*)	/e/		/o/
Low (*abierta*)		/a/	

6.3 What Are the Vowels in Latin and How Are They Organized?

We know from written documents that offer a guide to pronunciation, like the rhymes and meter of poetry and comments by grammarians, that Classical Latin had the same five vowels as Modern Spanish, but each of these vowels could be pronounced as a long or a short vowel. By a long vowel we mean that speakers actually held the pronunciation of the vowel for a longer time in the same way that a half note in music is held for a longer time than a quarter note. This difference in vowel length could even distinguish between different words. For example, LĪBER with a long vowel means 'free' (Spanish *libre*), whereas LĬBER with a short vowel means 'book' (Spanish *libro*). Other such **minimal pairs** (*pares mínimos*), that differ only in vowel length, are MĀLUM 'apple' and MĂLUM 'evil'; ŌS 'mouth' and ŎS 'bone'; and the verb forms VĒNIT 'he/she came' and VĔNIT 'he/she comes.' The line placed over a vowel to indicate that it is long is called a **macron** (*un macrón*) and the semi-circle placed over a short vowel is called a **breve** (*una breve*). These symbols were not used by Classical Latin authors, but were added later to help learners of Latin. When we cite Classical Latin words, we will indicate vowel length when you need to know it to trace the evolution of a Latin word into Spanish. If a vowel has no mark above it, assume that it is short. Table 6.2 shows the ten Classical Latin vowels with the written letters on the first line and the phonetic symbols on the second line, where /:/ indicates greater length.

You will notice that Table 6.2 also includes three Latin **diphthongs** (*diptongos*), made up of a vowel and a semi-vowel or glide in the same syllable. These diphthongs include OE /oj/, as in POENAM 'pain,' AE /aj/, as in CAELUM 'sky,' and AU /aw/, as in TAURUM 'bull.' In these Latin diphthongs, the vowel /o/ or /a/ is followed by the semi-vowel /j/ or /w/. These diphthongs lost their semi-vowel to become a single vowel or **monophthong** (*monoptongo*). This monophthongization took place through **assimilation** (*asimilación*) whereby sounds become more similar to each other, as shown in Table 6.3. The arrows in this table show how the positions for the vowel and the semi-vowel move closer to each other resulting in a new vowel.

TABLE 6.2 The Classical Latin vowel system (represented as letters and phonemes)

	Front	Central	Back
High	ī ĭ /i:/ /i/		ū ŭ /u:/ /u/
Mid	ē ĕ /e:/ /e/		ō ŏ OE /o:/ /o/ /oj/
Low		ā ă AE AU /a:/ /a/ /aj/ /aw/	

TABLE 6.3 Monophthongization of Classical Latin diphthongs

	Front	Central	Back
High	/j/		/w/
Mid high	/oj/ > /e/ ←		/o/ /aw/ > /o/ ↗
Mid low	/aj/ > /ε/ ↙		
Low		/a/ ↗	

In each case, the single vowel resulting from the diphthong emerges due to assimilation of the vowel and the semi-vowel that make up the diphthong. When /oj/ monophthongizes, the resulting vowel /e/ maintains the tongue height of mid /o/ but moves forward toward the position of the semi-vowel /j/. In the diphthong /aj/, the /a/ raises one degree toward the front of the mouth toward /j/, thereby becoming /ε/, whereas in /aw/ the tongue raises one degree backward in the mouth toward the position for /w/. We know that these changes occurred early in the evolution of the vowel system because these diphthongs follow the same changes into Spanish as the monophthongs that they changed to. Therefore, in our summary of the sound changes from Latin to Spanish we will list these diphthongs alongside the corresponding monophthongs: OE alongside ē /e/, AE alongside ĕ /ε/, and AU alongside ŏ /o/.

TABLE 6.4 From Latin ten-vowel to seven-vowel system (CL = Classical Latin, SL = Spoken Latin)

CL quantity	SL quality 9 vowels	SL merger 7 vowels		SL merger 7 vowels	SL quality 9 vowels	CL quantity
Ī /i:/ →	/i/ →	/i/		/u/ ←	/u/ ←	Ū /u:/
Ĭ /i/ ↘						Ŭ /u/
	/ɪ/ ↘				/ʊ/ ↗	
Ē /e:/ →	/e/ →	/e/		/o/ ←	/o/ ←	Ō /o:/
Ĕ /e/ ↘						Ŏ /o/ ↗
	/ɛ] →	/ɛ/		/ɔ/ ←	/ɔ/	
Ā /a:/ ——————→			/a/			
Ă /a/						

Table 6.4 shows how the ten-vowel system in Latin changed to a seven-vowel system in Spoken Latin. It was likely that, as occurs in many languages, speakers began to articulate the short vowels with the tongue lower in the mouth than the high vowels. Thus, the Classical Latin distinction according to vowel length, a distinction according to quantity, became a distinction according to tongue position in the mouth, a distinction of quality (Pulgram 1983: 112–14, Menéndez Pidal 1987: 43). This means that each of the five pairs of vowels developed a distinction in quality according to the opening or **aperture** (*la abertura*) of the vowels. The long vowels remained closed and the short vowels became more open. The symbol, /ɪ/, like the vowel in English *sit*, is the more open version of /i/ and the symbol, /ʊ/, like the vowel in English *good*, is the more open version of /u/. Note also that since /a/ was already an open vowel, it did not maintain a distinction between a more closed and a more open vowel (Menéndez Pidal 1987: 43). The next important step in this process is the further lowering of /ɪ/ and /ʊ/ which caused their merger with /e/ and /o/. This results in seven-vowel system of Spoken Latin that is the point of departure for all subsequent changes in Spanish.

Study Table 6.4 for a moment to see for yourself which vowels stayed the same and which vowels lowered. We see that the closed (long) vowels were all retained with the same vowel height without the feature of length, whereas the open (short) vowels lowered by one degree: ĭ /ɪ/ > /e/, ĕ /e/ > /ɛ/, ă /ɐ/ > /a/, ŏ /o/ > /ɔ/ and ŭ / ʊ/ > /o/. This lowering resulted in three mergers: the merger of ĭ and ē as /e/, of ă and ā as /a/, and of ŭ and ō as /o/. Thus, the three changes brought about by the merging of the high open and mid closed vowels and the low open and closed vowel reduced the ten-vowel system to a seven-vowel system.

6.4 Which Vowel Is Stressed in Latin?

The changes we have seen so far in Latin vowels apply to all vowels regardless of stress, that is, whether they bear the accent. But in order to trace the evolution of the Latin seven-vowel system into Spanish, we need to be able to determine which Latin vowel was stressed. Complete Practice 6-2 to see some examples of tonic or stressed vowels in Latin and Spanish.

Practice 6-2

Write an accent mark above the tonic vowel in the following Spanish words and determine which vowel is tonic in Latin by assuming that this is the vowel that developed into the tonic vowel in Spanish.

> MŎVET > *mueve*, TĔRRAM > *tierra*, PLĒNUM > *lleno*, PĬLUM > *pelo*, PRĀTUM > *prado*, HŌRAM > *hora*, CŬPPAM > *copa*, CATĒNAM > *cadena*, BALLAENAM > *ballena*, INFĔRNUM > *infierno*, VĬRĬDEM > *verde*

We identify the stressed or tonic vowel in Latin based on the number of syllables in a word and whether the next to last syllable, **the penultimate syllable** (*la sílaba penúltima*), is a **heavy syllable** (*una sílaba pesada*) or a **light syllable** (*una sílaba ligera*). If a word has only one syllable, then that syllable contains the tonic vowel, unless it is a word that is not stressed at all. In two-syllable or **disyllabic words** (*palabras disilábicas*), the stress always falls on the vowel in the penultimate syllable. In **polysyllabic words** (*palabras polisilábicas*) with three or more syllables, the stress is determined by whether the penultimate syllable is heavy or light. If the penultimate syllable is heavy then it bears the stress. If the penultimate syllable is light, then it does not bear the stress. Instead the stress passes to the **antepenultimate syllable** (*la sílaba antepenúltima*), the third syllable from the end of the word.

In order to determine whether the penultimate syllable in a Latin word is heavy and therefore stressed, or light and therefore unstressed, look first at the vowel in this syllable. If the vowel is long or a diphthong, then the syllable is heavy and it bears the stress, as in CATĒNAM (> *cadena*) and BALLAENAM (> *ballena*). If this vowel is short, then you must determine whether this syllable ends in a vowel or a consonant. If it ends in a consonant, then this syllable is known as a **closed syllable** (*una sílaba cerrada o trabada*) and it is heavy. If it ends in a vowel, it is known as an **open syllable** (*una sílaba abierta*) and it is light. In order to determine whether the syllable is closed or open, try dividing the syllable after the vowel. If a single consonant or a group of consonants that can begin a word follows the vowel, then this syllable is open. If this is a penultimate syllable containing a short vowel, then this syllable is light and the stress will fall on the antepenultimate syllable. This is the case in a word like OCŬLUM, divided as ['o-ku-lum]. If, however, the consonants following the vowel cannot begin a word, then one or more of these consonants will have to be placed at the end of the syllable containing the vowel in question, which means that the syllable is closed. If this is a penultimate syllable, then the syllable is heavy and it will bear the stress. This is the case in words with double or geminate consonants, like CASTĒLLUM, divided as [ka-'stel-lum], since double /ll/ cannot start a word, and INFĔRNUM, divided as [in-'fer-num], since the groups /nf/ and /rn/ cannot begin a word.

What we have just explained can be formulated simply and succinctly as the penultimate syllable rule, a name adapted from Alkire, Rosen, and Scidas's (2010: 6–8) "penultimate rule." It states that, in words of three syllables or more, if the penultimate syllable consists of a short vowel in an open syllable, then it does not bear the stress. Instead the stress falls on the antepenultimate syllable. In all other cases, namely if the vowel in the penultimate syllable is long or the syllable is closed, then the stress falls on the penultimate syllable. It is important to remember this simple rule because the vowel changes in the history of Spanish depend crucially on whether a vowel is stressed (tonic) or unstressed (atonic). Thus far we have seen that vowel changes depend on the type of vowel (high, mid, low, and long or short) and whether it is stressed or not.

Summary of Latin rules of accentuation:

The stress falls on the penultimate syllable . . .

- in all two-syllable words
- in any word of three syllables or more with a heavy penultimate syllable, that is, one with a long vowel or a closed syllable

The stress falls on the on antepenultimate syllable . . .

- in words of three or more syllables with a light penultimate syllable, namely a short vowel in an open syllable.

In practical terms, if you have a word of three syllables or more, begin by looking at the penultimate syllable. If it has a short vowel in an open syllable, the stress is on the antepenultimate syllable. If not, then the stress is on the penultimate syllable.

Complete Activity 6-1 on page 126.

6.5 How Do Vowels Change in Tonic Position?

Now that you know how to identify the tonic vowel in Latin words, we can look at the evolution of Latin tonic vowels in Spanish. Complete Practice 6-3 to discover these changes.

Practice 6-3

Take a look at the Latin words below and their corresponding forms in Modern Spanish.

Latin word	Spanish word	Latin after loss of vowel quantity	Spoken Latin seven-vowel system	Spanish vowel
VĪTAM	*vida*	/i/		
PĬLUM	*pelo*	/ɪ/		
PLĒNUM	*lleno*	/e/		
POENAM	*pena*	/oj/		
PĔTRAM	*piedra*	/ɛ/		
CAELUM	*cielo*	/aj/		
PRĀTUM	*prado*	/ɑ/		
MĂREM	*mar*	/a/		
PŎRTAM	*puerta*	/ɔ/		
PŌNIS	*pones*	/o/		
AURUM	*oro*	/aw/		
BŬCCAM	*boca*	/ʊ/		
LŪNAM	*luna*	/u/		

a. First, review what you just learned about the Spoken Latin seven-vowel system by writing the corresponding vowel from this system in the column labeled "Spoken Latin seven-vowel system."

b. Next, write the vowel in the resulting word in Spanish in the column marked "Spanish vowel."

c. Now compare these two columns to state how the vowels in tonic position in Spanish are different from the vowels in the Spoken Latin seven-vowel system.

d. What conclusion can you draw so far as to why Spanish has only five vowels whereas Spoken Latin had seven?

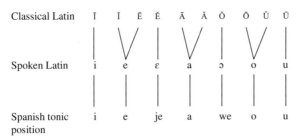

Figure 6.1 Evolution of Spoken Latin seven-vowel to Spanish five-vowel system

As shown in Practice 6-3, the difference between the Spoken Latin seven-vowel system and the Spanish vowels in tonic position is the diphthongization of Ĕ to /je/ and ŏ to /we/. The resulting diphthongs combine a vowel, in this case /e/, and a semi-vowel, /j/ or /w/, in the same syllable where only the vowel receives the stress. This provides part of the answer to the question posed in the title of this chapter. FĔSTA became *fiesta* through the diphthongization of Latin /ɛ/ in stressed position to Spanish /je/. Diphthongization in the Latin stressed vowels /ɔ/ and /ɛ/ also explains why we have words such as *bueno* from BŎNUM, *hueso* from ŎSSUM, and *hierba* from HĔRBAM. Figure 6.1 summarizes the changes that we have discussed in the evolution of Modern Spanish stressed vowels. This shows how the ten Latin vowels have given us five Spanish vowels, as well as two diphthongs.

Complete Activities 6-2 and 6-3 on page 128.

6.6 How Do Vowels Change in Atonic Position?

The vowels in a Latin word that are not stressed are called unstressed or **atonic vowels** (*vocales átonas*). We can identify three different positions for atonic vowels that determine their evolution: initial, final, and medial position. Medial position includes **pre-tonic vowels** (*vocales pretónicas*), which precede the tonic vowel, and **post-tonic vowels** (*vocales postónicas*), which follow the tonic vowel.

A four-syllable word like CASTĪGĀRE [ka-sti-ˈgá-re] 'to castigate, punish' can serve to illustrate these positions. We can first identify the tonic vowel as the /a/ in the penultimate syllable, since the long vowel Ā creates a heavy penultimate syllable and therefore bears the stress. We then identify the first /a/ as being in **initial position** (*la posición inicial*). Note that by initial position we mean atonic initial position, so initial position will refer to the first vowel in a word only when it is in atonic position. Therefore, if the first vowel in a three-syllable word is tonic, as in OPĔRA (> *obra*), then there will be no initial (atonic) vowel in these words. Returning now to CASTĪGĀRE we can identify the final /e/ as being in final position. A vowel is in **final position** (*la posición final*) if it is in the last syllable of the word. It does not have to be the last sound in the word, so that the /e/ in MŌVET is in final position. Note that the last vowel in a Latin word that has at least two syllables is always in final position, since the stress in a two-syllable word always falls on the penultimate syllable and never on the final syllable. Finally, the vowel /i/ in CASTĪGĀRE is in **medial position** (*la posición media*), specifically pre-tonic position, since it precedes the tonic vowel /a/ and is neither initial nor final. An unstressed medial vowel is in post-tonic position when it follows the tonic vowel, as does the /e/ in OPĔRA.

Let us look now at how the vowels in the Latin seven-vowel system develop in each of these positions by considering their results in Spanish. Practice 6-4 shows their development in initial position.

Practice 6-4

Take a look at the initial vowel of the Latin words below and their corresponding forms in Modern Spanish.

Spoken Latin vowel	Latin word	Spanish word	Spanish vowel
/i/	HĪBĔRNUM	*invierno*	
/e/	CĬRCĀRE	*cercar*	
	SĒCŪRUM	*seguro*	
/ɛ/	LĔŌNEM	*león*	
/a/	MĀTŪRUM	*maduro*	
	ĂPĬCŬLAM	*abeja*	
/ɔ/	CŎRŌNAM	*corona*	
/o/	NŌMĬNĀRE	*nombrar*	
	CŬMĬNĬTĬĀRE	*comenzar*	
/u/	SŪDĀRE	*sudar*	

a. Determine the tonic syllable for each Latin word by applying the rules of accentuation. Then underline this vowel and place an accent mark above it.
b. Write the result of each initial vowel in Spanish. What is the difference between the vowels in the seven-vowel system and the vowels in the Spanish reflexes?

We see that in initial position the short mid vowels do not diphthongize as they did in tonic position, but rather merge with the other mid vowels /e/ and /o/. This means that in initial position we find the five Spanish vowels /i/, /e/, /a/, /o/, and /u/.

The Latin words in Practice 6-5 allow us to determine the results for these seven vowels in final position.

Practice 6-5

Take a look at the final vowel of the Latin words below and their corresponding forms in Modern Spanish. If the vowel is lost in Spanish, write Ø (phonetic zero) for its result.

Spoken Latin vowel	Latin word	Spanish word	Spanish vowel
/i/	IERĪ	*ayer*	
	VĒNĪ	*vine*	
/e/	LĔŌNĒS	*leones*	
	PŌNĬS	*pones*	
	TŬRREM	*torre*	
/ɛ/	LĔŌNEM	*león*	
	PŎNTEM	*puente*	
	CĬRCĀRE	*cercar*	
/a/	VĪTAM	*vida*	
	ĂPĬCŬLAM	*abeja*	
/ɔ/	N/A		
/o/	AMĪCŌS	*amigos*	
	PĬLUM	*pelo*	
	SĒCŪRUM	*seguro*	
/u/	N/A		

a. Determine the tonic syllable for each Latin word by applying the rules of accentuation. Then underline this vowel and place an accent mark above it.
b. Write the result of each final vowel in Spanish. What is the difference between the vowels in the seven-vowel system and the Spanish reflexes?
c. For which vowels are two different results possible in final position?

In final position, we observe retention of /a/ and the merger of all the front vowels as /e/ and of all the back vowels as /o/. Therefore, only three vowels appear in final unstressed position in Spanish: /e/, /a/, and /o/. We also observe a new process in final position, namely the loss of a vowel, which in final position is called **apocope** (*la apócope*).

Furthermore, we see that apocope is a **conditioned sound change** (*un cambio fonético condicionado*), occurring in some phonological contexts and not in others. For example, in a word like PŎNTEM > *puente* the vowel is retained, but in LĔŌNEM > *león*, the /e/ is lost through apocope. We can consider the following words to determine the phonological environment in which apocope does or does not occur in Spanish.

Apocope: Latin > Spanish	No apocope: Latin > Spanish
SĬTEM > *sed*	SĔPTEM > *siete*
SALEM > *sal*	ŎLĔT > *huele*
MARE > *mar*	TŬRREM > *torre*
MĒNSEM > *mes*	FŎRTEM > *fuerte*
PĀCEM > *paz*	RŌMĀNICĒ > *romance*
PĀNEM > *pan*	PŎNTEM > *puente*
VĔNĪ > *ven*	NŎCTEM > *noche*
	NŎVEM > *nueve*

We see that apocope occurs after these single consonants: /d/, /l/, /r/, /s/, *c* or *z* /θ/, /n/, but that it does not occur after the Spanish consonants *rr* /r/, *ch* /tʃ/, and [β], pronounced as /w/ in Latin, nor after consonants groups, like /rt/, /nt/, and /nθ/. Apocope does not occur in verb forms either, like *huele*, except in certain second person imperatives, like *ven, ten, haz, sal,* and *pon*. In a word like *siete* from Latin SĔPTEM, the /e/ is not lost even though this word now ends in a single consonant, presumably because the group /pt/ was maintained until a fairly late date. The same also occurs in DUODECIM > *doce* 'twelve,' TREDECIM > *trece* 'thirteen,' PECTINEM > *peine* 'comb,' and SALICEM > *sauce* 'willow' (Lloyd 1987: 207).

In Old Spanish texts, we find cases of **extreme apocope** (*la apócope extrema*), the loss of final /e/ where it does not occur in Modern Spanish, as seen in many words in the Appendix, for example, in verb endings, like *diz* for *dice* (C108) or after a consonant group, like *fuert* for *fuerte* (D229B). Box 6.1 offers further information on the popularity of extreme apocope and its possible motivations.

Box 6.1 Extreme apocope: an extreme fad

During the 1990s, Southern California skater/hip hop style took the United States by storm. A staple of this style was baggy or loose-fitting jeans. One company in particular, JNCO Jeans, took this fashion to extremes by offering ultra-wide Crime Scene Jeans, with leg openings measuring 50 inches in diameter (Gorenstein 2016). This extreme fad fizzled out by the early 2000s. Much like extreme fashion trends, extreme apocope was a linguistic trend in Spanish between the eleventh and thirteenth centuries.

By the end of the eleventh century cases of extreme apocope were becoming more common. This trend is attributed to increased contact between Castilian and French speakers, since Latin final vowels, except /a/, were lost in French. One reason for this contact was the rerouting of the pilgrim road to Santiago de Compostela, well traveled by French pilgrims, through the heart of Castile and León by Sancho el Mayor, king of Navarre from 1000 to 1035. Another reason was the arrival of French priests and monks in Iberia during the reign of Alfonso VI (1072–1109) to teach the new Roman liturgy which had originated in northern France.

By the middle of the thirteenth century, however, the strong ties between Castile and France began to weaken with fewer marriages between Castilian and Gallic royalty. The decrease in intermarriages led to fewer French officials in positions of power. Castile became more independent and French linguistic models such as extreme apocope lost their prestige. In the thirteenth century, cases of extreme apocope were on their way out, a practice hastened by Alfonso X "the Wise" (1221–84). In the royal prologues he wrote for the learnèd works under his sponsorship, he used very few forms with extreme apocope. Much in the same way that JNCO Jeans' ultra-wide straight legged jeans came and went in American fashion in the 1990s, so too did extreme apocope during the eleventh and thirteenth centuries in Spain.

Complete Activity 6-4 on page 129.

The last vowel position to consider is medial position, whether pre-tonic or post-tonic. Practice 6-6 gives an idea of the evolution of Latin vowels to Spanish in these positions. Keep in mind that a post-tonic vowel in a three-syllable word, like LĪTTĔRAM cannot be long. If it were, it would be in tonic position.

Practice 6-6

Take a look at the medial vowels of the Latin words below and their corresponding forms in Modern Spanish.

Spoken Latin vowel	Latin word	Spanish word	Spanish vowel
/i/	N/A		
/e/	VĔRĒCŪNDĬAM	*vergüenza*	
	LŪMĬNĀRE	*lumbrar*	
	VĬRĬDEM	*verde*	
/ɛ/	APĔRĪRE	*abrir*	
	LĪTTĔRAM	*letra*	
/a/	ORNĀMĔNTUM	*ornamento*	
	ŎRPHĂNUM	*huérfano*	
/ɔ/	TĔMPŎRĀNUM	*temprano*	
	RŌBŎREM	*roble*	
/o/	LABŌRĀRE	*labrar*	
	PŎPŬLĀRE	*poblar*	
	PŎPŬLUM	*pueblo*	
/u/	N/A		

a. First, identify the tonic syllable for each Latin word by applying the rules of accentuation, and underline this vowel and place an accent mark above it.
b. Identify the medial vowel in each word and draw a circle around it.
c. Indicate whether the medial vowel is pre-tonic or post-tonic by writing PRE or POST after the Latin word.
d. Finally indicate the evolution of each vowel in Spanish by writing its result in the column "Spanish vowel."

We see that all vowels are lost in medial position except /a/ which is retained. The loss of a vowel in medial position is called **syncope** (*la síncopa*).

It is also possible to find words of four syllables or more with two medial vowels in succession, as in RECŪPĔRĀRE where the underlined /u/ and the second /e/ are pre-tonic. In such cases, the first of the two medial vowels evolves as if it were in initial position and the second one evolves as expected for a vowel in medial position. In this word, Ŭ > /o/ according to the rules for initial position, whereas the medial Ĕ is lost, resulting in the verb *recobrar*. We can refer to the evolution of a medial vowel as if it were in initial position as the **first medial vowel rule**.

Another important vowel development is the **yodization** (*la yodización*) of /i/ and /e/ when they directly precede another vowel, that is, when they are **in hiatus** (*en hiato*) with a following vowel. Two vowels are in hiatus when they are in immediate contact with one another but belong to different syllables. This occurs in Modern Spanish words, for example, between the /e/ and /a/ of *teatro* and the /i/ and /a/ of *encía*. There were only three diphthongs in Classical Latin, represented by the letters *ae*, *oe*, and *au*; otherwise two vowel sounds in Latin were in hiatus, as in VĪNEAM, pronounced ['wi-ne-am] in three syllables. In the evolution into Spanish, though, the /e/ becomes [j], so that this word becomes ['wi-nja] and eventually *viña* ['bi-ɲa]. We can refer to this as the "**yodization rule**" ("*la regla de la yodización*"). As a side note, we will see in Chapter 7 that the yod can also have an effect on the evolution of consonants, like the change of /n/ to /ɲ/ seen in *viña*.

Complete Activities 6-5, 6-6, and 6-7 on pages 130–32.

6.7 What Is the Relative Strength of Each Vowel Position?

Having considered the results for vowels according to each of four positions, we can now determine the strength of each position by studying the results of the vowels in that position. We can consider diphthongization to be a strengthening process because a single vowel becomes a diphthong by adding a semi-vowel, thereby making the syllable longer. We can consider retention to be the next strongest process, since the vowel is maintained. The weakest process, of course, is loss in the form of apocope or syncope. Given these criteria, which position can we identify as the strongest? Which can we identify as the weakest?

The strongest position would be the tonic position, since this is the only position in which diphthongs occur. The next strongest would be initial position, since there is no loss in this position. Next in order would be final position, since there is loss only of the front vowels after certain consonants. Finally, medial position would be the weakest, since all vowels are lost in this position except /a/.

6.8 Why *fiesta* but *festivo*?

We can now return to the question at the beginning of this chapter. Why is it that words in Modern Spanish related in meaning, such as *fiesta* and *festivo*, have a diphthong in one word and a monophthong in the other? What are some of the word pairs that you identified? Were you able to see a linguistic pattern in the pairs? Over the course of this chapter you may have already begun to suspect that the difference is due to the evolution of stressed and unstressed vowels.

We see in the pair *fiesta* and *festivo* that the diphthong in *fiesta* is in a stressed syllable and the monophthong in *festivo* is in an unstressed syllable, since the stressed vowel in *festivo* is the /i/. In *fiesta*, from FĔSTA, the plural form of FĔSTUM 'holiday, feast,' the short Ĕ in tonic position diphthongized to /je/. However, in *festivo* from FĔSTĪVUM, what is the position of this same Ĕ? Because FĔSTĪVUM has a long vowel ī in the penultimate syllable, we now know that the accent falls on this syllable. Therefore, the Ĕ of the antepenultimate syllable is in initial position and so it becomes /e/ in Spanish. As presented above, the short mid vowels Ĕ and Ŏ in Classical Latin, which became the open mid vowels /ɛ/ and /ɔ/ in later Spoken Latin, underwent diphthongization only in stressed syllables. In unstressed syllables, these vowels were retained as monophthongs. This explains the difference in the vowels in related pairs of words, such as *fiesta/ festivo*, *puerta/portal*, and *fuerza/fortaleza*.

Practice 6-7

Look at the present tense conjugation of *dormir* and *querer*.

dormir	querer
duermo	quiero
duermes	quieres
duerme	quiere
dormimos	queremos
dormís	queréis
duermen	quieren

How do you explain the pattern of diphthongs and monophthongs in these words? Should we consider these verbs to be irregular? Explain your answer.

Now that you know that diphthongs occur only in stressed vowels in Spanish, you can see that these regular sound changes created pairs of words with different forms, such as *fiesta/festivo, puerta/portal, fuerte/fortaleza*, and *duermo/dormimos*. Understanding the vowel changes in the history of Spanish allows you to see that the alternation between diphthongs in stressed syllables and monophthongs in unstressed syllables is due to regular sound changes.

6.9 Chapter Summary

- The evolution of Latin vowels into Spanish depends on their stress and place in the word. We can identify four positions:
  - Tonic or stressed position, like the /a/ in SĒMĪNĀRE.
  - Initial unstressed position which refers to the first vowel in the word if it does not bear the stress, like the first /e/ in SĒMĪNĀRE.
  - Medial unstressed position which refers to an unstressed vowel in the middle of the word, which can be pre-tonic, like the /i/ in SĒMĪNĀRE, or post-tonic, like the /u/ in ŎCŬLUM.

○ Final position, which refers to an unstressed vowel in the final syllable of a word, like the second /e/ in SĒMĬNĀRE.

• In words of three or more syllables, the penultimate syllable rule allows you to determine which Latin vowel is stressed. If the penultimate syllable of a Latin word contains a short vowel in an open syllable, as in ŎCŬLUM, then the stress falls on the antepenultimate syllable and the penultimate syllable is unstressed. If, on the other hand, the penultimate syllable contains a long vowel, as in SĒMĬNĀRE, or is a closed syllable, as in INFĔRNUM, then it bears the stress and its vowel is the tonic vowel. In words of two syllables, the penultimate syllable always bears the stress. In one-syllable words, the stress falls on the only syllable.

• The vowel changes themselves are summarized in Figure 6.1. In short, in tonic position the long vowels in Latin stay long, the short high vowels lower by one degree (ĭ > /e/ and ŭ > /o/), the short mid vowels diphthongize (ĕ > /je/ and ŏ > /we/), and the long and short /a/ merge to a single /a/. In initial atonic position, vowels follow the same evolution as in tonic position, but there is no diphthongization, so ĕ > /e/ and ŏ > /o/. In medial atonic position, all vowels are lost, except /a/ which is retained as /a/. In final position, /a/ is retained, all the back vowels (ū, ŭ, ō, ŏ, and AU) become /o/, and all the front vowels (ī, ĭ, ē, ĕ, AE, and OE) become /e/ after a consonant group or the single consonants *rr* /r/, *ch* /tʃ/, and *v* [β], but are lost through apocope after other single consonants.

Activities

Activity 6-1

Identify the stressed vowel in each Latin word according to the rules of accentuation presented in this chapter. First, underline the vowel in the penultimate syllable. If it is short and in an open syllable, then place the accent mark over the vowel in the antepenultimate syllable. If this vowel is long or short in a closed syllable, then place the accent mark over the vowel in the penultimate syllable. Then select the Spanish reflex for the Latin words from the alphabetical list of Spanish words after the table.

VĪNĔAM	GANGRAENAM
CLAMĀRE	RĔCŬPĔRO
*AURŬNDUM	CATĒNAM
CŎRPUS	ACŪTUM
MŎLĪNUM	CĒRAM
INFĔRNUM	TĔNET
LĪMPĬDUM	ARBŎREM
CŎLLŎCŌ	PERFĔCTUM
LŬPUM	SAGĬTTAM
THĒSAURUM	DĬGĬTUM
JŎCUM	PŎPŬLUM

Choose from among these Spanish words: *agudo, árbol, cadena, cera, cuelgo, cuerpo, dedo, gangrena, infierno, juego, limpio, llamar, lobo, molino, orondo, perfecto, pueblo, recobro, saeta, tesoro, tiene, viña.*

Recopy each of the words above in the appropriate place in the table below according to its stress. One of each type has been done for you as a model.

Two-syllable words (accent falls on penultimate syllable):

Latin | Spanish
LŬPUM | *lobo*

Polysyllabic words (accent falls on heavy penultimate syllable):

Latin | Spanish
*AURŬNDUM | *orondo*

Polysyllabic words (accent falls on antepenultimate syllable):

Latin | Spanish
VĪNĔAM | *viña*

Activity 6-2

Tonic vowels: In the chart below, fill in the empty boxes with the corresponding Spanish word preceded by the evolution of the tonic vowel. The first two have been done for you.

Latin	Spanish
ī /i/ FĪLUM	/i/ *hilo*
ĭ /ɪ/ LĬNGUAM	/e/ *lengua*
ē /e/ TĒLAM OE /oj/ FŒDUM	
ĕ /ɛ/ PĔDEM AE /aj/ CAECUM	
ă /a/ PĂTREM ā /a/ MĀLUM	
ŏ /ɔ/ BŎNUM	
ō /o/ TŌTUM AU /aw/ CAUSAM	
ŭ /ʊ/ CŬPPAM	
ū /u/ FŪMUM	

Activity 6-3

Give the reflex in Modern Spanish for the Latin words below. Indicate the vocalic change in the tonic vowels by writing R for retention, L for lowering, D for diphthongization, or M for monophthongization after the Spanish word.

a. DŪRŬM

b. PŬLLUM

c. PAUCUM

d. AMOENUM

e. FLŌRES

f. FŎRTEM

g. CĂPRAM

h. vīnum

i. mĭnŭs

j. cĕntum

k. grānum

l. graecŭm

m. sētam

Activity 6-4

Corpus Search on Apocope

Investigate the prevalence of extreme apocope in Old Spanish texts by searching for apocopated and non-apocopated forms in the *Corpus del español*. Choose two of the sets of words provided below which pair an apocopated form, a case of extreme apocope, with its corresponding non-apocopated form. Write these in the spaces provided in the left column of the table below. Then perform a search on each of these forms in the *Corpus del español* by following these steps. We have included the example of *pus/puse* 'I put' in the chart for you as an example.

1. Go to corpusdelespanol.org and then click on the Genre/Historical corpus to bring up the search box.
2. Select "Chart" and then one at a time write each of the words you have selected in the search box and click on "see frequency by section." This will bring up a chart with your results.
3. In the table below write down the number under "freq" for four time periods, the 1200s, the 1300s, the 1400s, and the 1500s. This is the total number of times the word you searched appears in the texts included in the corpus for each century.
4. Also write down the number under "per mil" for each century. This is the number of times this word appears per million words in texts from this time period.

After you have recorded your results, compare the frequencies for the apocopated and non-apocopated forms. Do they coincide with the description in Box 6.1? Is there a decrease in the frequency of apocopated forms with an increase in the frequency of non-apocopated forms? In the results for *pus/puse* we see a sharp decline after the thirteenth century, the 1200s.

diz/dice 'he/she says'	ond/onde 'where'
fuert/fuerte 'strong'	suert/suerte 'luck'
puent/puente 'bridge'	regnant/regnante 'reigning'
vall/valle 'valley'	present/presente 'present'

	1200s		1300s		1400s		1500s	
Word	freq	per mil	freq	per mil	freq	per mil	freq	per mil
Example								
pus	77	11.47	11	4.12	42	5.15	7	0.41
puse	13	1.94	64	23.97	180	22.06	369	21.66
Your first pair								
Your second pair								

Activity 6-5

Summary chart of vowel changes with examples: In each cell of the chart below, write the resulting vowel along with one sample word from this chapter that will help you remember these changes.

Latin ten-vowel	Latin seven-vowel	Tonic	Atonic		
			Initial	Final	Medial
Ī	/i/	/i/ VĪTA > *vida*			
Ĭ					
Ē Œ					
Ĕ AE					

(cont.)

Latin ten-vowel	Latin seven-vowel	Tonic	Atonic		
			Initial	Final	Medial
Ă Ā					
Ŏ					
Ō, AU					
Ŭ					
Ū					

Activity 6-6

Summary chart of just the vowels without examples: Complete this chart, which summarizes the vowel changes from Latin to Spanish according to the position of the vowel in the word.

Chart A: In this chart the Latin vowels are given and the cells have been drawn for you.

Latin ten-vowel	Ī	Ĭ, Ē, OE	Ĕ, AE	Ā, Ă	Ŏ	Ō, AU, Ŭ	Ū
Latin seven-vowel	i	e	ɛ	a	ɔ	o	u
tonic							
initial							
final							
medial							

Chart B: Here is a blank table without the cells drawn for you to complete on your own. You can recopy it and complete it from memory.

Activity 6-7

Using the chart in Activity 6-5, indicate the evolution in Spanish of each vowel in the following Latin words. Follow these steps:

1. Determine first for each word whether there is an /i/ or /e/ in hiatus with a following vowel. If so, this vowel will not follow the regular evolution, but will instead become a yod [j]. This is the yodization rule referred to in Section 6.6.

2. Identify the tonic vowel and the position of the other vowels. Remember to apply the first medial vowel rule mentioned in Section 6.6, if applicable.

3. For each vowel determine its outcome in Spanish according to its position. Once you have identified the evolution of each vowel, try to guess the resulting word in Spanish.

Example 1: SĒCŪRUM > *seguro*
The penultimate syllable is stressed because it contains a long vowel.
Ē initial > /e/
Ū tonic > /u/
Ŭ final > /o/

Example 2: VĬRĬDEM > *verde*
The antepenultimate syllable is stressed because the penultimate syllable
    contains a short vowel (ĭ) in open syllable.
Ĭ tonic > /e/
Ĭ medial > Ø

E final > /e/ after a consonant group rather than Ø

Example 3: VĪNĔA > *viña*

The antepenultimate syllable is stressed because the penultimate syllable contains a short vowel (Ĕ) in open syllable.

Ī tonic > /i/

Ĕ before /a/ in hiatus > [j]

A final > /a/

1. PŎPŬLUM	6. INFĔRNUM
2. PŎPŬLĀRE	7. ACŪTUM
3. ŌRPHĂNUM	8. APĔRĪRE
4. CŌLLŎCŌ	9. DĬGĬTUM
5. FABŬLĀRE	10. CŬMĬNĬTĬĀRE

Further Reading

Álvarez Rodríguez, Adelino 1996. "¿Irregularidades en la apócope 'normal' de la /e/? Intento de explicación," in A. Alonso González, L. Castro Ramos, B. Gutiérrez Rodilla, and J. A. Pascual Rodríguez (eds.), *Actas del III Congreso Internacional de Historia de la Lengua Española*, 33–41. Madrid: Arcos Libros

Mackenzie, Ian 1999–2017. "History of Spanish vowels," in *The linguistics of Spanish*. www.staff.ncl.ac.uk/i.e.mackenzie/vowels.htm

Moreno Bernal, Jesús 2004. "Los condicionamientos de la apócope en los textos castellanos antiguos," *Revista de Filología Románica* 21: 187–99

"Romance languages: Pronunciation of Vulgar Latin and Romance," NativLang. YouTube video

Schürr, Friedrich. 1951. "La diptongación ibero-románica," *Revista de dialectología y tradiciones populares* 7(3): 379–90

7 How Did ACŪTUM Become *agudo?*

Regular Consonant Changes

Lead-in Questions

7-1 Study the following sets of related words in Spanish:

agudo 'sharp' and *agudeza* 'acuteness, sharpness' vs. *acuidad* 'sharpness' (< ACŪTUM 'sharp')

agua and *aguacero* 'downpour' vs. *acuático* 'aquatic' and *acuario* 'aquarium' (< AQUAM 'water')

vida vs. *vital* 'vital, lively' and *vitalidad* 'vitality' (< VĪTAM 'life')

cabo 'end piece' vs. *descapotable* 'convertible (car)' (< CAPUT 'head')

Which consonant is different in the sets of words and how is it different? What might have caused this difference?

7-2 Pronounce the following sentence in English: *Did you eat yet?*

First pronounce it slowly and then pronounce it quickly.

What happens to the /d/ at the end of *did* and the /t/ at the end of *eat* when you pronounce this sentence quickly?

Write some other examples in English where this happens, like *I want you to do it.*

What happens when /d/ and /t/ come in contact with a following /j/, as in *you* and *yet?* Why does this happen?

This chapter introduces the consonant sounds of Spanish and how they have changed over time from Latin to Old Spanish to Modern Spanish. You will see that certain processes of change increased the number of consonants from Latin to Old Spanish and then other changes decreased their number from Old Spanish to Modern Spanish. Whereas the placement of stress was all-important in the evolution of vowels, in the evolution of consonants what is important is the position of the consonant within the word and whether it is a single consonant or part of a group of two or more consonants. After completing this chapter, you will be able to trace all the sound changes from Latin words to Spanish, except for the special vowel changes that are the topic of Chapter 8.

7.1 What Are the Consonants in Spanish and How Are They Organized?

In the previous chapter, we saw that a vowel is a sound articulated without any obstruction or audible friction in the oral cavity. Consonants, on the other hand, are produced when the speaker creates a narrow channel or a complete closure in the mouth. The way the air flows or does not flow out of the mouth during the pronunciation of a consonant is called **the mode of articulation** (*el modo de articulación*). For example, the consonant /p/ is **a stop** (*una oclusiva*) because the flow of air is blocked completely. If you say *pan* [pan] while placing your hand in front of your mouth, you will notice that no air comes out of your mouth while it is closed to produce the /p/. Because there is a restriction or blockage of air flow in consonants, they are also classified by the place in the mouth where this restriction or blockage occurs. This second criterion for the classification of consonants is called **the place (or point) of articulation** (*el punto de articulación*). For /p/ the blockage is created by a complete closure of both lips and so the point of articulation for /p/ is **bilabial** (*bilabial*). The third and final characteristic of consonants is their **voicing** (*la sonorización*). Whereas all vowels are voiced, consonants can be either **voiced** (*sonoras*), if the vocal cords vibrate during their production, or they can be **voiceless** (*sordas*), if the vocal cords do not vibrate. For example, /p/ is a voiceless consonant, since the vocal cords do not vibrate when it is pronounced. You can verify this by placing your hand on your throat while you say *pan*. Notice that there are no vibrations in your throat during the /p/, only during the vowel /a/ and the consonant /n/. If you produce vibrations of the vocal cords during the production of a /p/, you will end up pronouncing its voiced counterpart, the consonant /b/. A complete articulatory description of a consonant includes its voicing, point of articulation, and mode of articulation. We can thus classify /b/ as a **voiced bilabial stop** (*una oclusiva bilabial sorda*). Like the vowels we studied in Chapter 6, we again follow the linguistic convention of representing phonemes, the distinctive sounds of a language, between slashes //.

Table 7.1 shows the complete inventory of consonants in Spanish. Let us look first at the mode of articulation. We have already seen that the air flow is blocked completely during a stop. During the production of a **fricative** (*una fricativa*), air flows out through a restricted channel in the mouth, but is not blocked completely. Thus, during a fricative, like /s/, one hears the hissing or shushing sound created by the flow of air. Because the air is not blocked, it is also possible to prolong the sound of a fricative, so that you can say /s/ for as long as your breath holds out. For stops, by contrast, you can hold the closure for a long time, but you do not hear any sound. This is why you have the impression that you cannot prolong a stop. In fact, you can prolong the closure, which is why a language like Italian can distinguish between short and long stops, as in *fato* 'fate' and *fatto* 'done.'

Affricates (*las africadas*) are essentially a stop followed by a fricative. In a word like *chulo*, the first consonant is produced by creating a complete closure /t/ followed by a fricative /ʃ/. This combination of stop plus fricative is considered in Spanish to be a single sound, the voiceless palatal affricate /tʃ/, written with the letters *ch*. Another mode of articulation is used for the two sounds for the letters *r* or *rr*. One is the **flap** (*la vibrante simple*) /ɾ/, as in *pero*, produced by a single tap of the tongue against the alveolar ridge, the bony ridge right behind the teeth. The other is the **trill** (*la vibrante múltiple*) /r/, as in *perro*, produced by multiple taps of the tongue against the alveolar ridge. A **lateral consonant** (*una consonante lateral*) is produced when air flows around the sides of the tongue, as in the consonant /l/ in the word *lateral*. Finally, a **nasal consonant** (*una consonante nasal*) is produced when air is obstructed in the oral cavity, but escapes through the nose. You can verify that air is coming out through the nose by holding the pronunciation of /m/ and then pinching your

TABLE 7.1 Spanish consonants: articulatory classification

		Bilabial (*bilabial*)	Labio-dental (*labio-dental*)	Dental (*dental*)	Alveolar (*alveolar*)	Palatal (*palatal*)	Velar (*velar*)	Glottal (*glotal*)
Stops (*oclusivas*)	Voiceless (*sordas*)	/p/		/t/			/k/	
	Voiced (*sonoras*)	/b/		/d/			/g/	
Fricatives (*fricativas*)	Voiceless		/f/	(/θ/)	/s/		(/x/)	(/h/)
	Voiced	[β]		[ð]		/ʝ/	[ɣ]	
Affricates (*africadas*)	Voiceless					/tʃ/		
	Voiced							
Flaps and trills (*vibrantes*)	Voiced				/ɾ/, /r/			
Laterals (*laterales*)	Voiced				/l/	(/ʎ/)		
Nasals (*nasales*)	Voiced	/m/			/n/	/ɲ/		

nose shut. Notice that the sound stops completely because you have now blocked the flow of air through the nose necessary to produce this nasal consonant. When this happens, you end up instead with the voiced bilabial stop /b/. This also explains why you cannot produce nasals when a cold blocks your nasal passages.

Turning now to point of articulation, we see that sounds can be pronounced with both lips in the bilabial position, like /p/ and also /b/ and /m/. There is also a bilabial fricative in Spanish [β] produced when the phoneme /b/ is between vowels, as in *haba* 'broad bean.' The square brackets indicate a sound that is **an allophone** (*un alófono*), a non-contrasting sound or a sound that does not distinguish between words, rather than a phoneme. Sounds are classified as **dental** (*dental*) when the tongue comes in contact with the back of the teeth during their production, as in /t/ and /d/. There is also a dental fricative [ð] produced when the phoneme /d/ is between vowels, as in *hada* 'fairy.' We have also included in this category the interdental voiceless fricative /θ/, pronounced in northern Spain in words like *cielo, hacer*, and *vez*. The parentheses around a sound in Table 7.1 mean that it is not produced by speakers of all dialects of Spanish.

Alveolar consonants (*las consonantes alveolares*) are pronounced with contact between the tip of the tongue and the alveolar ridge. This is the case for /s/, /l/, /n/, and the two types of *r* in Spanish. The **palatal consonants** (*las consonantes palatales*) in Spanish include the voiced fricative /j/, the most widespread pronunciation of the sound represented by *y* in a word like *mayo* and by *ll* in a word like *castillo*. There is dialectal variation in the pronunciation of this sound, but we have not included all the dialectal variants of Spanish in Table 7.1, only those sounds necessary to understand the changes from Latin to Old Spanish to Modern Spanish. Other palatal sounds include the affricate /tʃ/ as in *chulo*, and a palatal lateral /ʎ/, a pronunciation in some dialects of *ll*, as in *ella*. Finally, the palatal nasal /ɲ/ is the sound represented by *ñ*, as in *niño*. The **velar consonants** (*las consonantes velares*) are the stops /k/ and /g/ and the voiceless fricative /x/, known as the jota, as in *mujer* [mu-ˈxeɾ]. This sound is pronounced as a voiceless glottal fricative in some American Spanish varieties, as in *mujer* [mu-ˈheɾ]. The voiced velar fricative [ɣ] is an allophone of /g/ between vowels, as in a word like *haga* '1sg., 3sg. present subjunctive of *hacer*.'

7.2 How Has the Consonant Inventory Changed since Latin and Old Spanish?

As mentioned above, Latin had fewer consonants than Modern Spanish and Old Spanish had more consonants than either Latin or Modern Spanish, as seen in Table 7.2. In order to compare the consonants in each stage of the history of

TABLE 7.2 Comparison of consonants in LATIN, *Old Spanish*, and Modern Spanish

		Bilabial	Labio-dental	Dental	Alveolar	Palatal	Velar	Glottal
Stops	voiceless	P *p* p		T *t* t			K *k* k	
	voiced	B *b* b		D *d* d			G *g* g	
Fricatives	voiceless		F *f* f	(θ)	S *s* s	ʃ	(x)	H *h* (h)
	voiced				z	ʒ, *j* j	w	
Affricates	voiceless				ts	tʃ tʃ		
	voiced				dz	dʒ		
Flaps and trills	voiced				R *ɾ, r* ɾ, r			
Laterals	voiced				L *l* l	ʎ (ʎ)		
Nasals	voiced	M *m* m			N *n* n	ɲ ɲ		

Spanish, the Latin consonants are shown in the upper left-hand corner of the appropriate cell in the table in small capitals. The Old Spanish consonants are shown in the middle of the cell in italics and the Modern Spanish consonants are shown in the bottom right-hand corner of each cell in regular letters. In order to make the table more readable, we have dispensed with the slanted and square brackets and have omitted the allophones [β], [ð], and [γ]. We have kept the parentheses, though, for sounds that do not appear in every modern variety of Spanish.

A word is in order regarding Latin /w/. This sound is a labio-velar approximant. Labio-velar means that it is pronounced with rounded lips while the back of the tongue approaches the velum, the soft palate in the back of the mouth. It is called **an approximant** (*una aproximante*) because, unlike a fricative, there is no audible friction during its production nor is there a complete closure. This sound is represented in Latin by the letter v, as in VĪTAM /'wi-ta/, which is sometimes written u in inscriptions, as in UITAM.

Complete Activity 7-1 on page 159.

7.3 How Did Consonants Change from Latin to Modern Spanish?

We saw in Chapter 6 that vowel changes depended on whether a vowel was tonic or atonic and, if it was atonic, on its position in the word. The changes in consonants, summarized in Table 7.3, depend on their position in the word and on the surrounding sounds. The table is organized so that you can identify the position of each consonant in a Latin word and then look up its result in Spanish. By applying the vowel changes you learned in Chapter 6 with the consonantal changes summarized in Table 7.3, you will be able to determine the changes of all the sounds in a Latin word so as to arrive at the resulting word in Spanish.

TABLE 7.3 Consonantal changes from Latin to Spanish

	Single consonants				Consonant groups (organized by first consonant in the group)				
	Initial	**Intervocalic**	**Before yod**	**Final**	**Initial**	**Medial geminates**	**Medial changes**	**Medial reduction**	**Medial retention**
[p]	[p] PĔRDIT > *pierde* PĬRA > *pera*	[b] > [β] SAPĔRE > *saber* OPĔRA > *obra* PŎPŬLUM > *pueblo*	[pj] APIUM > *apio* [jp] (metath-esis) SAPIAT > *sepa*	–	[pl] > [pl] PLŪMAM > *pluma* [pl] > [ʎ] PLĒNUM > *lleno* [pr] > [pr] PRĀTUM > *prado*	[pp] > [p] CŬPPAM > *copa*	[pl] > [bl] DUPLUM > *doble* [pl] > [t·] AMPLUM > *ancho* [pr] > [br] CAPRAM > *cabra*	[ps] > [s] IPSAM > *esa* [pt] > [t] SĒPTEM > *siete*	[pl] EXEMPLUM > *ejemplo* [pr] COMP(E)RĀRE > *comprar*
[t]	[t] TĔRRAM > *tierra*	[d] > [ð] ACŪTUM > *agudo* AMĀTUM > *amado*	[sʲ],[θ] RATIŌNEM > *razón*	Ø AMAT > *ama* SUNT > *son*	[tr] > [tr] TRĪSTEM > *triste*	[tt] > [t] GŬTTAM > *gota*	[tl] > [x] VETŮLUM > *viejo* [tr] > [dr] PATREM > *padre*	–	[tr] INTRĀRE > *entrar*
[k] before [a], [o], [u]	[k] CAUSAM > *cosa* CŎRIUM > *cuero* CŪPAM > *cuba*	[g] > [ɣ] FŎCUM > *fuego* [k] after [w] PAUCUM > *poco*	–	Ø PER HŌC > *pero* SIC > *sí* NEC > *ni*	[kl] > [kl] CLARUM > *claro* [kl] > [ʎ] CLAVE > *llave*	[kk] before [a], [o], [u] > [k] VACCAM > *vaca* [kk] before [e], [i], [ae] > [sʲ], [θ] TUCCĪNUM > *tocino*	[kl] > [x] OC(Ŭ)LUM > *ojo* [kl] > [t·] MASC(Ŭ)LUM > *macho*	[ks] > [s] SĔX > *seis* [ksk] > [sk] EXCURRŌ > *escurro*	–

TABLE 7.3 (cont.)

	Single consonants				Consonant groups (organized by first consonant in the group)				
	Initial	Intervocalic	Before yod	Final	Initial	Medial geminates	Medial changes	Medial reduction	Medial retention
[k] before [e], [i], [ae]	[s],[θ] (OS [ts]) CAELUM > cielo CINCTAM > cinta	[s],[θ] (OS [dz]) FACĔRE > hacer VICĪNUM > vecino	[s],[θ] MISTĪCIUM > mestizo	–	[kr] > [kr] CRŪDUM > crudo		[kr] > [gr] *SOCRAM > suegra [ks] > [x] AXEM > eje [kt] > [t·] *LACTEM > leche	[ksp] > [sp] EXPANTĀRE > espantar [kst] > [st] SEXTAM > siesta [kt] > [t] FRUCTUM > fruto	
[kw] before [a]	[kw] QUATTUOR > cuatro	[gw] AQUAM > agua	–	–	–	–	–	–	–
[kw] before other vowels	/k/ QUID > qué QUĔM > quien	/g/ AQUĬLAM > águila Ø CŪBĬTUM > codo	–	–	–	–	–	–	–
[b]	[b] BŎNUM > bueno BALNEUM > baño	[β] CABALLUM > caballo	[bj] RUBĔUM > rubio	Ø AB > a SUB > OS so	[bl] > [bl] BLANDUM > blando [br] > [br] BRACCHIUM > brazo	[bb] > [β] ABBATEM > abad	–	–	[bl] OBLATAM > oblada [br] COLŪBRAM > culebra

TABLE 7.3 (cont.)

	Single consonants				Consonant groups (organized by first consonant in the group)				
	Initial	Intervocalic	Before yod	Final	Initial	Medial geminates	Medial changes	Medial reduction	Medial retention
[w]	[b] VĪRĬDEM > *verde*	[β] VĪVĔRE > *vivir* Ø RĪVUM > *río*	–	–	–	–	–	–	–
[d]	[d] DĀRE > *dar* DĬGĬTUM > *dedo*	[ð] GRĂDUM > *grado* Ø FOEDUM > *feo* FĬDEM > *fe*	[j] RADIUM > *rayo* [x] or [h] ENODIĀRE > *enojar* [s] o [θ] GAUDIUM > *gozo* Ø FASTIDIU > *fastío*	Ø AD > *a* ISTUD > *esto*	[dr] > [dr] DRACŌNEM > *dragon*	[dd] > [ð] ADDŪCĔRE > *aducir*	–	[dr] > [r] CATHĒDRAM > *cadera*	[dr] QUADRUM > *cuadro*
[g] before [a], [o], [u]	[g] GALLĪNAM > *gallina* GŬRDUM > *gordo*	[ɣ] AUGUSTUM > *agosto* Ø LĒGĀLEM > *leal*	–	–	[gl] > [gl] GLŬTTŌNEM > *glotón* [gl] > [l] GLANDEM > *lande* [gr] > [gr] GRADUM > *grado*	–	[gl] > [x] RĒGŬLAM > *reja* [gn] > [ɲ] COGNĀTUM > *cuñado*	[gr] > [r] INTĔGRUM > *entero*	[gr] NĬGRUM > *negro*

TABLE 7.3 (cont.)

	Single consonants				Consonant groups (organized by first consonant in the group)				
	Initial	Intervocalic	Before yod	Final	Initial	Medial geminates	Medial changes	Medial reduction	Medial retention
[g] before [i], [e]	[j] GĒLUM > *hielo* Ø GERMĀNU > *hermano*	Ø DIGĬTUM > *dedo* FRIGĬDUM > *frío*	[j] FŪGIO > *huyo* EXAGIUM > *ensayo*	—					
[f]	[h] > Ø FŪMUM > *humo* FILUM > *hilo* [f] FĒSTA > *fiesta* FŎCUM > *fuego*	[h] > Ø REFŪSĀRE > *rehusar* [β] PRŌFĒCTUM > *provecho* STEPHĂNUS > *Esteban*	—	Ø IŌSĒPH(US) > *José*	[fl] > [fl] FLŌREM > *flor* [fl] > [ʎ] FLAMMAM > *llama* [fr] > [fr] FRĒNUM > *freno*	[ff] > [h] > Ø OFFŌCĀRE > *ahogar*	—	—	—
[s]	[s] SŌLEM > *sol* SĔRRAM > *sierra* [x] SĂPŌNEM > *jabón* SĒPIAM > *jibia*	[s] (OS [z]) CASAM > *casa* THĒSAURUM > *tesoro*	[sj] > [s] CAMĪSIAM > *camisa* [sj] > [js] (metathesis) BĀSIUM > *beso* [ss] > [x] or [h]	[s] AMĪCŌS > *amigos* AMĪCĀS > *amigas* MĀTRĒS > *madres* AMĀS > *amas*	[sk] > [esk] SCŌPAM > *escoba* [skl] > [eskl] SCLAVUM > *esclavo* [skr] > [eskr] SCRĪBŌ > *escribo*	[ss] > [s] GROSSUM > *grueso*	[sk] > [s],[θ] CRĒSCĔRE > *crecer*		[sk] MŪSCAM > *mosca* [sm] *BAPTISMUM > *bautismo* [sp] VĔSPAM > *avispa*

TABLE 7.3 (cont.)

	Single consonants				Consonant groups (organized by first consonant in the group)				
	Initial	**Intervocalic**	**Before yod**	**Final**	**Initial**	**Medial geminates**	**Medial changes**	**Medial reduction**	**Medial retention**
			*RUSSEUM > rojo		[sp] > [esp] SPONSUM > esposo [st] > [est] STĀRE > estar [str] > [estr] STRĬCTUM > estrecho				[st] CASTĒLLUM > castillo [str] NŌSTRUM > nuestro
[m]	[m] MĔTUM > miedo MĀTRĒS > madres	[m] FŪMUM > humo	[mj] VINDĒMIAM > vindimia	Ø NUNQUAM > nunca CANTĀBAM > cantaba YAM > ya TURREM > torre [n] QUĒM > quien TAM > tan CUM > con	–	[mm] > [m] FLAMMAM > llama	[mn] > [n] SŎMNUM > sueño [mn] > [mbr] HOMINEM > hombre	[mb] > [m] PALŪMBAM > paloma [mpt] > [nt] CŌMPĬTUM > cuento	[mp] TĔMPUS > tiempo [mpr] *COMPERŌ > compro
[n]	[n] NATAM > nada	[n] LŪNAM > luna	[ɲ] ARANEAM > araña	Ø NON > no	–	[nn] > [n] ANNUM > año	[ng] > [ns],[nθ] GINGĪVAM < encía	[nkt] > [nt] IŪNCTUM > junto	[nd] QUANDO > cuando

TABLE 7.3 (cont.)

	Single consonants				Consonant groups (organized by first consonant in the group)				
	Initial	Intervocalic	Before yod	Final	Initial	Medial geminates	Medial changes	Medial reduction	Medial retention
	NON > *no*		HISPANIAM > *España*	[n] IN > *en*			[ng] > [n] CINGĔRE > *ceñir* [nk] > [ns],[nθ] CONCĬLIUM > *consejo*	[ns] > [s] MĒNSAM > *mesa* [nst] > [st] CONSTĀRE > *costar* [nstr] > [str] MŌNSTRĀRE > *mostrar*	[nf] INFĬRMUM > *enfermo* [ng] FUNGUM > *hongo* [nk] TRUNCUM > *tronco* [nt] [ntr] PŎNTEM > *puente* INTER > *entre*
[l]	[l] LACŪNAM > *laguna*	[l] CAELUM > *cielo*	[x] CILIA > *ceja* MULIĔREM > *mujer*	[l] MĔL > *miel*		[ll] > [ʎ] BELLUM > *bello* CABALLUM > *caballo*	[lk] before [e], [i] > [ls],[lθ] DULCEM > *dulce* [lt] > [tʃ] MULTUM > *mucho*	[lp] > [p] TALPAM > *topo* [lt] > [t] ALTARIUM > *otero*	[lb] ALBA > *alba* [ld] CALĬDUM > *caldo* [lg] ALGAM > *alga*

TABLE 7.3 (cont.)

	Single consonants				Consonant groups (organized by first consonant in the group)				
	Initial	Intervocalic	Before yod	Final	Initial	Medial geminates	Medial changes	Medial reduction	Medial retention
									[lk] SULCUM > *sulco* [lp] PALPĀRE > *palpar* [ls] FALSUM > *falso* [lt] ALTUM > *alto*
[j]	[x] JOCUM > *juego* [j] JUGUM > *yugo* Ø IACTĀRE > *echar*	[j] MAIUM > *mayo* Ø PEIŌREM > *peor*	–	–	–	–	–	–	–
[h]	Ø HŎMĬNEM > *hombre*	–	–	–	–	–	–	–	–
[r]	[r] RŌTAM > *rueda*	[ɾ] TAURUM > *toro*	[rj] > [r] MATERIAM > *madera*	[r] (metathesis) INTER > *entre*	–	[rr] > [r] TURREM > *torre*	[rg] before [i], [e] > [rs],[rθ] ARGILLAM > *arcilla* [rk] before [i], [e] > [rs],[rθ]	[rs] > [s] URSUM > *oso*	[rb] BARBAM > *barba* [rd]

TABLE 7.3 (cont.)

	Single consonants				Consonant groups (organized by first consonant in the group)				
	Initial	Intervocalic	Before yod	Final	Initial	Medial geminates	Medial changes	Medial reduction	Medial retention
				SEMPER > siempre			MERCĒDEM > merced		SURDUM > sordo [rf]
				QUATTUOR > cuatro					ORPHĀNUM > huérfano [rg]
									GURGŪLIO > gorgojo [rk]
									ARCUM > arco [rm]
									ARMA > arma [rn]
									FORNĀRE > hornar [rp]
									CŌRPUS > cuerpo [rt]
									CHARTAM > carta [rv]
									SĒRVUM > siervo

In order to do this, you first need to learn to read the chart of consonantal changes. Part A of the chart shows the results for single consonants, those that are not in contact with another consonant. These may occur in initial position when they are the very first sound of the word, like the /t/ in TERRAM. When the consonant is in the middle of the word and is preceded and followed by vowels, then it is in **intervocalic position** (*la posición intervocálica*), as is the /t/, and also the /k/, in ACŪTUM. A consonant may also be followed by the semi-vowel [j], as is the /t/ in RATIŌNEM. This semi-vowel did not exist in Latin, but rather is formed when the vowel /i/ or /e/ is followed immediately by another vowel, according to the yodization rule presented in Chapter 6, at the end of Section 6.6. In RATIŌNEM the /i/ is immediately followed by the vowel /o/ and so it becomes the semi-vowel yod [j]. We will see that contact with a yod leads to changes in many consonants and vowels. Single consonants may also occur in final position when they are the last sound in the word, like the /t/ in AMAT. Notice also that for the consonants /k/ and /g/ you need to see which vowel follows the consonant, since their evolution is different before /a/, /o/ and /u/, on the one hand, and /i/ and /e/, on the other hand.

Consonants are considered to be in a group when at least two consonants are together in a word. Groups can occur in word-initial position, such as the /pr/ in PRATUM. Otherwise, they occur in medial position in the middle of a word. Here we distinguish between **double or geminate consonants** (*consonantes dobles o geminadas*) in which the same consonant is repeated, such as the /pp/ in CUPPAM, and other groups. For other groups, the table organizes them according to the type of change that occurred. The column labeled **change** (*cambios*) lists the consonant groups where at least one of the consonants changed, such as the /p/ in CAPRAM > *cabra*. The column labeled **reduction** (*reducción*) shows the groups where one of the consonants was lost, such as the /p/ in SEPTEM > *siete*. Finally, the column **retention** (*conservación*) lists the groups where both consonants were maintained, such as the /pl/ in EXEMPLUM > *ejemplo*. Please note that sometimes consonant groups are created when a vowel is lost through syncope. Note also that some groups may have more than one possible outcome. For example, the group /m'n/ is created through syncope, where /'/ indicates the lost vowel. In DOMĪNUM this group becomes /ɲ/ in Spanish *dueño*, but in HOMĪNEM this group becomes /mbr/ in *hombre.* One often finds *omne* for *hombre* in Old Spanish, as in the Appendix D234A, with syncope, with neither of the changes just mentioned.

It is time now for you to try your hand at deriving Spanish words from Latin words by applying the rules you learned for vowel changes and by determining consonant changes from Table 7.3.

Complete Activity 7-2 on page 159.

7.4 What Are the General Processes of Consonantal Change?

We can identify certain processes of change among all the individual changes listed in Table 7.3. These are summarized in Table 7.5 which you might want to refer to as you read the explanation of each process. The most straightforward of these is retention, which is essentially a lack of change. A consonant pronounced in the same way in Spanish as in Latin is considered to be retained, like the initial /p/ in PIRA > *pera.* Another straightforward process is **loss** (*la pérdida*) whereby a consonant ceases to be pronounced. This often happens with Latin final consonants, when AMAT becomes *ama* and and TURREM becomes *torre.*

The other three processes affecting consonants involve a change in mode or point of articulation and perhaps also voicing. In most cases these changes result from **assimilation** (*la asimilación*), the process by which a sound becomes more similar to other sounds near it. Note that the term for a linguistic process always refers to its result, so that assimilation means the process of becoming more similar. The first of these changes is **lenition** (*la lenición*), which generally means weakening and refers specifically to a series of changes including voicing and **fricativization** (*la fricativización*) and sometimes loss. This series of changes is called weakening because it can end in loss. The entire process for the voiceless dental stop /t/ has these steps:

/t/ > /d/ (voicing) > [ð] (fricativization) > Ø (loss)

We can see these steps in the change from TŌTUM to *todo*. In the voicing step the voiceless intervocalic /t/ becomes /d/, so that Latin ['to-tu] becomes *['to-do]. In the next step, fricativization, the dental voiced stop /d/ becomes the interdental voiced fricative [ð], which is its sound in Standard Spanish *todo* ['to- ðo]. In many varieties of Spanish, one also finds the last step in the process, loss, as in the pronunciation of *todo* as ['to-o] or [to]. In Old Spanish, on the other hand, we often find the letter *d* still written in words where it does not appear in Modern Spanish, as in *piedes* for *pies* (D227B) and *vido* for *vio* (E26).

The first step, voicing, is an assimilation to the surrounding vowels, which are voiced, as in TŌTUM > *todo*, or to a preceding vowel and following /r/, as in MATREM > *madre*. This change occurs when a speaker continues the vibration of the vocal cords for the preceding vowel and the following vowel or consonant during the pronunciation of the voiceless stop. It is interesting to observe that this type of voicing occurs in American English so that a word like *latter* now sounds like *ladder*.

The fricativization step is also assimilation. In this case, the stop becomes more similar to the surrounding vowels by becoming a fricative. Since the stop blocks the passage of air from the mouth completely and a fricative lets some air escape, the fricative is more similar to the vowels, which do not impede the flow of air. A former student described fricativization as a kind of "rolling stop." The speaker brings the articulators closer together as if to produce a stop, but then doesn't stop the flow of air all the way. The last step, loss, cannot be considered to be assimilation, but it does of course reduce the articulatory movement required to produce the sound, since that movement is omitted entirely.

Table 7.4 shows that the other voiceless stops, /p/ and /k/, can undergo voicing and fricativization and sometimes loss and that the voiced consonants, /b/, /d/, and /g/, can undergo fricativization and sometimes loss. Wherever a consonant starts on this path, a change to the next step is considered to be lenition. The stages attested in Modern Spanish are the pronunciations followed by Modern Spanish words.

We observe in Table 7.4 that the endpoint of the lenition process is not the same for the different consonants. The voiceless consonants in Latin, /p/, /t/, and /k/, generally end up at the fricativization stage, except for the loss of intervocalic [ð] that is prevalent in Modern Spanish. The voiced consonants in Latin

TABLE 7.4 Steps in the process of lenition with illustrations

Consonant	1. Voiceless	2. Voiced	3. Fricative	4. Ø (zero)
Process		Voicing	Fricativization	Loss
/p/	[p]	[b]	[β]	
	CAPUT	[ˈka-bo]	[ˈka-βo] *cabo*	
	CAPRAM	[ˈka-bra]	[ˈka-βɾa] *cabra*	
/t/	[t]	[d]	[ð]	Ø
	TŌTUM	[ˈto-do]	[ˈto-ðo] *todo*	[to] *todo*
	MATREM	[ˈma-dre]	[ˈma-ðɾe] *madre*	
/k/	[k]	[g]	/γ/	
	LACUM	[ˈla-go]	[ˈla-γo] *lago*	
	LACRIMAM	[ˈla-gɾi-ma]	[ˈla-γɾi-ma] *lágrima*	
/b/		[b]	[β]	
		CUBUM	[ˈku-βo] *cubo*	
		COLOBRAM	[ku-ˈle-βɾa] *culebra*	
/d/		[d]	[ð]	Ø
		MODUM	[ˈmo-ðo] *modo*	
		SEDĒRE	[ˈse-ðeɾ]	[seɾ] *ser*
		CATHEDRAM	[ˈka-ðe-ðɾa]	[ka-ˈðe-ɾa] *cadera*
		QUADRUM	[ˈkua-ðɾo] *cuadro*	[ka-ˈðe-ɾa] *cadera*
/g/		[g]	/γ/	Ø
		RĒGĀLEM	[re-ˈγal]	[re-ˈal] *real*
		INTEGRUM	[en-ˈte-γɾo]	[en-ˈte-ɾo] *entero*

in intervocalic position and between a vowel and [ɾ] are more likely to end up being lost. This is the regular outcome in this position of Latin /g/, the most common outcome of Latin /d/, and a very rare outcome of Latin /b/. Two of the rare examples of loss of intervocalic Latin /b/ are SABŪCUM > *sauco* 'elderberry' and SUBUNDĀRE > *sondar* 'to probe' (Lathrop 2003: 116).

Lenition is of course the process that explains the difference between the first consonant in the Spanish words *agudo* and *acuidad* presented in Lead-in question 7-1 (page 134 above). In a derived word like *agudo* the /k/ from ACŪTUM underwent voicing and then fricativization. In a learnèd word like *acuidad* the Latin /k/ remains unchanged because these words do not undergo regular sound changes.

Another important process in consonantal evolution is **palatalization** (*la palatalización*), which is in most cases also a type of assimilation. As its name implies, palatalization is a change in point of articulation of a non-palatal sound to a palatal sound. This occurs, for example, when a consonant followed by yod [j] becomes palatal, as in the change of /n/ plus yod to /ɲ/, as in VĪNEAM > ['winja] > ['bi-ɲa]. Since the yod is a palatal semi-vowel, speakers change the point of articulation of the alveolar nasal consonant /n/ to the palatal region to produce /ɲ/. Palatalization before a yod occurs in American and British English as well. In American English palatalization is frequent when a word ending in /t/ or /d/ is followed by a word beginning with [j]. This explains the pronunciation of *did you eat yet*, from Lead-in question 7-2 (page 134), as [dʒit-'tʃɛt]. The /d/ plus [j] in *did you* palatalizes to [dʒ] and the /t/ plus [j] in *eat yet* ends up as [tʃ], although it may also voice to [dʒ] because of the first consonant, so that entire question could be written *jeet jet?* In British English, this type of palatalization also occurs within certain words, not just across words, so that the /d/ in *dual* palatalizes to [dʒ], so that a *dual carriageway*, a two-lane highway in American English, can sound like a *jewel carriageway*.

In Spanish, /t/ before yod became /ts/ after a consonant or /dz/ in intervocalic position. Thus, *FORTIA became Old Spanish *fuerça* ['fwer-tsa] and PUTEUM became Old Spanish *pozo* ['po-dzo]. The affricate /ts/ or /dz/ in these words later changed to /s/ or /θ/ in Modern Spanish, as in *fuerza* 'strength' and *pozo* 'well.' Whether the result is /s/ or /θ/ depends on the dialect, as we will see in greater detail in Chapter 9. You may be wondering at this point why a change to /ts/ and /dz/, and later /s/ and /θ/, is considered to be palatalization, since these are dental rather than palatal sounds. Linguists have typically expanded the definition of palatalization to include changes to /s/ and /θ/ as well as actual palatal sounds, since these changes result from a movement toward and across the palatal region, even though the resulting sound is not palatal. Latin /k/ before [j] follows the same changes as /t/ before [j], so that *MINACEA becomes

Spanish *amenaza* 'threat.' The consonant /d/ before [j] is usually lost so that only the /j/ remains, as in HODIE > *hoy*, but palatalization of /dj/ to /dz/ and then /s/ or /θ/ occurs in the rare cases where [dj] follows a consonant, as in *VIRDIA > *berza* 'cabbage.'

Other examples of palatalization that result in /s/ or /θ/ occur when the velar consonant /k/ or /g/ is followed by a front vowel, /i/ or /e/. This change is clearly an assimilation in point of articulation, since the velar stops /k/ and /g/ adopt a point of articulation more similar to that of the front vowels /i/ and /e/. This occurs when Latin /k/ is in initial position, as in CENTUM > *ciento*, intervocalic position, as in FACERE > *hacer*, medial geminate position, as in *TUCCĪNUM > *tocino* 'bacon,' and in medial position where /k/ follows a consonant, as in DULCEM > *dulce* and MERCĒDEM > *merced* 'mercy.' The consonant /g/ palatalizes in medial position after a consonant to /s/ or /θ/, like /k/ does, as in ARGĪLLAM > *arcilla* 'clay.' In initial position, however, /g/ is usually lost, as in GERMĀNUM > *hermano* and GINGĪVAM > *encía* 'gum (of the mouth).' When it does palatalize to [dʒ], which then becomes /x/ in Modern Spanish, as in GENTEM > *gente* and GENĔRUM > *género*, the word is considered to be a learnèd word that was borrowed directly from Latin and so has not followed the regular sound changes. One can compare the learnèd *género* 'gender, genre' with the derived word *yerno* 'son-in-law.' One finds *yente* in Old Spanish, as in the Appendix C114, so the learnèd form *gente* must have been borrowed later.

Palatalization also occurs in certain consonant groups, although it is hard to explain these changes as cases of assimilation. For example, in the palatalization of /mn/ to /ɲ/, as in SOMNUM > *sueño*, it is clear that the /m/ adopts a point of articulation closer to that of /n/, but why does this group end up as a palatal nasal, given that this sound is farther back in the mouth than either /m/ or /n/? The palatal nasal also results from the groups /gn/ and /ng/, as in COGNĀTUM > *cuñado* 'brother-in-law,' and CINGĔRE > *ceñir* 'hug, cling,' and from the geminate /nn/, as in ANNUM > *año*. Other groups result in the palatal lateral consonant /ʎ/, more often pronounced as [j] or [ʝ] today, as do the initial groups /pl/, /kl/ and /fl/, as in PLANUM > *llano* 'flat,' CLAVEM > *llave* 'key,' and FLAMMAM > *llama* 'flame' and the medial geminate /ll/, as in CABALLUM > *caballo*. Finally, some consonant groups palatalize to /tʃ/. These include medial /pl/, /lt/, /kt/, and /kl/, as in AMPLUM > *ancho*, MULTUM > *mucho*, OCTO > *ocho*, and MASCŬLUM > *masclum* > *macho*, respectively.

The last process is **velarization** (*la velarización*), which is the change of a non-velar consonant to the velar consonant jota /x/. Three words that illustrate this process were mentioned as examples of syncope in the *Appendix Probi*, presented in Chapter 2: SPECULUM NON SPECLUM, OCULUS NON OCLUS, and VETULUS NON VECLUS. In all three the loss of medial /u/ created a consonant cluster /kl/ or /tl/ which then velarized to /x/ in the Modern Spanish words *espejo, ojo,* and *viejo.* Two other consonant clusters also velarize, namely /gl/ as in RĒGŬLAM > *reja* 'grill,' and /ks/, as in EXEMPLUM > *ejemplo.* The medial consonants /d/, /ss/, and /l/ velarize before yod, as in RADIUM > *rayo* 'ray of light, lightning bolt,' *RUSSEUM > *rojo,* and ALIUM > *ajo* 'garlic.' Finally, there are two initial consonants that sometimes velarize: /s/ as in SAPŌNEM > *jabón* and /j/ as in JOCUM > *juego.* As we will see in Chapter 9, the sounds that have become velar in Modern Spanish were the palatal consonants /ʃ/ and /ʒ/ in Old Spanish. Thus, the cases of velarization before a yod are clearly examples of assimilation. The clusters that velarize can also be seen as assimilation because, except for /tl/ which one assumes changed to /kl/, they begin with a velar consonant (/k/ or /g/) and end with an alveolar consonant (/l/ or /s/) and the palatal region is between the velar and alveolar points of articulation. The subsequent change from a palatal fricative to a velar one is not assimilation, but it does reduce articulatory movement since the root of the tongue travels a shorter distance to produce friction in the velar region than when the blade of the tongue travels to the palatal region.

The processes of consonantal change are summarized in Table 7.5. This table was compiled directly from Table 7.3 by recording each consonantal change in the appropriate place in Table 7.5. For example, the first row of Table 7.5 shows the result for every single initial consonant. We see in the leftmost cell of the first row that most initial consonants were retained. In the next row to the right we see that there are no examples of initial consonants undergoing lenition. In the next column under palatalization we see that only /k/ and /g/ before front vowels palatalize and under "velarization" we see that only two consonants velarize. Under "loss" we see that only Latin /f/, /g/ before a front vowel, /j/, and /h/ are sometimes lost in initial position. Activity 7-4 asks you to study this chart further so as to capture generalizations about the consonantal changes from Latin to Spanish.

TABLE 7.5 Processes of consonantal change (parentheses around a change indicate that this is one of at least two possible outcomes)

Position	Retention	Lenition	Palatalization	Velarization	Loss
(a) Single consonants					
Initial	p, t, k^{a,o,u}, (f), (s)		k^{i,e,ae} > s, θ	(s), j ^{a,o,u}	(f > h)
	b, d, g ^{a,o,u}, m, n, l, r (j), w > b		g^{i,e} > j		(g^{i,e}), (j), h
Intervocalic	s, m, n, l, r, (j)	p > β	k^{i,e,ae} > s, θ		(b)
		t > ð,			(d)
		k^{a,o,u} > γ			(w)
		kw > γw			(g)
		(f > β)			(f), (j)
		(b > β)			
		(d > ð),			
		(w > β)			
		(g $^{a,o/e}$ > γ)			
Final	s, l, r, (n), (m > n)				do not occur in final position in Latin:
					p, g, j, w, h
					are lost: t, k, b, d, f, (m), (n)
(b) Consonant groups					
Initial	pr, (pl), tr, kr, (kl), br, bl, dr, gr, (gl), fr, (fl)		(pl > ʎ)		(gl > l)
			(kl > ʎ)		
			(fl > ʎ)		
Medial geminate	geminate becomes single		kk ^{i,e,ae} > s, θ		ff > h
	pp > p, tt > t, kk^{a,o,u} > k, bb > β, dd > ð, ss > s, mm > m		nn > ɲ		
			ll > ʎ		

Medial before yod	pj > pj ~ jp			(dj), ssj, lj	(dj > j)
	bj		tj > s, θ		(dj > Ø)
	sj > sj ~ js		kj > s, θ		(gj > j)
	m		(dj) > s, θ		
	rj > r ~ jr		nj > ɲ		
Medial other	(pl), pr	pr > br	pl > tʃ	tl, (kl), ks, gl	pt > t
	tr	pl > bl	kt > tʃ,		ps > s
	bl, br	tr > dr	(kl > tʃ)		ks > s
	dr	kr > gr	(ng > ɲ)		kt > t
	gr		(gn > ɲ)		ksp > sp
	rp, rt, rk^{a,o,u}, rb, rd, rg, rf, rm, rv		mn > ɲ,		kst > st
	sp, st, str, sk^{a,o,u}, skr, sm		nk^{i,e,ae} > ns, nθ		ksk > sk
	mp, mpr, (mb)		rk^{i,e,ae} > rs, rθ		(dr > r)
	nt, ntr, nk^{a,o,u}, nd, (ng), nf		lk^{i,e,ae} > ls, lθ		(gr > r)
	lp, lt, lk^{a,o,u}, lb, ld, lg, ls		sk^{i,e,ae} > s, θ		mpt > nt
			ng^{i,e,ae} > ns, nθ,		(mb > m)
			rg^{i,e,ae} > rs, rθ		nkt > nt
			ffl > ʎ		nst > st
					nstr > str
					ns > s

Complete Activities 7-3 and 7-4 on pages 160-62.

7.5 Chapter Summary

- Consonants are classified according to their mode of articulation, point of articulation, and voicing.
- A comparison of the consonant inventory, the complete set of consonants in each language, in Latin, Old Spanish, and Modern Spanish, showed that new consonants were created in Old Spanish, especially palatal fricatives, affricates, and nasals, some of which were later lost in Modern Spanish. A new consonant created in Modern Spanish is the jota /x/.
- Consonants changed from Latin to Spanish according to whether they were single consonants in Latin or in a group and according to their position in the word, whether initial, medial, or final position or before a yod.
- The individual sound changes that occurred from Latin to Spanish, shown in Table 7.3, can be classified according to five major processes of change: retention, lenition or weakening (which includes voicing, fricativization, and possibly loss), palatalization, velarization, and loss. As shown in Table 7.5, retention is most frequent in initial position, weakening in intervocalic position, palatalization before a yod or when /k/ or /g/ is before a front vowel /i/ or /e/, velarization in consonant clusters like /kt/ and /ks/, and loss in final position.
- Now that you have studied regular vowel and consonant changes, you are able to trace all of the sound changes of a Latin word so as to arrive at its Spanish reflex.

Activities

Activity 7-1

Overview of Consonantal Changes

In order to determine which consonants were created during the history of Spanish, answer the following questions based on Table 7.2:

1. Look first at the Latin consonants. Which of them no longer exist in Old Spanish and Modern Spanish?

2. Which consonants in Old Spanish did not exist in Latin? In other words, which new consonants were created between Latin and Old Spanish? Underline these in the table. What is their point of articulation?

3. Which Old Spanish consonants did not survive in Modern Spanish? Circle these in the table. What is the mode of articulation of these consonants?

4. There are two consonants that are new in Modern Spanish. List them here and state their mode and point of articulation.

5. What conclusions can you draw about consonantal development in the history of Spanish based on your responses to questions 1–4? For example, the fact that Latin /w/ no longer appears in Spanish indicates that it either changed to another sound or was lost completely. We will see below that it changed to /b/.

Activity 7-2

For each Latin word below, indicate the position and the evolution of each sound and give the resulting Spanish word. You may also write the process of change, if you like. You may consult the table of vowel changes in Chapter 6 and the table of consonant changes (Table 7.3) in this chapter in order to do this.

Here are two words to serve as an example:

Example 1: PLĪCĀRE > *llegar*

/pl/ initial > /ʎ/

/ ĭ / initial > /e/

/k/ + /a/ intervocalic (V__V) > /g/ > [ɣ]
/ā/ tonic > /a/
/r/ intervocalic (V__V) > /ɾ/
/e/ final > Ø (apocope)

Example 2: NŌMĬNEM > *nombre*
/n/ initial > /n/
/ō/ tonic > /o/
/ ĭ / medial > Ø (syncope)
/mn/ (group resulting from syncope) > /mr/ > /mbr/
/e/ final > /e/
/m/ final > Ø

1. CŬPPAM	13. ALĬUM
2. CĔNTUM	14. LENTĬCŬLAM
3. RŎTAM	15. DŎMĬNUM
4. SECŪRUM	16. SĒMĬNĀRE
5. CABALLUM	17. STRĬCTUM
6. FĀBULĀRE	18. DĬRĒCTUM
7. PĔTRAM	19. SĒNIŌREM
8. TABŬLAM	20. PĒNSĀRE
9. *TŬCCĪNUM	21. ĪNSŬLAM
10. *FŎRTĬA	22. DĬGĬTUM
11. CLAVEM	23. PĬGRĬTĬAM
12. GĔLUM	24. RECŬPERĀRE

Activity 7-3

Review of Regular Sound Changes in Vowels and Consonants

Write in the chart below one more example of each process and one position in which it occurs. There may be more than one position in which each process occurs, so you can pick one of them. You will need to consult Chapter 6 and this chapter to complete this chart.

Process of vowel change	Example	Position
1. diphthongization	PĔTRAM > pi̯edra	
2. retention	PLĬCĀRE > llegar	
3. apocope	PANĚM > pan_	
4. syncope	ŎPĔRA > ob_ra	

Process of consonant change	Example	Position
1. retention	PŎPŬLUM > pueblo	
2. lenition	PŎPŬLUM > pueblo	
3. palatalization	CĬLĬA > ceja /k/ > /s/	
4. velarization	CĬLĬA > ceja /l/+[j] > /x/	
5. loss	MĒNSAM > me_sa_	

Activity 7-4

Refer to Table 7.5 in order to answer the following questions about tendencies in consonantal change.

1. Which process is the most frequent in each of the positions? Simply write the process next to the position. We have completed the answer for single consonant in initial position for you.

    Single consonant
        initial position: retention
        intervocalic position
        final position
    Consonant groups
        initial position
        medial position before yod
        medial other position

2. We can rank the processes from the least change to the most change as follows: retention, palatalization, velarization, lenition, and loss. Based on this information, in which position would you say consonants change the least? the next least? the most? the next most? What conclusions can you draw about the susceptibility of consonants to change according to their position in the word?

Further Reading

Mackenzie, Ian 1999–2017. "History of Spanish consonants," in *The linguistics of Spanish*. www.staff.ncl.ac.uk/i.e.mackenzie/cons.htm

Pensado Ruiz, Carmen 1996. "La velarización castellana /ʃ/ > /x/ y sus paralelos romances," in A. Alonso González, L. Castro Ramos, B. Gutiérrez Rodilla, and J. A. Pascual Rodríguez (eds.), *Actas del III Congreso Internacional de Historia de la Lengua Española*, 153–70. Madrid: Arcos Libros

Ranson, Diana L. 1998. "Velarización y posteriorización: Variantes, paralelos, y mecanismo del cambio," in Claudio García Turza, Fabián González Bachiller, and Javier Mangado Martínez (eds.), *Actas del IV Congreso Internacional de Historia de la Lengua Española*, I: 279–87. Logroño: Universidad de La Rioja

Recasens, Daniel 2002. "Weakening and strengthening in Romance revisited," *Rivista di Lingüística* 41(2): 327–73

2014. "Interpretación de algunos cambios fonéticos en las lenguas romances," *Revista de Filología Románica* 31: 135–50

8 | Why Is 'milk' *leche* but 'Milky Way' Is *Via Láctea*?

Special Tonic Vowel Changes

Lead-in Question

8-1 For the following words, what would their reflexes have been in Spanish if the tonic vowel had undergone regular sound changes? What are the Modern Spanish reflexes instead? How are they different? What might account for this?

   a. VĪTREUM and MŬLTUM; *LACTEM and ALTĔRUM

   c. MATĔRIAM and NŎVIUM

   d. CASTĔLLUM and *CŎLŎBRAM

This chapter presents special changes in the tonic vowel that differ from the regular changes you studied in Chapter 6. You will see that all of these changes are brought about through the raising effect of a yod or another sound in the word. This illustrates the important principle that sounds sometimes change differently depending on the other sounds around them.

8.1 What Are the Special Tonic Vowel Changes?

The three parts of the Lead-in question illustrate three types of special vowel changes. The first is **vowel raising** (*la cerrazón vocálica*). We see this raising in the evolution of the tonic vowels /i/ and /u/ in vĭtreum > *vidrio* 'glass' and mŭltum > *mucho* and also /a/ in *lactem > *leche* and altĕrum > *otro*. You will recall from Chapter 6 that the short tonic vowels lowered by one degree so that we would expect the reflexes **vedrio* and **mocho*, just like pĭlum > *pelo* and cŭppam > *copa*. The vowel /a/, already an open vowel, normally remains unchanged, as in lacum > *lago*. When it raises, it can become fronted to /e/, as in *leche*, or it can become backed to /o/, as in *otro*. In all these examples, because the vowel is higher than the expected result, we call this raising.

The second exceptional change is the **lack of diphthongization** (*la falta de diptongación*) that results from vowel raising in words with a tonic short /e/ and /o/, like matĕriam > *madera* and nŏvium > *novio*. If the tonic vowels had diphthongized in these words the way they did in sĕptem > *siete* and nŏvem > *nueve*, the results would be **madiera* and **nuevio*.

The third exceptional change is the change of the diphthong /je/ to /i/ and of /we/ to /e/, as in castĕllum > *castillo* and *cŏlŏbram > *culebra* 'snake.' Through regular diphthongization these words would have become *castiello* and *culuebra*. This process is typically known as **secondary monophthongization** (*la monoptongación secundaria*), because the first monophthongization occurred in Latin when the three Latin diphthongs became monophthongs, like the change from /oj/ to /e/ as in poenam > *pena*, as seen in Chapter 6.

In order to explain these exceptional changes, this chapter focuses on how sounds are affected by their **phonological environment** (*el contexto* or *entorno fonológico*), the other sounds around them.

Complete Activity 8-1 on page 174.

8.2 What Accounts for These Special Vowel Changes?

In simple terms, these changes are caused by the raising effect of a yod or other high or palatal sound. You also saw in Chapter 7 that yod has a palatalizing effect on consonants, such as the /n/ in vīneam > *viña* 'vineyard.' Its widespread effects on both vowels and consonants are no doubt why our students have concluded over the years that yod is the reason for every exceptional change. More often than not they are right. The changes due to the yod are caused by assimilation as other sounds become more similar to it. Because yod is a high front semi-vowel, vowels become more similar to it by raising by one degree, as shown in Figure 8.1. The raising of /a/ to /e/ when followed by a yod is the same change we have already seen in Table 6.3 when the Latin diphthong /aj/ became /ɛ/. In fact, this same change also occurred in English and explains why the letters *ai* in *maid* and *tail* are pronounced /e/.

We can illustrate the raising process with two words from the Lead-in question. In vītreum the e in hiatus with the following u becomes a yod through the yodization rule from Chapter 6. Then the tonic vowel ĭ, through assimilation to the yod in the following syllable, raises from short ĭ to long ī, as shown in Figure 8.1. From there it follows the regular sound change for tonic /i/ to become the /i/ in *vidrio*. The lack of diphthongization in a word like matĕriam > *madera* is also explained through raising. The yod in this word comes from the /i/ in hiatus with /a/. Then the tonic short ĕ raises one degree to long ē and then evolves normally to /e/. Recall that diphthongization occurs only in the short vowels ĕ and ŏ, so when they raise to ē and ō they no longer diphthongize.

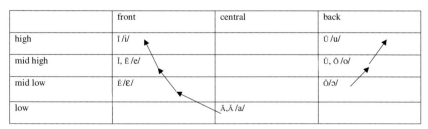

	front	central	back
high	ī /i/		ū /u/
mid high	ĭ, ē /e/		ŭ, ō /o/
mid low	ĕ /ɛ/		ŏ /ɔ/
low		ā,ă /a/	

Figure 8.1 Effect of yod on Latin vowels in their evolution to Spanish

Up until now we have been talking only about the yod, but there is another semi-vowel /w/, known as **waw** (*el wau*), that can also raise the tonic vowel. You may recall from Table 6.3 that it is a high semi-vowel, like yod, but it is pronounced in the back of the mouth, rather than the front. So when it affects the /a/, it not only causes it to raise, but also to become more backed. In a word like ALTĔRUM > *otro* the /l/ changes to /w/ and then /aw/ changes to /o/. This same change was seen in the monophthongization of the Latin diphthong /aw/ to /o/, as in PAUCUM > *poco*.

The tonic vowel can also raise not because of a yod but because of a word-final Ī /i/ through the process known as **metaphony** (*la metafonía*). This is the same process that accounts for singular and plural pairs in English like *foot/feet, tooth/teeth*, and *goose/geese*. This process is not nearly as common as raising by yod because few words ended in /i/ in Hispano-Romance. However, when metaphony did occur, it had the effect of raising the stressed vowel one degree, just like yod did, so that Ĕ > /e/ and Ē > /i/, as in the following verb forms:

VĔNĪ 'come!' > *¡ven!*, instead of **¡vien!*
VĒNĪ 'I came' > *vine*, instead of **vene*
FĒCĪ 'I did' > *hice*, instead of **hece*

Complete Activity 8-2 on page 175.

8.3 How Is the Yod Formed?

The semi-vowel yod did not exist in Classical Latin and so all the examples of yod that have such a powerful effect on the evolution of vowels and consonants in Spanish have been created in Spoken Latin. Most often a yod is created through the means already familiar to you, namely the process of yodization. This occurs when an /i/ or /e/ in hiatus with a following vowel becomes yod, as in the examples VĪTRĔU and MATĔRIA above. The vowel /i/ or /e/ can also end up in hiatus with another vowel when a consonant is lost, as when /w/ is lost in CANTĀ(V)I > [kan-'taj] > *canté* or when /d/ is lost in TŬRBĪDUM > *turbio* 'murky, unclear.' The consonants /k/, /l/, and /g/ may change to yod before another consonant, as in *LACTEM > *leche*, AXEM > *eje* 'axis,' SPĔCŬLUM > *espejo*, MŬLTUM > *mucho*, and LĬGNA > *leña* 'firewood.' This process is called **vocalization** (*la vocalización*), since a consonant becomes a semi-vowel. For example, one possible sequence of changes for *LACTEM > *leche* is ['lak-te] > ['laj-te] > ['lej-te] > ['le-tje] > ['le-ʧe]. Notice that the yod changes places through metathesis to end up after the consonant /t/, which then palatalizes to /ʧ/. Penny (2002: 50) proposes /l/ to /w/ as a first step in MŬLTUM > *mucho*, so that the steps would be ['mul-tu] > ['mow-to] > ['moj-to] > ['muj-to] > ['mu-tjo] > ['mu-ʧo]. In short, a yod can be created when /i/ or /e/ are in hiatus with another vowel, a situation which may have existed in Latin or may have been created by the loss of a consonant, or through the vocalization of the first consonant of the groups /kt/, /ks/, /kl/, /lt/, or /gn/.

8.4 Which Vowels Does the Yod Raise?

Having identified the ways a yod is created, we can now observe that the yod can appear in different places in the word and that its position determines whether it has a raising effect on the tonic vowel. We can identify these three positions:

1. immediately after the tonic vowel in the same syllable, as in *LACTEM > ['laj-te] > *leche*
2. in the following syllable, as in VĪTREU > ['bi-dɾjo] > *vidrio*
3. formed from the group [gn], as in LĬGNA > *leña*, or from /n/ plus yod, as in *CŬNEA > ['ku-nja] > *cuña* 'cradle'

It is important to keep in mind that a yod can change from the syllable following the tonic vowel to the same syllable through metathesis, as in SAPIAM > ['sa-pi-am] > ['sa-pja] > ['saj-pa] > ['se-pa] *sepa*.

Not all of the tonic vowels are affected by the same conditions in the same way. We will first examine the effect of yod on A /a/, Ĭ /e/, and Ŭ /o/ to see whether raising occurs and then we will look at Ĕ and ŏ to see whether the yod impedes diphthongization.

Complete Practice 8-1 in order to determine the effect of yod on the vowels A, Ĭ, and Ŭ in the three positions just mentioned.

Practice 8-1

Examine the following words to determine whether yod raised the vowels A, Ĭ, and Ŭ in each position. Circle the Spanish words that result from raising.

Vowel environment	Latin	Formation of yod	Spanish
Position 1 (same syllable)	*LACTEM	['laj-te]	*leche*
	STRĬCTUM	[es-'trej-to]	*estrecho*
	ĬMPŬLSAT >	[em-'poj-sat]	*empuja*
Position 2 (next syllable)	LABIUM	['la-βjo]	*labio*
	VĬTREUM >	['be-drjo]	*vidrio*
	TŬRBĬDUM >	['tor-βjo]	*turbio*
Position 3 (followed by [ɲ])	ARĀNEAM	[a-'ra-nja]	*araña*
	LĬGNA >	['le-ɲa]	*leña*
	*CŬNEA >	['ko-nja] > ['ko-ɲa]	*cuña*

We see that yod raises /a/ only when it follows it in the same syllable and it raises /e/ only when it is in the next syllable. The back vowel, /o/, on the other hand, is raised in all three positions.

Take a look at the Spanish results for the Latin vowels Ĕ and ŏ in Practice 8-2 to determine whether the yod raises these vowels and impedes their diphthongization.

Practice 8-2

Examine the following words to see whether the yod raised the vowels ĕ and ŏ in each position. Circle the Spanish words that show a lack of diphthongization.

Vowel environment	Latin	Formation of yod	Spanish
Condition 1 (same syllable)	DĪRĔCTUM	[di-ˈrɛj-to]	*derecho*
	NŎCTEM	[ˈnɔj-te]	*noche*
Condition 2 (next syllable)	SPĔC(Ŭ)LUM	[es-ˈpɛ-ʎo]	*espejo*
	NŎVIUM	[ˈnɔ-βjo]	*novio*
Condition 3 (followed by [ɲ])	VĔNIŌ	[ˈbɛ-njo]	*vengo*

It is clear from these examples that the yod raises ĕ in all three positions, impeding its diphthongization and raising the vowel to /e/. The yod also raises the vowel ŏ in positions 1 and 2. In position 3 we were unable to find a clear-cut example of ŏ before /nj/. In a word like CICŌNIA 'stork' with a long ō, one finds nevertheless /we/ in its reflex *cigueña*, because scholars assume that the yod comes in contact with the ō through metathesis and then /oj/ changes to /we/ (Wireback 2009: 57).

We have seen that a yod, and also a waw and a final /i/, can raise the tonic vowel under certain conditions. Figure 8.2 provides a summary of the regular vowel changes seen in Chapter 6 along with a summary of the results produced by raising from yod.

Complete Activities 8-3 and 8-4 on page 176.

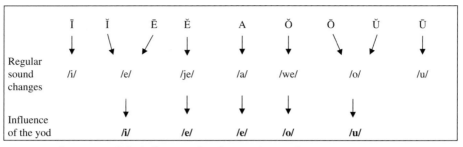

Figure 8.2 Summary of the influence of yod on tonic vowels

Box 8.1 Which came first: the chicken or the egg? The palatalization of consonant clusters

The age-old question of the chicken or the egg is often applied to causality dilemmas when it is difficult to determine which of two events is the cause and which is the effect. One such causality dilemma is the basis for the two different approaches to the palatalization of the consonant clusters /ks/, /kt/, and /gn/ from Latin and the secondary consonant clusters /k'l/ and /g'l/ resulting from syncope, as discussed by Wireback (2009). These approaches are the yod-based approach and the consonant-based approach.

The yod-based approach claims that the /k/ or /g/ in these clusters changed first to a yod, which then triggered the palatalization of the following consonant. In some words the yod also raised the preceding vowel, but in others it was absorbed by the newly palatalized consonant without vowel raising. In this scenario the yod comes before palatalization. The consonant-based approach, on the other hand, maintains that palatalization is the result of assimilation between the two consonants of the group. For example, mutual assimilation between a velar /k/ and a dental /t/ could result in a palatal consonant like /tʃ/. In this scenario palatalization comes before the yod which, if it occurs, is explained as the result of anticipating the new palatal consonant formed through assimilation.

Wireback (2009) finds both approaches to be problematic. He observes that the yod-based approach falls short by failing to explain why the proposed yod does not form a diphthong with some preceding vowels. If /k/ becomes yod in the /kt/ group of OCTO 'eight,' then why is the Spanish reflex *ocho*, instead of **huecho*? One would expect /o/ plus a following /j/ to become /we/ in the same way that CORIUM becomes *cuero*, after the yod comes in contact with the preceding /o/ through metathesis: /koɾju/ > /kojɾu/ > /kweɾo/. The consonant-based approach in which the consonant group palatalizes first and then creates a yod in anticipation of the palatal consonant is not entirely satisfactory either. According to this approach, the /kt/ in FACTUM, which becomes *hecho*, would first become palatal /tʃ/ and then speakers would produce a yod before /tʃ/ to arrive at /jtʃ/, so /faktu/ > /atʃo/ > /ajtʃo/ > /etʃo/. Yet the fact that no yod develops in many other consonant clusters, even though it does in other Ibero-Romance languages, leads one to wonder whether a yod would really be produced in such cases. For example, BASSĀRE becomes Old Spanish *baxar* (> Modern Spanish *bajar*), whereas it is *baixar* in Portuguese with a yod following the initial /a/. One also finds CAPSA which becomes Old Spanish *caxa* 'box' and Modern Spanish *caja* versus Portuguese *caixa*. So, if the yod did not come first (yod-based approach) and neither did palatalization (consonant-based approach), then what did?

According to Wireback (2009), it is necessary to combine both approaches. He claims that palatalization is the result of the evolution of /k/ and /g/ into a palatal but more consonantal sound. This sound had the same palatalizing properties as the yod but it did not raise the preceding vowel. After the formation of this palatal-consonantal reflex, other linguistic factors then either caused or impeded yod formation "resulting in both cases of palatalization with no apparent presence of yod as well as cases of palatalization that produced a palatal semi-vowel" (Wireback 2009: 62). So, which came first: the yod or consonantal palatalization? Well, neither. According to Wireback, there was an option that was neither a chicken nor an egg, but something in between.

8.5 Why Is *castillo* Written *castiello* in Some Old Spanish Texts?

In Old Spanish texts we encounter the spelling *castiello* for *castillo* 'castle' and by the same token *Castiella* for *Castilla* 'Castile.' This is because the pronunciation of the tonic vowel as [je], resulting from the regular diphthongization of Latin Ĕ, was maintained long enough to be attested in writing. Other examples of secondary monophthongization of the tonic vowel before the palatal lateral consonant /ʎ/ include SĔLLAM > *siella* > *silla* and CULTĔLLUM > *cuchiello* > *cuchillo*. Menéndez Pidal (1987: 55) explains that assimilation of /e/ to the palatal /ʎ/ resulted in complete assimilation of /e/ to /i/. To understand the articulatory process better, repeat the words *castiello* and *castillo* several times. You notice that in *castiello* both /j/ and /ʎ/ are palatal sounds, so you have to move your tongue down to pronounce the /e/. If you reduce the articulatory movement by keeping your tongue in the high palatal position, then the /e/ is eliminated and the diphthong /je/ monophthongizes to [i], as in *castillo*.

Menéndez Pidal (1987: 56–57) points out that the *-illo* form doesn't appear in literary texts until the fourteenth century, but non-literary documents, such as notarized letters, show the use of the form as early as the tenth century in the northern part of the Iberian Peninsula in Castile and Burgos. He believes that the form began there and slowly expanded throughout the peninsula. However, even today the Leonese and High Aragonese dialects conserve the older *-iello* forms. You can see examples of the *-iello* ending in the Appendix, for example, *Castiella* in B15, *capiello* in C118, and *aniello* in C119.

Secondary monophthongization can also occur before before syllable-final /s/ followed by a consonant, as in VĔSPĔRAM > *viespera* > *víspera* 'eve, the day before' and VĔSPAM > *aviespa* > *avispa* 'wasp.' However, we do not always see this change, as witnessed in the words FĔSTA > *fiesta* and SĔXTAM > *siesta*. Not all scholars agree, however, that this monophthongization is based on the sounds in question. Malkiel (1976, 1980a) proposes instead that *-iello* changes to *-illo* by analogy to diminutive suffixes like *-ito, -ico*, and *-ino*. This position has been refuted, however, by Mendez Dosuna and Pensado (1986).

This process of monophthongization also affected the diphthong /we/, a process which was most likely complete around the fourteenth century when the last examples of *fruente* were found in writing (Menéndez Pidal 1987: 61). This monophthongization of /we/ to /e/ occurred after groups of labial consonant plus a liquid consonant /l/ or /ɾ/, as in FLŎCCUM > *flueco* > *fleco* 'bangs,' FRŎNTEM > *fruente* > *frente* 'forehead,' or before such a group, as in *COLŎBRAM > *culuebra* > *culuebra* 'snake.' An example of *fruente* is found in the Appendix C60. Menéndez Pidal (1987: 61) explains that the combination of a labial sound, such as /f/ + alveolar /l/ or /ɾ/ + labial /w/ before a palatal /e/, required movement from the front of the mouth to the back for the /w/ and then to the front again. Eliminating the /w/ removed the movement to the back of the mouth.

Complete Activity 8-5 on page 178.

8.6 Chapter Summary

- The yod has the effect of raising Latin vowels by one degree in the evolution into Spanish.
  - Thus, the yod raises Ī and Ē from [e] to [i], as in VĪTREUM > *vidrio*, and Ŭ and Ō from [o] to [u], as in MŬLTUM > *mucho*.
  - It also raises Ĕ to [e] and Ŏ to [o], thereby impeding their dipthongization, as in as in MATĔRIAM > *madera* and NŎVIUM > *novio*.
  - The low vowel [a] raises only when the yod or waw follows it immediately, so that [aj] > [e], as in *LACTEM > *leche*, and [aw] > [o], as in ALTĔRUM > [ˈaw-tɾo] > *otro*.
- The yod is produced in several ways:
  - through the yodization rule when [i] or [e] is in hiatus with another vowel in Latin
  - when [i] and [e] come into contact with a vowel through loss of a consonant
  - when the first consonant of a group like [kt], [ks], [lt], or [gn] vocalizes to [j].
- The effect of the yod is not the same on all vowels.

○ It raises [a] only when it follows it in the same syllable, as in *LACTEM > leche.

○ It raises [e] (< ĭ and ē) only when yod is in the following syllable, as in VĬTREUM > *vidrio.*

○ It raises and therefore impedes diphthongization of [ɔ] (< ŏ) in both the previous positions.

○ It raises [o] (< ō and ŭ) and [ɛ] (< ĕ) in both of these positions and also before palatal [ɲ].

• A final long ī can also have a raising effect on the tonic vowel through metaphony, as in VĒNĪ 'I came' > *vine.*

• The process of secondary monophthongization occurs during the Old Spanish period when a word like Old Spanish *castiello* (< CASTĔLLUM) becomes *castillo* and *culuebra* (< *CŎLŎBRAM) becomes *culebra.* The monophthongization of the diphthong reduces articulatory movement by eliminating the sound that is least like the surrounding sounds.

• Both Spanish *leche* and *láctea* come from the Latin stem LACT- 'milk.' The [e] in the derived word *leche* results from the vocalization of [k] to [j] in the [kt] group and then the raising of [aj] to [e]. The word *láctea* is a learnèd word that keeps the original vowel in Latin. So, the simple explanation for the difference is the raising effect of the yod in the derived word and not in the learnèd word.

Activities

Activity 8-1

In each of the following Latin words, underline the tonic vowel and then write in the blank the abbreviation for the process that occurred in its evolution into Spanish. RA = raising, LD = lack of dipthongization, SM = secondary monophthongization, SC = regular sound change

_____ 1. CANTĀVIT > *cantó*

_____ 2. CĪLIA > *ceja*

_____ 3. FŎLIA > *hoja*

_____ 4. FRAXĬNUM > *fresno*

_____ 5. FRĪCTUM > *frito*

_____ 6. FRŎNTEM > *frente*

_____ 7. HŎDIE > *hoy*

_____ 8. LĪMPIDUM > *limpio*

_____ 9. *LŪCTAM > *lucha*

_____ 10. PĔCTUS > *pecho*

_____ 11. PLŪVIAM > *lluvia*

_____ 12. SŎMNUM > *sueño*

_____ 13. SPĔCŬLUM > *espejo*

_____ 14. VĔSPAM > *avispa*

_____ 15. VĔTŬLUM > *viejo*

_____ 16. VĪNDĒMIAM > *vendimia*

Activity 8-2

Map each of the words above that you marked as undergoing raising in Activity 8-1 onto Figure 8.1 (copied below). Write the number of the word and then draw an arrow from its vowel in Latin to the vowel this raises to in order to give the Spanish reflex. We have provided two examples as a model.

	front	central	back
high	Ī /i/ 8 *limpio*		Ū /u/
mid high	Ĭ, Ē /e/ 8 LĪMPIDUM		Ŭ, Ō /o/
mid low	Ĕ /ɛ/		Ŏ /ɔ/ 1 *cantó*
low		Ā, Ă /a/ 1 CANTĀVIT	

Figure 8.1bis Effect of yod on Latin vowels in their evolution to Spanish

Activity 8-3

Many Latin verbs had an /i/ or /e/ only in the 1sg. ending of the present indicative that developed into a yod in Spanish. Give the regular result for these 1sg. Latin verb forms, paying special attention to the effect of the yod on the tonic vowel. Then give the result for 2sg. and compare these to the actual forms in Modern Spanish. We will explore this topic further in Chapter 14.

1sg. verb	By regular sound change	In Modern Spanish	2sg. verb	By regular sound change	In Modern Spanish
Example: MĒTIŌ	*mido*	*mido*	MĒTĪS	*medes*	*mides*
1. TĔNEŌ			TĔNES		
2. SŬBEŌ			SŬBES		
3. APĔRIŌ			APĔRĪS		
4. SĔNTIŌ			SĔNTĪS		
5. SĔRVIŌ			SĔRVĪS		
6. CŌŌPĔRIŌ			CŌŌPĔRĪS		
7. VĒSTIŌ			VĒSTĪS		
8. PROHĬBEŌ			PROHĬBES		
9. FŬGIŌ			FŬGIS		
10. bonus: SAPIŌ (with metathesis)			SAPIS		
11. bonus: HABEŌ			HABES		

Activity 8-4

For each of the following Latin words:

a. Underline the tonic vowel.
b. Circle the sound that becomes yod.
c. Give the Spanish reflex.
d. Decide whether there is a raising effect.

e. If there is a raising effect, identify the position of the yod: 1 = yod in the same syllable, 2 = yod in the following syllable, 3 = yod effect from [ɲ], 4 = yod in following syllable moves to same syllable through metathesis.

Latin word	Spanish reflex	Raising effect?	Position
Example: BASĬUM	beso	yes	4
1. CALŬMNIAM			
2. CASEUM			
3. *CERĔSIA			
4. CONSĬLIUM			
5. DIRĔCTUM			
6. EXTRĀNEUM			
7. FŎLIA			
8. FRAXĬNUM			
9. LĬMPĬDUM			
10. *LŬCTAM			
11. NŎCTEM			
12. ŎCŬLUM			
13. PĔCTUS			
14. PLŬVIAM			
15. PŬGNUM			
16. SĬGNA			
17. STRĬCTUM			
18. SUPĔRBIAM			
19. VĔTULUM			
20. VŬLTUREM			

Activity 8-5

Do a search for the words *castiello* and *castillo* in the CORDE. When do each of these words appear for the first and last times? Which form is most common in the tenth, twelfth, and fourteenth centuries? Are there any other spellings for this word?

Further Reading

O'Neill, Paul 2012. "New perspectives on the effects of yod in Ibero-Romance," *Bulletin of Spanish Studies* 89(5): 665–97

Wireback, Kenneth J. 1997. "On the Palatalization of /kt/, /ks/, /k'l/, /g'l/, and /gn/ in Western Romance," *Romance Philology* 50(3): 276–94

   2007. "Vocalization of /k/ or anticipatory epenthesis? Glide formation and consonant-based palatalization in the Western and Italo-Romance development of Latin /ks/ and /kt/," *Romanische Forschungen* 119(1): 3–37

9 Why *fieldad* but *lealtad*?

Special Consonant Changes

Lead-in Questions

9-1 Write down five words in Modern Spanish that end in -*dad* and five that end in -*tad*. Which ending is more common? (Tip: You can find examples by searching words ending in -*tad* and -*dad* in the dictionary at www.rae.es.)

9-2 Latin FUNDU has given Spanish *hondo, fondo,* and *profundo.* How are the modern forms different? What do you think caused this?

9-3 Do you know any native speakers who pronounce *caza* as [ˈka-θa]? And any who pronounce *caza* as [ˈka-sa]? Where are they from? Where do you think the /θ/ came from?

This chapter takes a closer look at three sound changes involving consonants in the history of Spanish in order to illustrate some general principles of sound change. By looking at the changes resulting in words like fieldad *and* lealtad *you will learn that sound changes take place in a certain order. You will also learn that variation may be a part of sound change, so that the same Latin sounds may end up with different results in Spanish. A closer look at the evolution of Latin initial /f/ in*

Spanish will reinforce the point, made in Chapter 8, *that sounds evolve differently in different phonological contexts. It will also illustrate the idea that sound changes occur during a certain time period, so that words introduced after this period will not be subject to that change. Finally, the history of the sibilants in Spanish shows clearly the phases of a sound change and also that sounds can undergo different changes in different geographical regions.*

9.1 Why *fieldad* but *lealtad?*

When you learned to trace the sound changes from a Latin word to its Spanish reflex in Chapters 6, 7, and 8, we were not concerned about the order the sound changes occurred in. The one exception was to identify the creation of a yod before identifying other changes, since this would certainly affect the evolution of other vowels and consonants in the word. Apart from the yod, though, you could apply the changes in any order and still end up with the same result in Spanish. In this section, we consider a special case where the result of the voiceless consonants /p/, /t/, and /k/ will be different depending on whether voicing or syncope occurs first. This is then a question of **relative chronology** (*la cronología relativa*), the order in which sound changes occur.

We can begin with a familiar example. When we apply the sound changes to Latin PŎPŮLUM, we say that the underlined /p/ is in intervocalic position. In this position, it undergoes lenition so that it voices to /b/ and then fricativizes to [β] to result in *pueblo*. We assume that the syncope of the medial /u/ does not take place until after the voicing has taken place so that the order of the changes or relative chronology is voicing then syncope. Now let us consider the changes in Latin CŌPŮLAM. If we apply the same changes here as in PŎPŮLUM, then the result will be *cobla*. However, we know that the resulting word in Spanish is *copla* 'four-line stanza, couplet' and so we need a way to account for the lack of voicing of the /p/ in this word. In order to explain the voiceless /p/, Menéndez Pidal (1987: 158) has proposed that *copla* is semi-learnèd. He specifies semi-learnèd rather than learnèd because syncope occurs in *copla*, but not in other learnèd words, like *másculo* alongside derived *macho*. However, another option, more probable in our opinion, is a different chronology of voicing and syncope in this word. If syncope occurs before voicing, then CŌPŪLAM becomes *copla* and the normal evolution of the consonant group /pl/ is retention.

The same question of relative chronology explains the -*dad* and -*tad* endings. Which one do you think results from voicing before syncope? If you said that -*dad* results from voicing before syncope, then you were right to realize that voicing in this word occurs before the intervocalic position that produces it is lost through syncope. In Latin FIDĒLITĀTEM, voicing occurs first while the under-lined /t/ is in intervocalic position, and then syncope brings the fricative [ð] in contact with the preceding /l/ to create *fieldad*. In LĒGALITĀTEM, we can assume that syncope occurred first, so that no voicing of /t/ occurred in *lealtad*. The group /lt/ was then retained through normal evolution.

The examples above and the ones in Activity 9-1 that demonstrate the importance of relative chronology also test the linguist's attitude toward sound change. A prevailing attitude toward sound change since the time of the Neogrammarians at the end of the nineteenth century was that sound changes admitted no exceptions. If you adopt this stance toward sound change, then there can be only one regular outcome and all other outcomes must have an alternative explanation. This stance explains why numerous scholars have sought to explain the lack of voicing in words like *copla* as cases of learnèd borrowings, contemporary borrowings from other languages, analogy to other words, or early syncope or later devoicing, as catalogued by Ranson (1999: 137–39). If you accept, though, as we do, that variation is a natural part of the process of sound change, then different results mean that one variant was selected in one word and another variant was selected in another word. This same attitude toward sound change may also explain why some words with an intial /f/ in Latin have a form with either /f/ or zero in Modern Spanish, like *fondo* and *hondo*, seen in the following section.

Scholars assume that all the sound changes we have studied, not only voicing and syncope, occur in a certain order. For the proposed order of these changes see the handy lists in Penny (2002: 109–10) and Pharies (2007: 85–90, 151–54) or the complete discussion of these changes in Pensado Ruiz (1984).

Complete Activity 9-1 on page 191.

9.2 Why *hondo* but *fondo*?

By looking more deeply into the evolution of Latin initial /f/ in Spanish, we continue the topic of the chronology of sound change. You are already familiar with this change from Chapter 4 where we discussed the possibility of Basque influence on Latin /f/ > [h] and from Chapter 7 where we observed that /f/ is one of the few Latin consonants to be lost in initial position. In this chapter we explore the stages of this change, its chronology, and its two different results, whether loss, as in *hondo* 'deep,' or retention, as in *fondo* 'bottom, depths.'

Some authors (Steiger 1932, Lloyd 1987, Penny 2002) believe that this change was a specific development of Castilian and other northern dialects. Although there is no documentation to confirm this hypothesis, they further suggest that the articulation of the word-initial labio-dental fricative /f/ was actually closer to a bilabial voiceless fricative [ɸ] and that the bilabial articulation had spread throughout the peninsula by the Middle Ages (Lloyd 1987: 213). Because the lips barely touch to produce the bilabial fricative [ɸ], the slightest relaxation of the lips would eliminate the lips as articulators, which would change this sound to [h]. Of course it is also possible to arrive at [h] from the labio-dental fricative [f] by removing the oral articulation needed for its production. The change from any fricative to [h], such as the aspiration of /s/ in Modern Spanish, is produced when speakers no longer make the corresponding gestures in the mouth.

Before the semi-consonant [w], there could have been a combination of a relaxation followed by a tensing of the lips in anticipation of the labio-velar [w]. Thus, Lloyd (1987: 215) proposes that there were three allophones of /f/ in early Castilian:

[h] before /o/ and /u/
[hɸ] before [w]
[ɸ] everywhere else

A further step then occurred in northern Castile and eastern León so that [hɸ] became [f] and was pronounced before the diphthong [we], the glottal fricative [h] was pronounced before all vowels, not just back ones, and [ɸ] or [f] was pronounced before all consonants. This would explain why one finds the reflex /h/ before vowels, as in FĪLUM > *hilo* 'thread,' but /f/ before consonants, as in FRŎNTEM > *frente*, and diphthongs, as in FŎCUM > *fuego*.

There is ample evidence in writing that /f/ had changed to /h/ by an early date. The earliest documented examples of the change are seen in the extreme north. For example, in a document from Castile dated 863 the Latin name FORTĪCIUS appears as *Ortiço*. In Aragon, the name FORTIS appears as *Hortiz* in a document dated 1099 and as *Ortíz* in a document from 1100 (Lloyd 1987: 216). Of course, words spelled with the letter *f* could also have been pronounced [h], so it is not always clear from the spelling what the pronunciation might have been. Lloyd (1987) feels confident, however, in attributing the confusion of the letter *f* with the articulation of [h] to the Castilian dialect based on several other documents. An Arabic history tells the tale of a certain *infante* 'prince' who died in Moorish lands in 1083. The author mentions that the people from La Rioja referred to him as the "il-hante," "changing the f to h in speaking" (Lloyd 1987: 216–17). Also, when Old French words that had word-initial /h/ were borrowed into the Castilian dialect, for example *héraut* 'herald' and *honte* 'shame,' they were sometimes written with an *f*, as *faraute* and *fonta*, although these words were most assuredly pronounced with [h]. Arabic words containing /f/ that were borrowed into the language, were sometimes written with *h*, such as SAFUNĀRIYA > *çanahoria* (*zanahoria* 'carrot'), further testimony not only of the confusion between /f/ (or its variant [ɸ]) and [h]), but also to the fact that interchanging the sounds had no effect on the meaning of words (Lloyd 1987: 217–18).

When large numbers of Latinisms were adopted into the Spanish lexicon from the twelfth century on, brought in mostly by the clergy, the use of [f] was reinforced and there was a weakening of the phonetic associations among the allophones of /f/, namely [h], [ɸ], and [hɸ]. The result was a phonological split of /f/ and /h/ into separate phonemes. This split allowed popular words to survive along with new words brought into the language, with different articulations and different meanings. Thus, we find doublets, two different words with the same origin as mentioned in Chapter 5, such as *horma* 'mold' and *forma* 'form' (< FŎRMAM), *habla* 'speech' and *fábula* 'fable' (< FABŬLAM), and *hondo* 'deep' and *fondo* 'bottom, depths' (< FUNDUM).

Complete Activity 9-2 on page 192.

While completing Activity 9-2, you probably noticed that the Latin words in the left column of that activity underwent the change /f/ > /h/ (and then > Ø in Modern Spanish), whereas those on the right conserved the /f/ in words with the same or a similar root. It is because the words in the left column were part of the lexicon during the time of the earliest Roman invaders and therefore underwent the regular sound changes. If the sound was word initial, it became aspirated (and later disappeared). If it was word medial, it was retained. Also, the words in the right column were derived Latin words that over the centuries underwent semantic changes so that the Modern Spanish words no longer mean literally what the root and the old prefixes meant. Many speakers of Modern Spanish would not even recognize that the words *confundir* and *hundir* 'to sink' are related. However, if a word underwent all of the regular phonological changes and then was made into a derived word (a prefix plus a root), the changes in the root would also be reflected in the derived words such as in *hacer* < FACĔRE and *deshacer* < DES + FACĔRE. Thus, when it was clear to speakers that the /f/ was word initial, this sound became aspirated /h/ and then Ø, and when it was not clear that the sound was word initial, the labio-dental fricative /f/ was retained, as in *confundir* from CONFŬNDĔRE. Further proof that speakers did not perceive a word as made from a prefix plus root is the voicing of an intervocalic /f/ at the beginning of the root, as in PRŌFECTUM > *provecho* 'benefit, advantage.' Learnèd words adopted during the lexical expansion during the Middle Ages, however, were unlikely to undergo the regular sound changes, so they are pronounced with /f/, as in PROFUNDUM > *profundo*. You can now answer Lead-in question 9-2 and explain how Latin FUNDUM could give us the Modern Spanish words: *hondo, fondo,* and *profundo,* a topic taken up further in Box 9.1. It is interesting to observe the many words in the Appendix written with an initial *f-* that now begin with an *h-* in Modern Spanish, such as *figo* for *higo* (A8), *fiziéronlo* for *lo hicieron* (E23), and even *fondo* for *hondo* (E43).

Once the split between /f/ and /h/ occurred, the next change to take place was the loss of /h/, which, according to Lloyd (1987: 325), "probably began in the region of Burgos, and then spread to both the urban and rural areas of Castile."

We know that this was a relatively late innovation in the Castilian dialect because the aspirated /h/ is part of the popular speech in many parts of southern Spain and Latin America to this day. The allophone [hɸ] may have been simplified and was substituted by either [h] or [ɸ]. This is evidenced in dialects that still retain [h] before semi-vowels (e.g. ['hwer-te] for *fuerte*), although [ɸ], as in ['ɸwer-te], was more common and closer to the educated norm which eventually gave way to [f].

As for the orthography of these sounds, the allophones [h], [ɸ], and [hɸ] could all be represented as *f* or *h* until the split into two phonemes. At least by the thirteenth century, scribes needed a way to distinguish between [f] and [h]. Since the letter *f* could represent [h], some writers in the mid thirteenth century started to adopt the *ff* to make clear that the sound was articulated as a labio-dental [f] (Blake 1988a: 268). There is also evidence of variation in thirteenth-century documents, such as the spellings *Haro, Ffaro*, and *Faro* for the same Riojan town (Blake 1988a: 275). However, the letter *h* gradually came to be the orthographic norm for the aspirated form which, to this day, is retained only in spelling. Rini (2010) found an ingenious way to determine when the /h/ might have been lost from pronunciation by looking to see whether the article *la* was used before nouns beginning with *h* plus a stressed /a/, such as *la hada* 'fairy,' in which case the /h/ was still pronounced, or whether the article *el* was used, as in *el hada*, in which case the /h/ may not have been pronounced. He reports that the first example indicating the possible deletion of /h/ is *el harpa* by Enrique de Villena in 1427 or 1428.

Box 9.1 *Hondo* and *fondo*: an alternative explanation

From Latin FUNDUM we get both *hondo* 'deep' and *fondo* 'bottom, depths.' We could assume that *fondo* is the learnèd member of the doublet because it does not display the change [f] > [h] to Ø. Historical linguists have suggested caution, however, in assuming that a word that has not undergone certain sound changes is always learnèd. Blake (1988b), for example, shows that the use of the letter *f* in medieval writing was ambiguous and could represent [f], [h], or even Ø. In fact, variation in the pronunciation of this sound, he believes, has always been a feature of Castilian from at least the eighth century.

In a study of documents of the Castilian region from the twelfth to the fifteenth century, Blake found that most words were written with *f*, but that a few of them appeared with either *f* or *h* for the same word in the same document. Although these tokens with *h* are suggestive of a change in progress, it is unclear what the actual articulation was. Then at some point in the thirteenth and fourteenth centuries there was an increase in *ff* for word-initial [f]. Blake believes this is evidence that /f/ and /h/ had by then become two separate phonemes among the literate population. But not all speakers, and especially the illiterate population, made the distinction. Thus, scribes attempted to prescriptively reinforce this difference in writing (Blake 1988b: 58). This type of scribal prescriptivism may have been at work in earlier centuries when the desire to prescribe a "correct" form resulted in the coexistence for a while of two forms, as in *hondo* and *fondo*. Both forms survived with slightly different meanings but both may be popular and not learnèd words. What other evidence do you think would lend weight to this explanation?

Complete Activity 9-3 on page 193.

9.3 Are *casa* and *caza* Pronounced the Same?

9.3.1 How Were the Old Spanish Sibilants Created?

As early as Chapter 2, in the pronunciation of the Old Spanish text of *El Conde Lucanor*, you learned that there were numerous sibilants in Old Spanish that do not exist in Modern Spanish. This idea became even more evident in Table 7.2, a comparison of the consonant phonemes of Old Spanish with those of Latin and Modern Spanish, where we once again saw sibilants in Old Spanish that did not exist in Latin or Modern Spanish. This section focuses on the creation of these sibilants and the steps in their evolution. Of particular interest is when these changes took place and how they led to a difference in pronunciation between

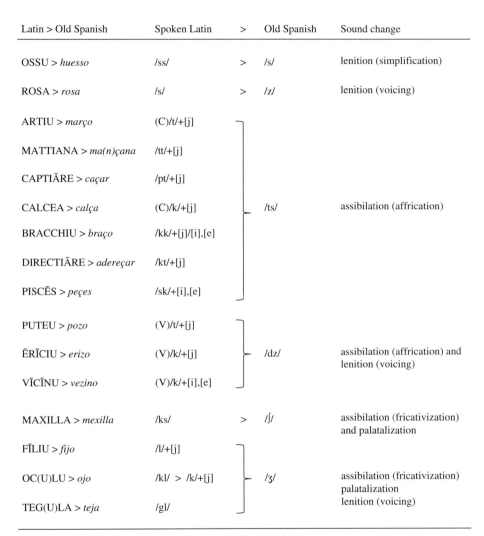

Latin > Old Spanish	Spoken Latin	>	Old Spanish	Sound change
OSSU > *huesso*	/ss/	>	/s/	lenition (simplification)
ROSA > *rosa*	/s/	>	/z/	lenition (voicing)
ARTIU > *março*	(C)/t/+[j]			
MATTIANA > *ma(n)çana*	/tt/+[j]			
CAPTIĀRE > *caçar*	/pt/+[j]			
CALCEA > *calça*	(C)/k/+[j]		/ts/	assibilation (affrication)
BRACCHIU > *braço*	/kk/+[j]/[i],[e]			
DIRECTIĀRE > *adereçar*	/kt/+[j]			
PISCĒS > *peçes*	/sk/+[i],[e]			
PUTEU > *pozo*	(V)/t/+[j]			
ĒRĪCIU > *erizo*	(V)/k/+[j]		/dz/	assibilation (affrication) and lenition (voicing)
VĪCĪNU > *vezino*	(V)/k/+[i],[e]			
MAXILLA > *mexilla*	/ks/	>	/ʃ/	assibilation (fricativization) and palatalization
FĪLIU > *fijo*	/l/+[j]			
OC(U)LU > *ojo*	/kl/ > /k/+[j]		/ʒ/	assibilation (fricativization) palatalization lenition (voicing)
TEG(U)LA > *teja*	/gl/			

Figure 9.1 Latin consonants that become sibilants in Old Spanish

northern Spain, on the one hand, and southern Spain and the Latin America, on the other hand.

A series of regular sound changes in Spoken Latin including lenition, assibilation, and palatalization produced a series of six Old Spanish sibilants arranged in three voiceless/voiced pairs. Figure 9.1 summarizes the evolution of these sibilant consonants from Spoken Latin to Old Spanish in word medial position.

Word-initial combinations of /k/+ [j] also produced the affricate /ts/ (e.g. CAELUM > *çielo* and CISTAM > *çesta*). In some cases, a consonant that was word-medial in Latin became final in Old Spanish because of the loss of the final vowel. Because the original context had been intervocalic, the consonant would have gone through the regular changes of lenition, assibilation and voicing before the loss of the final vowel, as in PĀCEM > *paz*, most likely pronounced /padz/ in Old Spanish.

As seen in Chapter 7 there is a seventh sibilant in Old Spanish, a prepalatal affricate /tʃ/, that was formed from the Latin consonant groups /kt/, as in FACTUM > *hecho*, /lt/ after /u/, as in MULTUM > *mucho*, and /pl/ after a consonant, as in AMPLUM > *ancho*. This consonant remained the same from Old Spanish to Modern Spanish. The first six that we summarized above, however, did continue to evolve during the Middle Ages, as shown in the following section.

9.3.2 How Did the Sibilants Change from Old Spanish to Modern Spanish?

The system of sibilants underwent three major changes during the Middle Ages. The first of these processes is the change of the affricates /ts/ and /dz/ to the fricatives /s̪/ and /z̪/, respectively, which came about through the loss of the initial stop element in the affricate. Because the change did not result in any change to the phonological system, there was no change in spelling. This makes it difficult to determine when the change began, but Penny (2002: 99) believes it was completed by the fifteenth century. The second change, which occurred sometime during the sixteenth century, is the devoicing of the voiced sibilants so that only voiceless sibilants remained. Penny (2002: 99) believes that the absence of voiced sibilants had very likely been a characteristic of the northern dialects of Castile. The contrast of voiced and voiceless sibilants was maintained for a longer time in the south, but the voiceless sibilants became the norm when Madrid was established as the capital of Spain in 1561 and northerners migrated to the capital. By the late sixteenth century, following deaffrication and devoicing, the sibilant system of standard Spanish contained only three voiceless sibilants: /s̪/, /s/, and /ʃ/. The third major change involves a change in place of articulation of the remaining fricatives. There were many sets of words whose meaning was determined by the perception and production of these different sibilants, such as *caça* ['ka-s̯a] 'hunt' (Modern Spanish *caza*), *casa* ['ka-sa] 'house' (Modern Spanish *casa*), and *caxa* ['ka-ʃa] 'box' (Modern Spanish *caja*). In northern Spain, the potential confusion was avoided by creating a greater distance between the points of articulation of these three fricatives so as to make the differences more perceptible. This resulted in the /s̯/ moving farther forward in the mouth to become an interdental fricative /θ/, and the /ʃ/ moving farther back to become a velar fricative /x/. Thus, *caça* became *caza* ['ka-θa] and *caxa* became *caja* ['ka-xa] and only *casa* ['ka-sa] maintained the same articulation. Because a distinction is maintained between the phonemes /θ/ and /s/, these dialects are said to maintain *distinción*. The process of articulatory separation was not complete and recognized as the standard norm until about the middle of the seventeenth century and spelling changes were not reflected until the eighteenth- and nineteenth-century reforms were established (Penny 2002: 101).

In Seville and most of Andalusia, the evolution of the sibilants followed a different path. The affricates /ts/ and /dz/ had already merged with /s̯/, and /z̯/, so that no distinction was maintained between /s̯/ and /s/ as occurred in northern Spain. These dialects are called *seseante*. The spelling in texts of the fifteenth and sixteenth centuries from southern Spain reflects the phonological adjustments taking place. Writers would often use the ç and z to represent /s̯/, as in *paço* for *passo* and *caza* for *casa*, an indication that there was no longer a distinction between /s̯/ and /s/ (Penny 2002: 101).

Another explanation for this merger is that Andalusian Spanish never developed alveolar fricatives, perhaps due to the influence of Mozarabic or Arabic which lack these consonants, and the dental fricatives emerged from a neutralization of /ts/ and /s̯/ in the voiceless sibilants and a union of /dz/ and /z̯/ in their voiced counterparts. The system underwent the process of devoicing that occurred in all of the peninsula at around the same time so that Old Spanish /ts/, /dz/, /s̯/, and /z̯/ all resulted in a single sibilant phoneme: /s̯/. In these dialects /ʃ/ also velarized to /x/, which in parts of Latin America became the glottal fricative /h/, as in *caxa* ['ka-ha] and *mejor* [me-'hoɾ].

A summary of all the changes of both the standard Castilian dialect and the Andalusian and American dialects can be seen in Figure 9.2.

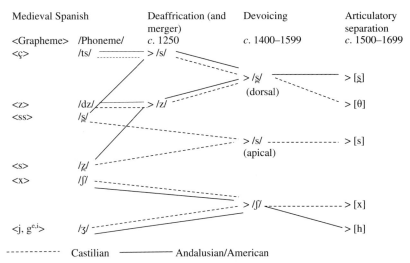

Figure 9.2 Development of sibilants from Old to Modern Spanish

Complete Activity 9-4 on page 194.

9.4 Chapter Summary

- The order in which voicing and syncope occur can determine whether a Latin voiceless consonant ends up as a voiced consonant in Spanish. If voicing occurs first, this consonant will be voiced, as in PŎPŬLUM > *pueblo*, but if syncope occurs first, depending on the resulting consonant group, then the consonant will be voiceless, as in COPULA > *copla*. The order in which sound changes occur is called their relative chronology. The Spanish word *fieldad* (< FIDĒLITĀTEM) shows voicing before syncope of the second to last /t/, whereas *lealtad* (< LĒGĀLITĀTEM) shows syncope first and therefore no voicing of the second to last /t/.
- Through regular sound change Latin /f/ remained /f/ before consonants and diphthongs and changed to /h/ and then was lost elsewhere. After /f/ had changed to /h/, a new consonant /f/ was reintroduced which led to the creation of doublets like *fondo* and *hondo*. The written records offer some

evidence of the stages in the change from /f/ > /h/ > Ø. Some historical linguists give alternative explanations for these doublets.

- A new series of sibilants was created in Old Spanish through palatalization of Latin consonants in various contexts. The six sibilants of Old Spanish were reduced to three sibilants in northern Spain, where a difference was maintained between /θ/ and /s/ (and /ʃ/ which later became /x/). This distinction was eliminated in southern Spain and then carried to Latin America when the affricates /ts/ and /dz/ merged with the fricatives, so that only /s/ and /ʃ/ remained. In both regions deaffrication and devoicing reduced the number of sibilants.
- A sound change takes place during a certain time period, but during this time different variants may be in competition.

Activities

Activity 9-1

In each of the Latin words below, first put parentheses around the vowel that is subject to syncope and underline the voiceless consonant that will no longer be intervocalic if syncope occurs. Then say whether the Spanish reflex shows evidence of voicing before syncope (VS) or syncope before voicing (SV), so that voicing does not occur. Explain your reasoning.

Example: EPĪSC(Ŏ)PUM > *obispo*. This shows evidence of SV because the /p/ that was intervocalic in Latin is not voiced in Spanish *obispo*. If syncope of the medial ŏ occurred before the /p/ voiced, then it formed part of a medial consonant group /skp/, which reduced to /sp/ without voicing of the /p/.

1. PŌLYPUM > *pulpo*
2. CAPITĀLEM > *caudal*
3. REPUTĀRE > *rebtar* > *retar*
4. *SIFILĀRE > *chiflar*
5. *MALIFAT(I)UM > *malvado*

6. ᴇxᴄᴀʟᴇꜰᴀᴄĕʀᴇ > *escalfar*

7. *ᴄᴏɴꜱᴜᴛūʀᴀᴍ > *costura*

8. *ɴᴀᴛĭᴄᴀ > *nalga*

9. ᴛʀīᴛĭᴄᴜᴍ > *trigo*

10. ᴘŏꜱĭᴛᴜᴍ > *puesto*

11. ᴄŏᴍĭᴛᴇᴍ > *conde*

12. ᴄᴏᴍᴘŭᴛāʀᴇ > *contar*

13. ʙᴏɴɪᴛāᴛᴇᴍ > *bondad*

14. ᴠᴇɴᴅĭᴛᴀ > *venta*

15. ꜱᴏʟūᴛᴜ > *suelto*

16. ʜᴜᴍɪʟɪᴛāᴛᴇᴍ > *humildad*

17. ᴍᴀꜱᴛɪᴄāʀᴇ > *mascar*

18. *ꜰɪxɪᴄāʀᴇ > *fisgar*

19. ᴘūʟĭᴄᴇᴍ > *pulga*

20. *ᴀʟɪᴄūɴᴜᴍ > *alguno*

Bonus: Which words show the same consonant group that ended up with two different results in Spanish?

Activity 9-2

Examine the sets of Latin and Spanish words below and explain why the Latin /f/ was maintained in the words in the left-hand column, yet lost in the words in the right-hand column. We provide the Latin origin of the word, but you will need to consult an etymological dictionary, such as the ones mentioned in Activity 17-3, to determine whether the /f/ is the result of:

a1. Regular sound change in word-initial position, where /f/ could be maintained or lost.

a2. Regular sound change in word-medial position, where /f/ could be maintained or lost, but was more likely to be maintained after a preposition.

b. Borrowing from another language where /f/ was maintained.

c. Learnèd borrowing from Latin.

Bonus: What is the similarity in meaning between the words with *f-* and the words with *h-*? For example, *confundir* could have arrived at the meaning 'to confuse' because 'melting with' leads to a loss of the identity of the elements mixed together and therefore to their confusion.

1. *fundir* 'to melt' (< FŪNDĔRE), *confundir* 'to confuse' (< CONFŪNDĔRE)	*hundir* 'to sink' (< FŪNDĔRE)
2. *aferrar* 'to anchor' (< AD + FERRUM)	*hierro* 'iron' (< FERRUM)
3. *infarto* 'heart attack' (< INFARTUM)	*harto* 'tired, fed up' (< FARTUM)
4. *fecha* 'date' (< FACTUM)	*hecho* 'done, made' (< FACTUM)
5. *fábula* 'fable' (< FABULAM)	*habla* 'faculty of (or variety of) speech' (< FABULAM)
6. *femenino* 'feminine' (<FEMININUM)	*hembra* 'a female' (< FEMINAM)
7. *fila* 'line, queue' (< FILAM, pl. of FILUM)	*hilo* 'thread' (< FILUM), *sobrehilar* 'whipstitch'
8. *folio* 'sheet of paper' (< FOLIUM), *folleto* 'leaflet'	*hoja* 'leaf' (< FOLIA, pl. of FOLIUM), *hojear* 'to leaf through'

Activity 9-3

Corpus Search

Do a word search in the CORDE for the forms *fablar, ffablar,* and *hablar* used from the twelfth to the seventeenth century. Be sure to use asterisks (*) as shown below in order to get as many tokens as possible. Fill out the table for the number of uses for each form in each century. When you finish, answer the following questions.

Form	12th c.	13th c.	14th c.	15th c.	16th c.	17th c.
*fabl**						
*ffabl**						
*habl**						

1. Until which century is the form *fablar* the most common? What happens after that?
2. When does the form *hablar* start to appear? What do you think is happening during this century?

3. What happens to *hablar* in the following century? Does its use increase or decrease? What accounts for this?

4. During which centuries do we see the use of *ffablar*? How was this word pronounced? Do you think the scribes that used this form were successful in making it a standard for that time? Why or why not?

Activity 9-4

Study Figure 9.2 on the development of sibilants in the history of Spanish. Write four statements to describe the overall tendencies you observe. Make sure that at least one of these focuses on the different results for Castilian Spanish and for Andalusian and Latin American Spanish.

Example: /ts/ and /dz/ merged with /s/ and /z/ in Andalusian/American Spanish, but they were kept distinct as /s̺/ and /s/ in northern Spain.

Further Reading

Bradley, Travis G., and Ann Marie Delforge 2006. "Systemic contrast and the diachrony of Spanish sibilant voicing," in Randall Gess and Deborah Arteaga (eds.), *Historical Romance linguistics: Retrospective and perspectives*, 19–52. Amsterdam: John Benjamins

Harris-Northall, Ray 1990. "The spread of sound change: Another look at syncope in Spanish," *Romance Philology* 44: 137–61

Malkiel, Yakov 1993. "The problem of 'the Old Spanish sibilants': Three consecutive new-style explanations," *Bulletin of Hispanic Studies* 70(2): 201–11

10 Why Do Spanish Speakers Sometimes Say *andé* Instead of *anduve*?

Morphological Changes

Lead-in Questions

10-1 Have you noticed that English speakers sometimes say *the data are important* while others say *the data is important*? What is the difference in these two sentences and why do speakers prefer one over the other?

10-2 Conjugate the verb *to shine: Today I shine, Yesterday I _____, I have _____*. Now do the same with *to show, to slay,* and *to weave*. For each verb say whether you used regular forms, like *Today I play, Yesterday I played, I have played*, or irregular forms, like *Today I begin, Yesterday I began, I have begun*.

This chapter begins with an overview of the grammatical categories and functions in use in Spanish today and the forms used to express them. This is followed by a look at the processes that have led to changes in these functions and forms. You will learn how speakers create new forms from existing elements and also how they reshape existing forms through analogy.

10.1 What Are Morphemes and Paradigms?

We have seen in Chapters 6–9 on phonological changes how speakers change their language by changing their pronunciation of certain sounds. In this chapter and the next four, Chapters 10–14, we will consider morphological changes in the history of Spanish, the ways in which speakers change the forms they use. The key to understanding morphology is first to realize that the forms in Spanish, like those of other languages, are organized into patterns or **paradigms** (*los paradigmas*). The next step is to learn to analyze these patterns. Therefore, the best way to understand morphology is to become a "pattern-seeking device" that learns to detect and analyze patterns in the forms in Spanish that express grammatical functions.

One paradigm that you are no doubt familiar with is a verb conjugation, such as the conjugation of the present indicative of the verbs *dormir* and *cantar*:

1sg. *duermo*	*canto*
2sg. *duermes*	*cantas*
3sg. *duerme*	*canta*
1pl. *dormimos*	*cantamos*
2pl. *dormís*	*cantáis*
3pl. *duermen*	*cantan*

When we compare these two paradigms, we can see that certain forms are associated with certain functions. It is easy to see that the stem of the verb, *duerm-* or *dorm-* for *dormir* and *cant-* for *cantar*, indicates the meaning of the verb, its lexical content, whether 'sleep' or 'sing,' and that the verb endings indicate grammatical person, such as the first person singular *-o* of *duermo* and *canto*.

Another example of a familiar paradigm is the different forms of an adjective like *bueno*:

m. sg.	*bueno*
f. sg.	*buena*
m. pl.	*buenos*
f. pl.	*buenas*

In this example the stem once again indicates the lexical content, so that *buen-* means 'good.' But the endings in an adjective, rather than indicating person, indicate gender, whether *-o* for masculine or *-a* for feminine, and number, whether singular with no ending or plural with an *-s*.

We can make another important observation based on these examples. What we call a form is not necessarily a word. Verb endings, even though they are not words, express meaning by indicating the person of the verb form. Adjective endings, like *-o* and *-a* and *-s* are not words, but they indicate masculine or feminine gender and singular or plural number. These minimal units of meaning are called **morphemes** (*los morfemas*) and they are the building blocks of all the forms in a language. The focus of the chapters on morphology will be to see how morphemes and their functions change over time.

Complete Activity 10-1 on page 209.

In the chapters on morphology we will be concerned with **inflectional morphology** (*la morfología flexiva*) rather than **derivational morphology** (*la morfología derivativa*). Derivational morphology, the process by which new words are created by adding prefixes and suffixes to roots, will be considered briefly in Section 17.2 on lexical creation. This includes the derivation from a base like *habitar* of words like *inhabitable, habitanza, habitante, habitador*, and *habitadora*. Inflectional morphology, on the other hand, studies paradigms, such as those presented above for verb and adjective endings, which are also known as **inflections** (*las flexiones*). In Spanish, these sets of forms indicate number and gender in adjectives, and many other nominal elements, and person, tense, and mood in the verb. The paradigms considered so far also show that it is useful to group forms into nominal elements, verbal elements, and other elements, since each type of element is inflected for different grammatical categories.

10.1.1 What Are the Nominal Elements of Spanish?

Most nominal elements, like the adjective *bueno*, are inflected for gender and number. One type of nominal element, personal pronouns, is also inflected for person, such as first person singular *yo* and *me* and second person singular *tú* and *te*. Nominal elements, whose development is the focus of Chapters 11 and 12, include nouns and the elements that occur along with them in a noun phrase, such as articles and adjectives, and the pronouns that serve in place of nouns. In order to make a comprehensive list of nominal elements we can begin with a noun and add elements before and after it, as long as they are not verbs. If we begin with the noun *amigos*, for example, we can add various elements in front of it, like *los amigos, unos amigos, estos amigos, mis amigos*, and *dos amigos*. These elements, known as **determiners** *(los determinantes)*, serve to further specify the noun referred to. We can also add adjectives before or after the noun to describe it, like *los buenos amigos* and *unos amigos simpáticos*. By doing this we are creating **noun phrases** *(los sintagmas nominales)*, parts of sentences that consist of a noun and other nominal elements. Rather than adding elements, like articles and adjectives, to nouns to form noun phrases, we can also replace nouns with pronouns. In a sentence like *mis amigos hablan español*, where *mis amigos* is the subject, we can replace this noun phrase with the subject pronoun, *ellos*, as in *ellos hablan español*, or with a demonstrative pronoun, *éstos*, a possessive pronoun, *los míos*, or an indefinite pronoun like *algunos* or *ningunos*. Some categories of forms, such as **possessives** *(los posesivos)* and **demonstratives** *(los demostrativos)*, have either a determiner/adjective form or a pronoun form. The way to determine whether an element is a determiner/adjective or a pronoun is whether it is used with or without a noun. For example, *mis* in *mis amigos son simpáticos* is a possessive adjective because it modifies the noun *amigos*. We can easily determine that *mis* cannot replace *mis amigos* because the sentence **mis son simpáticos* is not grammatical in Spanish. By contrast, *los míos* in *los míos son simpáticos* is a possessive pronoun because it stands in for *mis amigos*. Table 10.1 offers an overview of most of the nominal elements in Spanish, with adjectives and articles in the first column and pronouns in the second column.

Complete Activity 10-2 on page 211.

TABLE 10.1 Nominal elements in Spanish

Adjectives and articles	Pronouns
Definite articles: *el, la, los, las*	Definite relative pronouns: *él, la, los, las (que)*
Indefinite articles: *un, una, unos, unas*	Indefinite pronouns: *uno, una, unos, unas*
Demonstrative adjectives:	Demonstrative pronouns (can be written with or without the accent mark):
este, esta, estos, estas	*éste, ésta, esto, éstos, éstas*
ese, esa, esos, esas	*ése, ésa, eso, ésos, ésas*
aquel, aquella, aquellos, aquellas	*aquél, aquélla, aquello, aquéllos, aquéllas*
Possessive adjectives:	Possessive pronouns:
mi, mis	*mío, mía, míos, mías*
tu, tus	*tuyo, tuya, tuyos, tuyas*
su, sus	*suyo, suya, suyos, suyas*
nuestro, nuestra, nuestros, nuestras	*nuestro, nuestra, nuestros, nuestras*
vuestro, vuestra, vuestros, vuestras	*vuestro, vuestra, vuestros, vuestras*
su, sus	*suyo, suya, suyos, suyas*
Negative adjectives:	Negative pronouns:
ningún, ninguna, ningunos, ningunas	*ninguno, ninguna, ningunos, ningunas*
nulo, nula, nulos, nulas	*nada, nadie*
Indefinite adjectives:	Indefinite pronouns:
algún, alguna, algunos, algunas	*alguno, alguna, algunos, algunas*
	algo, alguien
Interrogative adjectives:	Interrogative pronouns:
cuál, cuáles	*cuál, cuáles*
	other interrogative pronouns: *qué, quién, quiénes*
Relative adjectives:	Relative pronouns:
cuyo, cuya, cuyos, cuyas	*que, quien, quienes*
Cardinal numbers: *dos, tres, cuatro*, etc.	Cardinal pronouns: *los dos, las dos, los tres, las tres, los cuatro, las cuatro*, etc.

TABLE 10.1 (cont.)

Adjectives and articles	Pronouns
Adjective quantifiers:	Pronoun quantifiers:
cada	*cada uno, cada una*
cualquier	*cualquiera*
todo, toda, todos, todas	*todos, todas*
mucho, mucha, muchos, muchas	*muchos, muchas*
poco, poca, pocos, pocas	*pocos, pocas*
tanto, tanta, tantos, tantas	*tantos, tantas*
demasiado, demasiada, demasiados, demasiadas	*demasiados, demasiadas*
bastante, bastantes	*bastantes*
cuánto, cuánta, cuántos, cuántas	*cuánto, cuánta, cuántos, cuántas*
Qualifying adjectives	Qualifying adjectives used as pronouns: *los buenos, los simpáticos, los alegres*, etc.
bueno, simpático, alegre, etc.	

10.1.2 What Are the Verbal Elements of Spanish?

Verbs, whose development is the topic of Chapters 13–14, are made up of stems followed by endings for different persons and tenses. As shown above, the verb *dormir* has the stems *duerm-* and *dorm-* in the present indicative. It also has the stems *dorm-* and *durm-* in the preterit, as in 1sg. *dormí* and 3sg. *durmió*. The fourteen different tenses in Spanish, illustrated by the verb *cantar* in Table 10.2, include the seven simple tenses of present, imperfect, preterit, future, conditional in the indicative, and present and imperfect in the subjunctive. There is also a series of seven compound tenses formed with the auxiliary *haber* plus the past participle, which include the present perfect, pluperfect, preterit perfect, future perfect, past conditional in the indicative, and the perfect and pluperfect in the subjunctive.

In the chapters on morphology we will focus on the inflected nominal and verbal elements rather than on unflected elements, such as adverbs, prepositions, conjunctions, and interjections.

Complete Activity 10-3 on page 212.

TABLE 10.2 Verb conjugations in Spanish illustrated by *cantar*

Simple tenses: indicative	Compound tenses: indicative
Present	Present perfect
canto	*he cantado*
cantas	*has cantado*
canta	*ha cantado*
cantamos	*hemos cantado*
cantáis	*habéis cantado*
cantan	*han cantado*
Imperfect	Pluperfect
cantaba	*había cantado*
cantabas	*habías cantado*
cantaba	*había cantado*
cantábamos	*habíamos cantado*
cantabais	*habíais cantado*
cantaban	*habían cantado*
Preterit	Preterit perfect
canté	*hube cantado*
cantaste	*hubiste cantado*
cantó	*hubo cantado*
cantamos	*hubimos cantado*
cantasteis	*hubisteis cantado*
cantaron	*hubieron cantado*
Future	Future perfect
cantaré	*habré cantado*
cantarás	*habrás cantado*
cantará	*habrá cantado*
cantaremos	*habremos cantado*
cantaréis	*habréis cantado*
cantarán	*habrán cantado*

TABLE 10.2 (cont.)

Simple tenses: indicative	Compound tenses: indicative
Conditional	Past conditional
cantaría	*habría cantado*
cantarías	*habrías cantado*
cantaría	*habría cantado*
cantaríamos	*habríamos cantado*
cantaríais	*habríais cantado*
cantarían	*habrían cantado*

Simple tenses: subjunctive		Compound tenses: subjunctive	
Present		Past	
cante		*haya cantado*	
cantes		*hayas cantado*	
cante		*haya cantado*	
cantemos		*hayamos cantado*	
cantéis		*hayáis cantado*	
canten		*hayan cantado*	
Imperfect in *-ra*	Imperfect in *-se*	Pluperfect in *-ra*	Pluperfect in *-se*
cantara	*cantase*	*hubiera cantado*	*hubiese cantado*
cantaras	*cantases*	*hubieras cantado*	*hubieses cantado*
cantara	*cantase*	*hubiera cantado*	*hubiese cantado*
cantáramos	*cantásemos*	*hubiéramos cantado*	*hubiésemos cantado*
cantarais	*cantaseis*	*hubierais cantado*	*hubieseis cantado*
cantaran	*cantasen*	*hubieran cantado*	*hubiesen cantado*

10.2 Which Changes Take Place in the Function and Shape of Spanish Forms?

Turning our attention now to morphological changes, we will see that speakers sometimes change the function of these forms, or how they use them, and sometimes they change the shape of the forms themselves.

10.2.1 What Are the Possible Changes in Function?

We can identify five possible outcomes in Spanish for the functions of a Latin form. The simplest outcome is **retention** (*la conservación*), which means that a form keeps the same function. For example, the Latin adjective BONAM remains an adjective in Spanish as *buena* and the Latin present indicative 1sg. CANTŌ maintains this same function in Spanish *canto.*

Another simple outcome for a function is **loss** (*la pérdida*), which occurs when a function ceases to exist. We will see in Chapter 11 that this is the outcome of the case functions in Latin, since there are no longer any cases in Spanish. This is why you were able to learn Spanish without ever learning about the nominative and accusative cases.

A third outcome is that a form can change its function through **repurposing** (*la reutilización*). One curious example in the history of Spanish is the repurposing of the Latin pluperfect subjunctive (1sg. CANTĀVISSEM), as the Spanish imperfect subjunctive (1sg. *cantase*). Another example, perhaps easier to imagine, is when a past participle, like *tinto* from TINCTUM 'dyed,' the past participle of the verb TINGĒRE, becomes an adjective as in *vino tinto* 'red wine' or even a noun, as in *Me tomo tinto, pero poco.* This same type of change has occurred in English, where a past participle like *drunk* becomes an adjective, as in *drunk driving*, or a noun, as in *a drunk*. We take up this topic further in Chapter 14.

A fourth outcome for forms or combinations of forms is the **expansion** (*la expansión*) of their functions. For example, in Latin most adjectives expressed the comparative by adding an -IOR suffix, so that the comparative of the adjective FORTEM 'strong' was FORTIŌREM 'stronger.' Latin adjectives ending in -IUS, like DUBIUS 'doubtful,' formed their comparative by adding the adverb MAGIS 'more' before the adjective so that 'more doubtful' was expressed as MAGIS DUBIUS. So when MAGIS came to be used in Spoken Latin with adjectives that did not end in -IUS, as in MAGIS FORTEM, which led to *más fuerte* in Spanish, its functions expanded. Similar options for the comparative exist in English today, a topic we explore further in Chapter 12.

The fifth outcome, and no doubt the most interesting, is **innovation** (*la innovación*) whereby speakers create a new form from the resources already available in their language. For example, speakers of Latin created a new future form by combining the infinitive with the present tense of the verb HABĒRE 'to have,' as in CANTĀRE HABEŌ, literally 'to sing I have,' which becomes Spanish *cantaré*. A second more recent innovation occurred when Spanish speakers created a new future form from the verb 'to go' plus the infinitive, as in *voy a cantar*. English speakers have created a similar construction, *I'm going to sing*, which exists alongside *I will sing* or *I'll sing*.

Most of the new constructions resulting from innovation, as well as expansion, are **analytical constructions** (*construcciones analíticas*), which means that their morphemes are separable and analyzable (Pulgram 1988). For example, the morphemes of *voy a cantar* are separable because one can say *voy inmediatamente a cantar*, but the morphemes of *cantaré* are not, since one cannot say **cantar- inmediatamente -é*. The future *cantaré*, with inseparable morphemes, is called a **synthetic construction** (*una construcción sintética*). The morphemes of *voy a cantar* are also analyzable because a native speaker can easily identify them as *voy a* plus the infinitive.

By contrast, most Spanish speakers cannot identify the parts of *cantaré*. They might know that this construction consists of the infinitive plus endings, but it is unlikely that they would know that these endings come from the verb HABĒRE. Another way to express the difference between analytical and synthetic constructions is to say that synthetic constructions contain **bound morphemes** (*morfemas ligados*) that cannot exist independently. For example, the -*é* of *cantaré* is a bound morpheme, whereas *voy* of *voy a cantar* is a **free morpheme** (*un morfema libre*) that can exist on its own. Thus, we will see that many of the new constructions created in the history of Spanish offer evidence of an **analytical tendency** (*la tendencia analítica*). The new forms are analytical constructions with separable and analyzable morphemes that compete with and may eventually replace the synthetic constructions with inseparable unanalyzable morphemes. Speakers may be motivated by a desire for clarity and regularity in creating these new constructions.

Complete Activity 10-4 on page 212.

10.2.2 What Are the Possible Changes in Form?

In addition to changes in functions, we will be concerned with changes to the forms themselves. The starting point for changes to forms, known as morphological changes, is the sound changes that affect all words. In some cases, these regular sound changes led to the same forms, so that the present indicative forms of *cantar* all have the same stem, as in 1sg. CANTŌ > *canto* and 1pl. CANTĀMUS > *cantamos*. Yet sometimes regular sound changes led to different forms. The different stems of 1sg. *duermo* and 1pl. *dormimos* result from the different place of the stress on these words in Latin. As we saw in Chapter 6, the stress in 1sg. DŎRMŌ falls on the stem DŎRM-, which means that the short tonic /o/ diphthongizes to [we]. In 1pl. DŎRMĪMUS, by contrast, the stress falls on the /i/ in the ending, which means that the short /o/ in the first syllable is in unstressed initial position and so remains [o]. Different forms for a single morpheme, like the stems *dorm-* and *duerm-* in the present tense of *dormir*, are called **allomorphs** (*los alomorfos*). The use of different stems is called **allomorphy** (*la alomorfía*), so we can talk about the allomorphy of the conjugation of *dormir*, which is another way of saying that it is irregular. Activity 10-1 offered two other examples of allomorphs. The stem *durm-* is another allomorph of *dormir* used in the 3sg. and 3pl. preterit. You also saw that the verb *andar* shows allomorphy with the stem *and-* in the present indicative and the stem *anduv-* in the preterit.

After undergoing regular sound changes, which may lead to regular or irregular forms, some forms then change by **analogy** (*la analogía*) when speakers reshape them based on the model of other forms. You may have created verb forms based on analogy yourself if you wrote in the answer to Lead-in question 10-2 *Yesterday I shined* and *I have shined*, instead of the inherited forms *Yesterday I shone* and *I have shone*. Rather than using the forms that result from regular sound change, speakers recreate forms based on the model of a regular verb, like *to fine: yesterday I fined him a dollar, I have fined him a dollar.* This type of analogy can be called **proportional analogy** (*la analogía proporcional*), since it can be represented as a four-part proportion, as described by Rini (1999a: 12): *fine/fined : shine/X = shined*. This means that the simple past *fined* is to the infinitive form *fine* as the analogical *shined* is to *shine*. In this way, the form *shined*, indicated by X in the proportion, is created following the model of *fined.* It then exists in English alongside the form *shone*, which developed through regular sound change.

Analogy is especially likely to occur if speakers do not use a verb often enough to be familiar with its irregular forms. This means that speakers may be even more likely to regularize the forms of *to slay* than the forms of *to shine*. So perhaps you wrote yest*erday I slayed* and *I have slayed* rather than the irregular forms *yesterday I slew* and *I have slain*. It is also interesting to note that figurative uses of language tend to be analogical. For example, someone might say "Saint George slew the dragon," but he would say that a funny story "just slayed me" instead of saying "it just slew me."

An example of proportional analogy in Spanish is the reflexes of 1sg. MŌSTRŌ. This word would have become Spanish *mostro* through regular sound changes, since the tonic ō in this word would have remained [o] in Spanish, unlike the ŏ in DŎRMŌ, which diphthongized in *duermo*. Thus, the Spanish form *muestro* is not the result of regular sound change, but rather the result of analogy to a verb like *duermo*, according to this analogical proportion: *dormir/duermo : mostrar/X = muestro*. Note that the forms of MŌSTRĀRE that undergo analogy are the ones where the stress falls on the stem, namely *muestro, muestras, muestra*, and *muestran*. The reflexes of MŌSTRĀMUS and MŌSTRĀTIS do not undergo analogy and end up as *mostramos* and *mostráis* through regular sound change. This is because their counterparts DŎRMĪMUS and DŎRMĪTIS do not develop a diphthong because ŏ is in initial position in these forms rather than tonic position and so does not diphthongize. Thus, the reflexes through regular sound change are *dormimos* and *dormís*.

An example of proportional analogy is the recent creation of new feminine forms for many professions. Even though the *Diccionario de la Real Academia* (*DRAE*) does not include *química* as the term for a female chemist, speakers have created this term using an analogical proportion such as *amigo/amiga : químico/X = química* (Epperson and Ranson 2010). Clearly other pairs of words could serve as models as well, such as *hermano/hermana* and *americano/americana*.

Another type of analogy is **leveling** (*la nivelación*) whereby speakers remodel a form based on other forms in the same paradigm. We saw an example of leveling in Section 3.1 in the paradigm of the verb *llevar*, where speakers extended the stem *llev-* throughout the paradigm. Through regular sound change the stem *llev-* would have occurred only in stems that bore the stress, known therefore as **strong stems** (*los radicales fuertes*). This is because the initial consonant results from initial /l/ in contact with the yod that results from the diphthongization of Latin Ĕ, for example, LĔVŌ ['lɛ-wo] > ['ljeβo] > *llevo* [ʎeβo]. There would have been no diphthongization and therefore no *ll-* [ʎ] through regular sound change in the **weak stems** (*los radicales débiles*) that did not bear the stress. For example, 1pl. LĔVĀMUS and 2pl. LĔVĀTIS would have become *levamos* and *leváis*, but speakers changed their stem to *llev-* through leveling, so that it is the same for all persons in the paradigm.

Another type of analogy is **reanalysis** (*el reanálisis*), whereby a form undergoes regular sound changes but then is reanalyzed or reinterpreted as having a different grammatical category. A simple example from English occurs when *data*, which was originally plural, as it was in Latin, becomes a singular noun (Rini 1999a: 26). One hears some English speakers say *the data are important* while others say *the data is important*. The same change has occurred with the word *media*, also of Latin origin, which was originally the plural of *medium*. An example from Spanish is the reanalysis of OPĔRA 'works,' the plural of the neuter noun OPUS, which changes to *obra* through regular sound change. Later speakers reinterpret it to be a feminine singular rather than a neuter plural noun. This reanalysis is no doubt due to the similarity between the /a/ ending in OPĔRA and the /a/ ending in many feminine singular nouns like PORTA, which becomes Spanish *puerta*. Once reanalysis takes place, then speakers create a new plural for *obra* using proportional analogy: *puerta/puertas : obra/X = obras*. Speakers determine that the plural of a feminine singular noun *obra* will be *obras* because the plural of *puerta* is *puertas*. Therefore, we can say that the new plural form *obras* is created first through the reanalysis of *obra* and then through proportional analogy of *obra* with other feminine nouns.

Box 10.1 What is backformation (*la derivación regresiva*)?

Backformation is a special type of reanalysis. It involves the reinterpretation of a form, just like reanalysis, but then the change resulting from proportional analogy involves the removal of a morpheme, usually a suffix. A simple example from English is the word *cherry*. This word was borrowed from French *cherise* 'cherry,' an earlier form of Modern French *cerise*. Because the singular form originally adopted into English ended in /z/, this form was then reanalyzed as a plural. If *cherise* is a plural, then the singular would be *cherry* based on a proportional analogy like: *apple/apples* : X = *cherry/cherise* (now *cherries*) (Rini 1999a: 25). An example of backformation from Spanish is the reanalysis of the neuter singular noun TEMPUS as a plural. By regular sound change it became *tiempos* which speakers reanalyzed as a plural because of its final /s/. A new singular was then created through an analogical proportion like: *amigo/amigos* : X = *tiempo/tiempos*. We see then that *tiempo* results through backformation from *tiempos*.

The importance of paradigms in morphological change is especially apparent in analogy, as speakers change the form of a word so that it follows the pattern of another word. You will see that analogy is rather chaotic, especially by comparison to sound change, because the associations speakers make between patterns are unpredictable. The result of many cases of analogy, though, is greater regularity in the resulting forms, which may also lead to fewer forms and patterns for speakers to remember.

Complete Activity 10-5 on page 213.

10.3 Chapter Summary

- Forms are made up of minimal units of meaning called morphemes, which are organized into patterns called paradigms or inflections.
- Inflections can indicate grammatical categories, like gender and number in nominal elements, or person, tense, and mood in the verb.
  - Nominal elements are elements that may be inflected for gender and number in Spanish. They include determiners, like definite articles and possessive adjectives, as well as qualifying adjectives, like *bueno*, that

describe the noun, the nouns themselves, and pronouns that stand in place of nouns.

○ Verbal elements include verb forms that are inflected for person, tense, and mood.

- The functions of forms can have one of five outcomes in the change from Latin to Spanish: conservation, loss, repurposing, expansion, and innovation.
- Expansion and innovation often increase the number of analytical constructions in Spanish, like *voy a cantar* instead of *cantaré*.
- The forms themselves change through regular sound change and sometimes later by analogy, a process where speakers change a form based on the model of another form.
- The types of analogy important in the history of Spanish include proportional analogy, leveling, and reanalysis, and a special type of reanalysis called backformation.

Activities

Activity 10-1

Let us study some more examples of paradigms in Spanish.

TABLE 10.3 Preterit conjugation for *cantar, mover, dormir,* and *andar*

Infinitive	cantar	mover	dormir	andar
1sg.	canté	moví	dormí	anduve
2sg.	cantaste	moviste	dormiste	anduviste
3sg.	cantó	movió	durmió	anduvo
1pl.	cantamos	movimos	dormimos	anduvimos
2pl.	cantasteis	movisteis	dormisteis	anduvisteis
3pl.	cantaron	movieron	durmieron	anduvieron

A. Answer the following questions by studying the forms of the preterit for regular -*ar* and -*er* verbs, one slightly irregular -*ir* verb, and one even more irregular -*ar* verb in Table 10.3.

   1. a. What is the preterit stem for each verb?

      b. Which verb has more than one stem?

   2. Draw a vertical line after the stem of each verb so that you can focus on the endings. Now state how the endings are similar and different for each person. The answers for 1sg. and 2sg. below serve as an example.

      1sg.: There is a single vowel for each conjugation, but the vowel is different: stressed /e/ in -*ar* verbs, stressed /i/ in -*er* and -*ir* verbs, and unstressed /e/ in *anduve*.

      2sg.: All the endings end in -*ste*, but the stressed vowels are different: stressed /a/ in -*ar* verbs and /i/ in the other three verbs.

      3sg.

      1pl.

      2pl.

      3pl.

   3. Does the stress fall on the stem or on the ending for these verb forms? Which are the only forms where the stress falls on the stem?

   4. Having detected the patterns above, summarize what is irregular about the preterit of *andar*, in other words, how is its conjugation different from the patterns for the regular verbs?

B. Answer the following questions by studying the forms of the Spanish third person personal pronouns in Table 10.4.

TABLE 10.4 Third person personal pronouns in Spanish

	Subject	Direct object	Indirect object
m. sg.	*él*	*lo*	*le*
f. sg.	*ella*	*la*	*le*
m. pl.	*ellos*	*los*	*les*
f. pl.	*ellas*	*las*	*les*

1. Gender:
   a. How is gender, the difference between masculine and feminine, indicated in the direct object forms?
   b. Which other forms indicate gender in the same way?
   c. Which forms do not indicate gender?
   d. Which forms indicate gender in a different way?
2. Number:
   a. How is number, the difference between singular and plural, indicated in all the forms?
   b. Which form is the only one not to indicate number in this way?
3. Grammatical function:
   a. How are the subject forms different from the direct object forms for f. sg., m. pl., and f. pl.?
   b. How are the direct object forms different from the indirect object forms?
   c. Summarize the ways in which the m. sg. subject form *él* is different from the other forms. What would its form be if it followed the same patterns for gender and number as the other forms?

Activity 10-2

Refer to the nominal elements in Table 10.1 for the following questions.

1. Write three sentences with a noun and its accompanying adjectives and then replace this noun phrase with a pronoun. Since you can write about anything you want, choose examples that are meaningful to you. Example: with a possessive adjective: *Nuestros colegas siempre nos ayudan*; with a pronoun: *Los nuestros siempre nos ayudan* or *Ellos siempre nos ayudan*.
2. Which pronouns do not have corresponding adjectives? Why do you think that is?
3. List three types of elements from the adjectives column that are inflected for gender. Which elements in the table are not inflected for gender? Indicate this by circling them.
4. Make up three noun phrases using the elements in the table. For one noun phrase, try to use as many elements as possible just because it's fun to challenge yourself. Here are some examples to get you started:

Muchos buenos ejemplos fascinantes
cada una de estas bonitas historias
tales grandes peras deliciosas

Activity 10-3

Refer to the conjugations for *cantar* in Table 10.2 for the following questions.

1. Which of these tenses do you use on a regular basis when you speak Spanish? Write a check mark (✓) next to these. Which ones do you use rarely? Mark these with a minus sign (–). Are there any that you have never used? Mark these with an X.

2. Write in the blank space next to the Spanish forms in each cell of the table the 1sg. form of what you consider to be the equivalent in English of the different tenses in Spanish. For example, next to the present tense *canto*, you would write *I sing*. Keep in mind that by equivalent we mean that the forms are similar and not necessarily that the tenses are used in exactly the same way in both languages. If a tense does not have an equivalent in English, write NE in the table for "no equivalent." If it has more than one equivalent, write two verbs in English.

3. What is the relationship in the time of the event expressed by the simple tenses and the corresponding compound tense? In other words, what is the time relationship between *canto* and *he cantado* and between *cantaré* and *habré cantado*?

4. In Activity 10-1 you considered the personal endings for the preterit. Look now at the personal endings for the other simple tenses in order to answer the following questions.

   a. 1sg. and 3sg. always end in a vowel. In which tenses do 1sg. and 3sg. have the same form? List them here:

   b. 2sg. always ends in /s/, except in which tense?

   c. What do all the 1pl. endings have in common?
      And the 2pl. endings?
      And the 3pl. endings?

Activity 10-4

A. Decide whether each of the following underlined constructions in English and Spanish is synthetic or analytical by writing S or A before the construction. Recall that a synthetic construction is one with inseparable morphemes, like *finished*, whereas an analytical construction is one with separable morphemes, like *have finished*. Show that an analytical construction is separable by placing an element between its parts and identifying these. Divide a synthetic construction into its morphemes and show that it is impossible to place anything in between these morphemes by marking this construction with an asterisk. The answers have been provided for the English example 1 to serve as a model. Examples from English:

1.a. __S__ I finished the homework. finish/ed *finish- already -ed
1.b. __A__ I have finished the homework. have already finished
1.c. __A__ I have the homework finished. *the homework* separates *have finished* so it is clearly analytical, but it would sound odd to put *already* in there: *I have already the homework finished.
2.a. ____ the tail of a dog
2.b. ____ a dog's tail
3.a ____ a clearer idea
3.b. ____ a more clear idea

Examples from Spanish (and one from Latin):

4.a. ____ Terminé la tarea.
4.b. ____ He terminado la tarea.
4.c. ____ Tengo la tarea terminada.
5.a. ____ FĪLIAE 'of the girl' (genitive case)
5.b. ____ de la hija
6.a. ____ una peor idea
6.b. ____ una idea más mala

B. Pick a pair of synthetic/analytical expressions in English or Spanish that you use yourself. Does the meaning of the analytical construction seem clearer to you than the meaning for the synthetic construction? Explain your reasoning.

Activity 10-5
Here are some additional examples of proportional analogy (A), leveling (L), and reanalysis (R). The type of analogy is already indicated, so your job is to

explain the classification of each example in your own words. Write out the analogical proportion for examples of proportional analogy.

1. A PĒNSŌ 'I weigh' would become *penso* (or *peso*, if the /n/ is lost) in Spanish by regular sound change. Instead it becomes *pienso* on the model of a verb like PĔRDŌ 'I lose' which becomes *pierdo* with the diphthongization of the short /e/.

2.a R The neuter singular noun CŎRPUS 'body' would become *cuerpos* through regular sound change. This is reinterpreted by speakers as a masculine plural noun.

2.b. A The neuter plural noun CŎRPŎRA 'bodies' would become something like *cuérpra* through regular sound change. Instead speakers create a new plural *cuerpos* on the model of masculine nouns like *amigo/amigos*.

3.a. R The neuter plural noun FĒSTA 'feast days, holidays' becomes *fiesta* through regular sound change which speakers perceive to be a feminine singular noun.

3.b. A After FĒSTA changes to *fiesta*, speakers create a new plural *fiestas* on the model of *puerta/puertas*.

4. L The present indicative 1sg. APĔRIŌ 'I open' would become *abero* through regular sound change (assuming the yod raises the tonic vowel Ĕ and prevents its diphthongization). Speakers change this form to *abro* instead, so that it has the same stem as *abres* from APĔRIS and *abre* from APĔRIT, which is also the stem for all the other persons in the paradigm.

Further Reading

"Grammar of words: Morphemes and allomorphs," NativLang. YouTube video

Bybee, Joan, Revere Perkins, and William Pagliuca 1994. *The evolution of grammar: Tense, aspect, and modality in the languages of the world.* University of Chicago Press. Chapter 1

Bustos Gisbert, Eugenio 1998. "Modelos morfológicos y cambio morfológico," *Revista de Filología Románica* 15: 35–49

Rini, Joel 1999a. *Exploring the role of morphology in the evolution of Spanish.* Amsterdam and Philadelphia: John Benjamins. Chapter 1

11 Why Is *mano* Feminine and *día* Masculine?

Changes in Case, Declension, Number, and Gender

Lead-in Questions

11-1 A noun like *student* in English or *estudiante* in Spanish can have many different functions in a sentence, for example, it can be a subject, a direct object, an indirect object, the object of a preposition, a possessive, as in *the student's book*, or it can be used in direct address, as in *Students, have you heard this joke?* Write down as many sentences as you need in English and Spanish to show *student* or *estudiante* in all these functions.

11-2 What terms do you use in English for males and females who perform the following professions: those who serve food, those who act in films, those who deliver the mail, and those who put out fires? What terms do you use in Spanish for a woman who is a chemist (*químico*), a doctor (*médico*), a pilot (*piloto*), a judge (*juez*), or a boss (*jefe*)? What conclusions can you draw about the ways that English and Spanish speakers refer to professional men and women?

In this chapter, you will continue analyzing patterns and paradigms in Spanish in order to get an overview of the major changes in the history of Spanish in nominal elements, namely nouns, articles, adjectives, and pronouns. An important paradigm in Latin are cases which were used to indicate the grammatical functions of nominal elements, whether they served as grammatical subjects, possessives, indirect objects, direct objects, or had other functions. These cases were organized into paradigms known as declensions. The story of cases and declensions shows how the typical singular–plural pattern arose in Spanish of singular without -s, as in amiga, *and plural with -s, as in* amigas. *Finally, we will explore the history of the gender of nouns in Spanish: those that show an -o/-a alternation in masculine and feminine, such as* el amigo *and* la amiga, *those that have the same ending for both genders, such as* el estudiante *and* la estudiante, *and those that show an alternation of -e or consonant for the masculine and -a for the feminine, such as* el infante/la infanta *and* el señor/la señora. *Finally, the loss of case distinctions and certain declensions or categories of nouns in Spanish explains why certain nouns, like* mano *and* día, *do not conform to the typical endings for masculine and feminine nouns.*

11.1 What Are the Changes in Nominal Elements from Latin to Spanish?

We learned in the previous chapter that speakers change the forms they use to express grammatical categories and functions. In this chapter, we will focus specifically on these changes in nominal elements by considering the changes in the Latin grammatical categories of case, number, and gender. Among these changes, the most radical one is the complete loss of cases and, along with them, declensions, the five categories of Latin nouns arranged according to their case endings. The loss of cases also led to a change in the way number is expressed in Spanish, making the relationship between singular and plural more regular. We will also see changes in the gender of nouns. The most important of these is the loss of the Latin neuter gender. This loss meant that neuter nouns from Latin were either lost completely or reanalyzed as masculine or feminine nouns. There are also some masculine and feminine words that have changed gender from Latin to Spanish and some nouns and adjectives that have come to mark gender that did not mark it before.

11.2 Why Does Latin Have Cases but Spanish Does Not?

11.2.1 What Are Latin Cases and What Do They Do?

In order to appreciate the consequences of the loss of Latin cases, you need first to understand what cases are and how they function. Cases (*los casos*) in Latin were used to indicate the grammatical function of nominal elements, such as the nouns, articles, pronouns, and adjectives presented in Chapter 10, Section 10.1.1. Cases were expressed by endings, as shown in Table 11.1 for the singular forms of the nouns AMICA 'female friend,' AMICUS 'male friend,' and CANIS 'dog.'

The different forms of AMICA serve to illustrate the six Latin cases. The case illustrated is underlined in the Latin sentence and the translation in Spanish shows how Modern Spanish expresses the grammatical functions previously expressed by cases.

Nominative: AMICA VIDET AMICUM. *La amiga ve al amigo.* 'The (female) friend sees the (male) friend.' The nominative case, AMICA, is used for the grammatical subject of the sentence, the person performing the action.

TABLE 11.1 Latin cases in the first, second, and third declension singular and their functions

Case	1st declension singular	2nd declension singular	3rd declension singular	Function
nominative	AMICA	AMICUS	CANIS	subject
genitive	AMICAE	AMICĪ	CANIS	possessor
dative	AMICAE	AMICŌ	CANĪ	indirect object
accusative	AMICAM	AMICUM	CANEM	direct object, also used after certain prepositions
ablative	AMICĀ	AMICŌ	CANE	means, also used after certain prepositions
vocative	AMICA	AMICE	CANIS	direct address

Genitive: Amicus videt canem amicae. *El amigo ve el perro de la amiga.* 'The (male) friend sees the (female) friend's dog.' The genitive case, amicae, is used to indicate the possessor of an object.

Dative: Amicus dat canem amicae. *El amigo da el perro a la amiga.* 'The (male) friend gives the dog to the (female) friend.' The dative case, amicae, which has the same form as the genitive case for this noun, is used to indicate the indirect object of the verb, the person to whom or for whom something is done. The best way to understand the function of an indirect object is to contrast it with the function of a direct object. The direct object answers the question *what?* What does the friend give? canem, 'the dog,' so canem is the direct object in the sentence above. The indirect object answers the question *to whom?* To whom does the friend give the dog? amicae, 'to the friend,' so amicae is the indirect object.

Accusative: Amicus videt amicam. *El amigo ve a la amiga.* 'The (male) friend sees the (female) friend.' In this sentence, amicam, in the accusative case, is the direct object of the verb. What (or whom) does the (male) friend see? amicam. The accusative is also used in Latin after certain prepositions, like ad as in vado ad Romam 'I am going to Rome.'

Ablative: Amicus cantat cum amicā. *El amigo canta con la amiga.* 'The (male) friend sings with the (female) friend.' The ablative, amicā, is used after certain prepositions, like cum 'with,' de 'from,' and ex 'out of, from.' The ablative can also be used without a preposition to express means or manner. For example, the ablative cultellō without a preceding preposition expresses the idea 'with a knife': amica pānem cultellō secat 'the (female) friend cuts the bread with a knife.'

Vocative: Amica, ubi est canem? *Amiga, ¿dónde está el perro?* '(female) Friend, where is the dog?' The vocative, amica, which for most nouns has the same form as the nominative, is used when speaking directly to someone. For example, Julius Caesar uses the vocative in his famous quotation Et tu, Brute? 'And you, Brutus?' when he asks whether his friend also betrayed him.

The cases of nominal elements that modify nouns, such as adjectives, are always the same as the case of the noun they modify. For example, if we describe amica in the previous sentences as bona 'good,' this adjective will be in the same case as amica. The sentence with amica in the genitive case would be Amicus

VIDET CANEM <u>BONAE AMICAE</u>. *El amigo ve el perro de la buena amiga.* This holds true for possessive adjectives as well. In order to say 'my friend,' for example, one would use the possessive adjective MEA in the same case as AMICA. The sentence in the vocative would be <u>BONA AMICA MEA</u>, UBI EST CANEM? *Mi buena amiga, ¿dónde está el perro?* We can also add a possessive adjective to 'dog.' The sentence 'My good (female) friend, where is your dog?' would be translated in Latin as BONA AMICA MEA, UBI EST <u>CANEM TUUM</u>?

Notice also that word order was very flexible in Latin, so that the words in any of the sentences above could be rearranged. For example, the first sentence where AMICA is in the nominative case could have any one of the possible orders:

AMICA VIDET AMICUM (as above). *La amiga ve al amigo.*

AMICA AMICUM VIDET. *La amiga al amigo ve.*

VIDET AMICA AMICUM. *Ve la amiga al amigo.*

VIDET AMICUM AMICA. *Ve al amigo la amiga.*

AMICUM VIDET AMICA. *Al amigo ve la amiga.*

AMICUM AMICA VIDET. *Al amigo la amiga ve.*

The Spanish sentences after the Latin ones show that these orders are all still possible in Spanish, given the right context, although the subject-verb-object (SVO) order of the first sentence is no doubt the most common.

Complete Activity 11-1 on page 234.

11.2.2 How Are the Forms of Latin and Spanish Nouns Organized?

Latin cases are organized into five different sets of case endings called **declensions** (*las declinaciones*) as shown in Table 11.2. Knowing which declension a noun or other nominal element belongs to allows you to know its endings in each of the six cases in the same way that knowing a regular verb's infinitive allows you to know its forms in different persons and tenses. If you know, for example, that PORTA is a first declension noun, then you know that its accusative singular is PORTAM, in the same way that knowing that

TABLE 11.2 The five Latin declensions

	First	Second		Third			Fourth		Fifth	
Singular	PORTA, -AE, f.	MODUS, -Ī, m.	LIGNUM, -Ī, n.	TURRIS, -IS, f.	AMOR, -IS, m.	MARE, -IS, n.	MANUS, -ŪS, f.	CORNŪ, -ŪS, n.	DIĒS, -ĒĪ, m.	SPECIĒS, -ĒĪ, f.
nominative	PORTA	MODUS	LIGNUM	TURRIS	AMOR	MARE	MANUS	CORNŪ	DIĒS	SPECIĒS
genitive	PORTAE	MODĪ	LIGNĪ	TURRIS	AMORIS	MARIS	MANŪS	CORNŪS	DIĒĪ	SPECIĒĪ
dative	PORTAE	MODŌ	LIGNŌ	TURRĪ	AMORĪ	MARĪ	MANUĪ	CORNŪ	DIĒĪ	SPECIĒĪ
accusative	PORTAM	MODUM	LIGNUM	TURREM	AMOREM	MARE	MANUM	CORNŪ	DIEM	SPECIEM
ablative	PORTĀ	MODŌ	LIGNŌ	TURRE	AMORE	MARĪ	MANŪ	CORNŪ	DIĒ	SPECIĒ
Plural										
nominative	PORTAE	MODĪ	LIGNA	TURRĒS	AMORĒS	MARIA	MANŪS	CORNUA	DIĒS	SPECIĒS
genitive	PORTĀRUM	MODŌRUM	LIGNŌRUM	TURRIUM	AMORUM	MARIUM	MANUUM	CORNUUM	DIĒRUM	SPECIĒRUM
dative	PORTĪS	MODĪS	LIGNĪS	TURRIBUS	AMORIBUS	MARIBUS	MANIBUS	CORNIBUS	DIĒBUS	SPECIĒBUS
accusative	PORTĀS	MODŌS	LIGNA	TURRĒS	AMORĒS	MARIA	MANŪS	CORNUA	DIĒS	SPECIĒS
ablative	PORTĪS	MODĪS	LIGNĪS	TURRIBUS	AMORIBUS	MARIBUS	MANIBUS	CORNIBUS	DIĒBUS	SPECIĒBUS

cantar is an *-ar* verb lets you know that its 1sg. form in the imperfect is *cantaba*. A Latin dictionary lists the nominative and genitive singular for every noun and these two forms allow you to determine the noun's declension.

Complete Activity 11-2 on page 236.

We have just seen that Latin nouns are organized into five declensions based on their case endings. Spanish no longer has cases, but we can sort Spanish nouns into three categories or classes based on their endings. The first class of nouns are those ending in *-a*, like *puerta* from first declension PORTA, and also *amiga, cosa, vida, casa,* and many others. The second class of nouns in Spanish ends in *-o*, like *modo* from MODUM and *amigo, libro, mundo, ejemplo,* and many others. Then we have Spanish nouns that end in *-e*, like *torre* from TURREM and also *madre, padre, hombre, gente,* and others, and nouns that end in a consonant, like *mar* from MARE and *pan, libertad,* and *ocasión.* Do the nouns ending in *-e* and those ending in a consonant belong to the same class? If you remember from Chapter 6 that the final vowel /e/ is lost after certain consonants in Spanish through apocope, then you know it makes sense historically to group these nouns together as the third class of Spanish nouns. The nouns ending in *-e* come from the Latin words where apocope did not take place, like TURREM > *torre,* whereas the nouns ending in a consonant are those where apocope did take place, like PANEM > *pan.*

Do the Latin nouns in the fourth and fifth declensions lead to any additional Spanish noun classes? The simple answer is no. Fourth declension nouns, like MANUM and CORNŪ, become second class nouns in *-o*, like *mano* and *cuerno.* Fifth declension DIEM joins the first class becoming *día,* while other fifth declension nouns join the third class, like FIDEM, which becomes *fe.* Some fifth declension nouns developed Spanish reflexes in different noun classes. SPECIĒM becomes both *especia* 'spice' in the first class and *especie* 'species' in the third class. Since nouns of the Latin fourth and fifth declensions join the forms of the first, second, and third declensions, the five Latin declensions are reduced to three noun classes in Spanish: the first class ending in *-a*, the second class in *-o*, and the third class in *-e* or a consonant.

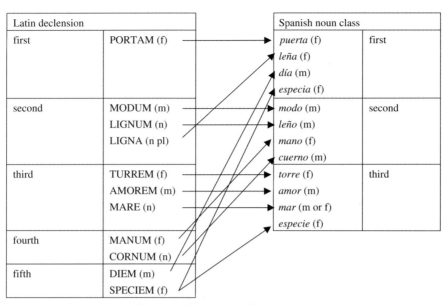

Figure 11.1 Comparison of Latin declensions and Spanish noun classes

Figure 11.1 summarizes the changes from Latin declensions to Spanish noun classes for the nouns in Table 11.3. The gender of each noun is indicated after the noun by (f) for feminine, (m) for masculine, and (n) for neuter nouns. All Latin nouns are listed in the accusative singular, except LIGNA 'wood, firewood, timber,' which is shown in the accusative plural (pl.).

Complete Activity 11-3 on page 237.

11.2.3 How Were Latin Cases Lost in Spanish?

There are two major changes that contributed to the loss of the six Latin cases. The first is the regular sound changes that erased case endings. The second is the expanded use of prepositions to take over the functions expressed by case endings. Looking first at sound changes, we can assess their effect on case endings by determining the case endings that would have resulted from regular sound change. We need to consider only the first, second, and third declensions,

TABLE 11.3 Latin cases of the first, second, and third declensions: hypothetical evolution through regular sound change

	First	Result	Second	Result	Third	Result
Singular						
nom.	PORTA	puerta	MODUS		TURRIS	
gen.	PORTAE	puerte	MODĪ		TURRIS	
dat.	PORTAE	puerte	MODŌ		TURRĪ	
acc.	PORTAM	puerta	MODUM		TURREM	
abl.	PORTĀ	puerta	MODŌ		TURRE	
number of forms	4	2				
sound changes	[m] > Ø					
	[a] and [a:] > [a]					
Plural						
nom.	PORTAE	puerte	MODĪ		TURRĒS	
gen.	PORTĀRUM	portaro	MODŌRUM		TURRIUM	
dat.	PORTĪS	puertes	MODĪS		TURRIBUS	
acc.	PORTĀS	puertas	MODŌS		TURRĒS	
abl.	PORTĪS	puertes	MODĪS		TURRIBUS	
number of forms	4	4				

since we know that these are the only noun classes that survived in Spanish. The cases for these three declensions are repeated in Table 11.3 with a column for their result in Spanish. We have already added the forms of the first declension. We see that in the singular these changes would have reduced the four Latin forms to only two forms. The genitive and dative forms, already identical in Latin, would become *puerte, since Latin final AE /aj/ develops like short /e/ and so would become /e/. The forms of the nominative, accusative, and ablative would all become *puerta. The loss of final /m/ makes the accusative identical to the nominative and the loss of the distinction between the short /a/ in the nominative and long /a:/ in the ablative would make those two cases the same. In the plural, by contrast, the sound changes would not have eliminated any distinctions.

Practice 11-1

Complete Table 11.3 by writing the results of the regular sound changes for the Latin cases in the second and third declensions. Below the forms for the singular and the plural for each declension write the number of different forms there were in Latin and then how many different forms would remain in Spanish. Also, list the sound changes that would have led to identical forms in Spanish in the singular. Keep in mind most of these forms did not survive in Spanish and so are hypothetical forms that allow us to determine the effect of regular sound changes on case endings.

We see in Table 11.3 that certain regular sound changes erased distinctions in case endings, especially in the singular. These sound changes include the loss of word-final /m/, which distinguished the accusative singular from other cases and the loss of distinctions among final vowels, like short and long /a/ in the first declension, long /o/ and short /u/ in the second declension, and long /e/ and short /i/ in the third declension. We can conclude that, even if speakers had wanted to maintain the functions of the Latin cases, many case endings would have become identical through regular sound changes.

We can now consider the syntactic changes that contributed to the loss of case endings. At the same time these sound changes were leading to a change in form, speakers were also expanding the function of the preposition plus noun construction, like CUM AMICĀ 'with the (female) friend.' Prepositions were already used with a noun in Latin to express meanings that case endings did not indicate, such as 'with' and 'from.' Either the accusative or ablative case was used after prepositions.

At some point speakers began to expand the functions of the preposition DE so that it could express possession or 'of' in addition to 'from.' The two ways of expressing possession, namely DE AMICĀ and the genitive case AMICAE, probably coexisted. Speakers also began using AD AMICAM for the indirect object alongside the dative AMICAE and prepositions, such as CUM or PRO, to express the means, like CUM CULTELLŌ 'with a knife,' rather than the ablative alone, CULTELLŌ.

An interesting chicken and egg question arises: Which came first: the sound changes or the syntactic changes? (Pulgram 1983: 114–16). Did speakers change sounds first and then start using prepositions to make up for identical case endings? Or did speakers begin expanding the functions of prepositions in order to regularize this system and achieve greater clarity? If the latter were the case, then the sound changes could proceed without creating too much ambiguity because case endings were no longer the only means of indicating possession, indirect objects, direct objects, and means. Which argument do you think is more plausible? Regardless of the relative chronology of sound changes and the expansion of the functions of prepositions, it is certain that both of these changes played a role in the loss of cases.

Complete Activity 11-4 on page 238.

Now that we have seen that there are no longer any cases in Spanish, we can ask: Which case do Spanish nouns come from? Take another look at the declensions presented in Table 11.2. A singular noun in the -a class in Spanish, like *puerta*, could come from the nominative, accusative or ablative, all of which would have become *puerta* through regular sound change. But, if we look at the plural forms, we see that only the accusative PORTĀS would become *puertas* through regular sound changes.

Let us see whether Spanish nouns in the other two noun classes appear to come from the Latin accusative form. For a Latin second declension noun MODUS, not only the accusative, but also the dative and ablative, with the same form in Latin, would have become *modo* in Spanish. If we look at the plural, we see that only the accusative MODŌS would become *modos* in Spanish.

In a third declension noun like TURRIS, the accusative, dative, and ablative would all have become *torre* in Spanish, just like for MODUS. The plural is unlike the second declension, though, since both the nominative and the accusative would have become *torres*. However, since we have already determined that the plural in the first and second declensions can come only from the accusative, we assume that the plural in third declension nouns comes from the accusative too.

Why would the form of the accusative rather than another case have survived in Spanish? One reason is that the accusative marked the singular/plural distinction in a regular way from one declension to the next. If we look at the declensions in Table 11.2 again, we will see that there was a regular pattern of singular without /s/ and plural with /s/ in the accusative. In the other cases by contrast there was no regular singular/plural pattern. Taking the nominative as an example, we find these singular/plural pairs in the three declensions: PORTA/PORTAE, MODUS/MODI, TURRIS/TURRĒS. Through regular sound changes, these would have become *puerta/ puerte, modos/mode*, and *torres/torres*, all of which show a different relationship of singular to plural. One can also assume that the accusative was more frequent than other forms, especially in the second and third declensions where the dative and ablative would also have given the same results as the accusative. Therefore, the possible greater frequency of the accusative case along with its regular means of marking plural favored the survival of its forms over those of other cases.

Box 11.1 Spanish words from cases other than the accusative

Even though the majority of Spanish nouns come from the accusative case, some nouns from other cases have survived. Some of the more common words and their Latin etyma are listed below according to the case they come from. For a more complete list see Lloyd (1987: 275–77).

Nominative: *Carlos* (< CAROLUS), *Marcos* (< MARCUS), *Jesús* (< JĒSUS), *diós* 'god' (< DEUS), *compaño* 'companion' (< COMPANIO), *maestre* 'master (of a military order)' (< MAGISTER), *avestruz* 'ostrich' (< AVIS STRUTHIO), *tizo* 'burning brand' (< TITIO), *gorgojo* 'weevil' (< CURCULIO).

Genitive: The names of three weekdays come from the genitive forms of Mars, Jupiter, and Venus in an expression meaning the day of each of these gods: *martes* 'Tuesday' < ((DIES) MARTIS '(the day) of Mars'), *jueves* 'Thursday' < ((DIES) JOVIS '(the day) of Jupiter'), *viernes* 'Friday' < ((DIES) VENERIS '(the day) of Venus'). Other words from the genitive include *condestable* 'high royal official' (< COMITE STABULI 'master of the stable'), *feligrés* 'worshiper, parishioner' (< FILIUS ECCLESIAE 'son of the church'), *pezuña* (< PEDIS UNGULA 'hoof,' literally 'nail of the foot').

Ablative: *ahora* 'now' (< HĀC HORĀ 'at this hour'), *hogaño* 'nowadays' (< HŌC ANNŌ 'in this year'), *luego* 'later' (< LOCŌ 'on the spot, place').

11.3 How Did Spanish Words End up as Masculine or Feminine?

11.3.1 What Is the Origin of Spanish Gender Endings?

In the discussion of Latin declensions, you have already observed the origins of gender marking in Spanish. The feminine ending /a/ traces its origins to the Latin first declension accusative ending in /a/. Most first declension nouns were feminine in Latin and kept their feminine gender in Spanish. Examples are plentiful, such as APICULAM > *abeja*, VESPAM > *avispa*, and LITTERAM > *letra*. There were, however, a handful of masculine first declension nouns in Latin, like SCRIBAM 'scribe' and POETAM 'poet.' These continue to be masculine in Spanish, as in *el escriba* and *el poeta*, but still end in /a/, since they evolved through regular sound change. Thus, some exceptional masculine nouns ending in /a/ trace their origins to Latin. Others, however, like *el clima, el tema, el problema,* and *el sistema*, trace their origins to Greek.

The masculine /o/ ending in Spanish comes from the Latin second declension where the final short /u/ of the accusative case became /o/. These Latin second declension masculine nouns have remained masculine in Spanish, such as CABALLUM > *caballo*, TAURUM > *toro*, and FOCUM > *fuego*. There were also a handful of second declension feminine nouns, but these kept the /o/ that resulted from regular sound change and have all become masculine in Spanish. These included the names of fruit trees, such as *CERASIUS 'cherry tree' (Classical Latin CERASUS), now *cerezo*, and Greek borrowings, such as DIALECTUS 'dialect,' now *dialecto*, and METHODUS 'method,' now *método*. As a side note, some tree names are feminine, since these derive from the adjective modifying the Latin noun for tree, ARBŌREM, which was feminine. For example, *higuera* 'fig tree' comes from the adjective FICARIA in the expression ARBOR FICARIA 'fig-bearing tree' (Penny 2002: 123).

Latin third declension nouns usually maintained their gender, but these nouns ended in /e/ or a consonant, so gender was not marked by a distinctive /a/ or /o/ ending. We saw above that TURREM remains feminine as *torre* and AMŌREM remains masculine as *amor*. Some third declension nouns changed gender, though, from masculine to feminine or feminine to masculine, no doubt in part because their endings did not indicate gender. We saw in Chapter 1, for example, that ARTEM was feminine, but that *arte* is very often used as a masculine noun in Spanish, as in *el arte poético*. This change of gender may have begun in the singular where the definite article *el* led speakers to perceive this noun as masculine. This same change from feminine to masculine occurred in ARBŌREM > *árbol*. Not only does this word begin with a tonic /a/ like *arte*, but the change may also have been favored by the fact that names of trees are masculine in Spanish. For example, an apple tree is a *manzano* and the fruit it bears is a *manzana*. Another example of a gender change is masculine FLŌREM 'flower,' which is now feminine *la flor*. Perhaps speakers perceived the flowers produced by plants as feminine in the same way they perceived their fruits as feminine.

11.3.2 How Does the Latin Neuter Get Lost?

In Latin there was a third gender, the neuter, in addition to the masculine and feminine genders that have survived in Spanish. As seen in Table 11.2, neuter nouns could occur in the second, third, or fourth declensions and always had identical forms for nominative and accusative cases in both singular and plural. For example, LIGNUM 'firewood, timber' is the nominative and accusative singular and LIGNA is the nominative and accusative plural. The neuter gender was lost in Spanish because all surviving neuter nouns changed gender to either masculine or feminine. Which gender they adopted depended in part on their Latin declension class, but many of these changes also appear to be arbitrary.

A second declension neuter noun could become masculine based on its singular form or feminine based on its plural form. For example, the singular form LIGNUM survives as the masculine noun *leño* 'log' and its plural LIGNA survives as the feminine noun *leña* 'firewood.' It is exceptional, though, for a single Latin noun to become two different words in Spanish. More often only the singular or plural form survives. Spanish *vino* comes from the singular VĪNUM and *pera* comes from the plural PIRA. These changes occur first through reanalysis and then through proportional analogy, concepts presented in Chapter 10. In the change from VĪNUM > *vino*, speakers first reanalyze this neuter singular noun as masculine because its -UM ending is identical to the -UM ending of the accusative case of a masculine second declension noun, like MODUM. The next step is the creation of a new plural form through proportional analogy. The plural of VĪNUM was VĪNA, but speakers create a new plural *vinos* by analogy to masculine second declension nouns based on the following proportion: *modo/modos : vino/*X = *vinos*.

A Latin neuter second declension noun can become feminine when speakers reanalyze its plural, like PIRA, as a feminine singular noun because its form is identical to the nominative case of a first declension feminine noun, like PORTA, and also to the accusative case, like PORTAM, after the regular loss of final /m/. Then speakers create a new plural through proportional analogy as follows: *puerta/puertas : pera/*X = *peras*.

A question that remains unanswered is why certain second declension neuter nouns became masculine while others became feminine. One might suspect that this depends on whether speakers used these nouns more often in the singular or plural. This seems to hold true for nouns like VĪNUM 'wine,' BALNEUM 'bath,' and CUBITUM 'elbow,' whose singular form survives, and for nouns like ARMA 'arms' and OPERA 'works,' whose plural survives. But why would GRANUM 'grain, seed' (> *grano*) and BRACCHIUM 'arm' (> *brazo*) be used more often in the singular and why would FĔSTA 'feast days' (> *fiesta*) and ALBA 'white colors' (> *alba*) be used more often in the plural?

Latin neuter nouns of the third declension most often stay in this declension but seem to end up as masculine or feminine arbitrarily. Neuter third declension nouns that became masculine include *NOMINEM > *nombre*, *ROBOREM > *roble* 'oak' and *AERAMINEM > *alambre* 'wire,' whereas those that became feminine include *LACTEM > *leche*, *LEGŪMINEM > *legumbre* 'legume,' and *ŪBEREM > *ubre* 'udder.' These forms are marked with an asterisk because they do not appear in Classical Latin. Instead we assume that a new analogical accusative was created in Spoken Latin. For example, the accusative of 'milk' was LAC, the same as the nominative. We assume, though, that a new accusative *LACTEM was created from the genitive LACTIS by analogy to third declension masculine nouns, such as the word for 'love' with genitive AMŌRIS and accusative AMŌREM. We can also mention third declension TEMPUS, plural TEMPORA, that became the masculine *tiempo* through backformation, as explained in Box 10.1. The same process explains the change of CORPUS, plural CORPORA, to *cuerpo/cuerpos*.

Latin neuter nouns of the fourth declension, since they end in /u/, end up as masculine nouns of the second class. These include ARCUM > *arco*, GRADUM > *grado* and GELUM > *hielo*. In summary, one finds Latin neuter nouns in the second, third, and fourth declensions. Neuter nouns of the fourth declension join the second declension and become masculine, like CORNŪ > *cuerno*, as do neuter nouns of the second declension, if their singular form survives, like VĪNUM > *vino*.

Complete Activity 11-5 on page 239.

11.3.3 How Are New Feminine Forms Created?

A process of proportional analogy that continues to the present day in Spanish is the creation of new feminine nouns and adjectives in -*a*, especially when they refer to women. Two notable examples are the fourth declension feminine nouns SOCRUS 'mother-in-law' and NURUS 'daughter-in-law.' Whereas the accusative forms SOCRUM and NURUM would have become *suegro* and *nuero* through the regular change of final /u/ to /o/, they instead adopt a final /a/ by analogy to other feminine nouns in /a/ to become *suegra* and *nuera*. This change was no doubt encouraged by the fact that the masculine noun *suegro* had already developed from second declension SOCERUM, meaning 'father-in-law.' We have evidence that these new feminine forms were in use by the third century, as attested by the examples SOCRUS NON SOCRA and NURUS NON NURA from the *Appendix Probi*, seen in Chapter 2.

Pairs of masculine and feminine words in /o/ and /a/ no doubt serve as the model for this type of proportional analogy. If we consider *amigo* (< AMICUM) and *amiga* (< AMICAM) to be the model, then we can write the proportional analogy as: *amigo/amiga : suegro/X = suegra*. No such masculine/feminine pair exists for *nuera*, though, since the word in Latin for 'son-in-law' is GENERUM, which becomes *yerno* in Spanish. The analogical proportion for this word cannot be based on a particular pair of words, then, but rather on the association of *nuera* with other feminine nouns that end in /a/. Other first and second declension nouns that could serve as a model for *suegro/suegra* in addition to *amigo/amiga* include ALUMNUM/ALUMNAM > *alumno/alumna*, DOMINUM/DOMINAM > *dueño/dueña*, and GERMĀNUM/GERMĀNAM > *hermano/hermana*. This pattern is also found in the first and second declension of adjectives, with the same endings as first and second declension nouns, like BONUM/BONAM > *bueno/buena*, MALUM/MALAM > *malo/mala*, and NOVUM/NOVAM > *nuevo/nueva*.

The process of creating new feminine forms in /a/ continues today when speakers refer to women performing jobs formerly reserved for men. Epperson and Ranson (2010), in a survey of 750 native speakers of Spanish living in the United States, found that over half the participants who completed the written questionnaire preferred feminine forms, such as *la química, la ingeniera*, and *la arquitecta*, to refer to female professionals.

Spanish speakers and writers also began adding the distinctive feminine /a/ to some third declension nouns that did not mark gender. For example, speakers created a feminine form *infanta* based on *infante* (< INFANTEM 'non-speaking'), which formerly referred to both men and women, in the same way they created a feminine *señora* by adding /a/ to *señor* (< SENIŌREM 'older'). You can see two examples of feminine *la mia señor* in the Appendix C106, C116. Among nouns that were originally third declension nouns, Epperson and Ranson (2010: 402) found that more than half of speakers preferred the new feminine forms *jefa* '(female) boss,' *presidenta* '(female) president,' *sirvienta* '(female) servant,' and *colegiala* 'schoolgirl.' However, *la estudiante* remains the more frequent form than *la estudianta*. The analogical addition of /a/ also occurs in some third declension adjectives, but not others. For example, speakers created *burguesa* alongside *burgués* 'bourgeois,' but *cortés* 'courteous' serves as both the masculine and feminine form; since there is no feminine form *cortesa*.

One example of the creation of a distinctive feminine form of a third declension adjective also appears in this example from the *Appendix Probi*: PAUPER NON PAUPERA [MULIER]. This change has not survived, however, since today one says *pobre mujer* rather than *pobra mujer*. Note that for nouns of the third class one finds *señora* alongside *señor*, but never the pattern *señoro/señora*. Thus, two new patterns have been created for gender pairs in addition to the /o/ – /a/ pair: one pairs a word ending in a consonant with a word ending in /a/, like *burgués/burguesa*, while the other pairs a word ending in /e/ with a word ending in /a/, like *infante/infanta* 'prince'/'princess.'

Complete Activity 11-6 on page 241.

11.3.4 Why Is *mano* Feminine and *día* Masculine?

By considering gender along with the loss of the Latin fourth and fifth declensions, we can now answer the title question for this chapter, a question often asked by learners of Spanish. Why is *mano* feminine even though it ends in /o/ and *día* masculine even though it ends in /a/? MANUS was already somewhat unusual in Latin as one of only twenty-two feminine fourth declension nouns ("Latin feminine nouns" 2016). In Spanish it becomes even more unusual. By keeping its feminine gender and following the regular sound change of final /u/ to /o/, *mano* ends up as the only Spanish feminine noun inherited from Latin that ends in /o/. The only other feminine nouns ending in /o/ are shortened forms of longer words, like *la radio* from *radiofonía* or *radiodifusión*, *la moto* from *motocicleta*, *la foto* from *fotografía*, *la disco* from *discoteca*, and words denoting women that use the masculine form, such as *la modelo* 'the (female) model,' *la reo* 'the (female) criminal,' *la soprano* 'the (female) soprano,' and *la testigo* 'the (female) witness' (Erichsen 2017). Feminines ending in /o/ seem odd in Spanish today, since most Spanish nouns in /o/ are masculine having come from masculine or neuter second declension nouns in Latin.

Día has even more exceptional origins than *mano*, since DIĒS was the only fifth declension noun that was not feminine. The irregularity of DIĒS in Latin continues in Spanish. By changing it to the first class of nouns ending in /a/, speakers ensured that it would continue to be one of the few masculine nouns in an overwhelmingly feminine class of nouns. Why would speakers not have kept the hypothetical **die* that would have resulted from regular sound change? The form **die* appears to be an especially attractive option, since a masculine noun would not be out of place in the third class of nouns where masculine nouns like *puente* and *viaje* are common. Perhaps the analogical change to first declension nouns occurred because so many other fifth declension nouns, all of which were feminine, changed to the first class of nouns, such as RABIĒS > *rabia* 'rabies, rage' and MATERIĒS > *madera*. Yet, other fifth declension nouns changed to the third class, such as FIDES > *fe*, and others changed to both first and third class, such as SPECIĒS > *especia* and *especie* mentioned above. This means that a change from DIĒM to **díe* was certainly possible.

Another reason DIĒS changed to *día* might have been the presence of other masculine nouns ending in /a/, most of which are borrowings from masculine words in Greek, like *clima* 'climate,' *cometa* 'comet,' *diagrama* 'diagram,' *dilema* 'dilemma,' *diploma* 'diploma,' *planeta* 'planet,' *problema* 'problem,' and *programa* 'program' (Erichsen 2017). This may explain why a masculine word ending in /a/ did not seem unacceptable to speakers. It is also possible that the use of DIĒS as a feminine noun may have played a part in the change. When DIĒS referred to a particular day in Latin it was feminine, as in the ablative expression CONSTITUTĀ DIĒ 'on the appointed day.' Of course, the fact that *día* is masculine suggests that the use of DIĒS in the feminine did not play a large part in the change of DIĒS to *día*. Learners of Spanish are right then to wonder why *mano* is feminine and *día* is masculine. These nouns were exceptional in Latin and they continue to be exceptional today.

11.4 Chapter Summary

- Latin had six cases. The nominative indicated the subject of a sentence, the genitive indicated the possessor, the dative indicated the indirect object, the accusative indicated the direct object, the ablative indicated the means, and the vocative was used for direct address.
- Latin cases were lost in Spanish through a combination of regular sound changes that erased case endings and a general tendency to replace synthetic constructions of noun plus case endings with analytical constructions consisting of a preposition plus a noun.
- Latin nouns were organized into five different declensions based on their case endings. The five Latin declensions were reduced to three noun classes in Spanish: a feminine first class ending in /a/, a masculine second class ending in /o/, and a masculine or feminine third class ending in /e/ or a consonant.
- Spanish nouns derived mostly from the accusative case, which most likely survived because it marked plural regularly across the declensions by adding

an /s/ to the singular and because it was perhaps more frequent than the other cases.

- Regarding gender, we saw that most masculine and feminine nouns in Latin kept their gender in Spanish, although a few changed from masculine to feminine or feminine to masculine, especially Latin third declension nouns that did not have a distinctive gender ending. Latin also had nouns with a neuter gender that became either feminine or masculine in Spanish.

- New feminine forms have been created throughout the history of Spanish when speakers added an /a/ ending to words by analogy to feminine words that ended in /a/ through regular sound change. For example, *señor* which originally had the same form for both masculine and feminine becomes *señora* in the feminine by analogy to feminine words ending in /a/, like *amiga*.

- The irregularity of *mano* and *día* is inherited from Latin where these words were already exceptional. Latin MANUM was one of the few feminine fourth declension nouns and DIĒS was one of the few masculine fifth declension nouns. In Spanish these nouns kept their Latin gender even though they end in a vowel associated with the other gender.

Activities

Activity 11-1

A. Underline each nominal element in sentence 1 below and then write what its case would be in Latin. The sentence is given in English, Spanish, and Latin to help you do this. Use these abbreviations for the cases: NOM = nominative (subject), GEN = genitive (possessor), DAT = dative (indirect object), ACC = accusative (direct object), ABL = ablative (means), and VOC = vocative (direct address).

1. English: Listen, Amelia, you told me you had seen the president of Mexico with your own eyes.

Spanish: *Oye, Amelia, tú me dijiste que habías visto al presidente de México con tus proprios ojos.*

Latin: Audī, Ameliā, tū mihi dixistī quod viderās praesidem Mexicī oculīs tuīs propriīs.

2. Make up a sentence yourself in English or Spanish that includes the functions of each of the six Latin cases. Suggestion: Begin with what is called a distransitive verb that takes both an indirect and a direct object like *to tell, to send, to write,* or *to give* (something to someone).

B. Underline each Latin noun in the sentences below and indicate its case. Then draw an arrow from any adjectives to the noun they modify to show that have the same case as the noun. We provide a translation of each sentence in English and Spanish and then the meanings of the individual words. (The sentences in this activity are taken from Wheelock (2005: 10, 16).)

1. Rotam fortunae non timent.
   'They do not fear the wheel of fortune.' *No temen la rueda de la fortuna.*
   (Cicero, rotam 'wheel,' fortūnae 'fortune,' non 'do not' timent '3pl. to fear')

2. Clementia tua multās vitās conservat.
   'Your clemency saves many lives.' *Tu clemencia salva muchas vidas.*
   (Cicero, clementia 'clemency,' tua 'f. sg. yours,' multās 'f. pl. many,' vitās 'lives,' conservat '3sg. to save')

3. Debētis, amīcī, de pcpulō Romanō cogitāre.
   'You should, friends, think about the Roman people.' *Debéis, amigos, pensar en el pueblo romano.*
   (Cicero, debētis '2pl. should,' amīcī 'friends,' de 'of, about,' takes the ablative case, populō 'people,' Romanō 'Roman,' cogitāre 'to think')

4. Fortuna adversa virum magnae sapientiae non terret.
   'Adverse fortune does not terrify a man of great wisdom.' *La fortuna adversa no aterroriza a un hombre de gran sabiduría.*
   (Horace, fortuna 'fortune,' adversa 'f. sg. adverse,' virum 'man,' magnae 'great,' sapientiae 'wisdom,' non 'does not,' terret '3sg. terrify')

5. NULLA COPIA PECUNIAE AVARUM VIRUM SATIAT.

'No abundance of money satisfies a greedy man.' *Ninguna abundancia de dinero satisface al hombre avaro.*

(Seneca, NULLA 'f. sg. no,' COPIA 'abundance,' PECUNIAE 'money,' AVARUM 'm. sg. avaricious, greedy,' VIRUM 'man,' SATIAT '3sg. satisfy')

Activity 11-2

Study Table 11.2 of the Latin declensions in order to answer the following questions:

A. First look for the cases that have identical forms. Write the number of the declension in which the following forms are identical:

1. genitive and dative singular
2. dative and ablative singular
3. dative and ablative plural
4. nominative and accusative (in which declensions and which gender)

B. Which vowel is found most often in the ending of the different declensions? For example, the vowel /a/ is found most often for the first declension. It appears in the nom. sg. PORTA, acc. sg. PORTAM, abl. sg. PORTĀ, gen. pl. PORTĀRUM, acc. pl. PORTĀS. State the vowel below and circle the endings that contain this vowel in Table 11.2. Feel free to list more than one vowel, especially if these vowels have the same evolution in Spanish, like final /i/ and /e/ and final /o/ and /u/.

2nd declension

3rd declension

4th declension

5th declension

C. Complete the following Latin expressions by writing the Latin noun in the appropriate case in the blank. Also write the declension that this noun belongs to and the case that you chose. You'll need to determine which case is needed in the sentence and then find the appropriate form in the declensions in Table 11.2. The nominative form and the genitive ending of each noun to be placed in the blank are provided so that you can determine the declension of each noun. (Source: "List of Latin phrases" 2017).

Example: Carpe _____. diēs, -ēī 'day, día' 'Seize the day, *Toma el día.*'

Answer: Carpe diēm. <u>5th</u> declension, <u>accusative</u> case

1. annō _____. dominus, -ī 'Lord' *Señor,* 'In the year of the Lord' *En el año del Señor.* Note that annō is the ablative case to indicate 'in the year' _____ declension, _____ case

2. Ave, _____. maria, -ae 'Maria' *María,* 'Hail, Mary' *Dios te salve, María* _____ declension, _____ case

3. _____ fugit. tempus, temporis 'time' *tiempo,* 'Time flies' *El tiempo vuela* _____ declension, _____ case

4. Hannibal ad _____. porta, -ae 'door or gate' *puerta,* 'Hannibal is at the gates' *Aníbal está en las puertas.* Roman senators would use this expression to describe any imminent danger. _____ declension, _____ case

5. _____ gratiās. deus, -ī 'God' *Dios,* 'Thanks to God' *Gracias a Dios* _____ declension, _____ case

6. de _____ non est disputandum. gustus, -us 'taste' *gusto,* 'Of tastes there is no disputing' *Sobre gustos no hay disputa* _____ declension, _____ case

7. Make up your own example of a Latin expression for your classmates to complete by looking one up online.

Activity 11-3

A. Figure 11.1 showed how certain nouns kept or changed their declension class from Latin to Spanish. Complete the similar figure below by . . .
   1. determining the Spanish reflex
   2. writing the Spanish reflex in the appropriate noun class in Spanish
   3. by drawing an arrow from the Latin word to its Spanish reflex.

Latin declension		Spanish class	
first	TĔRRAM (f)		first
	VĪTAM (f)		
second	PŎPŬLUM (m)		second
	VĪNUM (n)		
	PĬRA (n pl)		
third	PĔDEM (m)		third
	NOCTEM (f)		
	*LACTEM (n)		
fourth	LACUS (m)		
	GRADUS (n)		
fifth	FIDEM (f)		
	RABIEM (f)		

Figure 11.2 Comparison of Latin declensions and Spanish noun classes: additional examples

B. Based on Figure 11.1 and your completed Figure 11.2, list the different Latin declensions whose nouns change to:

the Spanish first class
the Spanish second class
the Spanish third class

C. Explain why the Latin fourth and fifth declensions are not maintained as separate noun classes in Spanish by explaining what happens to the nouns in these declensions.

Activity 11–4

For each of the following statements, indicate whether it is an argument in favor of (a) sound changes occurring first in the loss of Latin cases by writing S in the blank, or of (b) the expanded use of prepositions as occurring first by writing P in the blank. Explain your reasoning.

_____ 1. The sound changes that occurred in case endings occurred in all words, not just in case endings.

_____ 2. Prepositions express meaning more clearly than case endings alone. For example, DE FILIĀ expresses possession more clearly than the genitive FILIAE.

_____ 3. The sound changes that occurred in case endings follow a general tendency toward reduction of articulatory movement.

_____ 4. The expansion of prepositions follows a general tendency toward analytical constructions that express meaning more transparently.

_____ 5. Speakers might have decided to expand the use of prepositions after they realized that case endings were no longer distinct because of the sound changes.

_____ 6. Speakers may have decided to expand the use of prepositions in order to ensure comprehension even though case endings were still distinct.

Activity 11-5

A. You will see below Latin nouns listed in the accusative singular and plural, the forms that typically develop into Spanish nouns, along with their declension in parentheses. For each pair, write the singular and plural form of the noun in Spanish that derives from this Latin noun and the Latin declension and the Spanish noun class. Then evaluate the evolution of these forms in Spanish and write one of the following designations in the blank after each form:

S = the form undergoes regular sound changes only, with no analogy

R = the form undergoes regular sound changes but is reanalyzed so that it changes gender

A = the form results from proportional analogy

The answers for the first item serve as an example.

Latin acc. sg.	Latin acc. pl.	Meaning	Gender and declension	Gender and declension change	Spanish sg.	Change	Spanish pl.	Change
1. CŌRPUS	CŌRPŎRA	'body'	n, III	n > m III > II	cuerpo	A	cuerpos	R
2. CĪLIUM	CĪLIA	'eyelid'	n, II					
3. CŌLLUM	CŌLLA	'neck'	n, II					
4. EXEMPLUM	EXEMPLA	'example'	n, II					
5. FOLĬUM	FOLĬA	'leaf'	n, II					
6. FRAXĬNUM	FRAXĬNŌS	'ash tree'	f, II					
7. LABŌREM	LABŌRĒS	'labor'	m, III					
8. LEŌNEM	LEŌNĒS	'lion'	m, III					
9. LUPUM	LUPŌS	'wolf'	m, II					
10. NURUM	NURUS	'daughter-in-law'	f, IV					
11. PIRATAM	PIRATĀS	'pirate'	m, I					
12. SALEM	SALĒS	'salt'	m, III					
13. SERIEM	(NO PL)	'series'	f, V					
14. SPONSAM	SPONSĀS	'bride'	f, I					

B. Based on your answers to question A above, you will see that we can identify five types of nouns according to the change that occurs in singular and plural forms. The first of these, illustrated by *cuerpo/cuerpos* can be called the AR type because the singular changes by analogy (A) and the plural changes by reanalysis (R). The singular CŎRPUS changes to *cuerpos* through regular sound change. This form is reanalyzed by speakers as a plural form rather than a singular since it ends in /s/. Then a new singular form, *cuerpo*, is created based on the plural *cuerpos* through proportional analogy: *modo/ modos* : X = *cuerpo/cuerpos*.

List the other four types of nouns and give an example and explanation of each type.

Activity 11-6

Corpus Search

A. Track the creation of the new feminine form *infanta* by searching this term in the *Corpus del español* or the CORDE. Record the date it is first attested. Then search *la infante* to find the last date it is recorded. Over how many years did *la infante* and *la infanta* coexist?

B. Now track the popularity of new analogical feminines in Modern Spanish. Pick a feminine title, such as *la arquitecta* and *la arquitecto* or *la jefa* and *la jefe*, and search for both terms on www.google.es or www.google.com.mx or another site for a Spanish-speaking country. Record the number of tokens you found for each.

Bonus: If you found any statements about the use of each form, record one of those here.

Further Reading

Bengoechea, Mercedes 2006. "Lento deslizamiento del género gramatical femenino al centro del discurso: Nuevos aires en la identificación de mujeres en la prensa española," *Spanish in Context* 3: 139–57

England, John 1984. "Observaciones sobre las nuevas formas femeninas en el castellano del siglo XIII," in J. M Ruiz Veintemilla (ed.), *Estudios dedicados a James Leslie Brooks*, 31–44. Barcelona: Puvill Libros

1987. "New feminine forms in Spanish: The fourteenth and fifteenth centuries," *Bulletin of Hispanic Studies* 64: 205–14

Penny, Ralph 1980. "Do Romance nouns descend from the Latin accusative? Preliminaries to a reassessment of the noun morphology of Romance," *Romance Philology* 33: 501–09

12 Why Do Spanish Speakers Sometimes Say *más malo* instead of *peor*?

Origins of Nominal Elements

Lead-in Questions

12-1 Write a sentence with the word *la* in Spanish. Did you use it as a definite article, as in *la historia de la lengua es interesante*, or did you use it as a pronoun, as in *la encuentro interesante*? Had you ever noticed before that the definite article and the direct object pronoun *la* have the same form? Which other words have the same form for the definite article and direct object?

12-2 Have you ever said *this book here* or *that book there*? Or even *this here book* or *that there book*? If so, write a sentence using one of these expressions that seems natural to you. How is this different from just saying *this book* or *that book*?

12-3 Have you noticed that English speakers sometimes say *fairer* and *clearer* and sometimes *more fair* and *more clear*? Reflect on your own use of these comparative forms and list five adjectives you add the *-er* suffix to and five you use with *more*. Are there some adjectives you use with both constructions? Do they mean the same thing to you?

In Chapter 11, we explored the major changes in nouns in the history of Spanish. In this chapter, we examine other elements of the nominal system that determine or modify the noun or completely replace it, such as articles, demonstratives, personal pronouns, possessives, indefinites (including negative polarity items), and comparative adjectives. You will see many parallels between the noun changes you have already studied and the development of these nominal elements. Specifically, you will learn about the remarkable productivity of the forms of Latin ILLE as the origin of many of these forms. You will also discover how sound changes, analogical processes, and grammaticalization result in the modern forms.

12.1 What Is the Difference between Determiners and Pronouns?

When you wrote a sentence with the word *la* in it in Lead-in question 12-1, what function did the word have? Had you realized before that the word has more than one use? Did you realize the difference in function between a **definite article** (*el artículo definido*) (as in *la historia*) and a **pronoun** (*un pronombre*) (as in *la encuentro interesante*)? In Chapter 10 we mentioned that an article is a type of determiner that 'determines' or defines a noun. The definite article in *la historia*, further specifies the noun *historia*. If we use the indefinite article, as in *una historia*, we are not defining the noun in a particular way. A pronoun, unlike a determiner, can appear alone because it replaces a noun. Notice that the word *la* in *la encuentro interesante* does not precede a noun but appears alone. We typically use a pronoun only when we know what the pronoun refers to. In the case of *la encuentro interesante*, the word *la* is the direct object pronoun that refers to *la historia*. Other words that function as determiners and pronouns are demonstratives and possessives, as discussed in Section 10.1.1.

You probably realized that there are other forms that function both as a definite article and as a direct object pronoun, such as *las* (*las respuestas nos ayudan* and *las vuelvo a escribir*); *los* (*los ejercicios son buenos* and *los encuentro fascinantes*); and *lo* (*lo importante es estudiar mucho* and *lo he hecho ya*). Do all the definite articles have the same forms as the corresponding third person direct object pronouns? Yes, except for one, as shown in the following sentences.

1. (a) *No encuentro el libro que compré hoy.*
   (b) *¿No lo has visto?*

The singular masculine definite article, *el*, and the singular masculine direct object pronoun, *lo*, do not share the same form. In the next sections, you will learn the origins of these forms and the phonological and analogical processes that influenced their development.

12.2 Where Did Spanish Articles and Demonstratives Come from?

12.2.1 Where Did the Definite Article Come from?

Latin did not have definite articles, such as *el, la, los*, and *las* in Spanish. The Spanish definite articles evolved instead from the Latin demonstrative ILLE, which meant 'that' or 'yon,' like Spanish *aquel*. For example, the Latin phrase HABEŌ LIBRUM meant 'I have the book' or 'I have a book,' whereas HABEŌ ILLUM LIBRUM meant 'I have that book (over there).' The demonstratives were declined like nouns and other nominal elements in Latin, that is, they had distinct forms in the different cases, as seen in Table 12.1.

Practice 12-1

In order to understand the origins of the definite article in Spanish, indicate the following in Table 12.1:

1. Circle the forms that are different in Latin among the different genders. For example, the nominative singular is different because the masculine form is ILLE, the feminine is ILLA and the neuter is ILLUD, so each of those forms should be circled. All of the forms for genitive singular are the same as the form ILLĪUS, so you will not circle those forms. Which cases have different forms in the different genders? Which ones do not?

2. Then, draw a line between each Spanish form and the Latin form you think it comes from. What case do the Spanish forms come from?
3. Finally, explain whether you think the forms in Spanish result from regular sound changes or not.

By studying Table 12.1, you will have noticed that the masculine and feminine definite articles have different forms in Spanish, but that not all of the cases in Latin for the demonstrative ILLE show a gender difference. The nominative and accusative cases have a different form for all three genders in both singular and plural; the dative never shows a gender difference; the genitive shows a gender difference only in the plural; the ablative shows a gender difference

TABLE 12.1 Origin of Spanish definite articles

	Masculine		Feminine		Neuter	
Singular	Latin	Spanish	Latin	Spanish	Latin	Spanish
Nominative	ILLE	*el*	ILLA	*la/el**	ILLUD	*lo***
Genitive	ILLĪUS		ILLĪUS		ILLĪUS	
Dative	ILLĪ		ILLĪ		ILLĪ	
Accusative	ILLUM		ILLAM		ILLUD	
Ablative	ILLŌ		ILLĀ		ILLŌ	
Plural	Latin	Spanish	Latin	Spanish	Latin	Spanish
Nominative	ILLĪ	*los*	ILLAE	*las*	ILLA	–
Genitive	ILLŌRUM		ILLĀRUM		ILLŌRUM	
Dative	ILLĪS		ILLĪS		ILLĪS	
Accusative	ILLŌS		ILLĀS		ILLA	
Ablative	ILLĪS		ILLĪS		ILLĪS	

*   The feminine article *el* is used before nouns that begin with stressed /a/ (as explained in Chapter 1).
**   The neuter article is used in sentences such as *Lo bueno es poder comunicarse con más personas.*

only in the singular. This will become important when we look at other developments of ILLE in Spanish.

As far as the Latin origin of the Spanish forms is concerned, you will have noticed that the plural forms clearly derive from the accusative plural through regular sound changes, as ILLŌS > *los* and ILLĀS > *las*. As for the singular, Menéndez Pidal (1987: 259) claims that these forms derive from the nominative. But the feminine singular *la* could also come from the accusative ILLAM, with the regular loss of final /m/. The derivation from the accusative rather than the nominative is favored by the fact that most nouns derive from the accusative, as you saw in Chapter 11. The masculine singular, however, is more likely to derive from the nominative, since it is more likely that the final /e/ of ILLE would be lost through apocope (Menéndez Pidal 1987: 261, Penny 2002: 145) than the final vowel /u/ of the accusative ILLUM. There is also a feminine article *el*, as in *el agua*, used in Modern Spanish before nouns beginning with a stressed /a/. You will recall from Chapter 1 that this came from ILLA, whose second syllable was lost before a noun beginning with a vowel. The neuter article *lo* could come from either the nominative or accusative, since these always have the same form in the neuter. In fact, one possible explanation for the somewhat irregular masculine singular definite article *el* is that it maintained its first syllable instead of its last syllable so as to have a different form from neuter *lo* (Lloyd 1987: 279–80).

Table 12.2 summarizes the evolution of the Spanish definite articles by presenting only their Latin etyma and their two-syllable forms in Old Spanish. Because these forms always preceded a noun, they were unstressed and therefore

TABLE 12.2 Evolution of Spanish definite articles

Latin demonstrative	Old Spanish	Modern Spanish
ILLE (m. sg. nom.)	*el*	*el*
ILLA(M) (f. sg. nom. or acc.)	*ela*	*la, el*
ILLUD (n. sg. nom or acc.)	*elo*	*lo*
ILLŌS (m. pl. acc.)	*elos*	*los*
ILLĀS (f. pl. acc.)	*elas*	*las*

more likely to be reduced phonetically. This would explain why they were reduced from two syllables to one either through apocope, loss of the final vowel, in the masculine singular, or through the loss of the first vowel in the other forms, a process known as **apheresis** (*la aféresis*). Once this reduction took place, Latin LL was in either word-final or word-initial position and so changed to /l/, since /ʎ/ is rare in these positions.

12.2.2 Where Did the Indefinite Article Come from?

Latin did not have **indefinite articles** (*los artículos indefinidos*), such as Spanish *uno, una, unos,* and *unas,* in the same way it did not have definite articles. You may have noticed this from the translation 'I have a book' for HABEŌ LIBRUM. The indefinite articles come from the Latin number one, ŪNUS. Like ILLE, ŪNUS had different forms for each of the cases in the three different genders. It is not necessary to reproduce all these forms here, since we can assume that the accusative forms are the ones that survived in Spanish, as follows:

ŪNUM (m. sg. acc.) > *uno*
ŪNAM (f. sg. acc.) > *una*

Logically because ŪNUM meant 'one' it had only singular forms. The plural forms were created in Spanish through a simple case of proportional analogy. The masculine *unos* would result from an analogical proportion like *modo/ modos : uno/X = unos* and *unas* would result from an analogical proportion like *puerta/puertas: una/ X = unas.*

12.2.3 Where Did the Demonstratives Come from?

We have already seen that Latin had a demonstrative adjective and pronoun ILLE that evolved into the Spanish definite articles. Latin also had two other demonstratives, so that the complete set of Latin demonstratives is:

HIC '*este*' 'this'
ISTE '*ese*' 'that'
ILLE '*aquel*' 'that (over there), yon'

TABLE 12.3 Demonstratives in Latin and Spanish

	Latin	Spanish
'this'	HIC > Ø	este
'that'	ISTE	ese
'yon'	*(ACCU) ILLE	aquel
'himself'	(IPSE)	

(Forms in parentheses were not demonstratives in Latin.)

It is clear from a quick comparison of the Latin and Spanish forms that the Spanish demonstratives do not come directly from the Latin demonstrative with the same meaning. Several changes, summarized in Table 12.3, brought about the current Spanish demonstrative system. The forms of the first term HIC were lost entirely, except in certain expressions, such as HĀC HORĀ 'at this hour' > *ahora* 'now,' and HŌC ANNŌ 'in this year' > *hogaño* 'nowadays.' The second term, ISTE, changed its meaning from 'that' to 'this' to fill in the gap left by the loss of HIC, so that the demonstrative for 'this' in Spanish is *este*. The Spanish demonstrative *ese* came from IPSE, which was not a demonstrative in Latin. Rather IPSE meant 'self,' as in the sentence CICERO IPSE LAUDAT MĒ 'Cicero himself praises me.' We can imagine that IPSE could become a demonstrative because using IPSE to mean 'that same thing' or 'that very thing' could be a way of pointing something out.

The Spanish demonstrative *aquel* comes from ILLE reinforced by the addition of ECCE *'behold.'* ECCE must have had the variant *ACCU in Spanish because *ACCU ILLE would result in *aquel* through regular sound changes. You might find it interesting to know that in Old Spanish the other two demonstratives also had a reinforced form. One finds the form *aqueste* alongside *este* and *aquese* alongside *ese*. The excerpt from the *Auto de los Reyes Magos* in the Appendix contains three examples of the demonstrative from *ACCU ISTE written with a *ch* instead of *qu* in this text (A2, 14, 16), as in *achesta strela* 'esta estrella' (A2).

Why do you think speakers reinforced ILLE to form *aquel*? Consider the evolution of ILLE on its own in Section 12.2.1 and also your answer to Lead-in question 12-2. Once the meaning of ILLE had weakened to that of a definite article, speakers began to add ECCU/*ACCU to ILLE to emphasize the demonstrative function of the determiner. This reinforcement is very much like adding *here* or *there* to a demonstrative in English. We might say 'I want **this** book **here**,' or even 'I want **this here** book' to refer to the object that is right in front of us. The fact that *this* has lost its demonstrative function in English, just like ILLE lost its demonstrative function in the history of Spanish, no doubt encourages its reinforcement. For example, in a sentence like 'I was walking down the street when **this** guy shouted at me,' *this* is used as an indefinite determiner and not to refer to an object that is near us. It is similar to saying 'when **a** guy shouted at me.'

12.3 Where Did Personal Pronouns Come from?

In Latin, like Spanish, subject pronouns were optional, so that one could use the verb CANTAT 'he/she/it sings' with no subject pronoun in the same way a Spanish speaker can say simply *canta*. If a Latin speaker wanted to specify or emphasize who was singing, then she could use demonstrative pronouns, such as IS for 'he,' EA for 'she,' or ID for 'it.' It was also possible to use the forms of ILLE that you are already familiar with as third person pronouns. Below we will examine the evolution of third person pronouns, first the stressed pronouns and then the unstressed. Finally, we will look at the evolution of first and second person pronouns, both the Latin-derived pronouns and the Spanish innovations.

12.3.1 Third Person Pronouns

Table 12.4 shows the evolution of third person subject pronouns, such as *él* in *él canta bien* and *ellas* in *ellas cantan bien también*. These forms are all stressed.

As was the case for the definite articles, we assume that *él* derives from the nominative, whereas *ella* and *ello* could come from either the nominative or the accusative. Because the forms maintained their stress when functioning as

TABLE 12.4 Evolution of Spanish third person subject pronouns

Latin demonstrative	Modern Spanish
ILLE (m. sg.)	*él*
ILLA (f. sg.)	*ella*
ILLUD (n. sg.)	*ello*
ILLŌS (m. pl.)	*ellos*
ILLĀS (f. pl.)	*ellas*

TABLE 12.5 Evolution of Spanish third person object pronouns

Latin accusative	Modern Spanish direct object	Latin dative	Modern Spanish indirect object
ILLUM (m. sg.)	*lo*	ILLĪ (m. and f. sg.)	*le, se*
ILLAM (f. sg.)	*la*		
ILLUD (n.)	*lo*		
ILLŌS (m. pl.)	*los*	ILLĪS (m. and f. pl.)	*les, se*
ILLĀS (f. pl.)	*las*		

subject pronouns, they maintained both syllables, rather than losing the initial vowel through apheresis like the definite articles. The stress also meant that Latin LL changed to /ʎ/ (and later /j/ or /y/ in most dialects), in all forms, except for *él*, which underwent apocope. The third person pronouns used after prepositions are the same as the subject pronouns, as in *el libro es para ella* and *voy a ir con ellos*.

Table 12.5 shows the evolution of the third person unstressed object pronouns. Logically, the direct object pronouns came from the accusative case and the indirect object pronouns came from the dative case in Latin, thereby continuing the functions of those cases.

The object pronouns lost their stress and became clitic pronouns, which means that they do not exist independently, but rather form a single phonological unit with the verb. For example, one can say *la veo*, where *la* is followed by a verb, but one cannot say *la* by itself, as in *¿A quién ves?* *La. We will consider clitic pronoun placement in Chapter 15 on syntactic changes.

The indirect object pronouns *le* and *les* take the form *se* when followed by a direct object pronoun, as in *La madre se lo lee* 'the mother reads it to him/her/them.' This came about first through regular sound change and then through analogy. Latin ILLĪ ILLUM underwent the following regular changes on its way to Spanish *se lo* after the final /i/ of ILLĪ became yod before the initial vowel of ILLUM: [eljelo] > [ljelo] > [ʎelo] > [dʒelo] > [ʒelo], often written *ge lo* in Old Spanish, as seen in the Appendix (B28, C123, D227c, E34). Then this form became *se lo* when *ge* adopted the form of reflexive pronoun *se*. Thus, the indirect object pronouns *le* and *se* are allomorphs (discussed in Chapter 10) that both derive from ILLĪ.

Complete Activity 12-1 on page 261.

12.3.2 First and Second Person Pronouns

The first and second person subject pronouns came directly from the Latin nominative forms, as one would expect, whereas the stressed pronouns following a preposition came from the dative in the singular and from the nominative in the plural.

As seen in Table 12.6, Latin *vos* was originally the plural form of *tú*. However, in Spoken Latin, vōs was sometimes used as a singular form to show respect, a function that carried over into Old Spanish. Up until the fifteenth century, although there was variation in the use of the two forms, *vos* was used as a form

TABLE 12.6 Evolution of Spanish first and second person stressed pronouns

Latin	Modern Spanish subject	Latin	Modern Spanish post-prepositional
EGO (1sg. nom.)	*yo*	MIHI (1sg. dat.)	*mí*
TŪ (2sg. nom.)	*tú*	TIBI (2sg. dat.)	*ti*
NŌS (1pl. nom.)	*nos(otros)*	NŌS (1pl. nom.)	*nos(otros)*
VŌS (2pl. nom.)	*vos(otros)*	VŌS (2pl. nom.)	*vos(otros)*

of respect in both singular and plural and as the familiar form in the plural, and *tú* was reserved for the singular familiar form. By the sixteenth century, *vos* came to be used as the singular familiar form alongside *tú*. To this day in many South American and Central American countries and parts of Mexico, *vos* is the singular familiar form and in other regions of Latin America *tú* is used for the familiar singular. Since *vos* could be used for both singular and plural, a new form, *vosotros*, came into use to indicate the plural. Then *nos* became *nosotros* by analogy to *vosotros*. Box 12.1 provides further details on the evolution of *vosotros* and *nosotros*.

Box 12.1 Y'all comin' to dinner?

It can be confusing for learners of English that *you* and its corresponding conjugation express both the singular and plural forms of the second person. Depending on your variety of English, however, you probably use one of the many expanded forms of *you* for the plural pronoun. Rini (1999b: 210) offers this list of expanded forms in American English, many of which come from Spitzer (1947): *you all, y'all, yóu-two, yóu-three, yóu-people, yóu-folks, yóu-uns* (< *yóu-ones*, pronounced ['ju-əns]), *yous, you guys,* and *yous guys*. This same process explains why Spanish speakers created *vosotros*. It was a way of distinguishing plural *vos* from singular *vos* in the same way that Americans say *y'all* or *you guys* for the plural of *you*. Once *vosotros* was created, then *nosotros* was created by analogy on the same model.

Given the vast array of forms for *you* plural in English, Rini (1999b) wondered whether Medieval Spanish speakers used, along with *vos otros*, any other expanded plural forms, like **vos dos* 'you two,' **vos gente* 'you-people, you-folks,' **vos unos* 'yóu-uns,' **voses* 'yous,' and *vos todos* 'you all, y'all.' The only one of these found in Alfonsine texts is *vos todos* which occurs "almost to the total exclusion of *vos otros*" (Rini 1999b: 212). Even so, the number of tokens for these forms is small: 39 for *vos todos*, 23 for *nos todos*, 5 for *vos otros*, and 2 of *nos otros*. The higher number of tokens with *todos* (86%) suggests that *vos todos* emerged in Castilian before *vos otros*. If this is the case, what could have caused *vos* *todos* and *nos todos* to be replaced by *vos otros* and *nos otros?* Rini (1999b: 216) proposes that *vos otros* was preferred because it appeared to fit in better with the possessive adjectives and pronouns *vuestro, vuestra, vuestros, vuestras.* Even though *vosotros* (< VŌS ALTERŌS 'you others') and *vuestros* (< VOSTRŌS) had different origins, their similarity may have made speakers prefer *vosotros* to *vos todos* (Rini 1999b).

Now imagine if Spanish had continued the way of English with an expanded form of *vos todos.* This could have resulted in the synthetic and phonetically simplified form **votodos/as* which then could have extended by analogy to first person plural resulting in **notodos/as.* Now imagine if English had mirrored Spanish in its use of *vos* and *otros* as an expanded form. Instead of saying *y'all* or *you guys,* you might say the following: **Y'others comin' to dinner?*

Complete Activities 12-2, 12-3, and 12-4 on pages 263–66.

When *vos* was lost as a second person singular form of respect, another form was created to fill this void. Several forms were used, for example, *su señoría* 'your lordship,' *vuestra señoría* 'your lordship,' *su merced* 'your mercy,' *vuestra merced* 'your mercy,' among others. Which of these options do you think evolved to *usted?* That form was *vuestra merced,* which underwent several contractions, some of which included *vuesa merced, vuesarced, voacé, vusted,* and *vested,* on its way to becoming *usted.* The plural form *vuestras mercedes* contracted to *ustedes.*

Complete Activity 12-5 on page 266.

Turning our attention now to the pronouns following prepositions, we arrive at the interesting origin of *conmigo, contigo,* and *consigo.* These came from the combination of the Latin preposition CUM 'with' plus the ablative forms of the personal pronouns, MĒ, TĒ, and SĒ. In the flexible word order of Latin, the order MĒCUM, TĒCUM, and SĒCUM was more frequent than CUM MĒ, CUM TĒ, and CUM SĒ. Through regular sound change MĒCUM, TĒCUM, and SĒCUM would have changed to *mego, *tego, and *sego. At this point, speakers would no longer have been aware that the construction contained the preposition CUM, and so they added another CUM before the forms, thereby expressing the preposition twice. Through regular sound changes, this would result in *conmego, *contego, and *consego. The earliest attested forms in Spanish, though, are comigo, contigo, and consigo. One finds comigo in two of the excerpts in the Appendix (C132, E27, 40). One assumes that the stressed vowel changed from /e/ to /i/ by analogy to the forms of the pronouns used after other prepositions, namely mí, ti, and si. Furthermore, comigo eventually added an /n/ (> conmigo) to become like contigo and consigo. An interesting development in Modern Spanish is that one sometimes hears sinmigo 'without me' or sintigo 'without you' formed by analogy to conmigo. One popular example is the song Sinmigo by the Mexican artist, José Madero Vizcaíno.

We also find a similar development in the 1pl. and 2pl. forms after the preposition CUM. In the expressions NŌBĪSCUM and VŌBĪSCUM, the ablative forms NŌBĪS and VŌBĪS were replaced by the accusative to become NŌSCUM and VŌSCUM. With the addition of the initial CUM, these forms then became connusco/connosco and convusco/convosco, which are widely attested in Old Spanish. For example, one finds convusco in the Appendix (E38). These were of course replaced in Modern Spanish by con nosotros and con vosotros.

A word is in order regarding the change from TIBI > Spanish ti. Through regular sound change TIBI would become teve. We must conclude then that ti results from analogy to mí, which would result through regular change from MIHI, since the intervocalic /h/ would be lost and long /i/ would become /i/.

First and second person unstressed pronouns, both direct object and indirect object, all derive from the Latin accusative, unlike the third person unstressed pronouns whose indirect object forms came instead from the dative of ILLE. This explains why a form like me can be either a direct object, as in me entiendes, or an indirect object, as in me mandas un mensaje. Table 12.7 shows the evolution of first and second person unstressed pronouns.

Like the third person pronouns, the first and second person unstressed pronouns are also clitics and join with the verb to form a single unit. The only

TABLE 12.7 Evolution of Spanish first and second person unstressed pronouns

Latin accusative	Modern Spanish direct and indirect objects
MĒ	*me*
TĒ	*te*
NŌS	*nos*
VŌS	*(v)os*

irregular sound change in these forms is the loss of the initial /b/ of *vos*, so that it becomes *os*.

12.4 Why Does Spanish Have Two Possessives, like *mi* and *mía*?

As you know, Spanish possessives have short forms, like the determiner/adjective in *mi casa*, and long forms, like the adjective in *la casa mía* or the pronoun in *esa casa es mía*. Both forms derive from Latin possessive forms that also functioned as both determiners and pronouns. Table 12.8 shows the Latin forms for the masculine and feminine in the accusative case, since these are the forms that evolved into Spanish.

When the possessives functioned as determiners, the unboxed forms in Table 12.8, they became unstressed and the final vowel was eventually lost, except in the case of *nuestro* and *vuestro*. Note that the final vowel was maintained for a time in Old Spanish, which explains the form *mio Cid*, rather than *mi Cid*, in the title of the epic poem and throughout the poem (Appendix B). The masculine forms TUUM/TUŌS and SUUM/SUŌS when unstressed became *to/tos* and *so/sos* through regular sound changes when the short ŭ lowered to /o/ and the two vowels merged into one. By contrast, feminine singular TUA/TUĀS and SUA/SUĀS became *tu/tus* and *su/sus*. Penny (2002: 141) believes this is the result of **dissimilation** (*la disimilación*), whereby the regular result of the ŭ became /u/ instead of /o/ so as to be further differentiated from the final

TABLE 12.8 Evolution of Spanish possessives

Latin	Modern Spanish	Latin	Modern Spanish
Singular	Singular	Plural	Plural
MEUM, MEA	*mi,* mío, mía	MEŌS, MEĀS	*mis,* míos, mías
TUUM, TUA	*tu,* tuyo, tuya	TUŌS, TUĀS	*tus,* tuyos, tuyas
SUUM, SUA	*su,* suyo, suya	SUŌS, SUĀS	*sus,* suyos, suyas
Plural			
NŎSTRUM, NŎSTRA	nuestro, nuestra	NŎSTRŌS, NŎSTRĀS	nuestros, nuestras
VĔSTRUM, VĔSTRA	vuestro, vuestra	VĔSTRŌS, VĔSTRĀS	vuestros, vuestras

/a/. Lloyd (1987: 279), citing Meadows (1948), believes instead that the ŭ raised to /u/ because of a following yod that developed between the two vowels ŭ and A. You will recall from Chapter 6 that adjacent vowels in different syllables are said to be in hiatus and so a yod that develops between these vowels is called an **antihiatic yod** (*una yod antihiática*), a yod that breaks up the hiatus. This yod would then have been lost along with the final vowel, so that the resulting forms are *tu* and *tus*. The final step occurred when the masculine adopted the feminine forms, so that in the Modern Spanish forms *tu/tus* and *su/sus* the gender distinction has been lost. The antihiatic yod just mentioned was maintained in long stressed forms, such as *tuyo/tuya* and *suyo/suya*. The appearance of the yod may also have been a case of analogy to *cuyo* from CUIUS 'of whom.' A confirmed case of analogy is the change of VĔSTRUM to VŎSTRUM (> *vuestro*), no doubt by analogy with NŎSTRUM and the closely related subject pronoun VŌS.

12.5 Did *ninguno, nadie,* and *nada* Start out as Negative Words?

The negative adjective and pronoun *ninguno* (< NEC ŪNUM) is the only one of these three words to come from a negative word in Latin. The first syllable comes from NEC 'nor' kept no doubt because ŪNUM was already in use as the numeral and indefinite article *uno*. Through regular sound changes NEC ŪNUM would have become *neguno*, its form in Old Spanish. The initial vowel /i/ rather than /e/ may result from analogy to *ni* 'neither,' also from NEC, and the insertion or **epenthesis** (*la epéntesis*) of the second /n/ may result from the continued nasalization or nasal spreading of the initial /n/. (See Ranson 1996 on this last point.)

The negative pronoun *nadie* underwent a series of interesting changes in both meaning and form. How did a word that originally meant 'born' (< NATUM) end up meaning 'no one'? The first step was shortening of the phrase HOMINEM NATUM 'a man born' to just NATUM. This process where the noun is deleted and the adjective takes over the meaning of the entire noun phrase is fairly common. One example from Modern Spanish is using *postal* for *tarjeta postal*, as discussed further in Chapter 16. The next step was the broadening of the meaning from 'a human being born' to 'anyone at all.' Finally, this changed to the opposite meaning of 'no one at all' and then to 'no one' because of the use of this term in negative sentences. If such a change occurred in English, it would be like the word *soul* in the noun phrase *a living soul* taking on the meaning of 'anyone' and then from its use in *I don't see a living soul, soul* would come to mean 'no one.' As for the sound changes, NATUM would have evolved regularly to *nado*, but changed instead to *nadie* by analogy to *quien* (Penny 2002: 147–48). A similar process occurred with *nada*, which came from the feminine form of the same adjective, NATAM 'born,' in the noun phrase REM NATAM, literally 'a thing born.' In the same way NATUM came to mean 'anyone at all,' NATAM came to mean 'anything at all,' then 'nothing at all,' and finally 'nothing' from its use in negative sentences. Unlike *nadie, nada* comes from NATAM through regular sound changes.

12.6 Why Do Some Speakers Say *más malo* instead of *peor*?

The comparative expresses a comparison, like *clearer*, and the superlative expresses the highest degree, like *clearest*. In Latin, the comparative and superlative of adjectives could be expressed either with synthetic forms with inseparable suffixes, comparable to *clearer* in English, or with analytical constructions

TABLE 12.9 Comparative and superlative adjectives in Latin and Spanish

	Latin synthetic	Spanish	Latin analytical	Spanish
Positive	CARUM	*caro*	DUBIUM	*dudoso*
Comparative	CARIŌREM	*más caro*	MAGIS or PLŪS DUBIUM	*más dudoso*
Superlative	CARISSIMUM	*el más caro*	MAXIMĒ DUBIUM	*el más dudoso*

with separable forms, comparable to English *more clear*. The analytical forms were used with adjectives ending in -IUS, like DUBIUS 'doubtful' with the accusative DUBIUM. Thus, the Latin adjectives for *caro* 'expensive, dear' and *dudoso* 'doubtful' had the forms shown in Table 12.9 in the masculine accusative singular with their Spanish translations.

You have probably determined that the analytical comparative and superlative forms survived in Spanish, but with some differences. The analytical forms with PLŪS and MAXIMĒ fell out of use in Hispano-Romance, but the form with MAGIS gave rise to the Spanish comparative *más caro* and the superlative *el más caro*. Thus, we see another change from a synthetic form in Latin to an analytical construction in Spanish. It is interesting, though, that the Latin synthetic comparative forms of the adjectives 'good,' 'bad,' 'big,' and 'small' have survived as *mejor* (< MELIŌREM), *peor* (< PEIŌREM), *mayor* (< MAIŌREM), and *menor* (< MENŌREM). The meaning of *mayor* and *menor* has become more specific, though, so that it is now limited to age. A sentence like *Ella es mayor que yo* means that she is older than I am, not larger. To indicate size one would have to say *más grande* and *más pequeño*. Even *mejor* and *peor*, which have kept the same meaning, have the analytical counterparts *más bueno* and *más malo*, although the analytical comparatives are used more often to refer to the moral character of a person, as in *José es el chico más malo en esa pandilla* 'José is the worst kid in that gang.' If this surprises you, a simple internet search will return numerous examples of *más bueno* and *más malo*. It appears then that Spanish speakers are on the way to eliminating the synthetic comparatives altogether. In English as well, the ultimate result of the variation between forms like synthetic *clearer* and analytical *more clear* may be the use of the *more clear* construction with all adjectives.

The superlative ending -ISSIMUM has survived in Spanish as -*ísimo*, but it is no longer used as a superlative; rather it is used to express a high degree of the quality of an adjective, such as 'very' or 'extremely,' as in *carísimo* and *altísimo*. The four common adjectives mentioned above also had the irregular superlative forms OPTIMUM 'best,' PESSIMUM 'worst,' MAXIMUM 'most,' and MINIMUM 'least.' Activity 12-6 asks you to consider the results of these forms and other comparative and superlative forms.

Complete Activity 12-6 on page 268.

12.7 Chapter Summary

- Determiners are words that precede a noun, like the definite article *la* in *la historia*, whereas pronouns are words that replace a noun, like *la* in *la encuentro interesante*.
- The definite articles came from the different forms of the Latin demonstrative ILLE 'that over there.'
- The indefinite article in Spanish came from the Latin word ŪNUM 'one.' This number was only singular in Latin, so new plural forms *unos* and *unas* were created in Spanish by analogy to the plural forms of nouns.
- The demonstrative adjective and pronoun *este* comes from Latin ISTE with a change of meaning from 'that' to 'this.' The forms of Latin IPSE 'himself' develop into the demonstrative *ese* 'that.' The demonstrative *aquel* comes from *ACCU ILLE, which was made up of *ACCU, a variant of ECCE 'behold,' serving to reinforce ILLE.
- ILLE also developed into third person personal subject, direct object, and indirect object pronouns.
- Most of the first and second person possessives and subject, direct object, and indirect object pronouns are direct descendants from their counterparts in Latin, with only a few adjustments. One of the exceptional changes occurs in *conmigo*, and also *contigo* and *consigo*, which comes from CUM MĒ CUM, in

which the preposition CUM appears twice. Another change is the addition of *otros* to the second person plural pronoun *vos* to indicate plurality. The same change also occurred in *nosotros* by analogy to *vosotros*. The pronouns used to express respect and social distance, *usted* and *ustedes*, came from *vuestra merced* 'your mercy' and *vuestras mercedes* 'your mercies.'

- The changes in the nominal elements reviewed in this chapter mirror many of the changes in nouns from Chapter 11. The complex Latin system of cases and declensions has been lost, so that nouns and nominal elements distinguish only number and gender and person in the personal pronouns. Traces of the former Latin cases are seen only in the functions of subject, object, and indirect object in personal pronouns.

- The negative pronoun *ninguno* came from NEC ŪNUM 'not one' by undergoing reshaping through analogy. *Nadie* also underwent analogy and *nadie* and *nada* underwent semantic changes from positive terms to negative ones.

- Latin expressed the comparative and superlative of most adjectives through synthetic forms, like FORTIŌREM 'stronger' and FORTISSIMUM 'strongest,' or in a small set of adjectives through analytical forms, like MAGIS DUBIUS 'more doubtful' and MAXIMĒ DUBIUS 'most doubtful.' These have been replaced by analytical forms, like *más fuerte* and *el más fuerte* in Spanish, except for a few frequent comparatives that remain synthetic, like *mejor* and *peor*. Some of the other Latin synthetic comparatives and superlatives are still used, but with other meanings, like FORTISSIMUM > *fortísimo* with a change of meaning from 'strongest' to 'very strong.'

Activities

Activity 12-1
In Table 12.10 we reproduce ILLE in all its declensions, as in Table 12.1, in order for you to trace its evolution to all of its Spanish reflexes.

TABLE 12.10 Spanish reflexes of Latin ILLE

	Latin	Spanish				
		definite article *el libro*	demon-strative *aquel libro* < *ACCU + ILLE	subject *él habla*	indirect object *le hablo*	direct object *lo veo*
m. sg.						
nom.	ILLE	*el*	*aquel*	*él*		
gen.	ILLĪUS					
dat.	ILLĪ				*le*	
acc.	ILLUM					*lo*
abl.	ILLŌ					
neuter sg.						
nom./acc.	ILLUD					
m. pl.						
nom.	ILLĪ					
gen.	ILLŌRUM					
dat.	ILLĪS					
acc.	ILLŌS					
abl.	ILLĪS					
f. sg.						
nom.	ILLA					
gen.	ILLĪUS					
dat.	ILLĪ					
acc.	ILLAM					
abl.	ILLĀ					

TABLE 12.10 (cont.)

	Latin	Spanish				
		definite article *el libro*	demon-strative *aquel libro* < *ACCU + ILLE	subject *él habla*	indirect object *le hablo*	direct object *lo veo*
f. pl.						
nom.	ILLAE					
gen.	ILLĀRUM					
dat.	ILLĪS					
acc.	ILLĀS					
abl.	ILLĪS					

1. Write the Spanish forms that derived from ILLE in the appropriate cell in Table 12.10. The answers for the masculine singular have already been included as an example.
2. Which cases do not provide any of the surviving forms of ILLE?
3. Which Latin case do the subjects come from? And the indirect objects? And the direct objects? Does this correspond to the function of these cases in Latin?
4. What differences do you observe between the definite articles and the demonstratives? And between the subject pronouns and the direct and indirect object pronouns?

Activity 12-2

The first and second person pronouns in Spanish come from the same pronouns in Latin. The forms of these pronouns in Latin are displayed in Table 12.11.

1. Write down the pronouns in Spanish on the same line as their Latin etyma. The answers for the first person singular pronouns have been done for you.

TABLE 12.11 Spanish reflexes of the Latin first and second person pronouns

	Latin	Spanish			
		subject (stressed)	indirect object (unstressed)	direct object (unstressed)	object of preposition (stressed)
1sg.					
nom.	EGO	*yo*			
gen.	MEĪ				
dat.	MIHI				*mí*
acc.	MĒ		*me*	*me*	
abl.	MĒ				
2sg.					
nom.	TU				
gen.	TUĪ				
dat.	TIBI				
acc.	TĒ				
abl.	TĒ				
1pl.					
nom.	NŌS				
gen.	NOSTRĪ				
dat.	NŌBĪS				
acc.	NŌS				
abl.	NŌBĪS				
2pl.					
nom.	VŌS				
gen.	VĔSTRĪ				
dat.	VŌBĪS				
acc.	VŌS				
abl.	VŌBĪS				

2. What Latin case do the subject forms come from? And the indirect objects? And the direct objects? And the stressed post-prepositional objects? Does this correspond to the function of these cases in Latin?

3. What are the differences between the subject and object pronouns?

Activity 12-3 tú vs. vos

In the following passages from *Cantar de mio Cid*, determine whether each speaker addresses someone as *tú* or *vos* by writing this pronoun next to the name of this person below. What conclusions can you draw about the use of *tú* and *vos* in this passage?

Speaker	Speaking to	Pronoun used
Jimena	God	
Abbot Don Sancho	El Cid	
El Cid	Abbot Don Sancho	
	his wife and daughters	
	his nephew, Félez Munnoz	

1. [*Abbot Don Sancho invites Cid to stay with him and Cid gives him 50 marks (coins)*]

   - (A)gradézcolo a Dios, mio Çid, – dixo el abbat don Sancho – (247)
   pues que aquí vos veo, prendet de mí ospedado ('take lodging with me'). –
   Dixo el Çid, - Graçias, don abbat, e só(y) vuestro pagado ('I am indebted to you'), . . .
   mas porque me vo(y) de (esta) tierra, dó(y) vos çinquaenta marcos.

2. [*Jimena is praying to God to protect Cid*]

   Ya Señor glorioso, Padre que en çielo estás, (330) . . .
   Tú eres rey de los reyes e de todo el mundo padre, (361)
   a ti adoro e creo de toda voluntad,

3. [*Cid invites his wife and daughters to go with him to Valencia*]

   Vós, querida e ondrada ('honored') mugier, e amas ('both') mis fijas, (1604)
   mi coraçón e mi alma,
   entrad comigo en Valençia la casa

4. ¿O heres ('where are you'), mío sobrino, tú, Félez Munnoz? (2618)

   Primo eres de mis fijas amas d'alma y de coraçón

Activity 12-4

Vos vs. *tú* in Latin America

Find out whether *tú* or *vos* is the most frequent form of familiar address in four countries or regions in Latin America or the Caribbean. One way to do this is to use the *Corpus de Referencia del Español Actual* (CREA) (Real Academia Española). In the window for "consulta" enter either *vos* or *tú*. Under "medio" select "todos" and under "geográfico" select one at a time each country you are interested in. The number of tokens you find for *vos* and for *tú* for each search will give you an idea of its prevalence in each country. Report your results in a paragraph or a table.

Bonus: Why do some countries use *vos* and others *tú*? Conduct a brief internet search to find an answer.

Activity 12-5

Corpus Search: *vos todos* vs. *vos otros*

Investigate the two plural forms *vos todos* and *vos otros* in Old Spanish texts by performing a search on these forms in the *Corpus del español*, following steps 1–4 below. Record your results in Table 12.12. We have included the results for *vos todos* as an example.

1. Go to corpusdelespanol.org and then click on the Genre/Historical corpus to bring up the search box.
2. Select "Chart" and then one at a time write each of the forms you have selected in the search box and click on "see frequency by section." This will bring up a chart with your results.
3. In Table 12.12 write down the number under "freq" for six time periods, the 1200s, the 1300s, the 1400s, the 1500s, the 1600s, and the 1700s. This is the total number of times the word you searched appears in the texts included in the corpus for each century.
4. Also, write down the number under "per mil" for each century. This is the number of times this word appears per million words in texts from this time period.

TABLE 12.12 Frequency of *vos todos* vs. *vos otros* in different centuries

Word	1200s		1300s		1400s		1500s		1600s		1700s	
	freq	per mil	freq	per mil	freq	per mil	freq	per mil	freq	per mil	freq	per mil
Example												
vos todos	13	1.94	20	7.49	9	1.1	4	0.23	5	0.4	1	0.10
vos todas												
vos otros												
vos otras												
vosotros												
vosotras												

After you have recorded your results, compare the frequencies for the forms with *todos* and those with *otros*. Is there a preference for forms with *todos* in the twelfth century followed by a shift towards forms with *otros* as described by Rini (1999b)?

Activity 12-6 Comparative adjectives

Even though the Latin synthetic comparative and superlative forms are no longer used with this function in Modern Spanish, with the exception of the comparatives *mejor, peor, mayor,* and *menor,* many of these forms survive with other meanings. Table 12.13 presents Latin adjectives and their comparative and superlative forms.

1. Write the Spanish reflex under each one and give its meaning in Spanish. If the form no longer exists in Spanish, write the dagger symbol (†) next to it to

TABLE 12.13 Latin positive, comparative, and superlative adjectives and their Spanish reflexes

Adjective	Comparative	Superlative
1. BONUM 'good'	MELIŌREM	OPTIMUM
bueno 'good'	*mejor* 'better'	*óptimo* 'ideal, perfect'
2. MALUM 'bad'	PEIŌREM	PESSIMUM
3. MAGNUM 'large'	MAIŌREM	MAXIMUM
4. PARVUM 'small'	MINŌREM	MINIMUM
5. MULTUM 'much, many'	PLŪS	PLŪRIMUM
6. SUPERUM 'above, high'	SUPERIŌREM	SUPRĒMUM
7. EXTERNUM 'foreign, external'	EXTERIŌREM	EXTRĒMUM
8. INFERNUM 'underneath'	INFERIŌREM	INFIMUM
9. IUVENEM 'young'	IUNIŌREM	IUVENISSIMUM
10. POSTERUM 'following, next'	POSTERIŌREM	POSTRĒMUM
11. SENEM 'old'	SENIŌREM	SENISSIMUM
12. ULTRA 'beyond, on the other side''	ULTERIŌREM	ULTIMUM

indicate a lost form. The first example, BONUM, MELIŌREM, and OPTIMUM has been completed for you as an example.

2. What generalizations can you make about the change in meaning of these forms? Explain how these words are an example of repurposing.

3. Bonus question: List five words in English that come from the Latin words in this table. What is their relationship to the meaning in Latin?

Further Reading

Girón Alconchel, José Luis 1998. "Sobre el reajuste morfológico de los demostrativos en el español clásico," in Claudio García Turza, Fabián González Bachiller, and Javier Mangado Martínez (eds.), *Actas del IV Congreso Internacional de Historia de la Lengua Española*, I: 493–502. Logroño: Universidad de La Rioja

Líbano Zumalacárregui, Ángeles 1991. "Morfología diacrónica del español: las fórmulas de tratamiento," *Revista de filología española* 71(1): 107–21

Rini, Joel 1990. "On the chronology of Spanish *conmigo, contigo, consigo* and the interaction of phonological, syntactic, and morphological processes," *Hispanic Review* 58(4): 503–12

13 | Why Are There So Many Verb Tenses in Spanish?

Origins of Verbs

Lead-in Questions

13-1 Write down three sentences in English about your life. Now do the same thing in Spanish. Which verb tenses did you use in these sentences? Do you think these are the verb tenses you use most often? Are there other verb tenses that you are familiar with but do not use often? Which ones are these?

13-2 Which sentence do you prefer: *I'll go to the game this weekend* or *I'm going to the game this weekend*? Can you think of a context where the one you didn't prefer sounds better to you? Now try these sentences: *I ate the last apple. I have eaten the last apple.* Which sounds more natural to you? Do they mean the same thing?

Students of Spanish often want to know why there are so many verb tenses in Spanish. To arrive at an answer to this question, as for so many other questions about Modern Spanish, we will begin by looking at Latin. Whereas Latin had only ten verb tenses, six in the indicative and four in the subjunctive, Spanish has fourteen verb tenses, ten in the indicative and four in the subjunctive. Of the ten Latin tenses, four were kept, two were lost, and four were repurposed. In Spanish ten new tenses were created. This chapter outlines these changes and then focuses in particular on the new future and conditional forms, like cantaré *and* cantaría, *and the compound tenses, like* he cantado *and* había cantado. *We will see how these tenses were created and then look at the competition in Modern Spanish between two future forms,* cantaré *and* voy a cantar, *and two past tense forms, the preterit* canté *and the present perfect* he cantado.

13.1 What Is a Verb Tense?

Speakers of English and Spanish find it useful to indicate the time of an event, whether past, present, or future, by the tense of the verb they choose. In its most basic definition a verb tense is a verb form that indicates time. The word *tense* comes to English from Old French *tens* (Modern French *temps*), meaning 'time' from TEMPUS 'stretch of time,' which becomes *tiempo* in Spanish. If you have ever wondered why a verb tense seems to be tense or strained, it is because both meanings of *tense* in English go back to Latin TEMPUS, which comes from a Proto-Indo-European root meaning 'to stretch' (Harper 2001–17 "time"). By considering Spanish verb forms like the preterit *canté* and the imperfect *cantaba*, we see that tenses do not indicate only time, since both of these are past, but that they can also express other nuances of meaning. We will see in this chapter how Spanish speakers reorganized the verb tenses of Latin, by keeping some and losing some, repurposing others, and especially by creating new tenses. We will see that these new tenses arose as analytical constructions made up of existing elements that allowed speakers to express nuances of meaning not expressed through verb tenses in Latin. In this chapter, we will explore these changes with a special focus on the creation of new tenses in Spanish, their evolution, and how they entered into competition with existing tenses.

13.2 How Are Verb Tenses Reorganized from Latin to Spanish?

13.2.1 How Are Spanish Verb Tenses Organized?

In Chapter 10 (Table 10.2), in the introduction to morphology, you saw that the verb tenses in Spanish are organized into **simple tenses** (*tiempos simples*) and **compound tenses** (*tiempos compuestos*). A simple tense, like the present tense *canto*, consists of one synthetic form whose stem and ending are inseparable. For example, it is impossible to place anything between the stem *cant-* and the ending *-o*. One can say *yo canto* or *canto yo*, but not **cant- yo -o*. There are also compound tenses in Spanish made up of a form of the verb *haber* plus a past participle, such as the present perfect *he cantado*. These compound forms are analytical, meaning that the auxiliary is separable from the past participle and that speakers can analyze these verb forms into these two parts. One can say *yo he cantado, he cantado yo*, or *he yo cantado*. The last form, which illustrates the separability of *he* and *cantado*, is no doubt less frequent than the others.

The tenses in Spanish are organized so that for every simple tense, there is a corresponding compound tense. By a corresponding compound tense, we mean a tense where the auxiliary verb *haber* is in the same tense as the simple tense. Thus, for the present tense *canto* there is a corresponding compound tense *he cantado*, with *haber* in the present indicative. Table 13.1 summarizes the verb tenses in Spanish by presenting the simple tenses for *cantar* in the upper row and the corresponding compound tenses in the lower row.

Not only does each simple tense have a corresponding compound tense with a certain form, but each corresponding compound tense also has a certain meaning with respect to the simple form. Consider these examples of pairs of sentences with simple and compound tenses:

present / present perfect: *Vengo a clase. Ya he hecho la tarea.*
imperfect / pluperfect: *Venía a clase. Ya había hecho la tarea.*
future / future perfect: *Vendré a clase. Ya habré hecho la tarea.*
conditional / conditional perfect: *Vendría a clase. Ya habría hecho la tarea.*

TABLE 13.1 Spanish simple and compound verb tenses illustrated by 1sg. of *cantar*

Indicative

Simple tenses				
present	imperfect	future	conditional	preterit
canto	*cantaba*	*cantaré*	*cantaría*	*canté*

Compound tenses				
present perfect	pluperfect	future perfect	conditional perfect	past preterit
he cantado	*había cantado*	*habré cantado*	*habría cantado*	*hube cantado*

Subjunctive

Simple tenses		
present	imperfect	future*
cante	*cantara* or *cantase*	*cantare*

Compound tenses		
perfect	pluperfect	future perfect*
haya cantado	*hubiera* or *hubiese cantado*	*hubiere cantado*

* These tenses are no longer used in Modern Spanish, but appear in Old Spanish texts, in some legal documents, and in set phrases such as *Adónde fueres haz lo que vieres* ('When in Rome, do as the Romans do,' literally 'Wherever you might go, do what you will see'). Three future subjunctive forms appear in the Appendix: A17 *fure* 'fuere,' D231a *mandares*, E20 *levare*.

preterit / past perfect: *Vine a clase. Ya hube hecho la tarea.*

present subjunctive / present perfect subjuntive. *La profesora quiere que venga a clase. Quiere que haya hecho la tarea ya.*

imperfect subjunctive / pluperfect subjunctive: *La profesora quería que viniera a clase. Quería que hubiera hecho la tarea ya.*

We see that in each case, whether the verbs refer to present, past, or future actions, the compound tense expresses an action that occurs prior to the action in the simple tense. For example, in the present, I have done my homework before I go to class. In the past, I had done my homework before I went to class. And in the future, I will have done my homework before I will go to class. We can say then that the compound tenses express anteriority.

13.2.2 How Are Latin Verb Tenses Organized?

The ten verb tenses of the Latin active voice, for example, AMŌ 'I love,' rather than the passive AMOR 'I am loved,' are all synthetic forms consisting of a stem and an inseparable ending. These tenses can be organized into present-stem tenses and perfect-stem tenses. If you study the stems of the forms for the verbs CANTĀRE and SCRĪBĔRE 'to write' in Figure 13.1, you will observe that each verb has two different stems. The present stems, CANT- and SCRIB-, are found in the present, imperfect, and future indicative and in the present and imperfect subjunctive. These are left unshaded in the table. The other tenses, the perfect and pluperfect indicative and the perfect and pluperfect subjunctive, begin with a different stem: CANTAV- for CANTĀRE and SCRIPS- for SCRĪBĔRE. The perfect-stem tenses are shaded in the table. Thus, whereas Spanish verbs are organized into simple and compound tenses, Latin verbs are organized into present-stem and perfect-stem tenses. We will see that the Latin present stem corresponds to the simple tenses in Spanish and the Latin perfect stem corresponds to the compound tenses in Spanish.

13.2.3 How Did Verb Tenses Change from Latin to Spanish?

The possible outcomes of Latin verb forms in Spanish are organized in Figure 13.2 according to the possible changes in forms described in Chapter

Indicative							Subjunctive			
Present	Imperfect	Future	Perfect	Pluperfect	Future perfect		Present	Imperfect	Perfect	Pluperfect
CANTŌ	CANTĀBAM	CANTĀBO	CANTĀVĪ	CANTĀVERAM	CANTĀVERO		CANTEM	CANTĀREM	CANTĀVERIM	CANTĀVISSEM
SCRĪBŌ	SCRĪBĒBAM	SCRĪBAM	SCRĪPSĪ	SCRĪPSERAM	SCRĪPSERŌ		SCRĪBAM	SCRĪBEREM	SCRĪPSERIM	SCRĪPSISSEM

Figure 13.1 Latin present-stem and perfect-stem verb tenses illustrated by 1sg. of CANTĀRE and SCRĪBERE

	Indicative						Subjunctive					
	Present	Imperfect	Future	Perfect	Pluperfect	Future perfect	Present	Imperfect			Perfect	Pluperfect
Latin	CANTŌ	CANTĀBAM	CANTĀBŌ	CANTĀVĪ	CANTĀVERAM	CANTĀVERŌ	CANTEM	CANTĀREM			CANTĀVERIM	CANTĀVISSEM
Spanish												
1 loss			Ø					Ø	future			
2 conservation	canto	cantaba		canté			cante					
3 repurposing					cantara	cantare		cantase / cantara	cantare	cantare	cantare	cantase
4 innovation			cantaré / cantaría / habría cantado	he cantado	había cantado / hube cantado	habré cantado			hubiere cantado		haya cantado	hubiera or hubiese cantado

Figure 13.2 Changes in the organization of verb tenses from Latin to Spanish

10. Indicated on line 2 of the figure are the Latin verb forms that are maintained in Spanish with the same function, those whose result is conservation. These include the present indicative (CANTŌ > *canto*), the imperfect indicative (CANTĀBAM > *cantaba*), the perfect indicative to the Spanish preterit (CANTĀVĪ > *canté*) and the present subjunctive (CANTEM > *cante*). Of the changes in form from Latin to Spanish, the only one that does not undergo regular sound changes is CANTĀVĪ > *canté*. The /w/, written *v*, in Latin is lost, so that the vowel /a/ and /i/ come in contact. The /i/ then changes to yod /j/ and the resulting diphthong /aj/ changes to /e/. Thus, CANTĀVĪ [kan-'ta-wi] > [kan-'tai] > [kan-'taj] > [kan-'te] *canté*.

Another result of Latin verb forms in Spanish is repurposing, which occurs when the form is maintained in Spanish but with a different function. These changes are shown on line 3 of Figure 13.2, where a vertical arrow indicates the development of the form and a horizontal arrow indicates the change in function. We see that the Latin pluperfect indicative CANTĀVERAM loses the syllable VE /we/ and the final /m/ to become *cantara* in Spanish. Then it changes its function to the imperfect subjunctive, even though it could still function as a pluperfect indicative in Old Spanish, as in the Appendix C125 *ela la fiziera* 'she had made it.' The pluperfect subjunctive, CANTĀVISSEM, undergoes similar changes. It loses the syllable VI /wi/ and the final /m/, so that it becomes *cantase* in Spanish. This form also takes on the function of the imperfect subjunctive in Spanish, which explains why there are two competing forms of the imperfect subjunctive in Modern Spanish, even though the form *cantara* is much more frequent. Penny (2002: 201–05) provides an account of how the use of *cantara* and *cantase* in conditional sentences, such as *if I could, I would*, resulted in their having the same imperfect subjunctive function.

Two other forms also change function to become the future subjunctive, which is no longer used in Modern Spanish. These are the future perfect indicative and the perfect subjunctive. Since the forms of these two tenses were identical in Latin, except in the first person singular, it is impossible to tell on the basis of their forms alone which tense provided the forms of the future subjunctive. Admittedly, both of these changes in function are difficult to explain. The future perfect indicative at least expresses an action in the future like the future subjunctive, but why would a verb form change from indicative to subjunctive? The perfect subjunctive is subjunctive like the future subjunctive, but then we have to explain the change from perfect to future time reference.

The Latin verb forms which are not maintained or repurposed end up being lost. These include the future indicative and imperfect subjunctive, whose loss is indicated in line 1 by the zero symbol (Ø). Thus, four Latin verb tenses are maintained in Spanish with the same function (the present, imperfect, and perfect indicative, and the present subjunctive), four are repurposed (the pluperfect indicative as the imperfect subjunctive *cantara*, the pluperfect subjunctive as the imperfect subjunctive *cantase*, and the future perfect indicative and the perfect subjunctive as the future subjunctive *cantare*), and two are lost completely (the future indicative and imperfect subjunctive).

The fourth outcome in Spanish is the new forms that result from innovation. If we compare the Spanish and Latin verb tenses in Figure 13.2, we can see that ten new tenses are created. These include a new form for the future tense, since the Latin future tense forms were lost. These also include new forms for an entirely new function, the conditional, like *cantaría*, and the conditional perfect, like *habría cantado*. The other seven forms are all compound forms made up of the verb *haber* plus a past participle. These new forms continue the functions of perfect tenses in Latin that changed function through repurposing. The one exception is the new present perfect, which does not replace the preterit, but rather exists alongside it with a slightly different meaning. We now turn our attention to the development of these new forms.

Complete Activity 13-1 on page 286.

13.3 The Future and Conditional

13.3.1 How Were the Future and Conditional Created?

Speakers created a new analytical structure made up of the infinitive of the verb plus a conjugated form of the verb HABĒRE to express the future. At first the construction CANTĀRE HABEŌ meant literally 'to sing I have.' In practice, it expressed an obligation in the same way expressions made up of 'to have' and the infinitive express obligation in English (*I have to sing*) and Modern Spanish (*he de cantar* and *tengo que cantar*). Since something that one has to do is something that one will do in the future, this construction changes from a meaning of obligation to a reference to future time.

The conditional is an entirely new tense in Spanish that did not exist in Latin. It was created in the same way as the future, but the verb 'to have' is in the imperfect. Originally then CANTĀRE HABĒBAM, which becomes Modern Spanish *cantaría*, meant 'I had to sing' or '*tenía que cantar*.' Thus, the conditional is essentially a future form from a past perspective. For example, one says from the present perspective: *Digo que comprenderán* 'I say that they will understand' using the future tense. But from a past perspective, one says: *Dije que comprenderían* 'I said that they would understand' using the conditional.

13.3.2 How Have the Future and Conditional Changed?

The future and conditional were originally analytical forms with separable morphemes that speakers could identify as the infinitive and a form of *haber*. In Old Spanish these forms were still separable, since an object pronoun could be placed between them. One finds such examples in the Appendix for the future (A17 *aora lo he* for *lo adoraré* 'I will adore him' and E16 *dezirvos he* for *os diré* 'I will tell you') and the conditional (B23 *conbidar le ien* for *le convidarían* 'they would welcome him' and E17 *cuidarvos ía* for *os cuidaría* 'I would take care (to get this prize) for you'). In Modern Spanish, however, these forms are no longer separable. The change of *haber* from an independent verb to a grammatical ending is an example of grammaticalization, a process mentioned in Chapter 3.

Various changes take place during the process of grammaticalization, in this case, from a free-standing verb, like HABEŌ, to a verbal suffix. One is phonetic reduction or the loss of sounds. Notice that the Latin forms of this verb, 1sg. HABEŌ, 2sg. HABĒS, 3sg. HABET, 1pl. HABĒMUS, 2pl. HABĒTIS, and 3pl. HABENT are significantly reduced as the endings *-é, -as, -a, -emos, -eis*, and *-án*. For example, HABEŌ is reduced from five phonemes to one and the other forms all lose at least three phonemes as well. The same occurs with the conditional endings, where 1sg. HABĒBAM, 2sg. HABĒBAS, 3sg. HABĒBAT, 1pl. HABĒBĀMUS, 2pl. HABĒBĀTIS, and 3pl. HABĒBANT reduce to -*ía, -ías, -ía, -íamos, -íais,* and -*ían.* In all of these forms, the entire first syllable /hab/ is lost along with the second /b/ and the final /m/ and /t/, leaving only /ia/ and any other remaining consonants in the ending. Another change is the loss of meaning, so that the verb endings no longer have the meaning 'to have.' The independent verb also loses its syntactic properties, so that it can no longer change position within the sentence, but must always follow the infinitive and can no longer take objects of its own.

13.3.3 What Is the Periphrastic Future and How Does It Differ from the Simple Future?

At the same time the forms of the 'have-future' (infinitive + HABEŌ) were undergoing grammaticalization, speakers created a new analytical future. This new future is composed of the verb 'to go' followed by the preposition 'to' plus the infinitive, as in *voy a cantar* 'I am going to sing.' In this construction speakers use a metaphor of movement to indicate the future. If I am going (to a place) to sing, then I will sing when I get there: *voy a (un lugar para) cantar.* This new 'go-future,' which is also often called the periphrastic future, is now in competition with the simple or morphological future *cantaré.* In other words, when speakers wish to refer to future time, they can choose either the simple future, *cantaré,* or the periphrastic future, *voy a cantar.* Another choice which has existed since Latin is simply to use the present tense to express future time, as in *voy al partido este fin de semana* 'I'm going to the game this weekend.' This option can be called the **futurate present** (*el presente como futuro*). The history of a speaker's choice for future reference is summarized in Figure 13.3. The arrows mean that a form is replaced by another form whereas the symbol > indicates regular sound change.

Complete Activity 13-2 on page 286.

CL = Classical Latin, SL = Spoken Latin, MS = Modern Spanish

(S) = a synthetic form, (A) = an analytical form

CL CANTABO (S)			
	→ SL CANTARE HABEO (A)	> OS *cantar é* (A)	> MS *cantaré* (S)
			→ EM *voy a cantar* (A)
CL CANTO (S)		> OS *canto* (S)	> MS *canto* (S)

Figure 13.3 Verb forms referring to future time in the history of Spanish

13.4 The Compound Tenses

13.4.1 How Were the Compound Tenses Created?

We have seen in Section 13.2 that all the Latin verbs in the active voice were synthetic and that all the compound tenses in Spanish, like *he cantado, había cantado, habría cantado*, are new analytical creations. These new constructions came from an expression like HABEŌ EPISTOLAM SCRĪPTAM 'I have a letter written' '*tengo una carta escrita*' where HABEŌ expressed possession of an object, the letter, which was modified by a past participle. This sentence had a present tense meaning of 'I have a letter now and it is written.' The use of the past participle to modify the letter is the bridge that explains how the meaning of this sentence changed from present tense to past tense. If I now have in my possession a letter that is written, then someone must have written it in the past. If I am the person who wrote the letter, then 'I have a letter written' changes meaning to 'I have written a letter.'

The construction with HABEŌ, like HABEŌ EPISTOLAM SCRĪPTAM, requires that someone have an object, and so it would be used only with transitive verbs, that is, those that take a direct object. With intransitive verbs, like 'go, come, arrive,' a different expression was used. Here one would use a sentence like SUM VENTA, which meant literally 'I am come,' where the verb SUM is in the present tense and the past participle describes the subject of the verb. Here again the past participle is the bridge between present and past meaning. If I am "come" right now, then I have come in the past. Perhaps you are aware that English used to distinguish between the auxiliaries 'to have' and 'to be' with compound tenses, just like German still does, which is why the original words to the Christmas carol, *Joy to World*, say "Joy to the world, the Lord is come."

13.4.2 How Have the Compound Tenses Changed?

Two important differences have taken place in Spanish since the compound tenses were first attested in writing. As just mentioned, the past participle in the 'to have' construction modified the direct object and so in Old Spanish we still find that it agrees with the direct object like an adjective would. Two such examples from the Appendix are A3 *agora primas la e ueida* 'now for the first time I have seen it' where *la* refers to the star of Bethlehem, and C123 *yo ie las auia enviadas* 'I had sent them to her' where *las* refers to *las alfayas* 'the gloves.'

We also find in Old Spanish the verb *ser* still used as an auxiliary with agreement between its past participle and the subject. The very next line of the *Auto de los reyes magos* in the Appendix (A4) reads *poco timpo a que es nacida* 'a short time ago it was born' 'hace poco tiempo [literally 'poco tiempo ha'] que ha nacido.' In the process of grammaticalization of *haber* and *ser* from the verbs 'to have' and 'to be' to auxiliaries, speakers stopped using *ser* and generalized the use of *haber* as the auxiliary for both transitive and intransitive verbs. The past participles, because of the change from adjectives to part of the verb tense, no longer show agreement. If you happen to know French or Italian, then you know that these languages have kept a distinction between 'to have' and 'to be' auxiliaries and have maintained past participle agreement in certain cases, so that 'she has come' in French is *elle est venue* and in Italian *(lei) è venuta*. So between Old Spanish and Modern Spanish the auxiliary *ser* and the agreement of the past participle with the direct object of a transitive verb or the subject of an intransitive verb has been lost during the grammaticalization process.

CL = Classical Latin, SL = Spoken Latin, MS = Modern Spanish

(S) = a synthetic form, (A) = an analytical form

CL CANTAVI (S)		> OS *canté* (S)	> MS *canté* (S)	
	→ SL HABEO CANTATUM (A) SUM VENTA (A)	> OS *he (una canción) cantada* (A) > OS *soy venida* (A)	> MS *he cantado* (A or S?)	
				→ MS *tengo (una canción) cantada* (A)

Figure 13.4 Two verb forms referring to past time in the history of Spanish

There is another interesting change occurring in Modern Spanish. You are no doubt aware that *haber* was replaced by *tener* as the verb 'to have' in Spanish. The construction that gave rise to the compound tenses in Spanish, like HABEŌ EPISTOLAM SCRĪPTAM, has been recreated by speakers of Spanish today with the verb *tener*. One hears sentences like *tengo una carta escrita* or *tengo la tarea hecha*, which still have present meaning in Spanish. One day in the future, though, they might acquire a past meaning, like the Latin expression did in Old Spanish. It is interesting that this change has already occurred in Portuguese, which uses *ter* 'to have' as the auxiliary in compound tenses. However, in Portuguese the compound tense refers to a repeated action, so that *tenho cantado* means 'I have been singing.' These changes are shown in Figure 13.4.

13.5 Is There a Change in Progress in the Future and Past Tense Forms in Spanish?

We have just seen that there are currently two competing forms in Modern Spanish for expressing the future: the simple future, like *cantaré,* and the periphrastic future, like *voy a cantar.* We also find competing variants for past reference, namely the preterit, like *canté,* and the present perfect, like *he cantado.* We can call each of these different ways of saying the same thing a **variant** (*una variante*). As seen above in Section 3.3.6, a change in progress means that one of these variants will eventually be lost.

One of the ways that linguists can try to determine whether a variant will be lost is to see whether its use relative to the other variant is decreasing over time. For example, a linguist could record conversations with native speakers in Mexico City in 1970 and then record more conversations thirty years later, preferably with the same speakers. If the results show that the speakers used a smaller percentage of forms like *cantaré* to express future in relation to forms like *voy a cantar*, then we can conclude that *cantaré* may be in the process of being lost. This is called a **real time study** (*un estudio en tiempo real*).

Another way to determine whether variation represents a change in progress is to compare the use of variants by speakers of different ages, for example, their use among young speakers between 20 and 35 years old and among older speakers between 55 and 70 years old. If one variant is used less by the younger speakers and more by the older speakers, then we take this to be evidence that this variant may one day be lost. This is called an **apparent time study** (*un estudio en tiempo aparente*).

Linguists who have conducted apparent time studies on the future in Spanish have found that it is used very little (between 0 and 12.5%) in certain regions, like Chile, Puerto Rico, and Venezuela (Silva-Corvalán and Terrell 1992), but that it is used far more often in other regions, like Madrid (47%) (Cartagena 1995–96) and Las Palmas de Gran Canaria (71%) (Almeida and Díaz 1998). The same is true for the two past tense forms. The present perfect is used in only 15 percent of past tense tokens in Mexico City when compared to the preterit, but this percentage is 54 in Madrid (Howe and Schwenter 2008: 104). It appears then that the simple future and the present perfect are likely to be lost sooner in some areas than in others.

An interesting aspect of variation, especially when it involves a change in progress, is that the variants may develop different meanings. Languages tend to avoid synonyms and so *cantaré* may come to have different nuances of meaning from *voy a cantar*, in the same way that *canté* and *he cantado* may not have exactly the same meaning. Activity 13-4 asks you to discover differences in meaning between these variants.

Complete Activities 13-3 and 13-4 on pages 287–88.

13.6 Chapter Summary

- Latin had ten verb tenses in the active voice, all of which were synthetic.
- Only four of these were retained in Spanish with the same function: the present, imperfect, and perfect indicative, and the present subjunctive.
- Four were repurposed: the pluperfect indicative as the imperfect subjunctive *cantara*, the pluperfect subjunctive as the imperfect subjunctive *cantase*, and the future perfect indicative and the perfect subjunctive as the future subjunctive *cantare*. Note that the future subjunctive is no longer used in speech.
- Two of these were lost: the future indicative and imperfect subjunctive.
- Spanish speakers created new tenses: the future and conditional and a series of eight compound tenses made up of the verb 'to have' plus a past participle.
- The future comes from a new analytical construction like CANTĀRE HABEŌ 'I have to sing,' which then comes to mean 'I will sing.' The conditional comes from this same construction, but with 'to have' in the imperfect tense, as in CANTĀRE HABĒBAM 'I had to sing,' which comes to mean 'I would sing.'
- The compound tenses come from a new construction like HABEŌ EPISTOLAM SCRĪPTAM meaning 'I have a letter written.' It changes from present meaning to past meaning, 'I have written a letter.' Originally, and in Old Spanish, there was also a construction with the auxiliary *ser* and with past participle agreement with the object of *haber* or the subject of *ser*, but this has been lost. The other compound tenses are created by conjugating the auxiliary *haber* in different tenses.
- In both constructions, *haber* becomes grammaticalized by changing from an independent verb to a grammatical element, either a verb ending or an auxiliary verb.
- In Modern Spanish, the 'have' future is competing with a new 'go' future, *voy a ir*, and the present perfect is competing with the preterit. This variation may represent a change in progress where one of the variants may eventually be lost.

Activities

Activity 13-1

Reorganization of Verb Tenses

Just to summarize, Latin had the following verb tenses:

Indicative		Subjuntive	
present	CANTŌ	present	CANTEM
perfect	CANTĀVĪ	perfect	CANTĀVERIM
imperfect	CANTĀBAM	imperfect	CANTĀREM
pluperfect	CANTĀVERAM	pluperfect	CANTĀVISSEM
future	CANTĀBO		
future perfect	CANTĀVERŌ		

A. Classify the above forms into three groups according to their evolution in Modern Spanish and give the modern form. The first one has been done for you.

Form conserved with same function	Form conserved but repurposed with different function	If repurposed, provide new function	Form was lost
CANTŌ > *canto*			

B. Briefly summarize the newly created verbal forms (with *cantar*) in Modern Spanish that did not exist in Classical Latin.

C. Which of the Spanish forms that were originally retained have now fallen out of daily use and are only seen in older texts, legal documents, and set phrases?

Activity 13-2

Synthetic and Analytical Constructions

State to what degree the following statements about synthetic and analytical constructions are true by referring to Figure 13.1. You might also want to think about other examples we have seen from synthetic to analytical, like PORTAE → *de la puerta*, FORTIŌREM → *más fuerte*, and from analytical to synthetic, like *ACCU ILLE > aquel* and CON MĒCUM > *conmigo*.

1. There is an analytical tendency, but no synthetic tendency. Synthetic constructions are replaced by analytical ones, but analytical constructions do not become synthetic.
2. The change from analytical to synthetic reduces articulatory movement.
3. The change from synthetic to analytical reduces the number of forms a speaker has to remember.
4. The element in an analytical construction that grammaticalizes always becomes a suffix.
5. Speakers create new analytical constructions in order to express meaning more transparently, since the individual meanings of grammaticalized elements in a synthetic construction have been erased.

Activity 13-3

Indicate whether the following statements are arguments in favor of a change in progress toward the loss of the simple future and the preterit. Explain your reasoning.

1. Blas Arroyo (2008: 94–95) found that young people under 40 in the Spanish province of Castellón used the simple future in 44 percent of their future references in contrast to 55 percent for speakers over 40.
2. There are regions of the Spanish-speaking world where the simple future is hardly used at all, like Chile, Puerto Rico, and Venezuela.
3. The simple future is used in over 71 percent of future reference in Las Palmas de Gran Canaria.
4. The equivalent of the Spanish preterit, called the *passé simple* in French and the *passato remoto* in Italian, is no longer used in speech in the standard dialects of these latter languages.
5. The present perfect is now being used in Madrid for any action that took place in the same day and not just for actions that have some relevance in the present (Howe and Schwenter 2003: 63).
6. Schwenter (1994) found that young speakers in Alicante, Spain, used the present perfect more often than older speakers.

Activity 13-4

Complete the following sentences referring to events in the future by filling in the verb in Spanish. Examples are also provided in English for native speakers of English since it is sometimes easier to perceive nuances of meaning in your native language.

_____(yo ir) a Costa Rica si ahorro suficiente dinero.

Response: Iré a Costa Rica . . . o voy a ir a Costa Rica . . .

Example: _____(I go) to Costa Rica if I save enough money.

Response: I will go to Costa Rica . . . or I'm going to Costa Rica . . .

1. _____ (yo mirar) una película este fin de semana.

   _____(I see) a movie this weekend.

2. _____ (yo limpiar) mi cuarto más tarde.

   _____ (I clean) up my room later.

3. _____ (tú hacer) la tarea enseguida.

   _____ (you do) your homework right away.

4. ¡No te acerques a la bomba! _____ ((la bomba) explotar).

   Don't go near the bomb! _____ (it explode).

Try to decide why you used the tense that you selected in each case. What is the difference in meaning between them? Try each sentence using the other tense to see whether this changes the meaning. Write two other sentences in the future and decide why you used a particular tense.

Now fill in the verbs in these sentences referring to past events:

1. _____ ¿(tú oír) las noticias?

   _____ (you hear) the news?

2. _____ (yo ir) a Argentina el año pasado.

   _____ (I go) to Argentina last year.

3. _____ (yo nunca ir) a Paraguay en mi vida.

   _____ (I never go) to Paraguay in my life.

4. _____ (ella/estar contenta) desde su admisión a la facultad de derecho.

   _____ (she/be happy) since her admission to law school.

Did you use different past tenses? If so, describe the difference in meaning between the two. If not, use a different past tense to see how the meanings are different.

Further Reading

Aaron, Jessi Elana 2006. "*Me voy a tener que ir yendo*: A corpus-based study of the grammaticization of the *ir a* + INF construction in Spanish," in Nuria Sagarra and Almeida Jacqueline Toribio (eds.), *Selected proceedings of the 9th Hispanic Linguistics Symposium*, 263–72. Somerville, MA: Cascadilla Proceedings Project

Castillo Lluch, Mónica 2002. "Distribución de las formas analíticas y sintéticas de futuro y condicional en español medieval," in María Teresa Echenique Elizondo and Juan Pedro Sánchez Méndez (eds.), *Actas del V Congreso Internacional de Historia de la Lengua Española, Valencia 31 de enero – 4 de febrero 2000*, 541–50. Madrid: Gredos

Day, Meagan, and Sara Zahler 2014. "The continuous path of grammaticalization in Modern Peninsular Spanish," *University of Pennsylvania Working Papers in Linguistics* 20(1)

Juge, Matthew L. 2010. "Morphological mismatch and temporal reference in interaction with lexical semantics in Spanish," *Romance Philology* 64(2): 209–21

Luquet, Gilles 2004. "Los imperfectos de subjuntivo y la reestructuración del sistema verbal español a finales del siglo de oro," *Studia Romanica Posnaniensia* 31(1): 361–68

Mackenzie, Ian. 1999–2017. "History of the Spanish verb," in *The linguistics of Spanish*. www.staff.ncl.ac.uk/i.e.mackenzie/hisverb.htm

Pountain, Christopher J. 1985. "Copulas, verbs of possession and auxiliaries in Old Spanish: The evidence for structurally interdependent changes," *Bulletin of Hispanic Studies* 62: 337–55

Vincent, Nigel 1982. "The development of the auxiliaries *habere* and *esse* in Romance," in Nigel Vincent and Martin Harris (eds.), *Studies in the Romance verb: Essays offered to Joe Cremona on the occasion of his 60th birthday*, 71–96. London: Croom Helm

14

Why Is *comeré* the Future of *comer* but *sabré* Is the Future of *saber*?

How Regular Sound Change and Analogy Lead to Regular and Irregular Forms

Lead-in Questions

14-1 Which verb form do you use? *I have drank/drunk/drunken some water.* Which form of the adjective do you use? *I saw a drunk/drunken sailor.* Now try another verb: *The horses have treaded/trodden the ground. I have treaded/trodden water.* And another adjective: *The formerly downtreaded/downtrodden nation made remarkable progress.* What do you observe about the relationship between the past participle and the adjective?

14-2 In Spanish, do you say *he imprimido la tarea* or *he impreso la tarea*? Ask a few native Spanish speakers what they think about both forms. Why do you think there are two forms?

Chapter 13 *considered the organization of verb tenses from Latin to Spanish and the origins of the new Spanish tenses, the future and conditional and the compound tenses. This chapter focuses on the forms of these verbs. We will see that the sound changes in the history of the Spanish language, presented in* Chapters 6–9, *sometimes lead to regular verb forms in Spanish, but sometimes lead instead to irregular verb forms. In addition to sound changes, analogy is also at work, so that speakers sometimes change one verb form by analogy to another, just as they changed the form of certain nouns through analogy, such as* NURUM *to* nuera. *You will learn how speakers created regular and irregular verb forms and how they made many of these regular again through analogy.*

14.1 Why Are There So Many Irregular Verbs in Spanish?

We consider a verb to be irregular when its stem is not the same throughout its paradigm, in other words, when it shows stem allomorphy. Thus, a verb like *dormir* is irregular because it has two stems in the present, *duerm-* and *dorm-* and a third stem in the preterit *durm-*. The verb, *cantar*, on the other hand, is regular because it has the stem *cant-* in all persons and tenses. We will see in this chapter that many irregular stems resulted from regular sound changes. You will recall that regular sound changes produced the two present tense stems of *dormir: duerm-* when Latin /o/ was tonic, as in *duermo*, and *dorm-* when it was initial, as in *dormimos*. We will also see that analogy can either create or eliminate irregular verb stems. After showing how the three verb classes in Spanish came about, we consider the effects of regular sound change and analogy in the present tense, the future and conditional, the preterit, and in past participles.

14.2 Where Did Spanish -*ar*, -*er*, and -*ir* Verb Classes Come from?

In your language courses you no doubt learned that Spanish has -*ar*, -*er*, and -*ir* verbs, like *cantar, mover,* and *dormir*. These came from four conjugation classes in Latin. The first conjugation ending in -ĀRE, like CANTĀRE, became -*ar* verbs in Spanish. The fourth conjugation ending in -ĪRE, like DORMĪRE, became -*ir* verbs in

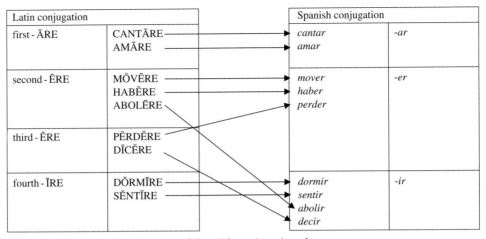

Figure 14.1 Comparison of Latin and Spanish conjugation classes

Spanish. The second conjugation ended in -ĒRE and the third in -ĔRE, so there was a difference in stress. The stress fell on the ending in -ĒRE infinitives because the /e/ was long, as in MOVĒRE [mo-'we-re], but on the stem in -ĔRE infinitives, as in PERDĔRE ['per-de-re]. This third conjugation class ending in -ĔRE was lost in Spanish, when the verbs in the third conjugation joined one of the other conjugations, in the same way that fourth and fifth declension nouns joined the other noun classes. For example, PERDĔRE became the -*er* verb *perder* but DĪCĔRE became the -*ir* verb *decir*. Figure 14.1 shows examples of changes in conjugation classes from Latin to Spanish.

When a verb changed conjugation class, not only did its infinitive change, but also the forms in the different tenses changed to those of its new conjugation class. For example, *abolir* 'to abolish' is conjugated just like other -*ir* verbs, with *abolimos* for the *nosotros* form in the present tense and the *abolido* for the past participle, even though it was in the second conjugation in Latin.

14.3 How Do Present Stems Evolve through Sound Change and Analogy?

We saw in Chapter 13 that the present indicative is one of only four Latin tenses still used with the same function in Spanish. When the present tense forms underwent the regular sound changes that apply to all words, the result was sometimes a regular conjugation, that is, a conjugation with the same stem for all six persons. For example, the present tense forms of the Latin verb CANTĀRE all have the stem *cant-* in Spanish:

Latin CANTĀRE 'to sing'	Spanish *cantar*
CANTŌ	*canto*
CANTĀS	*cantas*
CANTAT	*canta*
CANTĀMUS	*cantamos*
CANTĀTIS	*cantáis*
CANTANT	*cantan*

However, regular sound changes sometimes led to irregular patterns. We can identify three types of sound changes that led to allomorphy or different stems in the present tense. The first is the development of a consonant at the end of the 1sg. stem different from the consonant in other persons. This results from the different evolution of /k/ and /g/ before back vowels and front vowels. We can call this pattern of irregularity **stem-consonant allomorphy** (*alomorfía de la consonante radical*). For example, /k/ voices to /g/ and then fricativizes to [ɣ] before the 1sg. ending /o/, a back vowel, but it palatalizes to /s/ or /θ/ before front vowels, like the /i/ or /e/ that occur in the other persons. The forms of the Spanish verb *hacer* show this pattern. We have bolded the 1sg. stem to show that it is different from the others through regular sound change.

Latin FACĔRE 'to do'	Spanish *hacer*
FACIŌ → *FACO	**hago**
FACIS	*haces*
FACIT	*hace*
FACIMUS	*hacemos*
FACITIS	*hacéis*
FACIUNT → *FACENT	*hacen*

The two Latin forms marked with an asterisk are unattested in writing, but we believe they existed in Spoken Latin. Based on the Spanish result, we assume that the [i] was lost in FACIŌ and that the Latin 3pl. ending in -UNT changed to -ENT in all verbs, since all Spanish 3pl. verbs in the present tense end in -*en* rather than -*on*, the regular result of -UNT.

Whereas speakers maintained the different stems *hag-* [aɣ] and *hac-* [as] or [aθ] in *hacer*, most likely due to its frequency, in other verbs they changed one of the stems through analogy to the other stem, so that all persons in the paradigm had the same stem. By leveling the paradigm, speakers created regular verbs, even though the regular sound changes from Latin to Spanish had created an irregular paradigm. This occurs in the forms of the verb 'to cook.' Many of the Latin forms are starred forms because this verb changed from a third to a second conjugation verb and so its second conjugation present tense endings are not attested. The shading of the Modern Spanish 1sg. *cuezo* indicates that this form changed its stem by analogy to the stem of the other persons in the same paradigm. Thus, leveling of the paradigm occurred.

Latin COCĔRE → *COCĒRE 'to cook'	Old Spanish *cocer*	Modern Spanish *cocer*
COCŌ	***cuego***	*cuezo*
COCIS → *COCES	*cueces*	*cueces*
COCIT → *COCET	*cuece*	*cuece*
COCIMUS → *COCĒMUS	*cocemos*	*cocemos*
COCITIS → *COCĒTIS	*cocéis*	*cocéis*
COCUNT → *COCENT	*cuecen*	*cuecen*

Another example of stem-consonant allomorphy in Old Spanish is the verb *erguir* 'to straighten.' In this case the 1sg. form served as the model and the other persons adopted its stem. Leveling has occurred once again, but the majority stem changed by analogy to the minority stem. We will see that, in contrast to the relative regularity of sound changes, analogy operates in a haphazard way, so that it is impossible to predict which form will serve as the model for an analogical change. Shading once again indicates the forms that changed by analogy.

Latin ERIGĔRE → ERIGĪRE 'to straighten'	Old Spanish *erguir*	Modern Spanish *erguir*
ERIGŌ	*yergo*	*yergo*
ERIGIS	*yerzes*	*yergues*
ERIGIT	*yerze*	*yergue*
ERIGIMUS	*erezemos*	*erguimos*
ERIGITIS	*erezedes*	*erguís*
ERIGUNT →*ĔRIGENT	*yerzen*	*yerguen*

A second type of sound change that leads to different stems in the present tense is **stem-vowel allomorphy** (*alomorfía de la vocal radical*). This is caused by the diphthongization of Ĕ and Ŏ, which, as you recall, occurs only in tonic position. Thus, the stem for persons 1sg., 2sg., 3sg., and 3pl. is the strong stem because it bears the stress. The stem for persons 1pl. and 2pl. does not bear the stress and so is the weak stem. We have underlined the tonic vowel in Latin and bolded the familiar strong stems with their diphthong to illustrate this point.

Latin DORMĪRE 'to sleep'	Spanish *dormir*
DORMŌ	***duermo***
DORMIS	***duermes***
DORMIT	***duerme***
DORMĪMUS	*dormimos*
DORMĪTIS	*dormís*
DORMIUNT → *DORMENT	***duermen***

You may have heard the term stem-changing verbs or boot verbs applied to this pattern, because a line around the strong stems forms a boot, as seen in Figure 14.2.

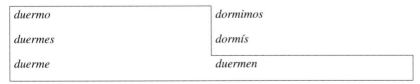

Figure 14.2 The boot shape of stem-changing verbs

In some verbs speakers eliminated the stem-vowel allomorphy by replacing the strong stems with the weak stems, as in the verb *confortar*.

Latin CONFORTĀRE 'to strengthen, comfort'	Old Spanish *confortar*	Modern Spanish *confortar* 'to comfort'
CONFORTŌ	**confuerto**	conforto
CONFORTĀS	**confuertas**	confortas
CONFORTAT	**confuerta**	conforta
CONFORTĀMUS	confortamos	confortamos
CONFORTĀTIS	confortáis	confortáis
CONFORTANT	**confuertan**	confortan

In other verbs speakers replace the weak stems with the strong stems, a process which applies also to the form of the infinitive. This occurred, for example, in the Old Spanish verb *atesar* 'to stiffen,' which became *atiesar* in Modern Spanish with a single stem *aties-*, and Old Spanish *encovar* 'to enclose in a cave,' which became Modern Spanish *encuevar*. We do not provide a table with Latin forms for these verbs, since they were first attested in Old Spanish.

In an example of proportional analogy rather than leveling, certain verbs adopt the stem-vowel allomorphy pattern by analogy to another verb. For example, MŌNSTRĀRE would not have a diphthong in the stressed syllable in Spanish, since the /o/ in this verb is long rather than short and only the short /o/ diphthongizes. However, by analogy to a verb like *dormir*, speakers change the vowel in the strong stems to a diphthong. We can call analogy from one verb paradigm to another **interparadigmatic analogy** (*la analogía interparadigmática*).

Latin MŌNSTRĀRE 'to show'	By regular sound change	Modern Spanish *mostrar*
MŌNSTRŌ	mostro	muestro
MŌNSTRĀS	mostras	muestras
MŌNSTRAT	mostra	muestra
MŌNSTRĀMUS	mostramos	mostramos
MŌNSTRĀTIS	mostráis	mostráis
MŌNSTRANT	mostran	muestran

The third type of allomorphy occurs when the first person singular forms in Latin developed a yod that was not present in other persons. This yod resulted from the -ĒŌ ending in a verb like HABEŌ 'I have' or the -IŌ ending in a verb like *MĒTIŌ 'I measure.' In these endings the /e/ or /i/ before /o/ became a yod which then raised the tonic vowel of the stem by one degree, as you recall from Chapter 8. This meant that the 1sg. stem would have a higher vowel than the other stems. We can call this **first person yod allomorphy** (*alomorfía de primera persona con yod*). For example, in the 1sg. form VENIŌ 'I come' the yod raises the tonic Ĕ, pronounced as /ɛ/ in Latin, to /e/, so that the tonic vowel does not diphthongize in the first person singular *vengo*. It does diphthongize, however, in the other strong stems through regular sound changes, like 2sg. *vienes*. As a side note, another change occurs in 1sg. VENIŌ in addition to vowel raising. The yod would normally palatalize the /n/ to /ɲ/, a change observed in Portuguese *venho* 'I come.' However, through analogy to verbs ending in -NGO, like FRANGŌ 'I break,' speakers change the form to *vengo* (Lloyd 1987: 294).

Latin VENĪRE 'to come'	By regular sound change	Modern Spanish *venir*
VENIŌ	**veño**	*vengo*
VENĪS	*vienes*	*vienes*
VENIT	*viene*	*viene*
VENĪMUS	*venimos*	*venimos*
VENĪTIS	*venís*	*venís*
VENIUNT → *VĔNENT	*vienen*	*vienen*

In other verbs, the allomorphy created through regular sound change by the influence of the yod on the tonic vowel is eliminated through leveling. This occurs, for example, in the evolution of the present tense forms of SUBĪRE. The yod in 1sg. SUBEŌ raises the tonic vowel to /u/, but in the other persons the short /u/ undergoes the regular sound change to /o/, whether in tonic or initial position. Then through leveling, all the other persons adopt the stem of 1sg., so that the verb paradigm has the same stem throughout.

Latin SUBĪRE 'to go under'	Old Spanish *sobir* 'to go up'	Modern Spanish *subir* 'to go up'
SUBEŌ	**subo**	subo
SUBĪS	sobes	subes
SUBIT	sobe	sube
SUBĪMUS	sobimos	subimos
SUBĪTIS	sobides	subís
SUBEUNT → *SUBENT	soben	suben

Sometimes the analogy is resolved in favor of the stem not affected by yod, as in the verb APERĪRE 'to open.' The yod in 1sg. would prevent diphthongization of the short ĕ, resulting in *abero* or even *aberio*, since sometimes the yod is maintained after /r/. However, in the other persons the short ĕ is in medial position and so is lost. Therefore, the stem for the other persons is ABR-. The 1sg. form adopts this stem through leveling so that this verb becomes regular.

Latin APERĪRE 'to open'	By regular sound change	Modern Spanish *abrir*
APERIŌ	***abero* / *aberio**	abro
APERĪS	abres	abres
APERIT	abre	abre
APERĪMUS	abrimos	abrimos
APERĪTIS	abrís	abrís
APERIUNT → *APERENT	abren	abren

Another verb in which the 1sg. stem, which we can call the yod stem, serves as the model is *MĒTĪRE 'to measure.' We mark all the forms of this verb with an asterisk because it was what is called a **deponent verb** (*un verbo deponente*) in Latin, meaning that it used passive forms with active meaning. Therefore, the active forms from which the Spanish forms derive are unattested in writing. However, in this verb the 1sg. stem is not adopted throughout the paradigm, only in the other strong forms, namely 2sg., 3sg., and 3pl. Since the tonic vowel in the 1sg. form MĒTIŌ is /e/, it raises to /i/ under the influence of the following yod. In the other forms, where this vowel is in tonic position or initial position, it would change to /e/ through regular sound change. In this verb, the other strong forms change to the *mid-* stem, whereas the weak forms retain the *med-* stem that developed through regular sound change. Thus, analogy follows the stem-changing verb pattern of a strong stem and a weak stem that we saw in *dormir.*

Latin MĒTĪRE 'to measure'	By regular sound change	Modern Spanish *medir*
*MĒTIŌ	**mido**	mido
*MĒTĪS	medes	mides
*MĒTIT	mede	mide
*MĒTĪMUS	medimos	medimos
*MĒTĪTIS	medís	medís
*MĒTIUNT → *MĒTENT	meden	miden

In the same way that a verb like *mostrar* adopted the stem-changing pattern of *dormir* through interparadigmatic analogy, other verbs adopt the pattern of *medir* by analogy. One such verb is SERVĪRE 'to serve.' The short Ĕ in this verb would become /e/ in 1sg. SĔRVIŌ after raising one degree because of the yod in the following syllable. In tonic position in the other strong stems, Ĕ would diphthongize to [je]. In the weak stems, persons 1pl. and 2pl., it would become /e/ in initial position. In Modern Spanish, the weak stem that develops through regular sound change is kept in 1pl. and 2pl., but speakers change the strong stem to *sirv-* by interparadigmatic analogy to the strong stem *mid-* of *medir.*

Latin SĔRVĪRE 'to serve'	By regular sound change	Modern Spanish *servir*
SĔRVIŌ	***servo**	sirvo
SĔRVĪS	sierves	sirves
SĔRVIT	sierve	sirve
SĔRVĪMUS	servimos	servimos
SĔRVĪTIS	servís	servís
SĔRVIUNT → *SĔRVENT	sierven	sirven

In the examples of analogy in the present indicative we have seen that regular sound changes can lead to three primary types of allomorphy, which we have called stem-consonant allomorphy, as in *hago* and *haces*, stem-vowel allo-morphy, as in *duermo* and *dormimos*, and first person yod allomorphy, as in *vengo* and *vienes*. We have also seen that these types of allomorphy are sometimes eliminated through leveling and so this type of analogy can change the irregular verb forms resulting from regular sound changes into regular verb forms. At the same time, other verbs that would have been regular, like *mostrar*, or that would have had a different pattern of allomor-phy, sometimes follow the model of irregular verbs and become irregular. Thus, we can conclude that analogy is an unpredictable change, since it is impossible to know which forms and patterns speakers will use as a model to change other forms.

Complete Activity 14-1 on page 308.

14.4 How Do Future and Conditional Stems Evolve through Sound Change and Analogy?

We have seen in Chapter 13 that the future and conditional tenses in Spanish are new forms made up of the infinitive plus a form of the verb 'to have.' The future endings come from the present indicative, like 1sg. HABEŌ, and the conditional endings come from the imperfect indicative, like 1sg. HABĒBAM. Over time these forms underwent sound changes, so that CANTĀRE HABEŌ became *cantaré* and CANTĀRE HABĒBAM developed into *cantaría*. In this section, we are interested in seeing how regular sound changes may have led to regular future and condi-tional stems, those identical to the infinitive, or irregular future and conditional stems, those different from the infinitive. After the regular sound changes run their course, speakers remodel some irregular stems through analogy so that they become regular again.

In future and conditional forms like CANTĀRE HABEŌ and CANTĀRE HABĒBAM, the stress came to fall on the ending rather than the stem. This meant that what had been the tonic vowel of the infinitive, like the /a/ in CANTĀRE, ended up in medial position. When this vowel was /a/, as in *cantaré* or *cantaría*, it was maintained, since the regular sound change for medial /a/ is retention. However, recall that other vowels are lost in medial position through syncope, and so the penultimate vowels in *-er* and *-ir* infinitives were lost through regular sound change. Thus, in SAPĔRE HABEŌ 'I will know,' the penultimate /e/ in SAPĔRE was lost through syncope, so that the stem became *sabr-*, the Modern Spanish stem, as in *sabré* and *sabría*. The regular sound change created an irregular future/conditional stem not identical to the infinitive *saber*.

In some verbs, other changes occurred after the loss of medial /e/. In PONĔRE HABEŌ/HABĒBAM, for example, the syncopated stem /ponɾ/ that resulted from the loss of the penultimate /e/ in PONĔRE, underwent further changes. In Old Spanish, one finds the stem *porn-* as in *porné* 'I will put,' which results from metathesis whereby the /n/ and /ɾ/ change places. Modern Spanish *pondré* results instead from epenthesis, in this case the insertion of /d/ between the /n/ and /ɾ/. In many verbs, the syncopated forms were later changed by analogy to the infinitive so as to become regular. RECIPĔRE HABEŌ/HABĒBAM and COMEDĔRE HABEO/HABĒBAM, for example, would have become *recibré/recibría* and *combré/combría* through syncope. Speakers later changed the future stem to *recibiré/recibiría* and *comeré/comería* in Modern Spanish by analogy to their infinitives *recibir* and *comer* and to the *-ar* verbs, which never were syncopated.

Complete Activity 14-2 on page 311.

14.5 How Do Preterit Stems Evolve through Sound Change and Analogy?

In this section, we will consider how regular sound change and analogy explain many Spanish preterit stems. Many preterits have regular stems resulting from regular sound changes. Just as the regular sound changes in a verb like CANTĀRE resulted in regular forms in the present indicative, they also resulted in regular forms in the preterit. We place the letter v, pronounced [w], and sometimes its entire syllable in parentheses to show that these sounds were routinely lost from Latin to Spanish. As a side note, it is fun to know that the loss of a syllable is referred to as **haplology** (*la haplología*), especially since if you apply haplology to the word itself you get **haplogy*.

Latin CANTĀRE 'to sing'	Modern Spanish *cantar*
CANTĀ(V)Ī	canté
CANTĀ(VI)STĪ	cantaste
CANTĀVIT	cantó
CANTĀ(VI)MUS	cantamos
CANTĀ(VI)STIS	cantasteis
CANTĀ(VE)RUNT	cantaron

Regular sound changes could also lead to irregular stems. One such example is the preterit forms of *dormir*. Look at the paradigm below to determine what might have created the stem *durm-* rather than *dorm-* in *durmió* and *durmieron*.

Latin DORMĪRE 'to sleep'	Modern Spanish *dormir*
DORMĪ(V)Ī	dormí
DORMĪ(VI)STĪ	dormiste
DORMĪVIT	durmió
DORMĪ(VI)MUS	dormimos
DORMĪ(VI)STIS	dormisteis
DORMĪ(VE)RUNT	durmieron

As you may have guessed, the raising effect of yod that we discussed in Chapter 8 caused the stem vowel to raise in 3sg. and 3pl. So in this verb regular sound change led to allomorphy which was not eliminated through analogy.

Another example where sound changes led to allomorphy occurs in the preterit of *hacer*. In this case, though, the allomorphy was later eliminated through leveling. In 1sg. FĒCĪ the long /i/ of the ending raises the stem vowel from /e/ to /i/ through metaphony, also discussed in Chapter 8, so that the result through regular sound change is Spanish *hice*. We can refer to this then as **allomorphy through metaphony** (*alomorfía por metafonía*). In all other persons, there is no ī in the final syllable to raise the stem vowel, so initial /e/ would remain /e/. But through leveling these forms adopt the same stem as *hice*.

Latin FACĔRE 'to do'	By regular sound change	Modern Spanish *hacer*
FĒCĪ	*hice*	*hice*
FĒCISTĪ	*heciste*	*hiciste*
FĒCIT	*heze*	*hizo*
FĒCIMUS	*hecemos*	*hicimos*
FĒCISTIS	*hecestes*	*hicisteis*
FĒCĒRUNT	*hecieron*	*hicieron*

A similar change occurs in the paradigm of *venir*, where 1sg. VĒNĪ changed to *vine* through regular sound change, and then 3sg. VĒNIT, which would have become *veno* through regular sound change, became *vino* by analogy to *vine*. We see the forms *fezo* and *veno* in writing until at least the fifteenth century.

An interesting case of interparadigmatic analogy explains the distinctive preterit forms with a stem vowel /u/, as in *hube*, *tuve*, and *anduve*. There were only two perfect forms in Latin that would have a /u/ in the stem through regular sound change, as illustrated by their 1sg. forms: POTUĪ 'I could' and POSUĪ 'I put.' In these verbs it is not a following yod that raises the stem vowel, but rather a following waw, the semi-vowel /w/. When the waw raised the /o/ in the stressed syllable the result was *pude* and *puse* in Spanish. These two forms then served as a model for the other preterits in /u/.

In other verbs the waw would have raised the stem vowel /a/ to /o/, and so the regular evolution would be HABUĪ > *ove* 'I had,' SAPUĪ > *sope* 'I knew,' CAPUĪ > *cope* 'I fit,' forms that are found in Old Spanish. Note that the waw changes /a/ to /o/ because it is a high back semi-vowel, whereas the front semi-vowel yod changes it to /e/, as seen in Chapter 8. Before these forms could arrive at their present-day forms, *hube*, *supe*, and *cupe*, by analogy to *pude* and *puse*, they served as a model for other verbs themselves. TENUĪ 'I held,' whose regular result would have been *tene or *tine, depending on the metaphony of the final /i/, became instead *tove*, by analogy to *ove*. In the same way, STĒTĪ 'I stood' became *estove* by analogy to a verb like *ove*, rather than *estide* through regular changes. The form *andove* was also created by analogy, yet we are unsure of the regular evolution of *andove*, since it is not clear whether *andar* comes from AMBULĀRE or AMBITĀRE. The final step is the change of all these preterits with stem vowels in /o/, *ove*, *sope*, *cope*, *tove*, *estove*, and *andove*, to stems in /u/ by interparadigmatic analogy to *pude* and *puse*. This final analogical step created modern *hube*, *supe*, *cupe*, *tuve*, *estuve*, and *anduve*.

Complete Activities 14-3 and 14-4 Part I on pages 313–14.

14.6 How Do Past Participles Evolve through Sound Change and Analogy?

Since participles are not inflected for person, a participle is considered to be regular when its stem is the same as the stem of the infinitive. Most Latin participles were weak participles with stress on the ending and these remained regular in Spanish through regular sound change, such as CANTĀTUM > *cantado* and DORMĪTUM > *dormido*. In most of the Latin strong participles, with stress on the stem, regular sound changes led to irregular participles, as in the following:

APERTUM > *abierto* 'opened'

COOPERTUM > *cubierto* 'covered'

DĪCTUM > *dicho* 'said'

FACTUM > *hecho* 'done, made'

FRĪTUM > *frito* 'fried'

JŪNCTUM > *junto* (now only adjectival) 'joined' (now 'together')

MORTUM > *muerto* 'died'

POSĬTUM > *puesto* 'put, placed, positioned'

RUPTUM > *roto* 'broken'

SATISFACTUM > *satisfecho* 'satisfied'

SCRĪPTUM > *escrito* 'written'

SOLŬTUM > *suelto* 'loosened'

TINCTUM > *tinto* 'dyed'

The simple answer to the question of why Spanish has so many irregular past participles is that they evolved through regular sound changes from irregular past participles in Latin.

The answer to the question of why Spanish does not have even more irregular past participles is that the great majority of these became regular in Spanish through analogy to the regular participles. For example, the strong past participle of MITTĔRE is MISSUM, which would give *meso* through regular sound. However, we find *metido* in Spanish from analogy to weak past participles, such as *dormido*. The analogical proportion would be: *meter*/X = *metido* : *dormir*/*dormido*. Other such cases include CURSUM → *corrido* rather than *curso*, QUAESITUM → *querido* rather than *quisto*.

A number of Spanish verbs have kept both Latin past participles, an irregular one from regular sound changes and a regular one from analogy, but with a difference in function. The new regular participle is used to form compound tenses (*he corregido la tarea, el libro me ha confundido*), whereas the older irregular participle has been repurposed as an adjective or noun (*la tarea es correcta, el libro es confuso*). A similar situation in English is the use of *proved* and *proven*. We can use either one as a past participle (*he has proved the theorem* or *he has proven the theorem*), but we use only the irregular form, as an adjective (*a proven fact*). Table 14.1 shows Latin past participles that have both a corresponding regular and irregular past participle in Spanish, even though the irregular past participle may be used now only as an adjective or noun.

It is interesting to realize that *vino tinto* 'red wine' originally meant 'dyed wine' and that *contento* 'happy, content' originally meant 'contained.'

Complete Activities 14-4 Part II and 14-5 on pages 314–15.

TABLE 14.1 Latin past participles with two Spanish forms

Latin verb	Spanish verb	Latin strong participle	Spanish irregular participle	Spanish regular participle
BENEDĪCĔRE	*bendecir*	BENEDĪCTUM	*bendito*	*bendecido*
CONFUNDĔRE	*confundir*	CONFŪSUM	*confuso*	*confundido*
CONTINĒRE	*contener*	CONTENTUM	*contento*	*contenido*
INCLUDĔRE	*incluir*	INCLŪSUM	*incluso*	*incluido*
PREHENDĔRE	*prender*	PRĒNSUM	*preso*	*prendido*
REDUCĔRE	*reducir*	REDUCTUM	*reducto*	*reducido*
REPRIMĔRE	*reprimir*	REPRISSUM	*represo*	*reprimido*
TINGĔRE	*teñir*	TINCTUM	*tinto*	*teñido*
TORQUĒRE	*torcer*	TORTUM	*tuerto*	*torcido*

14.7 How Did Verbs like *soy* Come about?

You may still be wondering at this point about one more set of irregular verb forms: *soy, doy, voy*, and *estoy*. The Latin forms SUM, DŌ, VADŌ, and STŌ, evolved regularly to *so, do, vo*, and *estó*, the forms found in Spanish texts from the thirteenth century, such as *yo só mandadero* in the Appendix E29. Our question then is where does the final -*y* (pronounced [j]) come from?

One possibility is that the [j] comes from the first sound of the subject pronoun *yo* placed after the verb. The /o/ of *yo* would presumably have been lost through apocope through a process like this: [so-ˈjo] > [ˈso + jo] > [so + j] > [soj] (Ford 1911, Schmidely 1988, Rini 1995–96). Gago-Jover (1997) is not convinced by this explanation citing the small number of tokens of *soy yo* between the fourteenth and seventeenth centuries compared to *yo so* and *yo do*.

Another explanation also appeals to agglutination of a final [j], but in this proposal [j] comes from the pronoun /i/ meaning 'there, about this' from Latin IBI 'there' written *y, i, hy*, or *hi* in Old Spanish texts. An expression such as *so y pagado/a* 'I am satisfied about this' could have resulted in *soy pagado*. An argument in favor of this is that this same pronoun is generally accepted as the origin of the [j] in *hay*, seen also in French *il y a* 'there is.' This view was originally presented by Molho (1969) and endorsed by Lloyd (1987) and Penny (2002). Wanner (2006), however, makes the same objection Gago-Jover (1997) made for *so yo*, citing the relatively small numbers of tokens of these verbs followed by the pronoun *y* in the available texts.

Wanner's (2006) own proposal is that the *y* of *soy* results from analogy of *so* to the 1sg. preterit form [fwi] from FUĪ 'I was.' Once the *y* was added to *soy* it was then adopted by *doy, voy*, and *estoy*. Wanner (2006) was inspired in this proposal by a similar proposal for French *suis* 'I am' by Pope (1952). One counterargument here, though, is that Wanner is proposing a fairly rare type of analogy, not seen in this chapter, from one tense in a verb paradigm to another.

It is also possible that all three elements proposed for the origin of the -*y* of *soy* could have had an effect. This position is what we call **multiple causation** (*la causación multiple*). Rather than seeing this as a failure to take a position, a "cop out," we can see it as a recognition that multiple influences may be at work on speakers' decisions at the same time.

Complete Activity 14-6 on page 316.

14.8 Chapter Summary

- The three conjugation classes in Spanish of -*ar*, -*er*, and -*ir* verbs come from four conjugation classes in Latin of -ĀRE, -ĒRE, -ĔRE, and -ĪRE verbs. The -ĒRE and -ĔRE classes combine to form one -*er* class in Spanish, but some verbs change from this class to the -*ir* class, like DĪCĔRE to *decir*.
- Regular sound changes may lead to irregular verb forms in Spanish. We observe three types of allomorphy in present tense verbs:
  ○ Stem consonant allomorphy, as in *hago* and *haces*
  ○ Stem vowel allomorphy, as in *duermo* and *dormimos*
  ○ First person yod allomorphy, as in *vengo* and *vienes*.

- In some verbs leveling occurs to restore one stem throughout the verb paradigm, as in *conforto/confortamos*, but sometimes speakers create stem allomorphy through interparadigmatic analogy to other verbs, as in *muestro/mostramos* created by analogy to a verb like *duermo/dormimos*.
- In the preterit regular sound changes created stem allomorphy in a verb like *dormir*, with one stem *dorm-* and another stem *durm-*. Analogy was also at work in preterit stems, so that *hube, supe,* and *cupe*, which would have been *hobe, *sope, and *cope through regular sound change, adopted the stem vowel /u/ by analogy to the verbs *puse* and *pude* where this /u/ resulted from the regular raising of tonic /o/ by a following /w/ from Latin POSUĪ and POTUĪ, respectively.
- In future and conditional stems, the same processes of regular sound change and analogy are also at work. Latin SAPĔRE HABEŌ became *sabré* through regular sound change. Other verbs developed irregular future stems in Old Spanish, like *combré* 'I will eat,' which speakers later changed to *comeré* by analogy to other verbs where the stem is the same as the infinitive, such as *cantaré*.
- The same processes of regular sound change and analogy also occurred in past participles. Latin IMPRESSUM, for example, became *impreso* in Spanish, but some speakers are now creating a regular participle *imprimido* instead, as mentioned in Lead-in question 14-2. In other verbs, the analogical past participle is already the norm, such as *contenido* for *contener*, whereas the form that developed through regular sound change is now the adjective *contento*.

Activities

Activity 14-1

Present Indicative Stems

In the following conjugations in Latin and Spanish, circle any forms in Modern Spanish that do not result from regular sound change. In the example, the analogical form appears in a shaded cell. Then write the form that would have resulted from regular sound change in the middle column. Finally, state the type of analogy that occurred in the line provided under the table, or state that all the forms resulted from regular sound change. For the types of analogy, choose from among leveling of stem-consonant allomorphy, stem-vowel allomorphy, first person yod allomorphy, or interparadigmatic analogy, analogy of one verb paradigm to another through proportional analogy.

Example:

Latin SPARGĔRE 'to scatter'	By regular sound change	Modern Spanish *esparcir* to 'scatter'
SPARGŌ	espargo	*esparzo*
SPARGIS		*esparces*
SPARGIT		*esparce*
SPARGĬMUS		*esparcimos*
SPARGĬTIS		*esparcís*
SPARGUNT →*SPARGENT		*esparcen*

Type of analogy: leveling of stem-consonant allomorphy

1.

Latin PĒNSĀRE 'to weigh'	By regular sound change	Modern Spanish *pensar*
PĒNSŌ		*pienso*
PĒNSĀS		*piensas*
PĒNSAT		*piensas*
PĒNSĀMUS		*pensamos*
PĒNSĀTIS		*pensáis*
PĒNSANT		*piensan*

Type of analogy: _____

2.

Latin PĔRDĔRE 'to lose'	By regular sound change	Modern Spanish *perder*
PĔRDŌ		*pierdo*
PĔRDIS		*pierdes*
PĔRDIT		*pierde*
PĔRDIMUS		*perdemos*
PĔRDITIS		*perdéis*
PĔRDUNT → *PĔRDENT		*pierden*

Type of analogy: _____

3.

Latin ĬMPLERE → ĬMPLĪRE 'to fill up'	By regular sound change	Modern Spanish *henchir* 'to fill'
ĬMPLIŌ		*hincho*
ĬMPLĪS		*hinches*
ĬMPLIT		*hinche*
ĬMPLĪMUS		*henchimos*
ĬMPLĪTIS		*henchís*
ĬMPLIUNT → *ĬMPLENT		*hinchen*

Type of analogy: _____

4.

Latin SĔNTĪRE 'to feel'	By regular sound change	Modern Spanish *sentir*
SĔNTIŌ		*siento*
SĔNTĪS		*sientes*
SĔNTIT		*siente*
SĔNTĪMUS		*sentimos*
SĔNTĪTIS		*sentís*
SĔNTIUNT → *SĔNTENT		*sienten*

Type of analogy: _____

5.

Latin VĚTĀRE 'to forbid'	By regular sound change	Modern Spanish *vedar* 'to ban, prohibit'
VĚTŌ		*vedo*
VĚTĀS		*vedas*
VĚTAT		*veda*
VĚTĀMUS		*vedamos*
VĚTĀTIS		*vedáis*
VĚTANT		*vedan*

Type of analogy: _____

6.

Latin COOPERĪRE 'to cover'	By regular sound change	Modern Spanish *cubrir*
COOPERIŌ		*cubro*
COOPERĪS		*cubres*
COOPERIT		*cubre*
COOPERĪMUS		*cubrimos*
COOPERĪTIS		*cubrís*
COOPERĪUNT → *COOPERENT		*cubren*

Type of analogy: _____

Activity 14-2

Future and Conditional Stems

For each of the verbs below, write the 1sg. future form in Modern Spanish and then indicate the changes that occurred between Latin and Old Spanish and between Old Spanish and Modern Spanish using these abbreviations:
S = syncope, M = metathesis, E = epenthesis, A = analogy to the infinitive, N = no change

Latin	Old Spanish	Changes from Latin to Old Spanish	Modern Spanish form	Changes from Old Spanish to Modern Spanish
Example: *POTĒRE HABEŌ 'I will be able to'	*podré*	S	*podré*	N
1. CAPĔRE HABEŌ 'I will fit'	*cabré*			
2. HABĒRE HABEŌ 'I will have'	*avré*			
3. BIBĔRE HABEŌ 'I will drink'	*bevré*			
4. MOVĒRE HABEŌ 'I will move'	*movré*			
5. COMEDĔRE HABEŌ 'I will eat'	*combré*			
6. PERDĔRE HABEŌ 'I will lose'	*perdré*			
7. PREHENDĔRE HABEŌ 'I will take'	*prendré*			
8. TENĒRE HABEŌ 'I will hold'	*terné*			
9. VENĪRE HABEŌ 'I will come'	*verné*			
10. SALĪRE HABEŌ 'I will go out'	*salré*			
11. QUAERĔRE HABEŌ 'I will want'	*querré*			
12. MORĪRE HABEŌ 'I will die'	*morré*			

Activity 14-3

Preterit Stems

For each pair of words, underline the Latin word whose Modern Spanish form has resulted from analogy. Then, for this word indicate:

A. the word that would have resulted had it evolved from regular sound changes
B. the form that actually has occurred in Modern Spanish
C. Explain the analogical change by saying how the actual form in Spanish is different from the form that would have resulted from regular sound change, and then give the model for this word and the analogical process. Note that in each pair one word is the model for the other.

Example: FĒCĪ/FĒCĪSTI

A. __heciste_____   B. __hiciste_____
C. The stem of the Modern Spanish form is *hic-* with an /i/ instead of /e/. This stem comes from analogy to 1sg. FECĪ > *hice* in which metaphony caused the stem vowel /e/ to raise to /i/. This is a case of leveling.

1. FĒCĪ / FĒCIMUS
A. _____   B. _____
C.

2. VĒNIT / VĒNĪ
A. _____   B. _____
C.

3. PŌSUĪ / HABUĪ
A. _____   B. _____
C.

4. CAPUĪ / PŌTUĪ
A. _____   B. _____
C.

5. HABUĪ / TENUĪ
A. _____   B. _____
C.

6. STĒTĪ / HABUĪ

A. _____   B._____

C.

Activity 14-4

Corpus Study

Part I Strong Preterits

In the CORDE search for the two words below in the centuries between 1100 and 1899, and fill in the table with the number of occurrences for each century.

Form A: *sope* Form B: *supe*

Part II Regular and Irregular Past Participles

COCĔRE 'to cook' had the strong participle COCTUM, which in Old Spanish became *cocho*. This form survived in Modern Spanish only in the compound form *bizcocho* 'sponge cake.' In the CORDE, search for the two words and fill in the table with the number of occurrences.

Form A: *cocho* Form B: *cocido*

Frequencies of occurrences

	1100s	1200s	1300s	1400s	1500s	1600s	1700s	1800s
Part I								
Form A								
Form B								
Part II								
Form A								
Form B								

Now answer the following questions:

1. In which document do Forms A and B appear for the first time and in which document do they appear for the last time? What are the dates of those documents?
2. For how many centuries did the two forms coexist?
3. Explain the evolution of A. Does it result from regular sound change or analogy? What about B? Why do you think B survived and A did not?

Activity 14–5

Past Participles

Fill in the following table with the Spanish infinitive that derives from the Latin infinitive. Then for each strong participle in Latin, write its Spanish reflexes. Indicate any resulting Spanish words that are not past participles by writing (A) for adjective or (N) for noun after the word. The first three have been done for you. Feel free to use Latin and Spanish dictionaries, if needed.

Latin verb	Spanish verb	Latin strong participle	Spanish irregular participle	Spanish regular participle
APERĪRE	abrir	APĔRTUM	abierto	–
CONFUNDĔRE	confundir	CONFŪSUM	confuso (A)	confundido
MITTĔRE	meter	MISSUM	–	metido
1. CORRIGĔRE		CORRECTUM		
2. MORĪRE		MORTUUM		
3. TENĒRE		TENTUM		
4. ELIGĔRE		ELECTUM		
5. FACĔRE		FACTUM		
6. EX(S)TINGUĔRE		EX(S)TĪNCTUM		
7. FRĪGĔRE		FRĪCTUM		
8. DĪCĔRE		DICTUM		
9. CURRĔRE		CURSUM		
10. IMPRIMĔRE		IMPRESSUM		
11. INCLŪDĔRE		INCLŪSUM		
12. RUMPĔRE		RUPTUM		
13. PŌNĔRE		PŎSĬTUM		
14. PRŌDŪCĔRE		PRŌDUCTUM		
15. SCRIBĔRE		SCRĪPTUM		
16. SALVĀRE		SALVUM		

(cont.)

Latin verb	Spanish verb	Latin strong participle	Spanish irregular participle	Spanish regular participle
17. VOLVĔRE		VOLŪTUM		
18. SUBSTITUĔRE		SUBSTITŪTUM		
19. QUAERĔRE		QUAESĪSTUM		
20. NASCĔRE		NATUM		

Activity 14-6

The forms *soy, doy, voy*, and *estoy*

1. Which of the proposals for the addition of /y/ in *soy* and other verbs do you find most convincing? Why?
2. Wanner (2006) observes that tokens of *so, do, vo*, and *estó* followed by the locative pronoun *y* are not frequent in old texts. Does this demonstrate conclusively that the *y* does not come from Latin IBI? What type of information could you collect in a corpus search to test the proposal you find most convincing?
3. Do you think linguists will be able to settle this question conclusively? Why or why not?

Further Reading

Maiden, Martin 1992. "Irregularity as a determinant of morphological change," *Journal of Linguistics* 28(2): 285–312
    2009. "From pure phonology to pure morphology: The reshaping of the Romance verb," *Recherches linguistiques de Vincennes* 1: 45–82
Maschi, Roberta 2005. "Analogy and irregularity in Romance verb morphology," In G. Booij, L. Ducceschi, B. Fradin, E. Guevara, A. Ralli, and S. Scalise (eds.), *On-line Proceedings of the Fifth Mediterranean Morphology Meeting* (MMM5), 125.140. University of Bologna. mmm.lingue.unibo.it
Moreno Bernal, Jorge 2004. "La morfología de los futuros románicos: las formas con metátesis," *Revista de Filología Románica* 21: 121–69
O'Neill, Paul 2015. "The origin and spread of velar allomorphy in the Spanish verb: A morphomic approach," *Bulletin of Hispanic Studies* 92(5): 489–518

15 Do You Say *veo el gato* or *veo al gato?*

Syntactic Changes

Lead-in Questions

15-1 In English, you can say *The dog ran after the cat* only with the words in this order. How can you say this in Spanish? Is it possible to change the order of the words in Spanish? Why is this so?

15-2 Do you say *quiero mi gato* or *quiero a mi gato* with the personal *a* before *gato*? Why?

15-3 What is the difference in meaning between *Juan cerró la ventana* and *La ventana se cerró*? Who is doing the action in each of these sentences? Why does one sentence use a reflexive marker *se* and the other one doesn't?

15-4 What is the difference in meaning between *la puerta es cerrada* and *la puerta está cerrada*? Why do you think Spanish has two verbs for 'to be'?

This chapter looks at the history of grammatical structures in Spanish that are quite different from English structures. By examining the origin of these structures and their evolution in Spanish, you will understand more clearly the grammar of Modern Spanish. This chapter begins by briefly examining how changes in the Latin case system contributed to changes in word order in Spanish. It then considers several other syntactic changes, including personal a, *the order of clitic pronouns, the expansion of the use of reflexives, and finally the functions of the verbs* ser *and* estar.

15.1 Changes in Word Order

We saw in Chapter 11 that the words in a Latin sentence, such as AMICA VIDET AMICUM 'The (female) friend sees the (male) friend,' could have numerous possible orders, because case endings indicated the grammatical functions of nouns and other nominal elements. However, word order in Latin was not completely free. The preferred order was subject-object-verb (SOV), as in AMICA AMICUM VIDET, literally 'The (female) friend the (male) friend sees.' Variations of this order were based on subtle differences of meaning, as they are today in Spanish (Ledgeway 2012: 59). As a result of the loss of the case system, word order and prepositions became the principal means in Spanish of indicating these grammatical functions and the language gradually shifted to the preferred subject-verb-object (SVO) word order that we mentioned in Chapter 11, although also with some flexibility.

If you are a native English speaker, Spanish word order may seem flexible to you, but it is less flexible than it was in Latin. For example, it means one thing to say *El perro corrió tras el gato* and another to say *El gato corrió tras el perro.* The word order and the preposition *tras* tell us who is running after whom, which is why we can also express the first sentence as *Corrió el perro tras el gato,* or *Tras el gato corrió el perro* where *el gato* is the object of the preposition. But we could not say **Corrió el perro el gato* or **El gato el perro corrió,* as was possible in Latin, because without case markings we would not know which noun phrase was the subject and which was the object of the preposition.

In fact, word order in Latin was so flexible that some linguists claim that such grammatical categories as noun phrases and verb phrases did not even exist. An example from the ancient poet Ovid of the first century BC shows how words that we now group together in noun phrases (noun + adjective or adjective + noun) could be completely separate:

GRANDIA	PER	MULTŌS	TENAUNTUR	FLUMINA	RIUŌS
great-NOM	through	many-ACC	are reduced	rivers-NOM	brooks-ACC

'great rivers are reduced to many streams' (Ledgeway 2012: 63)

You can see that the adjective GRANDIA 'great' is separated by three words from FLUMINA 'rivers,' the noun it modifies. Also, the quantifier MULTŌS 'many' is separated from the noun RIUŌS 'brooks.' Speakers or readers know that GRANDIA and FLUMINA go together because of the neuter nominative plural ending -A, and that MULTŌS and RIUŌS go together because of the masculine accusative plural ending -ōs (Ledgeway 2012: 63).

Gradually, however, with the loss of case endings, such flexibility gave way to the tendency to group words together in phrases and to separate noun phrases with a verb, so that the order SVO is now more common in Spanish. Word order, along with prepositions and agreement, now indicate the grammatical functions of nouns.

Thus, the sentence *The dog ran after the cat in Spanish* is most likely to be expressed as *El perro corrió tras el gato* with the more common SVO order. However, if we wanted to correct someone who thought that it was the boy who ran after the cat, we could also say *Corrió tras el gato el perro (no el niño),* with VOS word order or *Tras el gato corrió el perro*, with OVS order. In Spanish, as in Latin, there are subtle differences in meaning when the word order is different. In all three sentences, the preposition *tras* 'after' clarifies who is being chased and who is doing the chasing.

Complete Activities 15-1 and 15-2 on pages 329–30.

15.2 The Development of Personal *a* in Old and Modern Spanish

In Chapter 11, we mentioned briefly that most Latin prepositions were followed by either the accusative or the ablative. For example, the ablative case was used after the preposition CUM, as in AMICUS CANTAT CUM AMICĀ 'The (male) friend sings with the (female) friend' and the accusative was used after the preposition AD, as in VADŌ AD ROMAM 'I am going to Rome.' On the other hand, in sentences such as AMICUS DAT CANEM AMICAE 'the (male) friend gives the dog to the (female) friend,' prepositions were not used because the function of the nouns was clear from the case endings. We can tell that AMICUS is the subject by its nominative ending -US, that CANEM is the direct object because of its accusative ending –EM and that AMICAE is the indirect object because of its dative ending -AE. Whereas dative case in Classical Latin indicated the indirect object, in Spoken Latin it came to be expressed by the preposition AD 'to, toward' (and sometimes other prepositions) followed by the accusative case. So in Spoken Latin one could say AMICUS DAT CANEM AD AMICAM, where the indirect object AMICAM is marked with the accusative case ending -AM and preceded by the preposition AD. This tendency to use AD was passed down to Old Spanish, where it began to be used before a human direct object as well. One such example in the twelfth-century *Cantar de mio Cid* is *Dios salve a nuestros amigos e a vós más, señor* (line 3038) 'may God save our friends and (even) more you, sir.' The indirect object (underlined) in *se lo dio a su amigo* and the direct object in *vio a su amigo* are thus the direct evolution of the Latin construction AD + accusative (Penny 2002: 115).

We know that the personal *a* construction in Old Spanish was not obligatory because it was not completely fixed. Its use appears to be optional in *Cantar de mio Cid* where in the sentence *yo case sus fijas con yfantes de Carrion* 'I married his daughters to the princes of Carrion' (2956), the human direct object *sus fijas* does not appear with the personal *a*. Penny (2002: 115) suggests that it was used in Old Spanish to indicate clearly a human direct object that might otherwise be confused with the subject. Gradually, the use of *a* with personal objects, both direct and indirect, became obligatory. However, we can still see instances of its disambiguating function with non-human nouns for example, in sentences like *Persiguió el perro al gato* (Penny 2002: 116).

If you have heard Spanish speakers referring to a pet with the personal *a*, as in *Quiero mucho a mi gatito*, then you can be sure that they love their pets and see them as a part of the family. Using the personal *a* with a pet is a linguistic way of 'humanizing' and expressing affection for that pet.

Box 15.1 explains another use of the preposition *a* with verbs of movement.

Box 15.1 The preposition *a* with verbs of movement

Another use of the preposition *a* is in constructions with a verb of movement + *a* + infinitive, as in *El niño sale a pasear el perro*. Latin did not use a preposition between the verb of movement and the infinitive, as in VENERAT AURUM PETERE 'he had come to ask for his gold' (Melis 2005: 56). Thus, the use of the preposition *a* is an innovation in Spanish. In the first stage of development, both structures (with and without *a*) existed but with a semantic difference. The structure without *a* emphasized the fact that there were two separate but sequential events that occurred, as in *ve tomar aquel caballo* 'go (and) take that horse.' The structure with *a* emphasized that there was one complex event, where the verb of movement expressed the intention to complete the action of the infinitive, as in *ve a tomar aquel caballo* 'go (in order to) take that horse.'

In the first phase of grammaticalization, up until the middle of the fourteenth century, the structure without *a* was the norm, as in *e fueron poner sus escalas* 'and they went (to) put their scales' (*Fuentes cronísticas de la historia de España*, 1344, cited in Melis 2005: 67). The preposition *a* was used in only a small number of contexts, mostly in sentences where a place is mentioned in between the verb of movement and the infinitive, e.g. *e fizole ir al baño a lavar la cabeza* 'and he made him go to the bathroom to wash his head' (*Atalaya de las corónicas*, fifteenth century, cited in Melis 2005: 72). In later stages, during the second half of the fourteenth century through the fifteenth century, the use of *a* gradually increased and spread to more contexts. In the final stage, since the end of the fifteenth century, the use of *a* is almost obligatory and the structure without *a* is rarely used.

Complete Activities 15-3 and 15-4 on pages 330–31.

15.3 Changes in Clitic Pronoun Position

As we saw in Chapter 12, the personal pronouns in Spanish come directly from the Latin personal pronouns only in the first and second persons, whereas the third person pronouns come from the Latin demonstrative ILLE. This section focuses on the placement of clitic pronouns, those unstressed pronouns that join with the verb to form a single phonological word, as in *apágalo* 'turn it off' or *¿me oíste?* 'did you hear me?' You will recall from Chapter 12 that a clitic pronoun cannot exist without a verb. The word *clitic* comes from the Greek work *klitikos* 'inflexional,' which is derived from a word meaning 'to lean.' Clitics 'lean' on the verb because they cannot stand alone.

In Modern Spanish, clitic pronouns are **proclitic** (*proclíticos*), which means that they appear before the conjugated verb in declarative and interrogative sentences, as in *lo apagas así* 'you turn it off like this' and *¿lo apagaste?* 'did you turn it off?' They are **enclitic** (*enclíticos*), attached to the end of the verb, in imperative sentences, as in *¡Apágalo!* 'Turn it off!' When a modal verb is present, the clitic can appear before the conjugated modal verb, as in *lo voy a apagar* or *lo estoy apagando*, or after the infinitive, as in *voy a apagarlo*, or the gerund, as in *estoy apagándolo*.

Clitic placement in Old Spanish was different from that of Modern Spanish in that clitic pronouns were enclitic after a conjunction (*e, et*), as in *e mataronlo los christianos* 'and the Christians killed him' (*Gran crónica de Alfonso XI*, fourteenth century), and at the beginning of a sentence as in *llegóse a él* 'she came to him' (*La gran conquista de Ultramar*, 1295). Otherwise, clitic pronouns were proclitic, as in *que lo oyan los que están sobre la casa* 'that those on the house hear him' (*Calila e Dimna*, 1251). This placement is what is sometimes referred to as the Tobler-Mussafia "law" (Wanner 1991: 314). The rules were actually somewhat more complicated, though. It may have been that the default position was not proclitic, except after *et* and in initial position, but rather enclitic unless the verb was preceded by certain tonic words that could host the clitic pronoun, such as a stressed pronoun or noun, an adverb, or the negative *non* (Penny 2002: 137, Mackenzie 2017, Wanner 1991).

Another interesting feature of the clitic pronouns *me, te, le,* and *se* in Old Spanish is that they were subject to the extreme apocope mentioned in

Chapter 6. The following passages from *Cantar de mio Cid* show that apocope could occur in clitics in either enclitic position, as in sentences 1 and 2, or proclitic position, as in sentences 3 and 4:

1. *Espolonó el cavallo e metiól ('le metió') en el mayor az*
   'He spurred his horse and put it into the largest formation'
2. *déxem ('déjeme') ir en paz*
   'let me go in peace'
3. *Demos salto a él e feremos grant ganançia, antes quel ('que le') prendan los de Teruel*
   'Let's go after him and we will make lots of money, before those of Teruel capture him'
4. *Firmes son los moros, aún nos ('no se') van del campo*
   'The Moors are firm, they still do not leave the field'

By the fifteenth century, the final -*e* had been restored in most documents, although a few cases of apocope are still attested (Penny 2002: 137).

Complete Activity 15-5 on page 332.

15.4 The Rise of Reflexive and Middle Constructions

In Latin the pronoun SĒ had a reflexive use only, as in CICERO LAUDAVIT SĒ 'Cicero praised himself' (Wheelock 2005: 83). Spanish inherited both the forms and functions of the reflexive marker, but expanded its use to a wider variety of grammatical functions. Note that we will not be concerned here with the Spanish *se* that is a form of the indirect object, as in *se lo dio*, 'he gave it to her.' As we saw in Chapter 12, this comes from ILLI rather then SĒ.

One use of *se*, from the Latin reflexive SĒ, is what is called a quasi-reflexive, as in *Cuando María vio el anillo, se lo tomó* 'When Maria saw the ring, she took it (for herself)' and *Juan se lava los dientes tres veces al día* 'Juan brushes his teeth three times a day' literally 'Juan brushes to himself the teeth three times a day.'

In each case, the grammatical subject of the sentence is both the agent and the indirect recipient of the action of the verb in contrast to the direct object *el anillo* or *los dientes*. This contrasts with a true reflexive (also derived from SĒ) where the subject is also the direct object of the verb, as in *Juan se vio en el espejo* 'Juan saw himself in the mirror.' The quasi-reflexives are sometimes called **datives of interest** (*dativos de interés*) because the subject does something that is of benefit to him or herself.

There are other uses of *se* derived from reflexive SĒ that developed during the Middle Ages and became quite popular during the Renaissance. According to Whitley (1998), the **detransitivizing use** (*el uso destransitivizador*) of *se* is one of its most common functions. Spanish uses a reflexive marker to convert a **transitive verb** (*un verbo transitivo*), one that takes a direct object, such as *Juan cerró la ventana* (where *la ventana* is the direct object), into an **intransitive one** (*un verbo intransitivo*) as in *La ventana se cerró*, where there is no direct object. A construction like *la ventana se cerró* is called the **middle voice** (*la voz media*) because *se* in this kind of sentence is not a true reflexive; the window is not acting on itself, but rather is experiencing the action of being closed. Thus, in answer to Lead-in question 15-3, in *Juan cerró la ventana*, we know of course that Juan is closing the window; but in *La ventana se cerró*, we don't know who or how the window got closed. The transitive verb *cerrar* is converted into an intransitive verb with the use of *se*. Latin could also make use of the reflexive marker to transform the active voice to middle voice, as in ME DELECTŌ 'I please/ delight myself' alongside the non-reflexive ME DELECTAT 'he/she/it pleases/ delights me' (Wheelock 2005: 118).

Another way to **detransitivize** (*destransitivizar*) a verb is to convert it into **passive voice** (*la voz pasiva*). Like English, Spanish has the passive voice, so that a sentence such as *The plan was discussed at the meeting* can be expressed as *El plan fue discutido en la junta*. But it is more common for Spanish speakers to express the same idea as a middle passive, using the reflexive marker, as in *Se discutió el plan en la junta*.

To understand the multiple uses of the reflexive *se* in Modern Spanish, it is important to understand how they came about. Latin had morphological markers to express the passive voice. For example, the 1sg. form of the active voice for the verb DĒLECTĀRE 'to delight, please' was DĒLECTŌ 'I please,' and the 1sg. form of the passive voice was DĒLECTOR 'I am pleased.' Imperfect passive was 1sg.

DĒLECTĀBAR 'I was pleased' and future passive was 1sg. DĒLECTĀBOR 'I shall be pleased.' As previously mentioned, Latin also made use of the reflexive pronoun to transform the active voice to the middle voice with a similar meaning, so that MĒ DĒLECTŌ, literally 'I delight myself,' could mean 'I am delighted.' When Latin lost the passive verb forms with endings like -R and -RIS, the use of the reflexive marker to express middle voice, as well as true reflexives and quasi-reflexives, became more common (Whitley 1998).

As early as the tenth-century *Gloses Emilianenses*, mentioned in Chapter 5, one finds examples of the reflexive pronoun to mark middle voice, such as NON NOBIS SUFFICIT = *non conuienet a nob(is)* 'no nos conviene' 'it is not agreeable to us' and NON ERUBESCUNT = *non se bergundian* 'no se avergüenzan' 'they are not ashamed.' By the thirteenth century, as seen in *Cantar de Mio Cid*, one also finds phrasal combinations such as *ser* + past participle (*mucho eran (a) rrepentidos los i(n)fantes* 'the princes were very sorry (regretful)') alongside the middle constructions (*yo d'esso me pago* '*me conformo*' 'I am satisfied'). Thus, although Spanish lost the Latin morphological marker for expressing passive voice, it continued to express this function with the reflexive *se* and *ser* + past participle. From the Renaissance period onward, the use of the reflexive marker continued to expand resulting in a richer lexicon of reflexives and middle constructions.

Complete Activity 15-6 on page 332.

15.5 Why Does Spanish Have Two Verbs for 'to be': *ser* and *estar*?

The short answer to this question is that originally there was only one verb 'to be' in Spanish, which was *ser*. The forms of this verb derived in part from ESSE, the Latin verb meaning 'to be,' but some of its forms also came from SEDĒRE, the Latin verb meaning 'to sit.' For example, the imperfect indicative forms derive from the imperfect of ESSE, like 1sg. *era* < ERAM, whereas the present subjunctive forms derive from the present subjunctive of SEDĒRE, like 1sg. *sea* < SEDEAM. There is disagreement, however, about whether the infinitive *ser* comes from ESSE or SEDĒRE (Rini 1997). Later another verb, *estar*, from Latin STĀRE 'to stand,' began to take over some of the functions of *ser*. We will consider in this section these different functions and how *estar* came to be used alongside *ser* and sometimes in place of it.

Latin ESSE, like *to be* in English, had all the different functions of a true **copular verb** (*verbo copulativo*), a 'linking verb' that links subjects with nouns (VERGILIUS EST POĒTA 'Virgil is a poet') and adjectives (DŌNA SUNT MAGNA 'the gifts are large'). It was also used to express existence (COGITO ERGO SUM 'I think therefore I am') and location (PATER NOSTER, QUI ES IN CAELIS 'Our Father, who art in heaven'). Furthermore, it was the auxiliary verb used in the perfect of the passive voice with a past participle (LAUDĀTA EST 'she was praised'). As seen in Table 15.1, Old Spanish *ser* had many of the same functions as in Latin. It was used with noun and adjective complements, with locative adverbs expressing a place, and with past participles.

The verb STĀRE was not common in either Classical or Spoken Latin, but it eventually broadened its meanings of 'to stand' and 'to stand still' to include the more stative meanings of 'to remain' or 'to stay.' Gradually, as the original meanings became broader, the stative function gained traction as a copular verb. In early Old Spanish texts, *ser* and *estar* were both used to link a subject with a **locative complement** (*complemento locativo*), an adverb or prepositional phrase that locates the subject in a physical place, for example 'here,' 'over there,' 'in the yard,' 'with you.' However, when *ser* occurred with a human subject, its meaning implied 'to arrive,' as in *Antes sere con vusco que el sol quiera rayar* 'I will be with you before the sun begins to shine' (Pountain 1982: 152). *Estar*, on the other hand, when used with human subjects could express only the meaning of 'to remain,' as in *Firme estido Pero Vermue* 'Pedro Bermúdez remained firm' (Pountain 1982: 153). Gradually *estar* replaced *ser* in the locative function, except in the meaning 'to take place' still expressed by *ser* (Rojas 2004: 51–52). This is why one can say *la fiesta es en casa de Jorge* to say where an event is taking place. But in order to indicate the location of a person or thing, one would use *estar*, as in *Charo está en casa de Jorge* or *la buena comida está en casa de Jorge*.

Once *estar* began functioning as a linking verb with physical places, it was not difficult to associate *estar* with metaphorical and abstract places or positions.

TABLE 15.1 Functions of *ser* and *estar* in Old and Modern Spanish (based on Rojas 2004)

Function	Old Spanish		Modern Spanish	
	ser	*estar*	*ser*	*estar*
with noun complement	✓ (*Non pudet ser otra sennal* 'it can't be another sign' (A13, 12th cent.)	X	✓ *No puede ser otra señal*	X
with adjective complement	✓ (always more frequent) *Bla(n)ca era e bermeia* 'she was white and auburn' (C58, 13th cent.)	✓ (but scarce until 14th cent.) *la uva en aquel tiempo está muy madura* 'the grape at that time was very ripe' (16th cent.)	✓ (indicates inherent quality or member of a class): *Juan es enfermo* 'Juan is an invalid'	✓ (indicates a condition or acquired quality): *Juan está enfermo* 'Juan is sick'
with locative complement	✓ (more frequent in 13th cent.) *burgeses e burgesas por las finiestras son*, 'the bourgeois men and women are at the windows' (B19, 13th cent.)	✓ (more frequent since 14th cent.) *grado a ti, señor padre, que estás en alto!* 'thanks to you, Lord Father, who are on high' (B8,13th cent.)	✓ (only with events since 15th cent.) *La fiesta es en casa de Jorge*	✓ *Charo está en casa de Jorge*
with past participle	✓ (more frequent through 15th cent.) (auxiliary of passive): *La tienda es cogida* 'the tent is hit' (the result of an action): *ca echados somos de tierra!* 'for we are thrown out of (our) land' (B14, 13th cent.)	✓ (scarce until the 14th cent.) *el rio que estava una vez yelado* 'the river that was once frozen' (13th cent.) *estó agora mucho afincado de mengua de dineros* 'I am now very afflicted by a lack of money' (14th cent.)	✓ (auxiliary of passive): *El acueducto estaba totalmente destruido*	✓ (more frequent since 16th cent.) (a state as a result of an action): *El acueducto fue construido por los romanos*

These functions of *estar* are evident in the fourteenth-century *El Conde Lucanor*, in the sentence *podría escusar de aquel peligro en que estava* 'he would find a way to get out of the danger he was in' (Pountain 1982: 155). This idea could also extend to the use of *estar* with past participles and adjectives, as in *estó agora mucho afincado de mengua de dineros*, 'I am now very afflicted by a lack of money' and *el philósopho que estava cativo* 'the philosopher who was captive' (*El Conde Lucanor*, cited in Pountain 1982: 156).

These changes in *ser* and *estar* resulted in two different verbs for 'to be' in Modern Spanish with distinct functions: *ser* appears with **noun complements** (*complementos nominales*), as in *Erica es doctora* 'Erica is a doctor,' and *estar* combines with locative complements, except when the subject represents an event. With **adjective complements** (*complementos adjetivos*), *ser* can be followed only by an adjective that indicates a member of a class or an inherent property (*Juan es enfermo* 'Juan is an invalid, belongs to a class of invalids, or is inherently ill'), whereas adjectives following *estar* indicate the result of an action (*estoy enfermo* 'something has happened that has resulted in my being sick'), or indicate a state through which a subject is passing as in *la uva está madura en este momento*. The use of *estar* with an adjective can also express an unexpected reaction on the part of a speaker, as in *¡qué alto estás!* 'how tall you've suddenly gotten' (Pountain 1982: 141) or 'how tall you look!' With a past participle, *ser* forms a passive construction, as in *el acueducto fue construido por los Romanos* 'the aqueduct was built by the Romans,' and *estar* expresses a state that is the result of an action, as in *el acueducto ya estaba destruido cuando llegaron los moros* 'the aqueduct was already destroyed when the Moors arrived.'

Thus, the Latin system had one copular verb, ESSE, that combined with nouns, adjectives, locative complements and past participles. In Spanish this changed to a system with two copular verbs with distinct functions: *ser* is the only one of these verbs to take a noun complement, *estar* is more often used with locative complements and both combine with adjectives and past participles but with distinct meanings.

Complete Activity 15-7 page 333.

15.6 Chapter Summary

This chapter has examined some of the major syntactic changes in Spanish.

- Word order has become less flexible from Latin to Spanish, but it is still more flexible than English word order. For example, many more word orders are possible for the sentence *el perro corrió tras el gato* than for the English equivalent, *the dog chased after the cat.*
- The Spanish personal *a* developed from the Latin preposition AD 'to, toward' and is now an obligatory marker for human direct objects, in part to distinguish between subjects and direct objects after the loss of cases.
- Clitic pronoun placement has changed from Old Spanish to Modern Spanish. In Old Spanish, enclisis, that is the placement of the pronoun after the verb, was much more common, occurring after *et* 'and' and in sentence-initial and some other positions, whereas in Modern Spanish enclisis occurs only after the imperative. With constructions of modal verbs and infinitives or past participles, clitic position is still variable in Modern Spanish, as in *voy a hacerlo* or *lo voy a hacer.*
- The reflexive and middle constructions developed out of the Latin reflexive pronouns but gained more functions in Spanish and are now a predominant part of the grammar of Spanish.
- There are two copular verbs 'to be' in Modern Spanish. The forms of *ser* came from ESSE 'to be' and SEDĒRE 'to sit,' whereas those of *estar* came from STĀRE 'to stand.' Over time *estar* has taken on some of the functions that were previously the domain of *ser* and a difference in meaning has developed between the two.

Activities

Activity 15-1
Examine the following Latin text and translate it into Modern Spanish in order to learn more about word order in Latin. Then answer the following questions.

"The poet Horace contemplates an invitation" (Wheelock 2005: 7)

MAECĒNAS ET VERGILIUS MĒ HODIĒ VOCANT. QUID CŌGITĀRE DĒBEŌ? QUID DĒBEŌ RESPONDĒRE? SĪ ERRŌ, MĒ SAEPE MONENT ET CULPANT; SĪ NŌN ERRŌ, MĒ LAUDANT. QUID HODIĒ CŌGITĀRE DĒBEŌ?

> (CŌGITĀRE 'to think,' HODIĒ 'today,' MONENT '3pl. advise, warn,' QUID 'what, that,' SAEPE 'often,' VOCĀRE 'to call, convoke')

1. What do you notice about the placement of the verb? Where does it usually appear? When there is an auxiliary verb and an infinitive, where does the auxiliary verb usually appear? Is it always the same?
2. The accusative (direct object) form of the personal pronoun MĒ appears three times. Where does it appear in relation to the verb?
3. There are two adverbs in the text, HODIĒ and SAEPE. Where do they appear in the sentences?
4. In what ways is the word order in this text different from word order in Modern Spanish? How is it the same?

Activity 15-2

Examine one of the excerpts from a twelfth- or thirteenth-century text in the Appendix in this book. Write down three sentences where the word order is different from that of Modern Spanish. What can you conclude about the changes in word order that have occurred in Spanish since the twelfth or thirteenth century?

Activity 15-3

In the following Old Spanish texts of the late twelfth and early thirteenth centuries, identify the sentences in which personal *a* is used with human direct objects. What can you conclude about the use of personal *a* for direct objects in the language at that time? How does this contrast with the use of personal *a* in the language today?

1. *Adam ouo (tuvo) dos fillos, Kaym & Abel. Mató Kaym ad Abel* 'Adam had two sons, Cain and Abel. Cain killed Abel' (*Liber Regum*, 1194–1211)
2. *Et quando çercó (capturó) el Rey Don Sancho su hermano en Çamora, . . .* 'And when the King Don Sancho captured his brother in Zamora, . . .' (*Corónicas navarras*, 1205–09)
3. *Et quando mató Belid Alfons el Rey Don Sancho a traición* 'And when Vellido Dolfos killed the King Don Sancho by treason' (*Corónicas navarras*, 1205–09)

4. *prisó (recogió) el Rey Don Sancho de Castieylla a Rodic Diaz et criolo et fizolo cavayllero* 'the King Don Sancho of Castile took Rodrigo Díaz in and raised him and made him a knight' (*Corónicas navarras*, 1205–09)

Activity 15-4

A. In the following examples, what do you think is the difference in meaning between sentences (a) and (b)?

1. (a) *Cuando salgo de viaje, tengo que dejar el perro en la perrera.*
   (b) *Cuando salgo de viaje, tengo que dejar a mi perrito en la perrera. No me gusta hacerlo, pero no tengo otras opciones.*

2. (a) *¡Saca el gato de aquí! Deja sus pelos por todos lados.*
   (b) *Saca al gatito, ¿no? Está maullando y quiere salir.*

3. (a) *Suelta el caballo para que corra.*
   (b) *Suelta al caballo para que corra.*

Is the personal *a* in the (b) sentences used to disambiguate the subject and object or is it used as a personal *a*? Explain your reason(s). Why do Spanish speakers sometimes use *a* with certain animals? Do you think they would use them with all kinds of animals? Why or why not?

B. On a web page that explains what kind of pillow is best for sleeping and how to select one, we see the following title, as we would expect for an inanimate direct object:

¿Cómo elijo mi almohada? (www.innofisio.com/como-elijo-mi-almohada)

But in poetry and song lyrics, we see the use of the preposition *a* before the same inanimate object used as a direct object. How do you explain this use?

> *Solo quiero que tú sepas que te estoy queriendo,*
> *Que por las noches te sueño despierto y no estás*
> *Fuerte abrazo a mi almohada y pienso que te tengo*
> *Luego veo la realidad y me pongo a llorar.*
>   (Lyrics from *Solo quería que lo supieras* by
>   Eduardo Flores)

Activity 15-5

In the following Old Spanish sentences, the first six from *Calila e Dimna* (1251) and the seventh from *Documentos Castellanos* (1067), state whether the underlined direct and indirect object clitic pronouns are proclitic or enclitic. Then say whether their placement follows the Tobler-Mussafia Law.

1. *Despertó el dueño de la casa e sintió<u>los</u>* 'the owner of the house woke up and felt (heard) them'
2. *Et despertó a su muger et dix<u>ole</u>: "fabla quedo, que yo he sentido ladrones que andan sobre nuestra casa ..."* 'And he woke up his wife and said to her: "speak quietly, for I have felt (heard) thieves that walk on (the roof of) our house ..."'
3. *de guise que <u>lo</u> oyan los que están sobre nuestra casa* 'so that those who are on our house hear it'
4. *et dime quándo <u>los</u> sintieres çerca de aquí* 'and tell me when you feel them close to here'
5. *¿dónde <u>las</u> ayuntaste?* 'where did you get them?'
6. *Et fizo<u>lo</u> así como <u>le</u> mandó el marido et oyó el ladron* 'And she did it like that as the husband ordered her and the thief heard'
7. *Cognosco <u>me</u> in veritate* 'I truly know myself'

Activity 15-6

A. For each of the following transitive sentences, provide an intransitive (middle) version with the reflexive marker *se*. You will have to eliminate the subject and make the direct object the new subject.

| Example: | *Juan cerró la puerta.* |
| Middle with *se*: | *La puerta se cerró.* |

1. *Los piratas hundieron el barco.*
2. *Mamá quemó el pastel.*
3. *Perdimos las llaves del coche.*
4. *Papá despertó a Juanito.*
5. *El viento rompió los platos.*

B. Translate each one of the following English sentences into two Modern Spanish sentences, one in the passive voice with a form of *ser* and another one as a middle-passive construction with the reflexive marker *se*.

Example: *The plan was discussed at the meeting.*
Passive: *El plan fue discutido en la junta.*
Middle with *se*: *Se discutió el plan en la junta.*

1. The news was revealed on the radio program.
2. Many books were written in the twentieth century.
3. The movie had been filmed in Africa.
4. My favorite handicrafts are sold in that city.
5. The trees were cut down to build the new house.

C. In this exercise, you were asked to form passive sentences with *ser* and middle passives with *se*. How did these types of sentences evolve from Latin?

Activity 15-7

In the following verses from *Cantar de mio Cid*, analyze all of the instances of the use of *ser* (underlined). Translate these into Modern Spanish and say whether you continue to use *ser* today or whether you would use *estar*. Based on these examples, explain how the use of *ser* and *estar* has changed.

Non se abre la puerta, ca ('porque') bien era çerrada (39)
Non puedo traer el aver ('riquezas') ca ('porque') mucho es pesado (91)
De Castiella vos ides ('vais') pora las yentes estrañas, (176)
assí es vuestra ventura ('fortuna'), grandes son vuestras ganançias
En vuestras manos son las arcas (189)
Aún era de día, non era puesto el sol, (416)
Mandó ver sus yentes mio Çid el Campeador;
Sin las peonadas ('soldados') e omnes valientes que son,
Estas ganançias allí eran juntadas (506)
Firmes son los moros, aún no se van del campo (755)
Bien lo aguisa ('aprovecha') el que en buen ora nasco, (808)
Cuantos él trae todos son pagados ('satisfechos').
Con estas ganançias a la posada tornando se van; (943)
Todos son alegres, ganançias traen grandes,
Grandes son los poderes e apriessa se van llegando (967)

Respuso el conde: – ¡Esto non <u>será</u> verdad! (979)

¡Tan ricos <u>son</u> los sos que non saben qué se an ('tienen')! (1086)

Activity 15-8

Choose one of the five Old Spanish texts in the Appendix and answer the following questions for your text.

A. Clitic pronoun position (explained in Section 15.3): Underline six clitic pronouns. For each one, state whether its position follows the Tobler-Mussafia law and whether it has the same position in Modern Spanish.

B. *Ser* and *estar* (explained in Section 15.5): Underline six examples of *ser* and *estar*, three of each verb, if possible. Translate the Old Spanish verb into Modern Spanish and explain whether the same verb is used in Modern Spanish. Try to find examples where they are different.

C. Taking into account these two syntactic features and also general word order (from Section 15.1 and Activity 15-2), explain whether the language of the text you analyzed seems syntactically similar to or different from Modern Spanish.

Further Reading

Barry, A. K. 1987. "Clitic pronoun position in thirteenth-century Spanish," *Hispanic Review* 55 (2): 213–20

Bouzouita, Miriam 2008. "At the syntax-pragmatics interface: Clitics in the history of Spanish," in R. Cooper and R. Kempson (eds.), *Language in flux: Dialogue coordination, language variation, change and evolution*, 221–63. London: College Publications

Díaz, Miriam 2016. "Semantic changes of *ser*, *estar*, and *haber* in Spanish: A diachronic and comparative approach," in Eva Núñez-Méndez (ed.), *Diachronic applications in Hispanic linguistics*, 303–44. Newcastle upon Tyne: Cambridge Scholars Publishing

Fábregas, Antonio. 2013. "Differential object marking in Spanish: State of the art," *Borealis: An International Journal of Hispanic Linguistics* 2: 1–80

Rini, Joel 2009. "Dating the grammaticalization of the Spanish Clitic Pronoun," *Zeitschrift für romanische Philologie* 106 (3–4): 354–70

Tailya, Trần "How to use 'se' in Spanish – the most confusing word," YouTube video

Velázquez-Mendoza, Omar 2013. "Latín y romance en la Iberia del Medievo tardío y el complemento directo preposicional," *Zeitschrift für romanische Philologie* 129 (1): 115–27

Wanner, Dieter 1991. "The Tobler-Mussafia law in Old Spanish," in Hector Campos and Fernando Martínez Gil (eds.), *Current studies in Spanish linguistics*, 313–78 Washington, DC: Georgetown University Press

16

How Did MŪSCŬLUM 'little mouse' Become Spanish *muslo* 'thigh'?

Semantic Changes

Lead-in Questions

16-1 Think of a new expression that you have started using recently, like "it's lit" to describe a lively party. How has the meaning of the word *lit* changed in this new use? You may not be able to determine the exact change in meaning, but use your imagination to come up with a possible explanation.

16-2 You have no doubt noticed that many similar words in English and Spanish have different meanings, like *embarrassed* and *embarazada* 'pregnant' or *carpet* and *carpeta* 'folder.' Write down three other pairs of **false cognates** (*falsos cognados*) in English and Spanish, especially ones that you have used mistakenly yourself. Then determine for each pair of words the meaning they have in common. For example, English *carpet* and Spanish *carpeta* both refer to some type of covering, but a *carpet* covers a floor whereas a *carpeta* provides a cover for papers.

This chapter considers how speakers change the meaning of words by using them in new ways. You will learn that these semantic changes usually result from one of six primary processes, which may be accompanied by two secondary processes. Words can change meaning to that of an object or concept they resemble or with which they are in contact. A word can also change meaning because its form is similar to the form of another word or because it is used in an expression with another word that is then deleted. Words might also change their range, rather than their basic meaning. This occurs when a word's meaning becomes more general or broader or when it becomes more specific or narrower. Finally, any of the six primary processes can be accompanied by a change in affect, that is, a change in meaning to more positive or more negative connotations. Each of these types of semantic change is explained and illustrated below first with examples from English and then with examples from Spanish. By considering these semantic changes, you will arrive at a better understanding of the meanings of the words you use and how these meanings evolved. You will also learn how words of the same origin in Spanish and English can come to have different meanings, like embarrassed *and* embarazada *mentioned above in Lead-in question 16-2.*

16.1 What Are the Different Ways a Word Can Change Its Meaning?

In the previous chapters, we have considered in some detail how Spanish speakers change the sounds and forms of their language. In this chapter, we will consider how they change the meanings of words. Semantic change begins when a speaker uses a word in a new way in a particular context. This word thereby gains a new meaning that exists alongside the older meaning or may replace it altogether. For example, when people refer to a skilled and powerful athlete as a *beast*, they have created a new meaning for the word *beast* which exists alongside the original meaning of *beast* as 'a non-human animal.' This new use came about because speakers perceived a similarity between certain athletes and beasts in terms of strength and power.

A change of meaning like the new meaning of *beast* comes about through **metaphor** (*la metáfora*). As we have seen, this occurs when speakers perceive a resemblance between two items, which can be objects or actions or concepts, and so they apply the word of one item metaphorically to another item. Some other common examples of metaphor were created when speakers perceived a similarity between parts of the body and inanimate objects. Because the narrow strips on a comb sit together in a row like the teeth in the mouth, we refer to the *teeth of a comb*. We also talk about the *legs of a table* because they serve to support the table just as legs support the human body. The reverse can occur as well when we perceive that objects are similar to body parts. We talk about the *Adam's apple* in the throat or the *spinal column* that supports the body the way an architectural column supports a building.

Words may adopt the meaning not only of items that they resemble, but also of items with which they are in contact. The change in meaning through contiguity is called **metonymy** (*la metonimia*). An example from English is the use of the word *seat* to refer to the part of the body or the part of the pants that comes into contact with a seat or chair, as in the *seat of one's pants*. Another example in English is the change in meaning from Old English *ceace* 'jaw' to 'cheek,' the part of the face next to the jaw (Bloomfield 1933: 427). Metonymy can also include the process whereby part of an object takes on the meaning of the whole object, that is, when a part stands for the whole. This special type of metonymy carries its own name, **synecdoche** (*la sinécdoque*). We see this in the current use of *crib* in urban slang to refer to one's house or residence rather than to just a piece of furniture inside the house.

Whereas metaphor and metonymy are based on a similarity or contiguity of meaning, two other processes of change are based on a similarity or contiguity of form. The process of change based on a similarity of form is called **popular etymology** (*la etimología popular*). This process is typically included in discussions of semantic change (Ullmann 1959: 288–89, Penny 2002: 265), even though it does not always involve a change in meaning. One example is the word *crayfish* or *crawfish* which comes from the fourteenth-century English word *crevis,* borrowed from thirteenth-century French *crevice* (Modern French *écrevisse* 'shrimp'). The term popular etymology implies that this change came about because people invented an origin for a word and then changed its form accordingly. In this case, they changed *crevis* to *crayfish* on the assumption that it derived from the word *fish*, even though a crayfish is a crustacean, like shrimp and lobsters. Another example of popular etymology from English is the word *mushroom*. This is also a borrowing from Old French, this time from the word *meisseron* (Harper 2001–17: "mushroom"), now *mousseron* in Modern French. English speakers changed the ending to the recognizable word *room*, but it is hard to perceive a mushroom as a type of room, unless it is a dwelling for a forest fairy.

The process of change based on contiguity of form, known as **ellipsis** (*la elipsis*), occurs when one word takes on the meaning of an entire expression. For example, it is common for an adjective to take on the meaning of an entire noun phrase, as when the adjective *social* comes to stand for the expression *social security number*, as in *What's your social?* The adjective is kept in most cases rather than the noun because it contains the distinctive information. If someone were to ask simply *What's your number?*, keeping only the noun, you would not know which number to provide. This process is referred to as ellipsis because part of the expression, the noun in the example above, is elided or deleted.

The third general category of semantic change is a change in range, which means that a word's meaning becomes more general or more specific. When a word takes on a more general meaning we speak of **broadening** (*la ampliación*). This occurred in the English word *dog*, which originally referred only to a particular ancient breed of dog, but now refers to any type of dog. When the meaning of a word becomes more specific, we speak of **narrowing** (*la restricción*). An example of narrowing in English is the change in meaning of *hound* from 'dog,' the same meaning as German *Hund*, to a specific type of dog, namely 'a hound or hunting dog.' So while the meaning of *dog* underwent broadening by changing from a particular type of dog to the general term for dog, *hound* underwent narrowing, changing from the general term for dog to a particular type of dog.

The final two processes, amelioration and pejoration, can come about as a by-product of one of the other processes already mentioned. For example, the English word *knave* changed from its original meaning of a 'boy' to a 'rascal.' This is a case of narrowing, since a rascal is only one type of boy, and also a case of **pejoration** (*la peyoración*) whereby the meaning of the word acquires a negative connotation. A word can also acquire a more positive connotation through the process of **amelioration** (*la mejoración*) as in the case of *knight*,

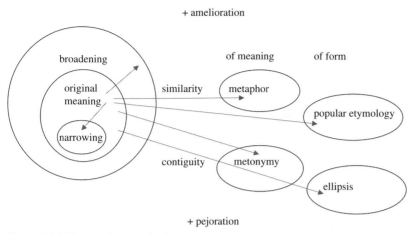

Figure 16.1 Types of semantic change

which also meant 'boy' originally. Like *knave*, it also underwent narrowing, but changed its meaning from a boy or servant to a knight, which since the sixteenth century has been a term of nobility (Harper 2001–17: "knight"). We have created the terms *peyoración* and *mejoración* in Spanish to distinguish between these linguistic processes and the general terms for worsening (*empeoramiento*) or improvement (*mejoramiento*).

Figure 16.1 provides a visual representation of the types of semantic change in order to serve as a guide as you read about these processes in the history of Spanish in the following sections of this chapter.

16.2 What Are Metaphor and Metonymy?

A popular type of metaphor in Spanish, as in English, is to apply names of body parts to other objects, so that one talks about *la boca del río* 'the mouth of a river,' *las entrañas de la tierra* 'the bowels of the earth,' and *las patas de la mesa* 'the legs of the table' (Ullmann 1959: 278–79, Penny 2002: 311–12). The reverse also occurs, so that body parts are often described metaphorically by other objects, such as *la nuez de la garganta* 'Adam's apple,' *el globo del ojo* 'eyeball,' and *la caja del pecho* 'rib cage' (Ullmann 1959: 279, Penny 2002: 312).

Throughout the history of Spanish, speakers have created new meanings based on other similarities as well. Because they no doubt thought that the peaks of mountains looked like the jagged edge of a saw, the Spanish word for 'saw,' *sierra* (< SERRAM 'saw'), took on the meaning of 'mountain range.' This is why one finds mountain ranges around the world with names such as the Sierra Morena in southern Spain and the Sierra Madre in Mexico. One humorous case of metaphor is the perception that a person's head looked like a cooking pot. Thus, one finds in Old Spanish the word *tiesta* for 'head' (< TESTAM 'cooking pot'), as seen in the Appendix B13, and also in the word for 'head' in French (*tête*) and Italian (*testa*). Another amusing metaphor between an object and a part of the body is the change mentioned in the title of this chapter. MŪSCŬLUM 'little mouse' changes its meaning to 'muscle,' since a well-developed muscle looks like a little mouse running under the skin. The new meaning 'muscle' then underwent narrowing in Spanish, so that *muslo* means 'thigh,' a specific muscle rather than a muscle in general.

Verbs can also undergo metaphorical change, although sometimes the similarity may be less obvious than with physical objects. For example, the words meaning 'to understand' in various languages often come from a word meaning 'to grasp' or 'to get.' That's why we often say in English "you get it?" to see whether someone has understood. In Spanish *comprender* 'to understand' comes from COMPRENDĚRE 'to catch, grasp.' One finds the same metaphorical path repeating itself in Modern Spanish, so that the words for 'to grasp,' such as *coger* and *pillar*, are now used to mean 'to understand' in some dialects (Dworkin 2006: 51). The other word meaning 'to understand' in Spanish, *entender*, also came about metaphorically. Latin INTENDĚRE meant 'to turn one's attention toward something,' literally 'to stretch out toward something.' The directing of one's attention then took on the meaning of understanding.

We saw another verb that has undergone a metaphorical change in meaning in Chapter 3 in the excerpt from *El Conde Lucanor* (line 14). The verb *cuidar* from CŌGITĀRE 'to think' was still used with the meaning 'to think' in Old Spanish, but it has since changed to meaning 'to care for.' One can see how thinking about someone is similar to caring for him or her, if one transfers one's thoughts into considerate actions. The Modern Spanish word for 'to think,' *pensar*, also resulted from a metaphor. It comes from PĒNSĀRE 'to weigh,' which also gives Spanish *pesar* in which it maintains the original meaning. Thinking can be a type of weighing, especially when weighing has the meaning of evaluating, as in *weighing one's options*, which is expressed by *sopesar* in Spanish. So we see that words can change meaning through metaphor when speakers apply a word to something that they view as similar to its original meaning.

Another frequent change in meaning, metonymy, results not from the perceived similarity between objects, but from their being in contact with one another. In the same way we speak in English about the seat of one's pants, the Latin word for 'seat' also gave its name to a body part in Spanish. CATHEDRAM 'armchair' changed to Spanish *cadera* 'hip,' the part of the body that touches the chair. Another metonymic change in Spanish is identical to one seen above in English. Just as the English word for 'jaw' became the word for 'cheek,' the Latin word for 'jaw,' MAXĪLLAM, became the Spanish word for 'cheek,' *mejilla*. This may have been motivated by the fact that the Latin word for 'cheek,' BUCCAM, had become the Spanish word for 'mouth,' *boca*, also through metonymy. The need for a new word for 'mouth' may have been brought about by the perception that the Latin word for 'mouth,' ŌREM, from which we get *oral*, was too short. To complete this facial carousel, we should mention that Latin had another word for 'jaw,' MANDIBULAM, which kept this meaning as Spanish *mandíbula*.

Metonymy can refer not only to objects in contact, but also to periods of time in contact or successive periods of time. The Spanish word *verano* 'summer' comes from VERĀNUM, an adjective derived from the Latin word for 'spring,' VĒREM. So what was once 'spring' or 'springlike' changed its meaning to 'summer,' the following season. The word for 'spring' in Spanish then changed its name to the first part of spring, namely *primavera* from Spoken Latin PRĪMA 'first' and VĒRA 'spring.' It is interesting to observe more recently that *ahora*, which originally meant 'now,' is often used to mean 'soon' and *ya*, which originally meant 'already,' is often used to mean 'now.'

We also find examples of synecdoche in Spanish in which a part of an object comes to refer to the whole object, as when one says *the crown* to mean *the king* or *the queen*. This explains how VŌTA 'vows,' the neuter plural of VŌTUM, came to refer to the entire wedding ceremony as *boda*. In another example, CAESPĪTEM 'sod, grass,' which is a part of the lawn, comes to refer to the entire 'lawn' as *césped*. It is also considered to be a type of metonymy when a product derives its name from the place where it is made. The word *moneda* 'coin, currency' derives its name from MONĒTA because Roman coins were minted in the temple of Juno Moneta. More modern products bear the names of their place of production, such as *jerez* 'sherry' from the city of Jerez in southwestern Spain, *champán* 'champagne' from the Champagne region of northeastern France, and *tequila* from the town of Tequila in the state of Jalisco in Central Mexico.

16.3 What Are Popular Etymology and Ellipsis?

Sometimes speakers associate the form of a word with other words through popular etymology. The change in form may or may not also have an effect on the word's meaning. One especially clear example in Spanish is the word *vagabundo* 'vagabond.' This is sometimes rendered as *vagamundo* through popular etymology on the assumption that it means 'someone who wanders throughout the world.' Another example is *tinieblas* derived from TENĒBRA 'concealment, darkness, gloom.' One finds this word written *tiniebra* in Old Spanish, a form attested along with *teniebra* and *tiniebla* until the early sixteenth century. It is possible that the change of ending from -*bra* to -*bla* results from an association of the form of this word with *niebla* 'fog' from NEBŬLA, since fog can also obscure one's vision. One last example is the change in form from POLLICĀREM, the adjective form of POLLĬCEM 'thumb,' to Spanish *pulgar* 'thumb.' You will recall that the initial /o/ of Latin becomes /o/ through regular sound change. In *pulgar*, however, it becomes /u/ perhaps by association with *pulga* 'flea,' since the thumb might have been a good instrument for smashing or removing fleas.

In the same way that English speakers shorten *social security number* to *social* through ellipsis, Spanish speakers may say *postal* for *tarjeta postal* 'postcard' and *móvil* for *teléfono móvil* 'mobile phone.' Historical examples include the Spanish word for 'plum' from PRŪNA CĒREOLA, where PRŪNA means 'plum' and CĒREOLA means 'wax-colored,' an adjective derived from CĒRA 'wax.' The Latin word for 'plum' is deleted so that the adjective CĒREOLA changes meaning from 'wax-colored' to 'plum' as *ciruela*.

16.4 Semantic Changes in Range: Broadening and Narrowing

Whereas metaphor and metonymy result in complete changes in meaning, broadening and narrowing are changes in range rather than basic meaning. In broadening, the meaning of a word changes from a more specific to a more general meaning. We can conceive of this in two different ways, depending on the type of item referred to. One way to conceive of broadening and narrowing is to establish a hierarchy where the more general term includes under its heading several more specific terms. We can refer to the more general term as the **superordinate term** (*el término superordinado*) and we can call the more specific items **subordinate terms** (*términos subordinados*). Figure 16.2 shows an example of this type of hierarchy for the words for 'bird.'

When a subordinate term takes on the meaning of the superordinate term, then we can say that its meaning has broadened. This is the case for the word *pájaro*, the superordinate term in Figure 16.2. Latin PASSĔREM, which becomes *pájaro*, originally meant 'sparrow,' but it takes on a more general meaning of any small bird, much in the same way that *dog* in English changed from a particular type of dog to the superordinate term for the species. We must specify that *pájaro* means any small bird because the Spanish word *ave* from AVEM 'bird' is an even more general word that also includes larger birds, like ostriches, penguins, vultures, and eagles.

When the change of meaning in a hierarchy is from a superordinate term to a subordinate term, then the meaning of a word has narrowed. This type of change occurred in the Spanish word *animal* from ANIMĀLEM 'a living thing,' literally anything that had an ANĬMA 'a soul.' In current popular usage, *animal* has a more specific meaning of non-human animals, especially mammals as opposed to birds and fish.

Superordinate term: *pájaro* '(small) bird'

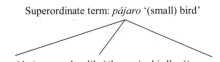

Subordinate terms: *gorrión* 'sparrow' *colibrí* 'hummingbird' *pájaro carpintero* 'woodpecker'

Figure 16.2 Superordinate term with subordinate terms for the semantic field 'bird'

TABLE 16.1 Distinctive semantic features for types of talking

	Produce utterances	In narrative form	To a higher power
hablar 'to speak'	+	−	−
contar historias 'to tell stories'	+	+	−
rezar 'to pray'	+	−	+

One can also conceive of broadening and narrowing in terms of semantic features. For example, we can say that talking is more general than telling stories or praying because talking has only the feature of producing meaningful sounds with one's vocal apparatus, whereas telling stories also has the feature of organizing these sounds into a narrative and praying has the additional feature of directing these sounds to a higher power to express requests or give thanks. The meaning that has fewer semantic features is more general, whereas the meanings that have more semantic features are more specific, as represented in Table 16.1.

In the history of Spanish, we see examples of broadening and narrowing within the semantic field of speaking. The word *hablar* came from FABULĀRE 'to tell fables.' The meaning of this word broadened when it lost the distinctive feature of telling fables, so that it came to mean producing any type of utterance. On the other hand, RECITĀRE 'to recite' narrowed in meaning to Spanish *rezar* by adding the feature of addressing oneself to a higher power. In Chapter 4 we saw that words borrowed from other languages often undergo narrowing. In English, *a party* can be any type of celebration, whereas *pari*, the English borrowing in Spanish, has the more specific meaning of a celebration in a bar. In Spanish, a *fiesta* is any type of celebration, but in English a *fiesta* is a specifically Spanish-themed type of celebration, such as a Cinco de Mayo party.

In summary, we have seen then that the meaning of a word can broaden when it takes on the meaning of a superordinate term in a hierarchy or when it loses a distinctive feature to become less specific and more general. The meaning of a word can also narrow when it takes on the meaning of a subordinate term in a hierarchy or when it adds a feature to its meaning thereby becoming more specific.

16.5 Semantic Changes in Affect: Amelioration and Pejoration

Changes in affect are considered to be types of semantic change in their own right by Penny (2002: 268–69), but we see them rather as by-products of other changes. Words can undergo a change in affect by changing to a more positive meaning through amelioration or to a more negative meaning through pejoration. One example of amelioration in Spanish is the word *caballo* from CABALLUM 'nag, workhorse.' The Latin word lost its connotation of a 'nag,' a horse in poor condition, to become the general word for horse, replacing EQUUM, whose stem is seen in words like *equestrian* in English and *ecuestre* 'equestrian' and *equitación* 'horseback riding' in Spanish. We see that the amelioration was accomplished by losing the distinctive feature 'in poor condition' which also resulted in broadening from a horse with a particular feature to the general term for 'horse.' So we can consider this change to be first and foremost an example of broadening. Since the broadening is accomplished by losing a negative feature, this is also a case of amelioration. A notable example of pejoration in Spanish is the change in meaning of SINISTRUM from 'left' to 'sinister.' This change had already begun in Latin where 'inauspicious' is listed as one of the meanings for SINISTRUM (latin-dictionary.net), no doubt because omens appearing on the left side in augury portended misfortune. In Old Spanish, as seen in the Appendix (B12, E25), *siniestro* still had the meaning of 'left.' It appears that the primary type of change in this example is metaphor whereby being on the left is similar to being unfortunate. Pejoration is a secondary feature of this change, since the metaphor results in a more negative meaning for this word.

16.6 Are There Other Types of Semantic Change?

The different proposals for the semantic change from Latin PLICĀRE 'to fold' to Spanish *llegar* serve to illustrate another possible pathway of semantic change. While there is general agreement that PLICĀRE is the **etymon** (*el étimo*) of *llegar*, the word it derives from, one finds different proposals as to how this change may have come about. One proposal is that the semantic change comes about through metaphor. Arrival is like folding since the parts of a sheet of paper come together when it is folded in the same way that a person or thing comes together with a destination by arriving there ("Plegar" 2017).

Corominas (1983: "*llegar*"), considered to be the standard reference on Spanish etymology, believes that PLICĀRE was formed from APPLICĀRE with the loss of the prefix AD- (which assimilated to AP- before the following /p/). Corominas lists the meaning of APPLICĀRE as 'arrimar,' 'abordar,' 'acercar,' which we can translate in English as 'put next to,' 'approach,' and 'bring closer,' respectively, meanings that are similar to 'arrive.' We believe, however, that it is more likely that APPLICĀRE derived from PLICĀRE with the addition of the prefix AD-, an idea supported by Ernout and Meillet (2001) in their etymological dictionary of Latin. Under the heading for AP-PLICŌ, written so as to show the prefix, they refer the reader to PLICŌ, saying that APPLICŌ did not appear until the time of Cicero. If APPLICĀRE is composed of AD- + PLICĀRE, then it would originally have meant something like 'fold toward.' This meaning would then have changed to 'to place near' and through narrowing to 'to land (a ship),' two definitions given for APPLICĀRE by latin-dictionary.net. If APPLICĀRE does indeed derive from PLICĀRE through prefixation, then this also means that PLICĀRE and its meaning 'to fold' is the appropriate starting point for Spanish *llegar*.

The most widespread explanation of the origins of Spanish *llegar* (Machado 1977: II, 135; Rohlfs 1970: 178–79, cited by Stolova 2015: 13), and the explanation we first learned in our classes, was that PLICĀRE changes meaning from 'fold' to 'arrive' because sailors folded the sails of their boats when they arrived at the shore. It has always troubled us, though, that this explanation did not correspond neatly to any of the types of semantic change already proposed in this chapter. Stolova (2015: 13), following Blank (1999: 74–75), provides a more satisfactory explanation by appealing to the notion of frame within cognitive linguistics: "within the frame of approaching the shore, the concept of arrival at one's destination and the concept of folding the sail have a strong and habitual relation between themselves, and as a result become designated with the same word, resulting in Spanish *llegar* 'to come'." We see then that words can change meaning based on their association within a habitual action without falling neatly under the heading of either metaphor or metonymy.

Another type of semantic change that does not fall neatly under the headings above is change through contrast, what Blank (2003: 13) calls "auto-antonymic polysemy." This results in **contronyms** (*un contrónimo*), words with the same form and opposite meanings. A striking example in English is the change in meaning of *bad* to 'good, tough, cool' in some contexts. Although this meaning was popularized in Michael Jackson's 1987 song, "Bad," it has existed since the 1890s and was first found in print in a 1928 jazz publication in the United States (Harper 2001–17: "bad"). It arose perhaps as a way for African Americans to turn a negative characterization of themselves as 'bad' into a positive description. This change results clearly in amelioration as well. One also finds contronyms in Spanish. One such example is the word *terrible* from TERRIBĪLEM 'frightening.' It has undergone a change very much like the one in English *bad*, from 'terrible, horrible' to 'incredible.' This may come about through a sarcastic use of the word. You tell someone something is terrible meaning that it is really wonderful. This type of change also happens in English when a speaker tells someone they have *sick skills*. This may have come from the idea that the person's skills are so amazing that they make the speaker sick. Or perhaps *sick* refers to the fact that the skills are so unusual as to be equated with being unhealthy.

Complete Activities 16-1 and 16-2 on page 350.

16.7 False Cognates in English and Spanish

The **false cognates** (*falsos cognados*), also known as false friends (*falsos amigos*), mentioned in Lead-in question 16-2, arise because a word undergoes different semantic changes in English and Spanish. Two pairs of words can serve as an illustration. Many English speakers learning Spanish have been embarrassed to find that *estoy embarazada* means 'I am pregnant' rather than 'I am embarrassed.' *I am embarrassed* would be translated instead by *estoy avergonzado* or *avergonzada*. Both words started out with a meaning of 'hamper or impede.' The

Oxford Dictionaries online (en.oxforddictionaries.com) list this as an archaic meaning in English, whereas the *DRAE* lists it as the first meaning of *embarazar*: "impedir, estorbar o retardar algo" 'to impede, hinder or delay something.' There is disagreement, though, about how each word came to have this meaning. According to the *Online Etymological Dictionary*, the English word traces its origins from Italian through French to a word formed from the prefix *in-* and the root *barra* 'bar.' Thus, the meaning of 'hinder' comes from placing a bar in one's way. Corominas (1983), however, derives the Spanish word from a root *baraço* meaning 'lazo,' 'a tie or trap,' so that the hindrance is created from being tied up or trapped. From the notion of hindered, the adjective in each language develops differently. In the Spanish meaning of 'pregnant' we see a case of metaphor, where the baby is like an obstacle, and also a case of narrowing, since the baby is a specific obstacle. In English, on the other hand, the focus is on the emotion created by this obstacle. A person who is hindered ends up feeling awkward and embarrassed.

Another pair of false cognates is English *exit* and Spanish *éxito* 'success.' Both words trace their origins indisputably back to EXĬTUM 'exit' derived from EXĪRE 'to go out, leave,' formed from the preposition EX- 'out of' and the verb ĪRE 'to go.' In English, this word has kept the same meaning of an 'exit,' that is, a door or road that leads out of a place. In Spanish *éxito* has taken on the meaning of 'success,' thereby undergoing narrowing to indicate only the result of this action and amelioration to refer only to a positive result. The study of semantic change explains how false cognates come to have different meanings even though they derive from the same word.

Complete Activities 16-3 and 16-4 on pages 351–52.

16.8 Chapter Summary

- Semantic change comes about when speakers change the meaning of words by using them in new ways.

- The different types of semantic changes and an example of each from the history of Spanish include:
  - Metaphor, where a word changes meaning to something that resembles it: SERRA 'saw' > *sierra* 'mountain range'
  - Metonymy, where a word changes meaning to something in contact with it: CATHĒDRA 'armchair' > *cadera* 'hip'
  - Popular etymology, where a word changes its form to resemble that of another word which may then affect its meaning: TENĒBRA 'darkness' > *tinieblas* 'darkness' by association with *niebla* 'fog'
  - Ellipsis, where one word takes on the meaning of an entire expression after the rest of the expression is deleted: PRŪNA CĒREOLA 'wax-colored plum' > *ciruela* 'plum'
  - Broadening, where the meaning of a word becomes more general: FABULĀRE 'to tell fables' > *hablar* 'to speak'
  - Narrowing, where the meaning of a word becomes more specific: RECITĀRE 'to recite, say aloud' > *rezar* 'to pray'
- The next two types of change occur in conjunction with one of the other changes listed above:
  - Amelioration, where a word's meaning takes on a more positive connotation: CABALLUM 'nag, workhorse' > *caballo* 'horse,' which occurs along with broadening.
  - Pejoration: SINISTRUM 'left' > *siniestro* 'sinister,' which occurs along with metaphor, since an omen on the left is inauspicious and therefore evil.
- There are also semantic changes that cannot be assigned to one of these categories, but that result instead from habitual use within the same frames or scenarios or from changes of contrast from one meaning to its opposite.
- We have also seen that semantic change helps to explain how false cognates, words with the same origin but different meanings, develop in Spanish and English. These words with a common starting point end up changing meaning in different ways in each language.

Activities

Activity 16-1

Classify the following semantic changes in the history of Spanish as one of the following six types by writing the abbreviation in the space provided: metaphor (MR), metonymy (MY), popular etymology (PE), ellipsis (EL), broadening (B), or narrowing (N). Add amelioration (+M) and pejoration (+P), if these changes also occurred.

_____ 1. Old Spanish *facera* 'façade' (< *faz* 'face' < FACIEM 'face, aspect') > *acera* 'sidewalk'

_____ 2. AFFECTĀRE 'to devote oneself' > *afeitar* 'to shave'

_____ 3. ARANEAM 'spider' > *araña* 'chandelier'

_____ 4. FĪCUM BIFĔRAM 'fig that bears fruit twice a year' > *breva* 'early fig'

_____ 5. CAUSAM 'lawsuit, case' > *cosa* 'thing'

_____ 6. FOCUM 'hearth' > *fuego* 'fire'

_____ 7. LIMPĬDUM 'clean, pure' > *lindo* 'pretty'

_____ 8. PARABŎLAM 'comparison, allegory' > *palabra* 'word'

_____ 9. PANARIAM 'bread basket' > *panera* 'basket'

_____ 10. CONSŌBRĪNUM PRĪMUM 'first cousin' > *primo* 'cousin'

_____ 11. SAPĔRE 'to taste of' > *saber* 'to know'

_____ 12. VILLĀNUM 'feudal tenant' (< VILLA 'country estate') > *villano* 'boorish'

Activity 16-2

Look up the etymon of each of the following Spanish words in a dictionary that gives etymologies, like www.rae.es or www.spanishetym.com. You may also need to look up the meaning of the Latin word in a Latin dictionary like www.latin-dictionary.net. Then compare the Latin and Spanish meanings to determine the type of semantic change that occurred. You can indicate this using the same abbreviations as in Activity 16-1.

Spanish word	Latin etymon	Meaning	Semantic change
1. *sucio* 'dirty'			
2. *cabeza* 'head'			
3. *manzana* 'apple'			
4. *casa* 'house'			
5. *cuero* 'leather'			
6. *avellana* 'hazelnut'			
7. *ceja* 'eyebrow'			
8. *compañero* 'companion'			
9. *comulgar* 'to take communion'			
10. *espalda* 'back'			
11. *accidente* 'accident'			
12. *estar* 'to be'			

Activity 16-3

For two pairs of false cognates below, look up the etyma of the English and Spanish words in an etymological dictionary, such as the *DRAE* for Spanish (www.rae.es) and the *Online Etymological Dictionary* for English (www.etymonline.com). Based on your research, indicate the common origin of the words in English and Spanish and how the meaning of these words changed differently in the two languages. Then add one pair of false friends not listed here that you are especially interested in and explain the change in meaning for this pair.

asistir and *assist*	*grosería* and *grocery*
carpeta and *carpet*	*lectura* and *lecture*
compromiso and *compromise*	*librería* and *library*
constipado and *constipated*	*operar* and *operate*
disgusto and *disgust*	*pariente* and *parent*
dormitorio and *dormitory*	*recordar* and *record*
fábrica and *fabric*	*sensible* and *sensible*

First pair of false cognates
Second pair of false cognates
Your own example of false cognates

Activity 16-4

Corpus Search

For a word that has changed meaning between Old Spanish and Modern Spanish, conduct a search in the *Corpus del español* or the CORDE to determine when this change occurred. Find at least three examples in three different centuries and read the passage in which they occur in order to determine their meaning. When you find the century where the meaning changed, check the previous century too, to see whether it had changed by that time. In this way you can find the century during which the meaning changed. Once you have found the century when the meaning changed, write down one or two examples of the new meaning or one or two examples where the meaning could have been either one.

For example, if you want to know when *cuidar* changed meaning from 'to think' to 'to care for' you could find at least three examples of *cuidar* in the thirteenth, fifteenth, and seventeenth centuries. We conducted this search in the CORDE by entering the dates, such as 1200 to 1300, in the spaces for the date and by selecting "párrafos" under "obtención de ejemplos" in order to read the larger context of each example. We found that the tokens in the seventeenth century had the meaning 'to care for,' whereas the tokens in the previous centuries had the meaning 'to think.' Therefore, we searched for examples in the sixteenth century as well. Apparently, this is the century when the meaning started to change because we found examples where the meaning was most likely 'to think,' but other examples where it was most likely 'to care for,' and especially examples where the meaning could be either one. Here is one such example:

> *y si no es en el verano no se puede criar ni cuidar en el ganado ninguno* 'and if it's not summer one cannot raise nor think about/take care of any livestock' (because there isn't enough grass for grazing) (Anonymous, 1575–80, *Relaciones histórico-geográficas-estadísticas de los pueblos de España*. Reino de Toledo)

Further Reading

Bybee, Joan, Revere Perkins, and William Pagliuca 1994. *The evolution of grammar: Tense, aspect, and modality in the languages of the world.* Chicago: University of Chicago Press. Chapter 8: "Mechanisms of semantic change"

Wright, Roger 1990. "Semantic change in Romance words for 'cut,'" in Henning Anderson and Konrad Koerner (eds.), *Historical Linguistics 1987: Papers from the 8th International Conference on Historical Linguistics*, 553–61. Amsterdam and Philadelphia: John Benjamins

"Why do word meanings evolve? Evolution & semantic change." The endless knot. February 22, 2017. YouTube video

17 | Why *perro* 'dog' instead of *can*?

Lexical Changes

Lead-in Questions

17-1 Think of any new words you have heard recently in English or in Spanish, like *kicks* for shoes in English or *cachos* in Spanish (in Honduras and Costa Rica), especially words that you have started using yourself. What words have they replaced? How were they created? Why have you and other people started using them?

17-2 Now try to think of some words in English and Spanish that have gone out of style and now seem dated. One such example is *groovy* in English or *azorado* 'amazed' in Mexican Spanish. These might be words that your grandparents used or words that you have read in books from an earlier time. For example, the first author's grandmother always asked her whether she had a *beau*, what we would now call a boyfriend, and Shakespeare wrote about scoundrels and scullions.

17.1 Is *decrementar* a Word?

Before we talk about the words that make up the Spanish language, the lexicon, we need to decide which words it includes. If someone asked whether *decrementar* 'decrease' is a word, what would you say? Most people not trained in linguistics will answer that a word exists if it is in the dictionary. But this just shifts the decision to lexicographers, the professionals who write dictionaries. They may not give the answer a linguist would give, but we can use their answer as a starting point. The forty-six members of the *Real Academia Española* add a new word to the *Diccionario de la Real Academia* (*DRAE*) once its usage has become sufficiently frequent in written sources, such as newspapers and books. Their decisions are also informed by consultation with various other organizations, such as the *Instituto de Lexicografía* and the *Asociación de Academias de la Lengua Española* (ASALE), which includes Spanish language academies throughout the Spanish-speaking world. In fact, it is even possible for anyone to suggest words for inclusion in the *DRAE* through an interactive service known as the *Unidad Interactiva* or UNIDRAE. This website states, though, that the recommended words must be documented in writing and cannot simply be part of one's personal usage. Even though dictionaries have played a role in prescribing standard usage throughout history and many people still see them in that role, Darío Villanueva, the director of the RAE, insists that the current purpose of the *DRAE* is simply to record the words used by Spanish speakers without promoting or censuring them. It appears then that the role of lexicographers is today more descriptive and less prescriptive than it was in the past.

If lexicographers seek to describe usage rather than prescribe it, then how would a linguist's description of the Spanish lexicon be different from theirs? First of all, a linguist would not limit the words that exist in Spanish only to those that can be found in writing, but would also include words found in the speech of native speakers. Many words that have not yet made their way into a dictionary can be found on websites such as the *Urban Dictionary* in English (www.urbandictionary.com) or *Jerga Urbana* (www.jergaurbana.com) or *Localismos* (www.localismos.com) in Spanish. One finds in the *Urban*

Dictionary, for example, the term *flip-flocks* for the "heinous combination of flip-flops and socks." In practical terms, linguists can adopt a broader definition than lexicographers because they are not required to compile and publish a dictionary listing all the words in Spanish. Therefore, a linguist will say that a word like *cliquear* 'to click with a mouse' exists in Spanish and a word like *smooshables* 'delicate grocery items you put on top of the bag' exists in English because native speakers use them, even though they have not yet been included in dictionaries like the *DRAE* or the *Oxford English Dictionary* (*OED*) or *Merriam-Webster*. In fact, the authors of a study of 4 percent of all the books in the English language "estimated that 52% of the English lexicon – the majority of the words used in English books – consists of lexical 'dark matter' undocumented in standard references" (Michel et al. 2011: 177). This shows why it is best not to limit the Spanish lexicon only to words found in dictionaries.

Of particular interest in this chapter are the changes that take place in the Spanish lexicon as native speakers create new words and stop using others. The two remaining sections of this chapter will consider the creation of new words like *selfie* and *autofoto*, mentioned in Chapter 3, and the loss of other words, like *raposo* 'fox' and *guisa* 'way,' found in the *Conde Lucanor* excerpt in Chapter 3.

Complete Activity 17-1 on page 367.

17.2 How and Why Do Speakers Create New Words?

The simple answer to why speakers create new words is that they want to express a concept or a nuance that does not already exist in their language. One way to do this is by creating new words out of existing elements, for example, by adding prefixes and suffixes to stems through the process known as **derivation** (*la derivación*). For example, the new entry in the *DRAE agroturismo* 'agroturism' adds the prefix *agro-* to the stem *turismo* 'tourism' and *pantallazo* 'screen shot' adds the suffix *-azo* to the stem *pantalla* 'screen.' New words can also be created through the process called **composition** (*la composición*) in which speakers combine words to form compound words, like *cortoplacista* 'someone who looks for short-term results' made up of *corto* 'short' and *plazo* 'term' plus the suffix *-ista*. Another type of composition is a **blend** (*un acrónimo*), like *amigovio*, formed from the fusion of *amigo* and *novio*, to refer to someone who is more than a friend but not quite a boyfriend or a fiancé. New expressions are also formed by combining existing nouns and adjectives to refer to new entities, as in the case of *red social* 'social network' in Spanish and *soft skills* in English. Note that in compound words both original words are still whole, as in *can opener* or *abrelatas*, whereas in a blend at least one word is partial, as in *brunch*, which combines *breakfast* and *lunch*, and *burrocracia*, which combines *burro* and *burocracia*. Note also that the difference between a blend and a new word created through prefixation or suffixation is that neither part of the blend serves as a prefix or suffix in other words. For example, we can determine that *agroturismo* is formed from the prefix *agro-* and the root *turismo* because *agro-* serves as a prefix in words such as *agroquímica* 'agrochemical industry' and *agropecuario* 'agriculture and livestock.' In the blend *burrocracia*, on the other hand, neither *burro-* nor *-cracia* serves as a prefix or suffix in other words.

An **acronym** (*una sigla* or *un acrónimo*, the same term in Spanish as a blend), can also provide a source of new words when speakers pronounce the initials for an expression as a word, as when the *Organización del Tratado del Atlántico Norte* is referred to as OTAN /otan/ in Spanish and as NATO in English. These have become especially popular in English recently because of their use in text messages. Some examples are FOMO 'fear of missing out,' YOLO 'you only live once,' and MOOC 'massive open online course.' In fact, most speakers are unaware that words such as *laser, radar*, and *scuba*, and even the *zip* in *zip code*, originated as acronyms. *Laser*, for example, is an acronym for "light amplification by stimulated emission of radiation." Speakers also create new words by shortening an existing word through the process known as **clipping** (*la abreviación*). An advertisement is often referred to as an *ad* or an *advert* and a public house as a *pub*, whereas in Spanish a *refrigerador* is *un refri* and a refrigerator/freezer combination can be called *una combi*.

New words may also enter the lexicon through borrowing, as we saw in Chapter 4. But today a speaker does not even have to travel to new places to discover a need for new words. Whenever a new invention hits the market, a word like *byte* is created or a new meaning is given to an existing word, like *ratón* or *mouse*. Spanish speakers create these new words either by borrowing them from other languages, especially English, or by using the resources in their language in new ways. Among the words admitted to the *DRAE* for the first time in its 23rd edition published in 2014, one finds borrowings from English referring to technology, such as *tuit* 'tweet,' *bloguero* 'blogger,' and *hipervínculo* 'hyperlink.' According to the taxonomy developed by Haugen (1950: 213–15), *tuit* is a **loanword** (*un préstamo*), since it borrows the sounds and meaning of the English word *tweet*, whereas *bloguero* is a **loanblend** (*un préstamo mezclado*), since it consists of a borrowed part, *blog*, and a native part, the suffix *-ero*. *Hipervínculo* is a **calque** (*un calco*), also called a loan translation, since it is a Spanish translation of the English term *hyperlink*.

Of course, the desire to name new objects and concepts, what Myers-Scotton (2002: 239) refers to as "cultural borrowings," is not the only reason for lexical creation. Sometimes speakers create new names for existing objects, like the English word *kicks* or the Spanish word *cachos* for shoes. When these words come from other languages, Myers-Scotton calls them "core borrowings," but they can also originate within the language itself. In such cases the new creation adds a different nuance to the meaning of the object. A speaker who uses the words *kicks* or *cachos* may be trying to show that he or she is up-to-date and a member of a particular group.

Complete Activity 17-2 on page 368.

We also saw in Chapter 4 that scholars can identify with a good degree of certainty the words that result from interlanguage influence, even though this influence is harder to establish for sound changes, like the change of initial /f/ to /h/. We assume then that a word like Spanish *chocolate* is borrowed from Nahuatl *xocolatl* because it would be too great a coincidence for Spanish speakers to create a word with similar sounds and meaning on their own. However, we can still have doubts about the origins or etymology of certain words, which are known as etymological cruxes, some of which are shown in Box 17.1. This can happen when we lack information about the existing words in the donor language. Such is often the case for languages with few written records at the time of their first contact with Latin or Spanish speakers, like the indigenous languages of the Iberian Peninsula and the Americas. Uncertainty can also occur with words that consist of so few sounds that different origins seem possible, like *álamo* 'poplar.' We can also have doubts about the path of transmission of certain words. For example, it can be difficult to determine whether a certain Spanish word is a borrowing from French or Provençal or whether it comes directly from Latin, since the sounds in the words in these related languages are similar. For example, is Spanish *flor* a Gallicism from French or Provençal or could FLŌREM have developed directly into *flor* rather than **llor* through regular sound change? Similarly, does *gente* come directly from GENTEM or is it a Gallicism from Old French or Old Provençal *gent*? (Dworkin 2012: 120–21). Often a scholar's answer to these questions depends on whether he or she believes that regular sound changes can yield different results, in which case *flor* and *gente* could come from Latin. If not, then scholars will assume that words containing different results for sound changes are borrowed from languages in which these sound changes would have occurred.

Box 17.1 What is an etymological crux?

An etymological crux is a word whose origin is uncertain because there is no single word attested in written records whose sounds and meaning can evolve without problems into the attested word. One such example in Spanish is *álamo* 'poplar' (Dworkin 2012: 32–33). One proposal is that it comes from Latin ALNUS 'alder,' but the meanings are different, since the words refer to different trees. Furthermore, ALNUS would not have resulted in Spanish *álamo* through regular sound change, but rather in *alno, auno*, or *ono*. Another proposal (García de Diego 1922: 149) is that *álamo* results from a blend of ALNUS with ULMUS 'elm tree.' This would yield ['al-mo], to which a medial [a] would have been inserted to yield *álamo*. However, like the first proposal, this one satisfies neither the semantic criterion of similar meaning nor the phonetic one, since there is no justification for the added medial [a]. Other scholars propose Gothic *ALMS as the etymon or a blend of ALBUS 'white poplar' with Celtic ELMOS. In summary, *álamo* is an etymological crux because none of the proposed etyma has the same meaning as *álamo* and sounds that would regularly evolve into this word.

Other etymological cruxes are presented below according to their proposed language of origin. Note that the words in boldface are listed in more than one category because even the language of their etymon is uncertain.

Words of disputed indigenous Iberian origin (Dworkin 2012: 31–38):

álamo 'poplar,' **perro** 'dog,' *corro* 'circle of spectators,' *corral* 'enclosed area,' *colmena* 'beehive,' *bruja* 'witch,' *arándano* 'cranberry,' *brío* 'gallantry; enthusiasm, vigor,' *zurdo* 'left-handed; awkward, clumsy,' *terco* 'stubborn,' *tosco* 'rude, rough, crude'

Words of disputed Latin origin (Dworkin 2012: 49–51):

tomar 'to take,' *matar* 'to kill'

Words of disputed Germanic origin (Dworkin 2012: 73–76):

álamo 'white poplar,' *broza* 'brushwood, underbrush,' *bramar* 'to bellow, roar, howl,' *sacar* 'to take out,' *gaita* 'bagpipe,' *cundir* 'to flow, ooze,' *lozano* 'arrogant (originally); handsome (now),' *amainar* 'to subside, abate, die down,' **aleve** 'treachery,' *adrede* 'on purpose, deliberately'

Words of disputed Arabic origin (Dworkin 2012: 91–95):

riesgo 'risk, danger,' *pato* 'duck,' *loco* 'mad, crazy,' **aleve** 'treachery,' *danzar* 'to dance,' *marrano* 'converted Jew,' *rincón* 'corner,' *naipes* 'playing cards,' *avería* 'damage, breakdown,' *faluca* 'type of vessel'

Words of disputed Portuguese origin (Dworkin 2012: 183–87):

afeitar 'to shave,' *cuitar* 'to afflict,' *cariño* 'affection,' *alguien* 'someone,' *echar de menos* 'to miss a person,' *bravo* 'wild, uncultivated; untamed,' *arisco* 'rude, surly,' *criollo* 'child born of European parents in Spain's American colonies; black born in these colonies'

Words of disputed indigenous American origin (Dworkin 2012: 207–09):

poncho, tabaco 'tobacco,' *baquiano* 'expert, skilled person,' *cigarro* 'cigar,' *boniato* 'sweet potato'.

Note: Dworkin lists no etymological cruxes for words entering Spanish from Gallo-Romance or English.

Complete Activity 17-3 on page 369.

Let us now take a closer look at the internal means for creating new words in Spanish through derivation and composition. Within the process of derivation, the addition of prefixes tends to change the meaning of words, whereas the addition of suffixes tends to change the grammatical class of a word. For example, the addition of the prefix *re-* to the verb *nacer* changes its meaning from 'to be born' to 'to be born again,' whereas the addition of the suffix *-miento* changes its grammatical category from a verb, *nacer*, to a noun, *nacimiento*. This tendency can be further confirmed by the examples in Table 17.1 of common prefixes associated with particular meanings and the suffixes associated with a particular grammatical class. However, there are of

TABLE 17.1 Common prefixes and suffixes in Spanish (adapted from Real Academia Española 2009: I, 337–38, 413, 670)

Prefix	Meaning	Examples
extra-	'outside of'	*extraterrestre*
sobre-	'over' or 'too much'	*sobrevolar, sobrecargar*
sub-	'under' or 'too little'	*subsuelo, subdesarrollo*
entre-, inter-	'between'	*entrepiso, interdental*
tras-/trans-	'across'	*trascurrir, transferir*
tele-	'at a distance'	*televisión*
ante-	'before'	*anteayer*
pos-/post-	'after'	*posguerra, postgrado*
multi-, pluri-	'many'	*multitarea, plurilingue*
re-, super-, archi-	'very'	*rebuscar, superatractivo, archiconocido*
re-	'again'	*reconstruir*
in-, des-, dis-, a-	'not X'	*ineficaz, desobedecer, disconforme, atemporal*
des-	'to undo'	*deshacer, desenchufar*
anti-, contra-	'against'	*antiaéreo, contraejemplo*
pro-	'in favor of'	*proamericano*
pro-	'in place of'	*pronombre*

TABLE 17.1 (cont.)

Suffix	Grammatical class	Examples
-ción	verb → noun	*rendir → rendición*
-ada	verb → noun	*llamar → llamada*
-aje	verb → noun	*almacenar → almacenaje*
-mento, -miento	verb → noun	*jurar → juramento,*
		atrever → atrevimiento
-dor, -dora	verb → noun	*nadar → nadador, nadadora*
-ería	verb → noun	*cazar → cacería*
	adjective → noun	*tonto → tontería*
-dad	adjective → noun	*feliz → felicidad*
-ez	adjective → noun	*viejo → vejez*
-eza	adjective → noun	*torpe → torpeza*
-itud	adjective → noun	*exacto → exactitud*
-al	noun → noun	*pera → peral*
-ero	noun → noun	*basura → basurero* (place for X)
		caballo → caballero (person related to X) (Alkire, Rosen, and Scida 2010: 71)
-ista	noun → noun	*guión → guionista*
-ado	noun → noun	*profesor → profesorado*
-able, -ible	verb → adjective	*aceptar → aceptable*
		temer → temible
-mente	adjective → adverb	*lento → lentamente*

course a few exceptions to this tendency. Sometimes a prefix is added along with a suffix for a change in grammatical class without a change in meaning, as in *entristecer* 'to sadden' based on the adjective *triste*. There are also cases where a suffix changes the meaning of a word rather than its grammatical class, as seen in the words listed as noun → noun in Table 17.1. For example, a *peral* is the tree producing *peras*, a *basurero* is the recipient for *basura*, and a *guionista* is a person who writes *guiones*. Other suffixes that change meaning rather than grammatical class are diminutive suffixes, which indicate affection or small size, and augmentative suffixes, which indicate a pejorative attitude toward this object or its large size. *Gatito* can refer to a kitten or a beloved grown cat, whereas *caserón* can refer to a large house or a run-down house and *delgaducho* can describe a person who is unattractively thin.

There can also be competition among various prefixes and suffixes. For example, do you say *to unfriend* or *to defriend* in English to remove a friend from your Facebook account? Or do you say *artificialness* or *artificiality* to refer to the quality of being artificial? In Spanish, such competition among suffixes was especially prevalent in Old Spanish where one finds alternative forms for nouns ending in *-dad*, *-dumbre*, *-eza*, and *-ura*, such as *pobredad* and *pobre-dumbre* alongside the modern *pobreza*, and *estrechura* and *estrecheza* alongside the modern *estrechez* (Dworkin 1989). Sometimes both forms survive but with different meanings, as in the case of *altura* which refers to literal height or altitude and *alteza* which is used figuratively as a title of nobility as in *Su Alteza Real* 'Your Royal Highness.'

Spanish speakers can also create words through composition, by combining two existing words into a new entity, as in *abrelatas* 'can opener' formed from the third person singular of the verb *abrir* and the noun *latas*, literally 'it opens cans.' The two words can be nouns, adjectives, or verbs or various combinations of these, as shown in Table 17.2. In some cases, especially when an adjective is

TABLE 17.2 Compound words in Spanish (adapted from Real Academia Española 2009: I, 737)

Grammatical class	Example without linking vowel	Example with linking vowel /i/
noun + noun	*motocarro* 'three-wheeled van'	*carricoche* 'covered wagon'
adjective + adjective	*sordomudo* 'deaf mute'	*agridulce* 'sweet and sour, bitterweet'
verb + verb	*duermevela* 'light sleep'	*quitaipón* 'removable'
noun + adjective	*aguardiente* 'moonshine, liquor'	*patitieso* 'gobsmacked'
noun + verb	*vasodilatar* 'vasodilate, to dilate the blood vessels'	*perniquebrar* 'to break a leg or both'
adjective + noun	*mediodía* 'midday'	
verb + noun	*sacapuntas* 'pencil sharpener'	

the first element, one finds the linking vowel [i], as in *pelirrojo/a* 'red-head' rather than **pelorrojo/a.*

Complete Activity 17-4 on page 369.

17.3 Why Do Speakers Stop Using Words?

We have seen in the previous sections that Spanish speakers create or adopt new words to refer to new objects or customs. On the other hand, speakers may cease to use a word when the thing it refers to becomes obsolete. In medieval times knights used weapons, such as a *halbert* and a *flail*, that are no longer in use today and so we are no longer familiar with these words. One also finds even more recent inventions that are no longer in use, having been replaced by newer technology, like *8-track tapes* and *floppy disks*. At other times, though, speakers adopt new words alongside existing words or they create several new words for the same item, such as the terms *flashdrive, thumbdrive*, and *memory stick* in English and *memoria* or *chupito* or *u ése bé* (for USB) in Spanish. When this happens two or more words enter into a period of lexical rivalry which may result in the loss of one of these words. Why then does a word get lost? What determines the eventual winner of this rivalry?

This is a difficult question to answer since many different reasons may be at work simultaneously. The primary reasons for the loss of a word are all based on some perceived defect of a particular word when compared to its rivals (see Dworkin 1989: 335 for a list of specific reasons). This defect most likely has to do with the sound of the word or its forms. With respect to sounds, a word may be lacking in phonetic substance after regular sound changes run their course. When this occurs, speakers may simply stop using the word or they may reinforce it, as happened with the word *hui* 'today' in French which was reinforced as *aujourd'hui*, literally 'on the day of today.' In Spanish, the lack of phonetic substance of *hoy* may have led speakers to say *el día de hoy* on occasion, but this expression is not lexicalized like Fr. *aujourd'hui*. This may also have played a role in speakers' using *pájaro* for some meanings of the shorter *ave* and the somewhat longer *perro* over the shorter Old Spanish *can* (< Lat. CANEM 'dog').

Another phonological defect may be the presence of disfavored sequences of sounds that result from regular sound change. The word *cola* may have been favored as the word for 'tail' over Old Spanish *coa*, the regular result of CAUDA, because speakers disfavored the sequence /oa/ in particular and all combinations of /o/, /a/, and /u/ in hiatus in general (Dworkin 1980). The diphthongs in the words *duendo* 'meek, tame,' *luengo* 'long,' and *muelle* 'comfortable' may also have played a role in their disuse, since speakers tended to favor diphthongs in primary adjectives associated with "vigor, energy, resistance, strength," according to Malkiel (1980b, cited by Dworkin 2011: 604). Another possible reason speakers would stop using a word is **homonymic conflict** (*el conflicto homonímico*) with another word with similar sounds, especially when this word's meanings are different. Dworkin (1994: 272–74) proposes, for example, that homonymic conflict could play a role in the loss of Old Spanish *acabdar* 'obtain, get, acquire' which was similar to *acabar* 'to finish.' The unusual consonant sequence /bd/ in this word could have played a role as well. Homonymic conflict may also play a role in the rejection of new creations. Epperson and Ranson (2010: 402) found in a survey of 750 Spanish speakers on their use of feminized titles that only 14 percent of speakers said they used *la pilota* for a female pilot, perhaps because of its homonymic conflict with *la pelota*.

Regarding the forms of a word, speakers may come to disfavor a word with irregular forms, especially if a rival with regular forms is available. Dworkin (1985) proposes this explanation for the loss of many *-ir* verbs, such as *gradir* 'to thank,' *padir* 'to suffer,' *podrir* 'to rot,' and their replacement by verbs ending in *-ecer*, respectively *agradecer, padecer, podrecer.* This same phenomenon occurs in Modern Spanish when regular verbs ending in *-ar* are used alongside verbs with more irregular conjugations, such as *enflacar* and *enflaquecer.* The replacement of irregular verbs with regular ones was happening at least as far back as Latin. For example, the regular verb form CANTĀRE 'to sing' was created by adding the infinitive ending -ĀRE to CANT-, the stem of the past participle of the irregular verb CANĔRE, with principal parts CANŌ, CANĔRE, CECINĪ, CANTUM. The same phenomenon occurs in English as well in which irregular verbs like *tread, trod, trodden,* and *slay, slew, slain* are gradually replaced by regular verbs like *to step* and *to kill*. The form of a noun like Old Spanish *can* 'dog' could also seem odd to speakers. Speakers might prefer a word with obvious gender marking to refer to an animal with biological gender. Therefore, the gender marking of *perro* and *perra* and the diminutive suffixes, like *perrito* and *perrita*, in addition to its greater phonetic substance, might have been a reason for speakers to prefer *perro* over *can*.

Complete Activity 17–5 on page 371.

17.4 Chapter Summary

- The Spanish lexicon, the set of words in Spanish, includes all the words that native speakers use in speaking and writing. Dictionaries like the *DRAE*, because of their limitations of space, include only words that are common in writing.
- Speakers can create new words from the resources already available in their language through:
  - derivation when they add prefixes and suffixes to existing words, like *agroturismo* and *pantallazo*. Prefixes usually change the meaning of a word, like *re-* in *renacer*, and suffixes usually change the grammatical class of the word, so that *-able* changes the verb *aceptar* into the adjective *aceptable*.
  - composition when they combine whole words to form compound words, like *abrelatas*, or to create a blend, like *amigovio*
  - acronymy when they create a new word from the initials of a phrase, like OTAN for *Organización del Tratado del Atlántico Norte*
  - clipping when they shorten a word like *refrigerador* to *refri* or *combinación* to *combi*
- Speakers can create new words in their language through borrowing.
  - A borrowing borrows the sounds and meaning of a foreign word, like *tuit* from English *tweet*.

- A loanblend borrows a stem and combines it with a native prefix or suffix, like *bloguero* for 'blogger.'
- A calque translates the foreign word into Spanish, like *hipervínculo* for 'hyperlink.'
- Certain words in Spanish are etymological cruxes, meaning that scholars are unsure of their etymology or origins, whether they come from Latin or whether they were borrowed from another language in a contact situation. One such example is *álamo* 'poplar.'
- There are several reasons for lexical loss, the loss of a word. These include:
  - A defect in the sounds of the word. It may have been too short, like Old Spanish *can* 'dog,' or it may have contained a disfavored sequence of sounds like *coa* 'tail.'
  - A homonymic conflict whereby this word sounded exactly or almost like another word, like Old Spanish *acabdar* 'to obtain' with *acabar* 'to finish.'
  - Irregular morphology so that the word was replaced by a word with more regular forms, like *padir* 'to suffer' by *padecer.*

Activities

Activity 17-1

1. Make a list of three new words in English, and also three words in Spanish, if you can think of any, that you encountered for the first time recently, especially ones you think might be unknown to people who do not belong to your same social network, like your professor or parents or grandparents. Write a sentence for each one to illustrate how it is used.

   Feel free to consult online dictionaries of recent terms to come up with these words:

   For Spanish: www.jergaurbana.com or www.localismos.com

   For English: www.urbandictionary.com or www.thefreedictionary.com

2. Next check to see whether these words appear in the following references with a more rigorous review process:

For Spanish: the *DRAE* at dle.rae.es

For English: the *OED* at www.oed.com or the *Merriam-Webster Dictionary* at www.merriam-webster.com

Were you surprised at all by which words were included or not included? Explain why.

Activity 17-2

Here are some words recently added to the 23rd and most recent edition of the *DRAE* in 2014 and to the *OED* in 2015.

1. First, put a check mark (✓) next to the new words you are familiar with. What do they mean to you? How do you use them?
2. For each word indicate the process of lexical creation by writing one or more of the following abbreviations next to each word.
   For borrowings use LW = loanword or LB = loanblend.
   For derivation use P = prefixation or S = suffixation.
   For composition use X = blend, C = compound word, or A = combination of adjective and noun.
3. Explain the process by which the words you listed in Activity 17-1 were created.

Words added to the *DRAE* in 2014	Words added to the *OED* in 2015
1. audioguía (n)	a. cisgender (adj)
2. bicicletería (n)	b. colorism (n)
3. conflictuar (v)	c. comedize (v)
4. egresar (v)	d. crowdfund (v)
5. externalizar (v)	e. declutter (v)
6. homoparental (adj)	f. freegan (n)
7. lonchera (n)	g. hard launch (n, v)
8. papichulo (n)	h. hot mess (n)
9. patalear (v)	i. photobomb (n, v)
10. precuela (n)	j. retweet (n, v)
11. teletrabajo (n)	k. staycation (n)
12. tunear (v)	l. voluntourism (n)

Activity 17-3

Select one of the words listed as an etymological crux and perform the following research:

1. Look up its etymology in at least three different sources. Summarize the different proposed origins of this word. Choose from among the following:

Diccionario de la Real Academia Española at dle.rae.es.

Corominas, Joan 1983. *Breve diccionario etimológico de la lengua castellana*, 3rd edn. Madrid: Gredos.

Meyer-Lubke, Wilhelm. 1935. *Romanisches etymologisches Wörterbuch*, 3rd edn. Heidelberg: Carl Winter Universitätsverlag. 1st edn. 1911.

Roberts, Edward A. 2014. *A comprehensive etymological dictionary of the Spanish language with families of words based on Indo-European roots*, vol. I (A–G), vol. II (H–Z). Bloomington, IN: Xlibris.

2. Find its first attestation in the *Corpus del español* and/or the CORDE.

Based on this information, which origin seems the most convincing to you? Explain your reasoning.

Activity 17-4

1. Derive new words from the following root words in Spanish by adding as many prefixes and suffixes as you can think of. Indicate the grammatical class of each word and explain the meaning or function of each prefix and suffix in the new words you derive. You will no doubt encounter prefixes and suffixes not listed in Table 17.2.

Tip: Feel free to consult a dictionary in order to find these words. The online *DRAE* at dle.rae.es allows you to search words that begin with, end with, or contain certain combinations of letters. For example, in the windows at the top of the page if you select "contiene" in the drop-down menu where you see "por palabras" as the default and then enter *fin* in the search box you will find all the words in Spanish containing *fin*.

Example: *fino* (adjective) 'fine'

New word	Grammatical class	Meaning	Prefix or suffix	Meaning of prefix or suffix
finura	noun	fineness	*-ura*	denotes a quality
fineza	noun	kindness	*-eza*	denotes a quality
refinar	verb	refine	*re-*	'very'
			-ar	forms a verb
afinar	verb	tune, polish, perfect	*a-*	forms a verb
			-ar	forms a verb
desafinar	verb	to be off key	*des-*	to undo
finamente	adverb	finely, elegantly	*-mente*	forms an adverb

a. *mover* (verb)

b. *hablar* (verb)

b. *verde* (adjective)

c. *triste* (adjective)

d. *pan* (noun)

e. *perro* (noun)

f. *honor* (noun)

2. Apply what you have learned about compound words to answer the following questions (adapted from Real Academia Española 2009: I, 760, 761, 767, 769, 778, 780)

a. If *tontivano* means 'an arrogant fool' (*un tonto vanidoso*), what does *tontiloco* mean?

b. If *rojinegro* means 'red and black,' what does *blanquiazul* mean?

c. If *bracicorto* means 'short-armed,' what does *nasilargo* mean?

d. If *ojitierno* means 'tender-eyed-,' what does *carialegre* mean?

e. If a *reposapiés* is an ottoman or footstool, what is a *calientapiés*?

f. If a *(chaleco) salvavidas* is a 'lifejacket,' what is a *salvapantallas*?

g. If a *quitanieves* is a snowplow, what is a *quitamanchas*?

h. If *clarividente* refers to someone who sees clearly, what does *grandilocuente* mean?

Activity 17-5

The following words have been replaced by other words in the history of the Spanish language. Offer possible reasons for this replacement choosing from among the following (adapted from Dworkin 1989: 335) or inventing reasons of your own.

a. obsolescence of the word's referent

b. excessive erosion of a word's phonetic substance

c. phonotactic awkwardness, in other words, disfavored combinations of sounds

d. homonymic conflict

e. paradigmatic complexity

1. Old Spanish *gulpeja* or *vulpeja* 'fox' and later *raposo* replaced by *zorro/zorra*

2. Old Spanish *vierme* 'worm' replaced by *gusano*

3. Old Spanish *olio* 'oil' replaced by Arabic *aceite*

4. Old Spanish *decir* 'to descend' replaced by *bajar* (< BASSIĀRE)

5. Old Spanish *can* 'dog' replaced by *perro* of uncertain origin

6. Old Spanish *façeruelo* 'pillow' replaced by Arabic *almohada*

7. Old Spanish *alface* from Arabic replaced by *lechuga* (< LACTŪCA)

8. Old Spanish *azogue/zoco* from Arabic replaced by *mercado* (< MERCĀTUM)

9. Modern Spanish *escorpión* 'scorpion' less common than *alacrán* from Arabic

10. Modern Spanish *oca* 'goose' less common than *ganso* from Germanic

Activity 17-6

In 2008 Anheuser-Busch came out with a new ad campaign to promote Bud Light. Their billboards and other ads read: "The difference is drinkability." Since the word *drinkability* is not in any English dictionary, the actors in the television ads explained the concept as "being easier to drink" or "having just the right taste, not too heavy, not too watered down." Not to be left behind, shortly after this period, ads and billboards in Mexico started popping up to tout Tecate Light which offered "Refrescancia Absoluta," with the word *refrescancia* not found in any Spanish dictionary.

Will the words *drinkability* and *refrescancia* increase in popularity so that they will be added to dictionaries one day like the word *dependability*? We owe this word to Theodore MacManus, an ad man who coined the term for use in a Dodge commercial back in the early 1900s. The word caught on and by the 1930s, it was appearing in dictionaries and now is commonly used in everyday language. (https://reedbrothersdodgehistory.wordpress.com/1950s-1960/dodge-dependability/)

List three words in advertising that you are familiar with or that you can find online that have been coined recently in English or Spanish. Conduct an online search to determine how long they have been in use and whether they are used in other contexts besides a specific advertisement. Which of these words do you think will survive as new words and which do you think will not? Why?

Further Reading

Dworkin, Steven N. 1981. "Phonotactic constraints and lexical loss in Old Spanish," *Zeitschrift für romanische Philologie* 97: 86–92

  2016. "Unique Latin lexical survivals in Ibero-Romance," in Eva Núñez-Méndez (ed.), *Diachronic applications in Hispanic linguistics*, 1–34. Newcastle upon Tyne: Cambridge Scholars Publishing

"El léxico español: La formación de palabras," livingspanish.com

"Spanish words that don't exist in English – Joanna Rants" Flama. Feb. 22. 2017. YouTube video

Appendix: Selections from Old Spanish Texts

Letters in italics in Appendices A and B are supplied by the editor of the texts. Line numbers for these texts have been changed to follow the lines of text as printed here.

Appendix A *Auto de los Reyes Magos* (end of the twelfth century; the earliest surviving fragment of Spanish liturgical drama) (Menéndez Pidal 1971: I, 71–72, cited by Pountain 2001: 35)

Scene I

(Caspar, solo)
¡Dios criador, qual marauila
no se qual es achesta strela!
Agora primas la e ueida,
poco timpo a que es nacida.
¿Nacido es el Criador   5
que es de la gentes senior?
Non es uerdad, non se que digo;
todo esto non vale uno figo.
Otra nocte me lo catare;
si es uertad, bine lo sabre. (pausa)   10
¿Bine es uertad lo que io digo?
En todo, en todo lo prohio.
¿Non pudet ser otra sennal?
Achesto es i non es al;
nacido es Dios, por uer, de fembra   15
in achest mes de december.
Ala ire o que fure, aoralo e,
Por Dios de todos lo terne.

Appendix B   *Cantar de mio Cid* (late twelfth – early thirteenth century) (Menéndez Pidal 1946)

1

De los sos ojos tan fuertemientre llorando,
tornava la cabeça i estávalos catando.
Vío puestas abiertas e uços sin cañados,
alcándaras vázias sin pielles e sin mantos
e sin falcones e sin adtores mudados.   5
Sospiró mio Çid, ca mucho avie grandes cuidados.
Fabló mio Çid bien e tan mesurado:
"grado a ti, señor padre, que estás en alto!
Esto me an vuelto mios enemigos malos."

2

Allí piensan de aguijar, allí sueltan las riendas.   10
A la exida de Bivar ovieron la corneja diestra,
e entrando a Burgos oviéronla siniestra.
Meçió mio Çid los ombros y engrameó la tiesta:
"albricia, Álbar Fáñez, ca echados somos de tierra!
Mas a grand ondra tornaremos a Castiella".   15

3

Mio Çid Roy Díaz por Burgos entróve,
En sue conpaña sessaenta pendones;
exien lo veer mugieres e varones,
burgeses e burgesas por las finiestras sone,
plorando de los ojos, tanto avien el dolore.   20
De las sus bocas todos dizían una razóne:
"Dios, qué buen vassallo, si oviesse buen señore!"

4

Conbidar le ien de grado, mas ninguno non osava:
el rey don Alfonsso tanto avie la grand saña.
Antes de la noche en Burgos dél entró su carta,   25

con grand recabdo e fuertemientre seellada:
que a mio Çid Roy Díaz, que nadi nol diesen posada,
e aquel que gela diesse sopiesse vera palabra
que perderie los averes e más los ojos de la cara,
e aun demás los cuerpos e las almas.   30

Appendix C *Razon feita d'amor con los denuestos del agua y el vino* (early thirteenth
century) (Bustos Tovar 1984)

Mas ui uenir una doncela;
Pues naçi no ui tan bella:
Bla[n]ca era e bermeia,
Cabelos cortos sobre'll oreia,
Fruente bla[n]ca e loçana,   60
Cara fresca como maçana;
Naryz egual e dreyta,
Nunca viestes tan bien feyta;
[...]
Dix le yo: "dezit, la mia señor,   106
si supiestes nu[n]ca d'amor?"
Diz ella; "a plan, con grant amor ando,
mas non conozco mi amado;
pero dizem un su mesaiero   110
que es clerygo e non caualero,
sabe muito de trovar,
de leyer e de cantar;
dizem que es de buenas yentes,
mancebo barua punnientes."   115
"Por Dios, que digades, la mia señor,
Que donas tenedes por la su amo[r]?"
"Estas luuas y es capiello,
est'oral y est'aniello
enbio a mi es meu amigo,   120
que por la su amor trayo conmigo."

Yo connoçi luego las alfayas
que yo ie las auia enbiadas;
ela connoçio una mi ci[n]ta man a mano,
qu'ela la fiziera con la su mano.   125
Tolios el manto de los o[n]bros,
besome la boca e por los oios;
tran gran sabor de mi avia,
sol fablar non me podía.
"Dios señor a ti loa[do]   130
quant conozco meu amado!
agora e tod bien comigo
quant conozco meo amigo!"
Una grant pieça ali estando,
de nuestro amor ementando [. . .]   135

Appendix D   *Milagros de Nuestra Señora,* Gonzalo de Berceo (first half of thirteenth
century) (Gerli 1985). The lines of a poem in this form are typically referred
to by the strophe number followed by a, b, c, or d for the line of verse within
that strophe. For example, the first line below is referred to as 220a.

El clérigo ignorante
Era un simple clérigo, pobre de clerecia,   220
dicié cutiano missa de la Sancta Maria;
non sabié decir otra, diciéla cada dia,
más la sabíe por uso que por sabiduría.

Dissoli el obispo: "Quando non as cïencia,   225
de cantar otra missa nin as sen nin potencia,
viédote que non cantes, métote en sentencia:
Vivi como merezes por otra agudencia."

Fo el preste su vía triste e dessarrado,   226
avié muy grand vergüenza, el danno muy granado;
tornó en la Gloriosa, ploroso e quesado,
que li diesse consejo, ca era atterado.

La Madre piadosa que nunqua falleció   227
a qui de corazón a piedes li cadió,
el ruego del su clérigo luego gelo udió:
No lo metio por plazo, luego li accorrió.

La Virgo glorïosa, madre sin dicïón,   228
apareciól al obispo luego en visïon;
díxoli fuertes dichos, un brabiello sermón,
descubrióli en ello todo su corazón.

Díxoli brabamientre: "Don obispo lozano,   229
¿contra mí por qué fuste tan fuert e tan villano?
Yo nunqua te tollí valía de un grano,
E tú ásme tollido a mí un capellano.

Si tu no li mandares decir la missa mía   231
como solié decirla, grand querella avría,
e tú serás finado hasta el trenteno día,
¿Desend verás que vale la sanna de María!"

Fo con estas menazas el bispo espantado,   232
mandó envïar luego por el preste vedado;
rogól quel perdonasse lo que avié errado,
ca fo él en su pleito durament engannado.

Tornó el omne bobo en su capellanía,   234
sirvió a la Gloriosa, madre Sancta María,
finó en su oficio de fin qual io querría,
fue la alma a gloria a la dulz cofradría.

Appendix E   *Calila e Dimna* (mid thirteenth century) (Cacho Blecua and Lacarra 1984)

DIXO DIGNA: –Dizen que un león estava en una tierra viçiosa, do avía muchas
bestias salvages et agua et pasto. Et las bestias que estavan en esa
tierra estavan muy viçiosas, fueras por el miedo que avían del
león. Et ayuntáronse todas las bestias et tomaron consejo, et
viniéronse para el león et dixéronle así: –Tú non puedes comer   5

de nos lo que tú quieres, a menos de lazrar; et nós vimos un consejo, que es bueno para ti et folgança para nos, de la lazería en que estamos, si tú nos quieres segurar du tu miedo.

DIXO EL LEÓN: –¿Qué es ese consejo?

DIXERON LAS BESTIAS: –Faremos contigo pleito que te demos cada día una bestia de nos   10
que comas sin lazería et sin trabajo, et que nos asegures que non te ayamos miedo de noche nin de día.

Et plogo al léon desto, et asegurólas et fízoles pleito.

Et acaesesçió un día a una liebre que la levasen al león et, queriéndola levar, dixo a las otras: –Si me quisiéredes escuchar,   15
dezirvos he cosa que vos non sería daño et vos será pro. Cuidarvos ía sacar desta premia deste león, et estorçería yo de muerte.

ET DIXÉRONLE: –¿Qué es lo que quieres que fagamos?

DIXO LA LIEBRE: –Mandad a quien me levare para él que me lleve muy paso, et que   20
me non lleve apriesa, et que tarde tanto fasta que pase la ora del comer del león.

Et fiziéronlo así et, quando fueron çerca del león, fue la liebre señera muy paso. Et el león [era] sollón et muy sañudo, et levantóse, et començó de andar et de catar a diestro et a siniestro   25
fasta que vido la liebre venir, et díxole: –¿Dónde venís et dó son las bestias? ¿Et por qué me mintieron el pleito que avían comigo puesto?

ET DIXO LA LIEBRE: –Non mande Dios, señor; yo só mandadero de las bestias para vos
et traíavos una liebre que vos enviaban que yantásedes; et yo que   30
venía cerca, fállome un león et tomómela, et dixo: Mayor derecho he yo de comer esta liebre que el otro a quien la levades.

ET DÍXELE YO: –Mal fazedes, que este conducho es del león que es rey de las bestias, que gelo envían para yantar. Pues conséjovos que non me lo tomedes nin fagades ensañar al léon; si non, avredes ende   35
mal.

Et él non lo dexó de tomar por eso, et denostóvos quanto pudo, et dixo que quería lidiar convusco, maguer sodes rey. Et quando yo vi esto, vine para vos quanto pude por vos lo querellar.

Et el león, quand lo oyó, asañóse, et dixo a la liebre: –Ve comigo   40
et muéstrame ese león que dizes.

Et la liebre fuese a un pozo en que avía muy clara agua, et era muy fondo, que podría bien cobrir al león, et díxole: –Este es el

lugar que vos dixe. Mas tomadme so vuestro sobaco et
mostrárvoslo he.   45

Et fizolo así, et él cató al fondo del pozo et vio su sonbra et la de
la liebre en el agua; et puso la liebre en tierra, et saltó en el pozo
por lidiar con el león, non dubdando qu' él era el león, et afogóse
en el pozo. Et tornóse la liebre, et estoçieron las bestias del miedo
en que era et fincaron seguras por siempre.   50

Glossary of Terms

The number after a term indicates the chapter where it first appears. A second number, if any, indicates a chapter that focuses on this concept.

acceptance (*la aceptación*) **5**   the adoption of one linguistic variety as the standard dialect, especially by speakers of other dialects (the acceptance of Castilian by speakers of Mozarabic)

acronym (*una sigla* or *un acrónimo*) **17**   a word based on the first letters of a phrase (*scuba* from *self-contained underwater breathing apparatus*)

actuation problem (*el problema de actuación*) **3**   understanding why speakers make certain changes to their language at a certain time

adjective complements (*complementos adjetivos*) **15**   complements of copular verbs (*happy* in *Jean is happy*)

adstratum (*el adstrato*) **4**   a language in contact with another language where both continue to be spoken (Basque in relation to Castilian)

affricate (*la africada*) **7**   a consonant formed by articulating a stop followed by a fricative (the /tʃ/ in *church*)

allomorph (*un alomorfo*) **10, 14**   each of the different forms of a single morpheme (*duerm-* and *dorm-* for the morpheme 'sleep')

allomorphy (*la alomorfía*) **10, 14**   the existence of allomorphs, i.e. different forms for a single morpheme (*duerm-* in *duermo* and *dorm-* in *dormimos*)

allophone (*un alófono*) **7**   a non-contrasting sound that does not distinguish between words ([pʰ] and [p] in *pot* and *spot*)

alveolar (*alveolar*) **7**   the place of articulation between the tip of the tongue and the alveolar ridge, the bony ridge right behind the teeth (/s/, /l/)

amelioration (*la mejoración/el desarrollo ameliorativo*) **16**   the process whereby the meaning of a word becomes more positive (CASA 'hut' > *casa* 'house')

analogy (*la analogía*) **2, 10**   the change of one form according to the model of another form (*anduve* → *andé* by analogy to *canté*)

analytical constructions (*las construcciones analíticas*) **10**   structures in a language with separable and analyzable morphemes (the future tense *voy a ir*)

analytical tendency (*una tendencia analítica*) **10**   the tendency of languages to replace synthetic constructions of inseparable unanalyzable morphemes with analytical constructions with separable and analyzable morphemes

antepenultimate syllable (*la sílaba antepenúltima*) **6**   the third to last syllable in a word (the syllable *rá-* in *rá-pi-do*)

antihiatic yod (*la yod antihiática*) **12**   a yod that develops between vowels in hiatus (*tuya* from *túa)*

aperture (*abertura*) **6**   the degree of opening of the mouth to pronounce sounds, usually vowels

apheresis (*la aféresis*) **12**   loss of the first sound in a word, usually a vowel (ILLAM > *la*)

apocope (*la apócope*) **6**   the loss of a vowel in final position of a word

approximant (*una aproximante*) **7**   a speech sound where parts of the mouth approach each other but do not make enough contact to create audible friction (the /w/ in *water*, the /β/ in *haber*)

articulatory movement (*el movimiento articulatorio*) **3**   the movement of the tongue, lips, jaws, and vocal cords in ways that produce linguistic sounds

assimilation (*la asimilación*) **6, 7, 8**   the process of a sound becoming more similar to other adjacent or neighboring sounds

atonic vowels (*vocales átonas*) **6**   unstressed vowels

backformation (*la derivación regresiva*) **10**   a morphological change where the new form results from the removal of a morpheme (Latin singular neuter TEMPUS is reinterpreted as plural *tiempos* and the new singular is backformed to *tiempo.*)

bilabial (*bilabial*) **7**   the place of articulation made by closing both lips (/p/ or /b/)

blends (*los acrónimos*) **3, 17**   the creation of a new word by fusing together parts of two words (*motor + hotel = motel*)

bound morpheme (*un morfema ligado*) **10**   a morpheme that cannot stand alone (*-o* in *gato* or *-s* in *cats*)

breve (*una breve*) **6**   a semi-circle placed over a Latin vowel to indicate that it is short (MĀLUM)

broadening (*la ampliación*) **16**   a semantic change whereby the meaning of a word becomes more general (Latin PASSĔREM 'sparrow' to Spanish *pájaro* 'bird')

calque or loan translation (*un calco o un préstamo traducido*) **17**   a word or phrase borrowed from another language by literal, word-for-word or root-for-root translation (*skyscraper → rascacielos*)

cases (*los casos*) **11**   sets of forms in a language like Latin that indicate the grammatical function of a noun or other nominal element (for example, the nominative case is the subject, the dative case is the indirect object)

change in progress (*un cambio en progreso* or *cambio en curso*) **3, 13**   the change in which a variant (sound, words, structure, etc.) is in the process of being lost (for example, the simple future like *iré*)

clipping (*la abreviación*) **17**   the shortening of a word (*lab* from *laboratory*) clitic pronoun (*un pronombre clítico*) **3, 12, 15**   a pronoun that cannot stand alone but is always attached to a verb to form a single phonological unit (*la vio* or *dígale)*

closed syllables (*las sílabas cerradas o trabadas*) **6**   syllables that end with a consonant (*vez*)

code (*el código*) **3**   a system of arbitrary symbols for expressing meaning; in other words, a language

codification (*la codificación*) **5**   a process of establishing the accepted and prescribed norms of the standard dialect

composition (*la composición*) **17**   a process of forming a new word by combining two existing words (*day+dreamer = daydreamer*)

compound tenses (*los tiempos compuestos*) **13**   tenses made up of an auxiliary and a past participle (*he cantado)*

conditioned sound change (*el cambio fonético condicionado*) **6, 7**   a change in a sound that occurs only in certain contexts (Spanish /b/ > [β] between vowels)

context (*el contexto*) **3**   elements surrounding an utterance including the physical setting, the knowledge shared by the participants, and the cotext

cotext (*el cotexto*) **3**   the words before and after a certain utterance

contronym (*un contrónimo*) **16**   a word with opposite meanings (*bad* meaning 'awful' and 'wonderful')

copular verb (*un verbo copulativo*) **15**   a verb that serves as a connector, a linking verb (*is* in *Jean is happy)*

cultismo trap (*la trampa del cultismo*) **6**   selecting a learnèd word as the reflex of the Spanish word instead of the derived word

dative of interest (*dativo de interés*) **15**   a quasi-reflexive where the subject does something that is of benefit to him or her (*Juan se compra un café*)

declensions (*las declinaciones*) **10, 11**   the list of all the cases of a noun and other nominal elements; Latin nouns and adjectives belonged to five different declensions

definite article (*el artículo definido*) **10, 12**   a type of determiner that defines a noun whose referent is known or specific (*the* in *the sun*)

demonstratives (*los demostrativos*) **10, 12**   words used to point out a certain person, place or thing (*this, that, these, those*)

dental (*dental*) **7**   the place of articulation between the tongue and the back of the teeth (/t/, /d/)

deponent verb (*un verbo deponente*) **14**   a verb in Latin with active meaning but passive forms (HORTOR 'I urge')

derivation (*la derivación*) or derivational morphology (*la morfología derivativa*) **10**   the process of adding lexical prefixes and suffixes to roots to form new words (*un-+tie = untie*; *drink+-able = drinkable*)

derived words (*las palabras derivadas*) 5   Spanish words passed down from Spoken Latin that underwent regular sound changes (ᴏᴘᴇ̆ʀᴀ > *obra*)

descriptive grammar (*una gramática descriptiva*) 2   a set of rules that describes what native speakers know about their language and how they use this knowledge

determiners (*los determinantes*) 10, 12   grammatical elements that serve to further specify a noun (*a*, *the*, *some*)

detransitivizing use (*el uso destransitivizador*) 15   the use of *se* to transform a transitive verb to an intransitive one (*Juan cerró la puerta→la puerta se cerró*)

detransitivize (*destransitivizar*) 15   to transform a transitive verb to an intransitive one through the passive or middle voice

diachronic description (*una descripción diacrónica*) 1   the study of a language at two or more points in time

dialect (*un dialecto*) 5   any linguistic variety used by speakers in a particular region or social group

diasystem *(un diasistema)* 5   a collection of dialects

diphthong (*un diptongo)* 6   a sound formed by the combination of a vowel and a semi-vowel in the same syllable (/fjesta/, /bweno/)

dissimilation (*la disimilación*) 12   a process where a sound becomes different from another nearby sound (ᴀʀʙᴏ̆ʀᴇᴍ > *arból*, the second /r/ changes to /l/ to be different from the first /r/)

disyllabic words (*palabras disilábicas*) 6   words with two syllables (*ha-blo*)

donor language (*la lengua donante*) 4   the source language from which a sound, word, or structure is borrowed into another language

double or geminate consonant (*una consonante doble o geminada*) 7   a consonant with a longer duration than a single consonant (/pp/ in ᴄᴜᴘᴘᴀ)

doublets (*dobletes*) 5   words with the same etymon (*obra* and *ópera* < ᴏᴘᴇ̆ʀᴀ)

elaboration (*la elaboración*) 5   a process during which speakers and writers expand the functions of a linguistic variety for wider use as a standard dialect

ellipsis (*la elipsis*) 16   when an adjective takes on the meaning of an entire noun phrase and the noun is then lost (*social* for *social security number*)

enclitic (*enclítico*) 15   clitics that attach to the end of a word (*la* in *apágala*)

epenthesis (*la epéntesis*) 12, 14   the insertion of a consonant in a word (*something* > *somepthing*)

expansion (*la expansión*) 10   when speakers use a form for additional functions

etymon (*el étimo*) 16   word from which another word derives (ᴏᴘᴇ̆ʀᴀ for *obra* and *ópera*)

extreme apocope (*la apócope extrema*) 6   loss of a word-final vowel in Old Spanish that is pronounced in Modern Spanish (*puent* instead of *puente*)

false cognates or false friends (*los falsos cognados o falsos amigos*) **16** words in different languages that have similar origins but different meanings (English *fabric* and Spanish *fábrica* 'factory')

final position (*la posición final*) **6** the position of an atonic vowel in the final syllable of a word (the position of U in AMICUM)

first medial vowel rule (*la regla de la primera vocal media*) **6** the evolution of the first atonic medial vowel as if it were in initial position (the change of U to /o/ in RECUPERARE)

first person yod allomorphy (*la alomorfía de yod de primera persona*) **14** different stems in a verb paradigm created by a yod only in the first person singular that raises the vowel in that stem (VĒNIŌ > *vengo* and VĒNĪS > *vienes*)

flap (*la vibrante simple*) **7** a consonant produced by a single tap of the tongue against the alveolar ridge (the /ɾ/ in *pero*)

free morpheme (*un morfema libre*) **10** a morpheme that can stand alone (*perro* in *perros*)

fricative (*una fricativa*) **6, 7** a consonant formed by a partial restriction of air flow that produces audible friction (/f/, /s/)

fricativization (*la fricativización*) **7** the process of a stop becoming a fricative to assimilate to other sounds that do not block the flow of air

futurate present (*el presente como futuro*) **13** the use of the present indicative to refer to future time (*voy* in *voy mañana* 'I'm going tomorrow')

grammaticalization (*la gramaticalización*) **3, 14** the process whereby a word becomes a grammatical element, such as an auxiliary or word ending (the change of HABEŌ in CANTĀRE HABEŌ to the ending -*é* in *cantaré*)

heavy syllable (*una sílaba pesada*) **6** an open syllable with a long vowel (CA-TĒ-NA) or a diphthong (BAL-LAE-NA) or a closed syllable ending in a consonant (AU-RŬN-DUM)

hiatus (*un hiato*) **6, 8** two vowels in immediate contact in different syllables (*te-a-tro*)

homonymic conflict (*el conflicto homonímico*) **17** a situation where two unrelated words sound similar (*pilota* and *pelota*) or the same (French *hui* 'today' and *huis* 'door')

human capacity for language (*el lenguaje*) **2** the ability of human beings to acquire and use a complex system of communication

hypercorrection (*una hipercorrección*) **2** a form that results from an erroneous attempt to correct a perceived error or less desirable form (*between you and I* instead of *between you and me*)

indefinite article (*el artículo indefinido*) **10, 12** a type of determiner that introduces a noun whose referent is nonspecific (*a* in *a cat*)

inflectional morphology (*la morfología flexiva*) **10** the set of morphemes that indicate gender, number, person, tense, and mood

inflections (*las flexiones*) **10** grammatical endings that indicate gender, number, person, tense, and mood

interparadigmatic analogy (*la analogía interparadigmática*) **14**   a change in the forms of one verb paradigm following the model of forms in another paradigm (MŌSTRŌ → *muestro* by analogy to *duermo* < DORMŌ)

initial position (*la posición inicial*) **6**   the position of an atonic vowel in the first syllable of a word (A in CABALLUM)

innovation (*la innovación*) **10**   when speakers use a form for a different function or meaning (*voy a cantar* to refer to future time)

Interface Hypothesis (*la hipótesis de la interfaz*) **3**   a hypothesis that proposes that grammatical, lexical, semantic, and pragmatic knowledge interact in different ways to determine the structure of a phrase or sentence

intervocalic position (*la posición intervocálica*) **7**   the position of a consonant in between two vowels

intransitive verb (*un verbo intransitivo*) **15**   a verb that takes no direct object (*María durmió*)

koineization (*la koineización*) **5**   the creation of a new linguistic variety from the features of different dialects (Standard Spanish is based on Castilian with features from other dialects)

lack of diphthongization (*la falta de diptongación*) **8**   the failure of a Latin vowel to diphthongize in Spanish because of the raising effect of a yod (NŎVIU > *novio* instead of **nuevio*)

language (*una lengua o un idioma*) **5**   a standard dialect or a diasystem, a collection of dialects

language change (*el cambio lingüístico*) **3**   any change in a language which comes about as speakers create or adopt new variants and lose others

lateral consonant (*una consonante lateral*) **7**   a consonant produced when air flows around the sides of the tongue (/l/ in *leche*)

learnèd words (*cultismos*) **5**   Spanish words borrowed directly from Classical Latin that did not undergo regular sound changes (OPĔRA > *ópera*)

lenition (*la lenición*) **7**   the weakening of a sound through voicing, fricativization, and/or loss (TUTU > ['to-do] > ['to- ðo] > [too] or [to] *todo*)

leveling (*la nivelación*) **10, 14**   analogical change where one form in a paradigm adopts the same stem as other forms (*levamos, levais* → *llevamos, llevais* adopting the stem *llev-* of *llevo, llevas, lleva,* and *llevan*)

lexical change (*un cambio léxico*) **3, 17**   changes to the lexicon or words of a language

lexical item (*una unidad léxica*) **3, 17**   a word

lexicon (*el léxico*) **3, 17**   the set of words in a language

light syllable (*una sílaba ligera*) **6**   an open syllable containing a short vowel (ŎR-PHĂ-NU)

loanblend (*un préstamo mezclado*) **17** a word that consists of a borrowed part and a native part (borrowed *blog* + native *-ero* = *bloguero*)

loanword (*un préstamo*) **17** a word adopted from another language (Spanish *tuit* from English *tweet*)

locative complement (*complemento locativo*) **15** adverb or prepositional phrase that locates the subject in a physical place (*here, in the yard*)

loss (*la pérdida*) **7** (**of a consonant**) the deletion of a consonant; **10, 13** (**of function**) when speakers stop using a form altogether or they stop using it for a particular function

macron (*un macrón*) **6** line placed over a long vowel (MĀLUM 'apple')

medial position (*la posición media*) **6** the position of an atonic vowel in the middle of a word (the E in OPĔRA and the A in ORNAMENTUM)

metaphony (*metafonía*) **8** the raising of the tonic vowel by a high final vowel (VĒNĪ > *vine*)

metaphor (*la metáfora*) **3, 16** a change in meaning through similarity (*crane* extended to a piece of machinery that also has a long neck)

metathesis (*la metátesis*) **8** the change of position of a sound or sounds in a word (*ask* > *aks*, PARABŎLA > *palabra*)

metonymy (*la metonimia*) **3, 16** a change of meaning of a word to that of an object with which it is in physical or temporal contact (the part of one's pants in contact with the seat is called the *seat of one's pants*)

middle voice (*la voz media*) **15** construction in which the subject receives the action or experience of the verb (*Juan se durmió*)

minimal pairs (*pares mínimos*) **6** words in a language that differ in only one phoneme (*pata/bata*)

mode of articulation (*el modo de articulación*) **7** the way air flows through the mouth during the pronunciation of a consonant, whether it is stopped, restricted, or unobstructed

monophthong (*un monoptongo*) **6** a single vowel (the /a/ in *pata*)

morphemes (*los morfemas*) **3, 10** the smallest meaningful units in a language (*cat, -s, button, -ed*)

morphological change (*un cambio morfológico*) **3, 10–14** a change in the form of a word

morphology (*la morfología*) **3, 10–14** the study of forms or morphemes

multiple causation (*la causación múltiple*) **14** the idea that a linguistic change can result from several influences working together (internal changes in articulation and contact with Basque could cause Latin /f/ > Old Spanish /h/)

mutual intelligibility (*la comprensión mutua*) **5** the ability of speakers of one linguistic variety to understand speakers of another linguistic variety and vice versa

narrowing (*la restricción*) **16** a semantic change to a more specific or narrower meaning (*deer* 'animal' to *deer* 'a particular type of ruminant')

nasal consonant (*una consonante nasal*) **7**   a consonant produced when the flow of air is obstructed in the oral cavity and escapes through the nose (/m/, /n/)

neologism (*un neologismo*) **3, 17**   a newly coined word, phrase or expression (*kicks* for 'shoes')

noun complements (*complementos nominales*) **15**   the complement of a copular verb (*a mother* in *Jean is a mother*)

noun phrase (*el sintagma nominal*) **10**   a phrase that consists of a noun and other nominal elements, such as determiners and adjectives (*the big book* in *the big book is very interesting*)

open syllables (*las sílabas abiertas*) **6**   syllables that end with a vowel (*si*)

orthographic change (*un cambio ortográfico*) **3**   a change in the spelling of a word

orthography (*la ortografía*) **3**   spelling

palatal (*palatal*) **7**   the place of articulation where the body of the tongue comes in contact with the hard palate, the middle part of the roof of the mouth (the /ɲ/ in *año*)

palatalization (*la palatalización*) **7**   the process of a non-palatal sound becoming palatal (the /n/ of VINEAM > /ɲ/ in *viña*)

paradigms (*los paradigmas*) **10**   a set of inflectionally related forms that reveal patterns in language, such as a verb conjugation

passive voice (*la voz pasiva*) **15**   construction where the item receiving the action is the subject of the sentence (*the ball was hit by Ann* vs. the active voice *Ann hit the ball*)

pejoration (*la peyoración/el desarrollo peyorativo*) **16**   the process whereby the meaning of a word becomes more negative (*knave* from 'boy' to 'rascal')

penultimate syllable (*la sílaba penúltima*) **6**   the second to last syllable in a word (the syllable /sa/ in *pensamos*)

phoneme (*un fonema*) **6**   the perceptually distinct units of sound in a language that distinguish one word from another (/p/ and /b/ in *pata* and *bata*)

phonological change (*un cambio fonológico*) **3, 6–9**   a change in the articulation of sounds (/k/ to /s/ in CAELUM > *cielo*)

phonological context (*el contexto fonológico*) **3, 8**   the sounds around the sound in question (the phonological context of the /o/ in *novio* includes a yod in the following syllable)

phonology (*la fonología*) **3, 6–9**   the study of the organization and distribution of meaningful sounds in a language

phonotactics (*la fonotaxis*) **4**   the rules or limits for how sounds can be put together in a particular language

place (or point) of articulation (*el punto de articulación*) **7**   the place in the mouth where articulators come together during the pronunciation of a consonant

polysyllabic words (*palabras polisilábicas*) **6**   words with three or more syllables (*pen-sa-mos*)

popular etymology (*la etimología popular*) **16**   a change in the form of a word caused by erroneous popular beliefs about its source (a change in the form of *crayfish* from French *crevice* 'shrimp,' to end in *fish* on the belief that it came from a word for 'fish')

possessives (*los posesivos*) **10, 12**   a determiner (*my phone, your dog*) or pronoun (*mine, yours*) to express belonging

post-tonic vowels (*vocales postónicas*) **6**   atonic vowels that follow the tonic vowel (the /i/ in NŌMI̱NEM following tonic ō)

pre-tonic vowels (*vocales pretónicas*) **6**   atonic vowels that precede the tonic vowel (the /i/ in NŌMI̱NĀRE preceding tonic ā)

prescribe (*prescribir*) **2**   the act of telling speakers how they should speak or write, that is, what is correct and incorrect

prescriptive grammar (*una gramática prescriptiva*) **2**   a set of rules that prescribes proper usage by telling native speakers how they should speak, that is, what is correct and incorrect

pronoun (*un pronombre*) **10, 12**   a word that replaces a noun or a noun phrase (*she* in *she is happy* where *she* replaces *Jean* in *Jean is happy*)

proportional analogy (*la analogía proporcional*) **10, 14**   analogy of one form to another in a different paradigm that can be represented as a proportion (*fine/fined : shine/*X = *shined*)

reanalysis (*el reanálisis*) **10, 11**   the reinterpretation of a form that has undergone regular sound changes as having a different function (Latin neuter plural FESTA reanalyzed as feminine singular *fiesta*)

recipient language (*la lengua recipiente*) **4**   the language that borrows or receives a sound, word, or structure from another language

Reconquest (*la Reconquista*) **5**   the gradual southward expansion of Castilians and other northerners into regions of the Iberian Peninsula that were under Arab control

reduction (*reducción*) **7**   loss of one consonant in a consonant group (the /p/ in SEPTEM > *siete*) or more generally a lessening in the number of sounds in a word

reflex (*reflejo*) **6**   the Spanish word that derives from a Latin word (*copa* is the reflex of CUPPA)

relative chronology (*la cronología relativa*) **9**   the order in which sound changes occur (e.g. whether syncope occurs before voicing)

repurposing (*la reutilización*) **10**   the process by which speakers use a form with a different function or meaning (the noun *friend* used as a verb)

retention (*la conservación*) **7, 10**   the process by which a sound remains the same or a form continues with the same function (CANTĀBAM > Spanish *cantaba*)

secondary monophthongization (*la monoptongación secundaria*) **8**   the change to a monophthong of an Old Spanish diphthong (Old Spanish *castiello* > Modern Spanish *castillo*)

selection (*la selección*) **5**   the process by which a particular linguistic variety is chosen as the basis for the standard language

semantic change (*un cambio semántico*) **3, 16**   a change in the meaning of words, phrases, or sentences

semantics (*la semántica*) **3, 16**   the study of meaning in language in words, phrases, or sentences

simple tenses (*los tiempos simples*) **10, 13**   a tense that consists of one synthetic form whose stem and ending are inseparable (*canto, cantaré*)

standard dialect (*el dialecto estándar*) **5**   the variety of a language approved by grammarians and generally taught in schools and to non-native speakers of the language

stem–consonant allomorphy (*alomorfía de la consonante radical*) **14**   the existence of stems with different consonants in a verb paradigm (*hag-* in *hago* and *hac-* in *haces*)

stem–vowel allomorphy (*alomorfía de la vocal radical*) **14**   the existence of stems with different vowels in a verb paradigm (*duerm-* in *duermo* and *dorm-* in *dormimos*)

stop (*una oclusiva*) **6, 7**   a consonant that is formed by completely stopping (obstructing) the flow of air

strong stems (*los radicales fuertes*) **3, 14**   stems that receive the stress (*duerm-* in *duermo* as opposed to *dorm-* in *dormimos*)

subordinate terms (*los términos subordinados*) **16**   the more specific terms in relation to a general term (*sparrow* and *robin* are subordinate terms of *bird*)

substratum (*el sustrato*) **4**   a language spoken in a region before the arrival of speakers of another language that is eventually abandoned (Iberian in the Iberian Peninsula in relation to Latin)

superordinate term (*el término superordinado*) **16**   the more general term in relation to specific terms (*bird* is the superordinate term in relation to *sparrow, robin*, etc.)

superstratum (*el superestrato*) **4**   a language spoken in a region after the arrival of speakers of another language that is eventually abandoned (Arabic in the Iberian Peninsula in relation to Spanish)

synchronic description (*una descripción sincrónica*) **1**   the study of a language at one point in time, usually the current time period

syncope (*la síncopa*) **2, 6**   the loss of an unstressed vowel in the middle of the word (OCŬLUM > OCLUM)

synecdoche (*la sinécdoque*) **16**   the process where part of an object can refer to the whole object (*Lend me your wheels* where *wheels* means 'car').

syntactic change (*un cambio sintáctico*) **3, 15**   a change in the order or the function of morphemes or words

syntax (*la sintaxis*) **3, 15**   the study of the formation of words into phrases and phrases into sentences

synthetic construction (*una construcción sintética*) **10**   structure in a language with inseparable unanalyzable morphemes (future *iré*)

tokens (*las occurrencias*) **1**   each representation of a linguistic item (we found ten tokens of *los artes poéticos* in our search)

tonic vowels 6   stressed vowels

transitive verb (*un verbo transitivo*) **15**   a verb that takes a direct object (*pegar* because it takes the direct object *la pelota* in *Juan pegó la pelota*)

trill (*la vibrante múltiple*) **7**   a consonant produced by multiple taps of the tongue against the alveolar ridge (the /r/ in *perro*)

value judgment (*juicio de valor*) **2**   an opinion about something's value or worth (e.g. it is wrong to say *cantastes*)

velar (*velar*) **7**   the place of articulation where the root of the tongue comes into contact with the velum, the soft palate at the back of the mouth (the place of articulation of the /g/ in *gato*)

velarization (*la velarización*) **7**   the process of a non-velar sound becoming velar (Old Spanish /ʃ/ > Modern Spanish /x/)

vocalization (*la vocalización*) **8**   the change of a consonant to a semi-vowel ([k] > [j] in the group [kt], as in *LACTEM > [laj-te] > leche*)

voiced bilabial stop (*una oclusiva biblabial sorda*) **7**   a consonant produced with vibration of the vocal cords and stoppage of air by both lips (/b/)

voiced consonant (*consonante sonora*) **7**   a consonant articulated with the vocal cords vibrating (/b/, /d/, /g/)

voiceless consonants (*consonantes sordas*) **7**   consonants articulated without the vocal cords vibrating (/p/, /t/, /k/)

voicing (*la sonorización*) **7**   the process of a voiceless sound becoming voiced (/f/ > /v/ in PRŌFECTU > *provecho*)

vowel (*una vocal*) **6**   a voiced speech sound made without any obstruction in the flow of air

vowel raising (*la cerrazón vocálica*) **8**   the change in the articulation of a vowel to a higher position in the mouth (the Ē of Latin VĒNĪ to /i/ in Spanish *vine*)

waw (*el waw*) **8**   the high back semi-vowel [w]

weak stems (*los radicales débiles*) **3, 14**   stems that do not receive the stress; the stress falls instead on the ending

yod (*la yod*) **8**   the high front semi-vowel [j]

yodization (**la yodización**) **6**   the process of /i/ and /e/ becoming /j/ when directly preceding another vowel (the change of /e/ to /j/ in VINEA)

Works Cited

Alatorre, Antonio 1989. *Los 1,001 años de la lengua española*, 2nd edn. México City: Fondo de Cultura Económica

Algeo, John 2010. *The origins and development of the English language*, 6th edn. Boston: Wadsworth Cengage Learning

Alkire, Ti, Carol Rosen, and Emily Scida 2010. *Romance languages: A historical introduction.* Cambridge University Press

Almeida, Manuel, and Marina Díaz 1998. "Aspectos sociolingüísticos de un cambio gramatical: La expresión de futuro," *Estudios filológicos* 33: 7–22

Asención, Yuly 2000. "English borrowing in computer-related Venezuelan Spanish: Use and policy." Unpublished ms., Northern Arizona University

Barbero, Abilio, and Marcelo Vigil 1988. *Sobre los orígenes sociales de la Reconquista.* Barcelona: Editorial Ariel

Barton, Simon 2004. *A history of Spain.* London and New York: Palgrave Macmillan

Behar, Doron M., Christine Harmant, Jeremy Manry, Mannis van Oven, Wolfgang Haak, Begoña Martinez-Cruz, Jasone Salaberria, Bernard Oyharçabal, Frédéric Bauduer, David Comas, Lluis Quintana-Murci, and the Genographic Consortium 2012. "The Basque paradigm: Genetic evidence of a maternal continuity in the Franco-Cantabrian region since Pre-Neolithic times," *The American Journal of Human Genetics* 90: 486–93

Blake, Robert 1988a. "*Ffaro, Faro*, or *Haro*? *F* doubling as a source of linguistic information for the early Middle Ages," *Romance Philology* 41(3): 267–89

1988b. "Sound change and linguistic residue: The case of [f-] > [h-] > [Ø]," in Thomas J. Walsh (ed.), *Georgetown University Round Table on Languages and Linguistics*, 53–62. Washington, DC: Georgetown University Press

Blake, Robert J., Diana L. Ranson, and Roger Wright (eds.) 1999. *Essays in Hispanic linguistics dedicated to Paul M. Lloyd.* Newark, DE: Juan de la Cuesta

Blank, Andreas 1999. "Why do new meanings occur? A cognitive typology of the motivation for semantic change," in Andreas Blank and Peter Koch (eds.), *Historical semantics and cognition*, 61–89. Berlin and New York: Mouton de Gruyter

2003. "Polysemy in the lexicon and in discourse," *Trends in Linguistics Studies and Monographs* 142: 267–96

Blas Arroyo, José Luis 2008. "The variable expression of future tense in Peninsular Spanish: The present (and future) of inflectional forms in the Spanish spoken in a bilingual region," *Language Variation and Change* 20: 85–126

Bloomfield, Leonard 1933. *Language.* New York: H. Holt

Bright, William 1997. "Notes," *Language in Society* 26: 469

Bustos Tovar, José Jesús de 1984. "Razón de amor con los denuestos del agua y el vino" in *El comentario de textos, 4: La poesía medieval*, 53–83. Madrid: Castalia

Cacho Blecua, Juan Manuel, and María Jesús Lacarra (eds.) 1984. *Calila e Dimna.* Madrid: Castalia

Cartagena, Nelson 1995–96. "La inestabilidad del paradigma verbal de futuro: ¿hispanoamericanismo, hispanismo, romanismo o universal lingüístico?" *Boletín de Filología* 35: 79–100

Cassano, Paul Vincent 1977. "Substratum hypotheses concerning American Spanish," *Word* 28: 239–74

"Celts" 2017. Wikipedia. Wikimedia Foundation. July 5. https://en.wikipedia.org/wiki/Celts

Corominas, Joan 1983. *Breve diccionario etimológico de la lengua castellana*, 3rd edn. Madrid: Gredos

Craddock, Jerry R. 1969. *Latin legacy versus substratum residue.* University of California Publications in Linguistics 53. Berkeley and Los Angeles: University of California Press

Davies, Mark 2002. *Corpus del español: 100 million words, 1200s–1900s.* www.corpusdelespanol.org

Domínguez Monedero, Adolfo J. 1984. "Reflexiones acerca de la sociedad hispana reflejada en la "Geografía" de Estrabón," *Revistas – Lucentum* III: 201–18. Online: https://rua.ua.es/dspace/bitstream/10045/4489/1/Lucentum_03_10.pdf

Dworkin, Steven N. 1980. "Phonotactic awkwardness as a cause of lexical blends: The genesis of Sp. *cola* 'tail,'" *Hispanic Review* 48(2): 231–37

    1985. *Etymology and derivational morphology: The genesis of Old Spanish denominal adjectives in* -ido. Beihefte zur Zeitschrift für romanische Philologie, 206. Tübingen: Max Niemeyer

    1989. "Studies in lexical loss: The fate of Old Spanish post-adjectival abstracts in -dad, -dumbre, -eza and -ura," *Bulletin of Hispanic Studies* 66: 335–42

    1994. "Near-homonymy, semantic overlap and lexical loss in Medieval Spanish: Three case studies," *Romanistisches Jahrbuch* 44: 271–81

    2006. "Recent developments in Spanish (and Romance) historical semantics," in Timothy L. Face and Carol A. Klee (eds.), *Selected proceedings of the 8th Hispanic Linguistics Symposium*, 50–57. Somerville, MA: Cascadilla Proceedings Project

    2011. "Lexical change," in Martin Maiden, John Charles Smith, and Adam Ledgeway (eds.), *Cambridge history of the Romance languages*, 585–605. Cambridge University Press

2012. *A history of the Spanish lexicon: A linguistic perspective.* Oxford University Press

Epperson, Belén Flórez, and Diana L. Ranson 2010. "¿La química, la químico o el químico? Cómo llamar a una mujer profesional," *Hispania* 93: 399–412

Erichsen, Gerald 2017. "Words that break the gender 'rule,'" *ThoughtCo.* March 20. www.thoughtco.com/words-that-break-the-gender-rule-3078133

Ernout, Alfred, and Antoine Meillet 2001. *Dictionnaire étymologique de la langue latine: Histoire des mots.* Reprint of 4th edn. Paris: Klincksieck

Ford, Jeremiah D. M. 1911. *Old Spanish readings.* Boston: Ginn

Gago-Jover, Fernando 1997. "Nuevos datos sobre el origen de *soy, doy, voy, estoy,*" *La Corónica* 25: 75–90

García de Diego, Vicente 1922. "Cruces de sinónimos," *Revista de Filología Española* 9: 113–53

García Fitz, Francisco 2009. "La Reconquista: Un estado de la cuestión," *Clio & Crimen* 6: 142–215

Gerli, Michael (ed.) 1985. Gonzalo de Berceo. *Milagros de Nuestra Señora.* Madrid: Cátedra

Glosas Emilianenses 2017. Wikipedia. Wikimedia Foundation. June 25. https://en.wikipedia.org/wiki/Glosas_Emilianenses

González Jiménez, Manuel 2002. "¿Reconquista? Un estado de la cuestión," in Eloy Benito Ruano (ed.), *Tópicos y realidades de la Edad Media (I)*, 155–78. Madrid: Real Academia de la Historia

Gonzalez Nieto, David 2007. "The emperor's new words: Language and colonization," *Human Architecture: Journal of the Sociology of Self-Knowledge* 5: 231–37

Gorenstein, Colin 2016. "12 oversized facts about JNCO jeans," Mental_Floss. http://mentalfloss.com/article/87246/12-oversized-facts-about-jnco-jeans

Gutman, Alejandro, and Beatriz Avanzati 2013a. *The language gulper: Native Meso-American languages.* www.languagesgulper.com/eng/Mesomap.html

2013b. *The language gulper: Native South American languages.* www.languagesgulper.com/eng/Southamer.html

Harper, Douglas. 2001–17. *Online etymological dictionary.* www.etymonline.com

Haspelmath, Martin 2008. "Loanword typology: Steps toward a systematic cross-linguistic study of lexical borrowability," in Thomas Stolz, Dik Bakker, and Rosa Salas Palomo (eds.), *Aspects of language contact*, 43–62. Berlin and New York: De Gruyter Mouton

Haugen, Einar 1950. "The analysis of linguistic borrowing," *Language* 26: 210–31

1972. *Ecology of language.* Palo Alto, CA: Stanford University Press.

Howe, Chad, and Scott A. Schwenter 2003. "Present perfect for preterit across Spanish dialects," *University of Pennsylvania Working Papers in Linguistics* 9: 61–75

2008. "Variable constraints on past reference in dialects of Spanish," in Maurice Westmoreland and Juan Antonio Thomas (eds.), *Selected proceedings of the 4th Workshop on Spanish Sociolinguistics*, 100–08. Somerville, MA: Cascadilla Proceedings Project

"Iberian Peninsula from 1247 to 1491." *Historical maps of Spain and Portugal*. Edmaps .com.

Izzo, Herbert 1972. "The layer-cake model in historical linguistics," *General Linguistics* 12: 159–68

Jakobson, Roman 1960. "Closing statement: Linguistics and poetics," in Thomas A. Sekeok (ed.), *Style in Language*, 350–77. Cambridge, MA: MIT Press

Jasanoff, Jay H., and Warren Cowgill 2017. "Indo-European Languages," *Encyclopaedia Britannica*. www.britannica.com/topic/Indo-European-languages

Jensen, John B. 1989. "On the mutual intelligibility of Spanish and Portuguese," *Hispania* 72: 848–52

Labov, William 1972. "Some principles of linguistic methodology," *Language in Society* 1: 97–120.

Lapesa, Rafael 1980. *Historia de la lengua española*, 9th edn. Madrid: Gredos

"Las nuevas palabras aprobadas por la RAE." 2014. *Universia: España*. Fundación Universia. October 23. http://noticias.universia.es/cultura/noticia/2014/10/23/111 3700/nuevas-palabras-aprobadas-rae.html

Lathrop, Thomas A. 2003. *The evolution of Spanish*, 4th edn. Newark, DE: Juan de la Cuesta

"Latin feminine nouns of the fourth declension" 2016. Wiktionary. Feb. 19. https://en .wiktionary.org/wiki/Category:Latin_feminine_nouns_in_the_fourth_declension

Ledgeway, Adam 2012. *From Latin to Romance: Morphosyntactic typology and change*. Oxford University Press

Lee, Tonia 2006. *Romeo and Juliet in urban slang*. School edition adapted by Tonia Lee. New York: Lulu.com

"List of Latin phrases" 2017. Wikipedia. Wikimedia Foundation. Jan. 27. https://en .wikipedia.org/wiki/List_of_Latin_phrases

Lloyd, Paul 1987. *From Latin to Spanish*. Philadelphia: American Philosophical Society

Lomax, Derek 1984. *La Reconquista*. Barcelona: Crítica

Lozano, Cristóbal 2006. "The development of the syntax-discourse interface: Greek learners of Spanish," in Vincent Torrens and Linda Escobar (eds.), *The acquisition of syntax in Romance languages*, 372–99. Amsterdam and Philadelphia: John Benjamins

Machado, José Pedro 1977. *Dicionário etimológico da língua portuguesa*, 3rd edn. Lisbon: Livros Horizonte.

Mackenzie, Ian 2017. "The rise and fall of proclisis in Old Spanish postprepositional infinitival clauses: a quantitative approach," *Bulletin of Hispanic Studies* 94: 127–46

Malkiel, Yakov 1976. "Multi-conditioned sound change and the impact of morphology on phonology," *Language* 52: 757–78.

　1980a. "Etymology as a challenge to phonology: The case of Romance linguistics," in Manfred Mayrhofer, Martin Peters, and Oskar E. Pfeiffer (eds.), *Lautgeschichte und Etymologie*, 260–86. Wiesbaden: Ludwig Reichert

　1980b. "The decline of Spanish *luengo* 'long': The disappearance of Old Spanish *lueñ(e)* 'far,'" in Jean-Marie d'Heur and Nicoletta Cherubini (eds.), *Études de philologie romane et d'histoire littéraire offertes à Jules Horrent*, 267–73. Liège: Université de Liège

Martinet, André 1986. *Des steppes aux océans: L'indo-européen et les «Indo-Européens»*. Paris: Payot

Meadows, Gail Keith 1948. "The development of Latin hiatus groups in the Romance languages," *PMLA* 63: 765–84

Melis, Chantal 2005. "El aspecto y la gramaticalización del nexo *a* en la construcción V_{mvt} + infinitivo," in Margaret Lubbers Quesada and Ricardo Maldonado (eds.), *Dimensiones del aspecto en español*, 55–97. México, DF: Universidad Nacional Autónoma de México/Universidad Autónoma de Querétaro

Mendez Dosuna, Julian, and Carmen Pensado 1986. "Can phonological changes really have a morphological origin?" *Diachronica* 3: 185–201

Menéndez Pidal, Ramón (ed.) 1946. *Cantar de mio Cid*. Madrid: Espasa-Calpe

　1971. *Crestomatía del Español Medieval*, I. Madrid: Gredos

　1987. *Manual de gramática histórica española*, 19th edn. Madrid: Espasa-Calpe

Meyer-Lubke, Wilhelm 1935. *Romanisches etymologisches Wörterbuch*, 3rd edn. Heidelberg: Carl Winter

Michel, Jean-Baptiste, Yuan Kui Shen, Aviva Presser Aiden, Adrian Veres, Matthew K. Gray, The Google Books Team, Joseph P. Pickett, Dale Holberg, Dan Clancy, Peter Norvig, Jon Orwant, Steven Pinker, Martin A. Nowak, and Erez Lieberman Aiden 2011. "Quantitative analysis of culture using millions of digitized books," *Science* 331: 176–82

Molho, Maurice 1969. *Linguistiques et langage*. Bordeaux: Ducros

Myers-Scotton, Carol 2002. *Language contact: Bilingual encounters and grammatical outcomes*. Oxford University Press

Nordquist, Richard 2017. "Hypercorrection (grammar and pronunciation)," *ThoughtCo.* March 3. www.thoughtco.com/hypercorrection-grammar-and-pronunciation -1690937

Núñez Méndez, Eva 2012. *Fundamentos teóricos y prácticos de la historia de la lengua española.* New Haven, CT: Yale University Press

O'Callaghan, Joseph F. 1975. *A history of medieval Spain.* Ithaca, NY: Cornell University Press

Palancar, Enrique L. 2009. *Gramática y textos del hñöñhö: Otomí de San Ildefonso Tultepec, Querétaro,* vol. II: *Textos.* México, DF: Editorial Plaza y Valdés/ Universidad Autónoma de Querétaro

Penny, Ralph 2002. *A history of the Spanish language,* 2nd edn. Cambridge University Press.

Pensado Ruiz, Carmen 1984. *Cronología relativa del castellano.* Ediciones Universidad de Salamanca

Pharies, David A. 2007. *A brief history of the Spanish language.* University of Chicago Press

"Plegar" 2017. Wiktionary. May 25. en.wiktionary.org

Pope, Mildred K. 1952. *From Latin to Modern French,* 2nd edn. Manchester University Press

Poplack, Shana 1979. "Function and process in a variable phonology." Unpublished PhD dissertation, University of Pennsylvania

Posner, Rebecca 1966. *The Romance languages: A linguistic introduction.* Garden City, NY: Doubleday

Pountain, Christopher 1982. "*ESSERE/STARE as a Romance phenomenon," in Nigel Vincent and Martin Harris (eds.), *Studies in the Romance verb: Essays offered to Joe Cremona on the occasion of his 60th birthday,* 139–60. London: Croom Helm

    2001. *A history of the Spanish language through texts.* London and New York: Routledge

Pulgram, Ernst 1983. "The reduction and elimination of redundancy," in Frederick B. Agard, Gerald Kelley, Adam Makkai, and Valerie Becker Makkai (eds.), *Essays in honor of Charles F. Hockett,* 107–25. Leiden: E. J. Brill

    1988. "Synthetic and analytic morphological constructs," in *Practicing linguist: Essays on language and languages,* vol. II: *On languages,* 193–203. Heidelberg: Carl Winter

Random House College Dictionary. 1980. www.geocities.ws/athens/forum/4737/indeur1 .html.

Ranson, Diana L. 1996. "Nombres y manzanas: Análisis fonético de la epéntesis consonántica en la historia de español," in Alegría Alonso González (ed.), *Actas del III Congreso Internacional de Historia de la Lengua Española,* 171–80. Madrid: Arco Libros

    1999. "Variation in voicing in Spanish syncopated forms," in Blake et al. (eds.), 125–54

2005. "Variation of the Spanish demonstratives *aqueste* and *este*," in Roger Wright and Peter Ricketts (eds.), *Studies in Ibero-Romance linguistics dedicated to Ralph Penny*, 187–214. Newark, DE: Juan de la Cuesta

Real Academia Española. *Corpus diacrónico del español (CORDE)*. http://corpus.rae.es /cordenet.html

Real Academia Española. *Corpus de referencia del español actual (CREA)*. http://corpus .rae.es/creanet.html

Real Academia Española 2001. *Diccionario de la lengua española*, 22nd edn. http://dle .rae.es/

Real Academia Española 2009. *Nueva gramática de la lengua española,* vol. I: *Morfología sintaxis.* Madrid: Espasa

Resnick, Melvyn C. 1981. *Introducción a la historia de la lengua española.* Washington, DC: Georgetown University Press

Resnick, Melvyn C., and Robert M. Hammond 2011. *Introducción a la historia de la lengua española*, 2nd edn. Washington, DC: Georgetown University Press

Rini, Joel 1995–96. "The 'clinching factor' in the addition of -*y* in Spanish *doy, estoy, soy, voy," Journal of Hispanic Research* 4: 1–11

1997. "The origin of Spanish *ser*: A phonosyntactic analysis," *Romance Philology* 50: 295–307

1999a. *Exploring the role of morphology in the evolution of Spanish.* Amsterdam and Philadelphia: John Benjamins

1999b. "The rise and fall of Old Spanish 'y'all': *vos todos* vs. *vos otros*," in Blake et al. (eds.), 209–21

2010. When Spanish *h*- went silent: How do we know? *Bulletin of Spanish Studies* 87: 431–46

Roberts, Edward A. 2014. *A comprehensive etymological dictionary of the Spanish language with families of words based on Indo-European roots.* Bloomington, IN: Xlibris

Rohlfs, Gerhard 1970. *From Vulgar Latin to Old French*, trans. Vincent Almazan and Lillian McCarthy. Detroit: Wayne State University Press

Rojas, Eunice 2004. "Análisis comparativo-diacrónico de los usos de *ser* y *estar* en español y en catalán." Unpublished master's thesis, University of Georgia

Ruiz de la Peña, Juan Ignacio 1995. "La monarquía asturiana (718–910)," in Juan Ignacio Ruiz de la Peña, Justiniano Rodríguez, and José Luis Martín (eds.), *El reino de León en la alta Edad Media,* vol. III: *Monarquía Astur-leonesa: De Pelayo a Alfonso VI (718-1109),* 11–127. León: Centro de Estudios e Investigación de San Isidoro

Schmidely, Jack 1988. "La -*y* de *doy, estoy, soy, voy*," in Manuel Ariza, Antonio Salvador, Antonio Viudas (eds.), *Actas del Primer Congreso Internacional de Historia de la Lengua Española,* 611–19. Madrid: Arco Libros

Schwenter, Scott A. 1994. "The grammaticalization of an anterior in progress: Evidence from a Peninsular Spanish dialect," *Studies in Language* 18: 71–111

Seklaoui, Diana R. 1989. *Change and compensation*. New York: Peter Lang

Silva Corvalán, Carmen, and Tracy Terrell 1992. "Notas sobre la expresión de futuridad en el español del Caribe," *Hispanic Linguistics* 2: 190–208

Simons, Gary F., and Charles D. Fennig (eds.) 2017. *Ethnologue: Languages of the world*, 20th edn. Dallas, Texas: SIL International.

Sorace, Antonella 2004. "Native language attrition and developmental instability at the syntax-discourse interface: Data, interpretations and methods," *Bilingualism: Language and Cognition* 7: 143–45

Spaulding, Robert K. 1943. *How Spanish grew*. Berkeley, Los Angeles, and London: University of California Press

Spitzer, Leo. 1947. "Vosotros," *Revista de Filología Española* 31: 170–75

Steiger, Arnald. 1932. *Contribución a la fonética del hispano-árabe y de los arabismos en el ibero-románico y el siciliano* (Revista de Filología Española, Anejo 17). Madrid: Casa Editorial Hernando

Stolova, Natalya I. 2015. *Cognitive linguistics and lexical change: Motion verbs from Latin to Romance*. Amsterdam and Philadelphia: John Benjamins

Thomason, Sarah G. 2001. *Language contact: An introduction*. Washington, DC: Georgetown University Press

Tuten, Donald N. 2003. *Koineization in medieval Spain*. Berlin and New York: Mouton de Gruyter

Tuten, Donald N., and Fernando Tejedo-Herrero 2011. "The relationship between historical linguistics and sociolinguistics," in Manuel Díaz-Campos (ed.), *The handbook of Hispanic sociolinguistics*, 283–302. Malden, MA: Blackwell

Ullmann, Stephen 1959. *Précis de sémantique française*, 2nd edn. Bern: A. Francke

"Visigothic Kingdom" 2017. Wikipedia. Wikimedia Foundation. June 30. https://en.wikipedia.org/wiki/Visigothic_Kingdom

Wanner, Dieter 1991. "The Tobler-Mussafia law in Old Spanish," in Hector Campos and Fernando Martínez Gil (eds.), *Current studies in Spanish linguistics*, 313–78. Washington, DC: Georgetown University Press

2006. "An analogical solution for Spanish *soy, doy, voy*, and *estoy*," *Probus* 18: 267–308

Weinrich, Uriel, William Labov, and Matin I. Herzog 1968. "Empirical foundations for a theory of language change," in Winfred Lehmann and Yakov Malkiel (eds.), *Directions for historical linguistics*, 95–189. Austin: University of Texas Press

Wheelock, Frederic M. 1963. *Latin: An introductory course based on ancient authors*, 3rd edn. New York: Barnes and Noble

2005. *Wheelock's Latin*, 6th edn, revised by Richard A. LaFleur. New York: HarperCollins.

Whitley, M. Stanley 1998. "Psych verbs: Transitivity adrift," *Hispanic Linguistics* 10: 115–53

Wireback, Kenneth J. 2009. "On palatalization and the origin of yod in Western Romance," *Romance Quarterly* 56(1): 55–67

"Word of the Year 2013" 2013. https://en.oxforddictionaries.com/word-of-the-year/word-of-the-year-2013

Wright, Roger 1982. *Late Latin and Early Romance in Spain and Carolingian France*. Liverpool: Francis Cairns.

Zimmer, Ben 2013. No, a drunken Australian man did not coin the word *selfie. LEX.I.CON valley: A blog about language.* Slate, Nov. 22. www.slate.com/blogs/lexicon_valley/2013/11/22/selfie_etymology_an_australian_man_takes_a_photo_of_his_lip_after_falling.html

Zipf, George Kingsley 1949. *Human behavior and the principle of least effort: An introduction to human ecology.* Cambridge, MA: Addison-Wesley

Zubizarreta, María Luisa. 1998. *Prosody, focus, and word order.* Cambridge, MA: MIT Press

Word Index

Subject Index